Advances in Study of Time-Delay Systems and Their Applications, 2nd Edition

Advances in Study of Time-Delay Systems and Their Applications, 2nd Edition

Guest Editor

Libor Pekař

MDPI

Basel • Beijing • Wuhan • Barcelona • Belgrade • Novi Sad • Cluj • Manchester

Guest Editor
Libor Pekař
Faculty of Applied
Informatics
Tomas Bata University in Zlín
Zlín
Czech Republic

Editorial Office
MDPI AG
Grossspeteranlage 5
4052 Basel, Switzerland

This is a reprint of the Special Issue, published open access by the journal *Mathematics* (ISSN 2227-7390), freely accessible at: https://www.mdpi.com/si/mathematics/time_delay_systems_II.

For citation purposes, cite each article independently as indicated on the article page online and as indicated below:

Lastname, A.A.; Lastname, B.B. Article Title. *Journal Name* **Year**, *Volume Number*, Page Range.

ISBN 978-3-7258-5553-7 (Hbk)
ISBN 978-3-7258-5554-4 (PDF)
https://doi.org/10.3390/books978-3-7258-5554-4

Contents

About the Editor

Libor Pekař

Libor Pekař is an Associate Professor at the Faculty of Applied Informatics, Tomas Bata University in Zlín, and the Department of Technical Studies, College of Polytechnics Jihlava, Czechia. He also serves as a temporary Guest Professor at the Frost Lab of the Beijing Institute of Technology, China. Assoc. Prof. Pekař is the author of two books and eight book chapters and (co-)author of more than 50 journal articles and 80 conference papers. His research interests include analysis, modeling, identification, and control of time-delay systems, algebraic control methods, heat-exchanger processes, relay-based autotuning, and optimization techniques. He serves as an Academic or Associate Editor of *Measurement and Control, Mathematics, AppliedMath, Frontiers in Energy Research* journals, and the *International Journal of Robotics and Control Systems.* He has also served as a Reviewer for over 30 international scientific journals, including *Automatica, IEEE Transactions on Automatic Control, IEEE Transactions on Industrial Electronics, ISA Transactions*, and *Applied Thermal Engineering.*

mathematics MDPI

Editorial

Advances in Study of Time-Delay Systems and Their Applications: A Second Edition

Libor Pekař

Faculty of Applied Informatics, Tomas Bata University in Zlín, Nad Stráněmi 4511, 76005 Zlín, Czech Republic; pekar@utb.cz

1. Introduction

The delay phenomenon is a common feature of industrial, communication, economic, biological, and similar systems and processes, and it significantly affects their stability and dynamics. It can markedly deteriorate the quality of control performance in feedback loops. Studying the influence of delays on system stability, dynamics, and control performance poses a challenging mathematical problem. System and control theories have addressed this issue for nearly a century, dating back to the seminal work by Volterra [1]. Modern control theory faces growing demands for enhanced quality and performance in both industrial applications and everyday life—demands that are difficult to meet using conventional methods. Achieving these goals requires a deeper understanding of controlled systems with delays. Despite significant advances in artificial intelligence techniques and strategies in recent years, distinguished scholars continue to propose innovative solutions to longstanding challenges and identify new open problems stemming from an increasingly profound understanding of this domain.

This collection focuses on recent developments in the analysis and control design of time-delay systems (TDSs). The goal was to attract quality and novel papers in the field of "Time-Delay Systems and Their Applications". It is anticipated that these top-tier research papers will have a considerable impact on the international scientific community and will inspire further advancements in the field.

2. Overview of Special Issue Contributions

The call for this Special Issue attracted 28 leading researchers in the field of TDSs, who collectively submitted 10 manuscripts. After a rigorous review process, however, only eight high-quality contributions were accepted and published. Based on the affiliation of the corresponding authors, three of the accepted papers are from China [2–4], while the remaining research papers were authored by scholars from Bulgaria [5], Jordan [6], Russia [7], Saudi Arabia [8], and Spain [9].

Two of the papers primarily investigate the exponential stability of TDSs. Sedova and Druzhinina [7] addressed the problem of uniform exponential stability for nonlinear time-varying TDSs. They applied the Razumikhin method to establish sufficient conditions for exponential stability and proposed an extension of the approach to time-varying systems. Specifically, they allowed the time-derivative of the constructed Razumikhin function to be indefinite and derived a new upper estimate on its rate of decrease. The results obtained can be viewed as extensions of those presented in earlier works [10,11], as well as a representation of known sufficient conditions for the exponential stability of linear delay equations. Applying the exponential stability conditions derived in this study to specific examples revealed that previously related results were either inapplicable or yielded different exponential estimates for the solutions. It was noted that the Razumikhin method led to stability conditions that were sufficient but unnecessary, resulting in overly conservative outcomes. Various approaches were then proposed to reduce this conservatism, and numerous results were reported in this area. The paper included a comparison with other findings [10,12–14], and the authors concluded that no universally good stability criterion currently exists.

Another paper in the Special Issue, authored by Lang and Lu [4], evaluates the exponential incremental stability of TDSs and presents the relevant criteria for both continuous and discontinuous right-hand sides. The authors proposed and proved sufficient conditions for the exponential incremental stability of solutions in systems with continuous right-hand sides. Before addressing the incremental stability of systems with discontinuous right-hand sides, they established conditions for the existence and uniqueness of the Filippov solution. Then, by constructing a sequence of systems with continuous right-hand sides and applying an approximation method, they derived sufficient conditions for the exponential incremental stability of systems with discontinuous right-hand sides. Numerical experiments with a linear TDS and a Hopfield neural network with time delay were conducted to verify the theoretical results. For future research, the authors aim to develop methods for constructing continuous TDSs to approximate discontinuous systems more effectively.

The stability of TDSs is closely related to their asymptotic behavior. Two other papers are primarily focused on the asymptotic behavior of solutions in a particular nonlinear neutral TDS and on novel criteria for oscillation [8], as well as the asymptotic behavior of another type of neutral TDSs [6], respectively. The former contribution, authored by Mesmouli et al., investigates stability, asymptotic stability, and exponential stability using the Banach fixed-point theorem. Under certain conditions, the matrix measure serves as the key tool for tackling these three types of stability in a system that includes two Volterra terms and a nonlinear term. The results obtained generalize the findings of [15] and the authors' recent research [16]. The work is another example of the advantage of using the fixed-point method over Lyapunov's method.

Batiha et al. [6] studied the oscillatory behavior of solutions to second-order differential equations (DEs) with neutrality conditions. They developed analytical criteria that highlight the dynamics of these equations and explain the associated oscillation patterns. Notably, the paper contributes to a deeper understanding of the mathematical properties of this class of DEs, enhancing the ability of researchers to address similar problems in various contexts. In particular, it emphasizes the dual effect of neutrality conditions in shaping the behavior of solutions, underscoring the potential to extend existing models to more complex, real-world applications. This research also adds to the existing literature [17,18] by providing precise criteria for assessing the nature of oscillatory solutions, laying a strong foundation for future studies. Further exploration of oscillatory effects in the context of higher-order DEs may reveal new patterns and offer deeper insight into the mathematical structure of these systems, enabling broader applications and greater understanding of more general systems.

The asymptotic behavior of solutions to nonlinear partial DEs (PDEs)—a key aspect in understanding their long-term dynamics—is the focus of another contribution to the Special Issue, authored by Ge and Du [3]. The paper addresses the global well-posedness and asymptotic behavior of solutions to non-autonomous Navier–Stokes equations (NANSEs) with infinite time delay and node determination. Using a mathematical framework based on a specialized function space, the authors demonstrated the well-posedness of the system, under the assumption of Lipschitz continuity with respect to time. In addition, they showed that the long-term behavior of strong solutions could be characterized by their values at a finite number of spatial nodes. The inclusion of an infinite delay term enabled the application of existing theoretical results to analyze the well-posedness and asymptotic behavior of the NANSEs under delay effects. This work provides theoretical support and specific examples for studying nonlinear PDEs with time-delay effects. It also validates the relevant conclusions obtained from time-delay DEs and offers insights into research methods applicable to nonlinear PDEs with other time-delay effects, further reinforcing findings from previous time-delay DE studies [19,20].

Nedzhibov [5] presented a detailed exposition of two spatio-temporal dynamic mode decomposition (STDMD) variants—the parallel and sequential STDMD methods. The author introduced the underlying matrix representations and highlighted their respective computational frameworks for analyzing spatio-temporal data. To address limitations inherited from the classic dynamic mode decomposition (DMD) algorithm, the study proposed extensions incorporating delay-embedding techniques [21]. In addition, numerical experiments were performed to validate the efficacy of the proposed extensions in overcoming the shortcomings of traditional DMD methods [22]. The results demonstrated the enhanced performance of delay-embedded STDMD, showcasing its utility in analyzing complex spatio-temporal datasets. Future research directions were also highlighted. This work advances spatio-temporal DMD methodologies by introducing extensions that enhance the robustness and accuracy of the analysis. The proposed approaches offer valuable tools for researchers and practitioners seeking more profound insights into the dynamics of complex spatio-temporal systems.

The problem of semi-global polynomial synchronization (SGPS) for high-order bidirectional associative memory neural networks (HOBAMNNs) with multiple proportional delays was addressed by Cong, Zhang, and Zhu in [2]. The authors initially derived delay-dependent SGPS criteria for the error dynamical system and then provided the corresponding controller gain. Illustrative examples were presented to demonstrate the applicability of their findings. The main contribution of this work lies in the first investigation of SGPS for HOBAMNNs with multiple proportional delays. By directly deriving easily implementable sufficient criteria based on the definition of SGPS, the proposed approach is applicable to a broader class of neural network models. Future research aims to explore general decay synchronization, which includes polynomial, exponential, logarithmic, and other forms of synchronization [23].

Finally, a comprehensive study on the evolution operator that generates the state trajectory of dynamical systems combining delay-free dynamics with several types of delays was conducted by De la Sen et al. [9]. In the first part of the study, explicit expressions were derived for the evolution associated with the state-trajectory solution of a class of linear time-varying differential delay-free systems. The impulsive-free part of the dynamics matrix function was assumed to be bounded, piecewise-continuous, and Lebesgue-integrable at all times. Both the absence and presence of impulsive actions in the system dynamics matrix were described. The obtained results were subsequently extended to systems with constant point delays, with the evolution operators that generate the trajectory solutions given explicitly. In the general case, these operators were non-unique in the impulsive scenario. The parameterization of impulsive actions at specific time instants occurred in the delay-free dynamics and in the various matrices of delayed dynamics, followed by an immediate return to the previous configuration. These impulsive actions were interpreted as instantaneous, abrupt switching changes in the parameterization, which might be non-unique, as the necessary impulsive gains to monitor the switched parameterizations can vary in achieving a suitable right limit of the solution trajectory. In addition, the boundedness of the solution trajectory of the impulsive TDS was investigated. It was found that an appropriate distribution of impulsive time instants can potentially stabilize a TDS, even if the delay-free dynamics is unstable.

3. Conclusions

All the above-mentioned authors deserve sincere gratitude for their valuable contributions to this Special Issue. We also extend our deep appreciation to the reviewers for their insightful comments and efforts in improving the quality of the submissions. We believe that these high-quality research papers will have a meaningful impact on the international scientific community and will further motivate research on the analysis and control of TDSs, both at the theoretical level and in real-world applications.

Funding: This author's work was funded by the internal research project of the Faculty of Applied Informatics, TBU in Zlín, No. RVO/CEBIA/2024/001.

Conflicts of Interest: The author declares no conflicts of interest.

Abbreviations

The following abbreviations are used in this manuscript:

DE	Differential equation
DMD	Dynamic mode decomposition
HOBAMNN	High-order bidirectional associative memory neural network
NANSE	Non-autonomous Navier–Stokes equation
PDE	Partial differential equation
SGPS	Semi-global polynomial synchronization
STDMD	Spatio-temporal dynamic mode decomposition
TDS	Time-delay system

References

1. Volterra, V. Sur la théorie mathématique des phénomenes héréditaires. *J. Math. Pures Appl.* **1928**, *7*, 249–298.
2. Cong, E.-y.; Zhang, X.; Zhu, L. Semi-global polynomial synchronization of high-order multiple proportional-delay BAM neural networks. *Mathematics* **2025**, *13*, 1512. [CrossRef]
3. Ge, H.; Du, F. Global well-posedness and determining nodes of non-autonomous Navier–Stokes equations with infinite delay on bounded domains. *Mathematics* **2025**, *13*, 222. [CrossRef]
4. Lang, Y.; Lu, W. Criteria on exponential incremental stability of dynamical systems with time delay. *Mathematics* **2023**, *11*, 2242. [CrossRef]
5. Nedzhibov, G. Delay-embedding spatio-temporal dynamic mode decomposition. *Mathematics* **2024**, *12*, 762. [CrossRef]
6. Batiha, B.; Alshammari, N.; Aldosari, F.; Masood, F.; Bazighifan, O. Nonlinear neutral delay differential equations: Novel criteria for oscillation and asymptotic behavior. *Mathematics* **2025**, *13*, 147. [CrossRef]
7. Sedova, N.O.; Druzhinina, O.V. Exponential stability of nonlinear time-varying delay differential equations via Lyapunov–Razumikhin technique. *Mathematics* **2023**, *11*, 896. [CrossRef]
8. Mesmouli, M.B.; Ardjouni, A.; Saber, H. Asymptotic Behavior of Solutions in Nonlinear Neutral System with Two Volterra Terms. *Mathematics* **2023**, *11*, 2676. [CrossRef]
9. De la Sen, M.; Ibeas, A.; Garrido, A.J.; Garrido, I. On the evolution operators of a class of time-delay systems with impulsive parameterizations. *Mathematics* **2025**, *13*, 365. [CrossRef]
10. Zhou, B.; Egorov, A.V. Razumikhin and Krasovskii stability theorems for time-varying time-delay systems. *Automatica* **2016**, *71*, 281–291. [CrossRef]
11. Ning, C.; He, Y.; Wu, M.; She, J. Improved Razumikhin-type theorem for input-to-state stability of nonlinear time-delay systems. *IEEE Trans. Autom. Control* **2014**, *59*, 1983–1988. [CrossRef]
12. Hou, C.; Gao, F. Criteria for quantitative stability for a class of Razumikhin-type retarded functional differential equations. *J. Math. Anal. Appl.* **1999**, *238*, 558–566. [CrossRef]
13. Hu, W.; Zhu, Q.; Karimi, H.R. Some improved Razumikhin stability criteria for impulsive stochastic delay differential systems. *IEEE Trans. Autom. Control* **2019**, *64*, 5207–5213. [CrossRef]
14. Zhou, B.; Luo, W. Improved Razumikhin and Krasovskii stability criteria for time-varying stochastic time-delay systems. *Automatica* **2018**, *89*, 382–391. [CrossRef]
15. Dung, N.T. New stability conditions for mixed linear Levin-Nohel integro-differential equations. *J. Math. Phys.* **2013**, *54*, 082705. [CrossRef]

16. Mesmouli, M.B.; Ardjouni, A.; Djoudi, A. Stability conditions for a mixed linear Levin-Nohel integro-differential system. *J. Integral Equ. Appl.* **2022**, *34*, 349–356. [CrossRef]
17. Tamilvanan, S.; Thandapani, E.; Džurina, J. Oscillation of second order nonlinear differential equations with sub-linear neutral term. *Differ. Equ. Appl.* **2017**, *9*, 29–35. [CrossRef]
18. Wu, Y.; Yu, Y.; Xiao, J.; Jiao, Z. Oscillatory behaviour of a class of second order Emden-Fowler differential equations with a sublinear neutral term. *Appl. Math. Sci. Eng.* **2023**, *31*, 224609. [CrossRef]
19. Chang, J. Solutions to non-autonomous integrodifferential equations with infinite delay. *J. Math. Anal. Appl.* **2007**, *331*, 137–151. [CrossRef]
20. Huang, A.; Huo, W.; Ma, J. Finite-dimensionality and determining modes of the global attractor for 2D Boussinesq equations with fractional Laplacian. *Adv. Nonlinear Stud.* **2018**, *18*, 501–515. [CrossRef]
21. Tu, J.H.; Rowley, C.W.; Luchtenburg, D.M.; Brunton, S.L.; Kutz, J.N. On dynamic mode decomposition: Theory and applications. *J. Comput. Dyn.* **2014**, *1*, 391–421. [CrossRef]
22. Clainche, S.L.; Vega, J.M. Spatio-temporal Koopman decomposition. *J. Nonlinear Sci.* **2018**, *28*, 1793–1842. [CrossRef]
23. Huang, Y.; Zhao, X. General decay synchronization of state and spatial diffusion coupled delayed memristive neural networks with reaction-diffusion terms. *Int. J. Control Autom. Syst.* **2024**, *22*, 2313–2326. [CrossRef]

mathematics

MDPI

Article

Semi-Global Polynomial Synchronization of High-Order Multiple Proportional-Delay BAM Neural Networks

Er-yong Cong [1,2,*], Xian Zhang [3,4,*] and Li Zhu [1]

[1] Department of Mathematics, Harbin University, Harbin 150086, China; zhuli1980@hrbu.edu.cn
[2] Heilongjiang Provincial Key Laboratory of the Intelligent Perception and Intelligent Software, Harbin University, Harbin 150080, China
[3] School of Mathematical Science, Heilongjiang University, Harbin 150080, China
[4] Heilongjiang Provincial Key Laboratory of the Theory and Computation of Complex Systems, Heilongjiang University, Harbin 150080, China
* Correspondence: cey1979@163.com (E.-y.C.); xianzhang@ieee.org (X.Z.)

Abstract: This paper addresses the semi-global polynomial synchronization (SGPS) problem for a class of high-order bidirectional associative memory neural networks (HOBAMNNs) with multiple proportional delays. The time-delay-dependent semi-global polynomial stability criterion for error systems was established via a direct approach. The derived stability conditions are formulated as several simple inequalities that are readily solvable, facilitating direct verification using standard computational tools (e.g., YALMIP). Notably, this method can be applied to many system models with proportional delays after minor modifications. Finally, a numerical example is provided to validate the effectiveness of the theoretical results.

Keywords: semi-global polynomial stability; high-order BAM neural network; semi-global polynomial synchronization; proportional delays; controller gains

MSC: 93D20

1. Introduction

Due to nonlinear computing capabilities and powerful parallel processing, neural networks (NNs) have played an important role in fields such as addressable memory, pattern recognition, and optimization control in recent decades [1,2]. A high-order NN capable of simulating auto-associative, hetero-associative, and multi-associative memory was proposed by Lee et al. [3] in 1986. Subsequently, various aspects of higher-order models have been extensively studied [4,5]. These higher-order NN models have higher fault tolerances, larger storage capacities, faster convergence speeds, and stronger approximation properties than first-order NNs.

Bidirectional associative memory NNs (BAMNNs) [6,7] consist of two layers of heterogeneous associative circuits, which extend the functionality of single-layer NNs and have the functions of memory and information association. In 1990, Simpson [8] put forward a class of HOBAMNNs. Since then, scholars had a strong interest in the research of delayed HOBAMNNs. In general, time delays considered for HOBAMNNs can be classified as constant delays [9], time-varying delays [10,11], leakage terms [12,13], and distributed delays [14]. In the implementation of NNs, in addition to the aforementioned types of delays, there also exists another crucial category of proportional delays. This is an unbounded time-varying delay that is different from constant delay, bounded time-varying delay, and distributed delay. The stability results of other types of time-delay systems cannot be applied to proportional delay systems directly too. For some time, an increasing number of scholars have started to pay attention to proportional-delay NNs (PDNNs) [15–18].

Pecora and Carroll proposed the concept of synchronization based on drive–response systems in [19]. It represents a state in which two or more systems exhibit common dynamic behaviors. When studying the dynamic behaviors of NNs, synchronization plays a crucial role. Since Zhou proposed the PDNNs in [20], the synchronization of PDNNs has also received much attention. A large number of manuscripts have emerged regarding the study of different types of synchronization problems for PDNNs: for example, asymptotic synchronization [21–23], exponential synchronization [24–27], finite-time synchronization [28–32], and fixed-time synchronization [33–35]. Regarding the implementation of synchronization between PDNNs, the majority of articles initially convert the proportional-delay drive–response systems into drive–response systems featuring constant delays and time-varying coefficients by means of nonlinear transformations. Then, corresponding methods are applied to derive sufficient conditions for synchronization: for example, the Lyapunov functionals (cited in [21,24,26,28,35]); the Lyapunov functionals and M-matrix method (cited in [27,36]); the matrix measure method (cited in [27]); the differential inequality techniques and the analysis approach (cited in [33,37,38]); the Lyapunov function and analytical methods (cited in [39]); the reciprocally convex technique combined with a new Lyapunov–Krasovskii functional (cited in [22]); the matrix measure strategy and the method based on the finite-time stability theorem of the Lyapunov approach (cited in [29]); the figure analysis method (cited in [30]); and the mean value inequality analysis (cited in [23]).

Polynomial stability differs from asymptotic stability and exponential stability. In terms of convergence rates, it is weaker than exponential stability and lies between asymptotic stability and exponential stability [17,18]. In the context of stability analyses for NNs, global power-rate stability and global polynomial stability are closely related concepts, both describing the convergence behavior of system trajectories over an unbounded state space. Global polynomial synchronization (GPS) is also an important synchronization method for PDNNs. It is a type of decaying synchronization, and its convergence rate is no higher than that of global exponential synchronization. In recent years, polynomial synchronization (PS) has emerged as a significant research direction in NN dynamics, achieving notable theoretical and practical advancements [40–46]. References [40,41] investigate the global power-rate synchronization (GP-RS) problem in different NNs. In [40], by utilizing the Leibniz rule for fractional-order derivatives and an extended comparison technique, the delay-dependent criteria for GP-RS were derived. In [41], by means of impulsive delay differential inequalities, sufficient conditions for achieving GP-RS in chaotic NNs under delay-dependent impulsive control laws are established. Zhou et al. [42] pioneered the concept of PS for recurrent NNs, employing inequality analysis techniques and constructing Lyapunov functionals to derive delay-dependent sufficient conditions for ensuring exponential synchronization and PS in drive–response systems. Subsequent studies expanded this framework to diverse NN architectures. For complex-valued inertial PDNNs, researchers developed synchronization criteria using a non-separated approach [43]. In the context of inertial PDNNs, scholars designed feedback controllers and reduced error systems to first-order differential equations through order reduction. By leveraging derivative definitions, matrix norm properties and Lagrange's mean-value-theorem novel proportional-delay differential inequalities were established, resulting in matrix-norm-based synchronization criteria [44]. Addressing high-dimensional quaternion-valued systems, researchers achieved GPS through nonlinear controllers that integrate quaternion algebra with advanced inequality techniques [45]. Practical applications were further explored in parameter-uncertain proportional-delay memristive NNs, where the Lyapunov stability theory and inequality analysis yielded synchronization criteria that successfully applied to image encryption systems [46]. Collectively, these works have systematically advanced PS methodologies, demonstrating theoretical completeness in model generality, controller design, mathematical tool innovation, and real-world implementation.

The central aim of this paper is to devise a control law capable of ensuring the SGPS of multiple proportional-delay HOBAMNNs. The main contributions of this paper are as follows:

(1) This is the first study on the SGPS of multiple proportional-delay HOBAMNNs, and the definition of SGPS here is obviously different from that of GPS.
(2) This paper proposes a direct derivation method based on the system's solution. Different from previous research results, it avoids using nonlinear transformation to convert PDNNs into constant delay NNs. This method simplifies the research process, avoids the complexity brought by constructing the Lyapunov–Krasovskii functional, and makes the structure of the paper more reasonable.
(3) The established SGPS criterion not only enhances the convergence rate and accuracy but also enables straightforward implementation using the MATLAB R2016b 9.1 toolbox.

The remaining portion is structured as follows. The elaboration and preparatory work of the problem will be conducted in the next section. The major achievements of this research, a new standard for SGPS, are presented in Section 3. Illustrative examples are provided in Section 4 to verify the validity of the obtained results. Finally, in Section 5, we present our conclusions.

Notation: The real number and positive integer sets are denoted by $\mathbb{R}$ and $\mathbb{N}^+$, respectively. The symbol $\mathbb{R}^{l\times s}$ denotes the set consisting of $l \times s$ matrices. $\mathbb{R}^{l\times s}_{\succeq}$ and $\mathbb{R}^{l\times s}_{\succ}$ are subsets of $\mathbb{R}^{l\times s}$, with the former containing all nonnegative matrices and the latter containing all positive matrices. In a similar vein, we also utilize $\mathbb{R}_{\succeq}$ and $\mathbb{R}_{\succ}$, among others. For $s \in \mathbb{N}^+$, let $\mathbb{R}^s$ be the linear space of all s-dimensional column vectors over $\mathbb{R}$. The column-vectorizing operator is denoted by $\mathrm{col}(\cdot)$. The notations $\|\cdot\|_2$ and $\|\cdot\|_\infty$ represent the Euclidean norm and ∞-norm on $\mathbb{R}^s$, respectively.

2. Problem Description

Consider a class of multiple proportional-delay HOBAMNNs, which can be described as follows:

$$\begin{aligned}\dot{\zeta}_i(t) = & -\mathfrak{a}_i\zeta_i(t) + \sum_{j\in\mathbb{Z}_m}\left[\mathfrak{b}_{ij}\, h_j(\vartheta_j(t)) + \mathfrak{c}_{ij} l_j(\vartheta_j(p_{ij}t))\right] \\ & + \sum_{j\in\mathbb{Z}_m}\sum_{l\in\mathbb{Z}_m} \mathfrak{d}_{ijl}\hbar_j(\vartheta_j(p_{ijl}t))\hbar_l(\vartheta_l(p_{ijl}t)) \\ & + I_i(t), i\in\mathbb{Z}_n, t\in[t_0,\infty),\end{aligned} \tag{1a}$$

$$\begin{aligned}\dot{\vartheta}_j(t) = & -\hat{\mathfrak{a}}_j\vartheta_j(t) + \sum_{i\in\mathbb{Z}_n}\left[\hat{\mathfrak{b}}_{ji}\tilde{h}_i(\zeta_i(t)) + \hat{\mathfrak{c}}_{ji}\tilde{l}_i(\zeta_i(\hat{p}_{ji}t))\right] \\ & + \sum_{i\in\mathbb{Z}_n}\sum_{r\in\mathbb{Z}_n} \hat{\mathfrak{d}}_{jir}\tilde{\hbar}_i(\zeta_i(\hat{p}_{jir}t))\tilde{\hbar}_r(\zeta_r(\hat{p}_{jir}t)) \\ & + \tilde{I}_j(t), j\in\mathbb{Z}_m, t\in[t_0,\infty),\end{aligned} \tag{1b}$$

$$\begin{gathered}\zeta_i(s) = \varphi_i(s), \vartheta_j(s) = \psi_j(s), \delta t_0 \le s \le t_0, i\in\mathbb{Z}_n, j\in\mathbb{Z}_m, \\ \delta = \min\left\{\min_{i\in\mathbb{Z}_n, j\in\mathbb{Z}_m} p_{ij}, \min_{i\in\mathbb{Z}_n, j\in\mathbb{Z}_m}\hat{p}_{ji}, \min_{i\in\mathbb{Z}_n, j,l\in\mathbb{Z}_m} p_{ijl}, \min_{i,r\in\mathbb{Z}_n, j\in\mathbb{Z}_m}\hat{p}_{jir}\right\}\end{gathered} \tag{1c}$$

where $\zeta_i(t)$ and $\vartheta_j(t)$ denote the ith and jth neuronal state of layer-X and layer-Y, respectively; $t_0 \geq 0$ is the initial time; $h_j(\cdot), \tilde{h}_i(\cdot), l_j(\cdot), \tilde{l}_i(\cdot), \hbar_j(\cdot)$, and $\tilde{\hbar}_i(\cdot)$ are nonnegative activation functions; $p_{ij}, \hat{p}_{ji}, p_{ijl}$ and $\hat{p}_{jir}$ denote the proportional delays: $0 < p_{ij} < 1$, $0 < \hat{p}_{ji} < 1, 0 < p_{ijl} < 1$, and $0 < \hat{p}_{jir} < 1$. $\mathfrak{a}_i$ and $\hat{\mathfrak{a}}_j$ are positive constants; constants $\mathfrak{b}_{ij}$, $\hat{\mathfrak{b}}_{ji}$, $\mathfrak{c}_{ij}$, and $\hat{\mathfrak{c}}_{ji}$ represent the connection weights; $\mathfrak{d}_{ijl}$ and $\hat{\mathfrak{d}}_{jir}$ are the second-order nonnegative connection weights; $\varphi_i(s), \psi_j(s) \in \mathbb{C}[\delta t_0, t_0]$ stands for the initial functions. $I_i(t)$ and $\tilde{I}_j(t)$ denote the external inputs on the i-th and j-th neuron at time t. $\mathbb{Z}_k = \{1, 2, \ldots, k\}, k \in \mathbb{N}^+$.

We require these assumptions:

Assumption 1. *There is $\bar{h}_j, \bar{\bar{h}}_i \in \mathbb{R}_{\succ}$ such that $h_j(0) = \tilde{h}_i(0) = 0$, $0 \leq \frac{h_j(\alpha_1) - h_j(\alpha_2)}{\alpha_1 - \alpha_2} \leq \bar{h}_j$ and $0 \leq \frac{\tilde{h}_i(\alpha_1) - \tilde{h}_i(\alpha_2)}{\alpha_1 - \alpha_2} \leq \bar{\bar{h}}_i$ for any $\alpha_1, \alpha_2 \in \mathbb{R}$ subject to $\alpha_1 \neq \alpha_2$, $i \in \mathbb{Z}_n$ and $j \in \mathbb{Z}_m$.*

Assumption 2. *There is $\bar{l}_j, \bar{\bar{l}}_i \in \mathbb{R}_{\succ}$ such that $l_j(0) = \tilde{l}_i(0) = 0$, $0 \leq \frac{l_j(\alpha_1) - l_j(\alpha_2)}{\alpha_1 - \alpha_2} \leq \bar{l}_j$ and $0 \leq \frac{\tilde{l}_i(\alpha_1) - \tilde{l}_i(\alpha_2)}{\alpha_1 - \alpha_2} \leq \bar{\bar{l}}_i$ for any $\alpha_1, \alpha_2 \in \mathbb{R}$ subject to $\alpha_1 \neq \alpha_2$, $i \in \mathbb{Z}_n$ and $j \in \mathbb{Z}_m$.*

Assumption 3. *There is $\bar{\hbar}_j, \bar{\bar{\hbar}}_i, \in \mathbb{R}_{\succ}$ suich that $\hbar_j(0) = \tilde{\hbar}_i(0) = 0$, $0 \leq \frac{\hbar_j(\alpha_1) - \hbar_j(\alpha_2)}{\alpha_1 - \alpha_2} \leq \bar{\hbar}_j$ and $0 \leq \frac{\tilde{\hbar}_i(\alpha_1) - \tilde{\hbar}_i(\alpha_2)}{\alpha_1 - \alpha_2} \leq \bar{\bar{\hbar}}_i$ for any $\alpha_1, \alpha_2 \in \mathbb{R}$ subject to $\alpha_1 \neq \alpha_2$, $i \in \mathbb{Z}_n$ and $j \in \mathbb{Z}_m$.*

Assumption 4. *The activation functions $\hbar_j(\cdot)$ and $\tilde{\hbar}_i(\cdot)$ satisfy $-\tilde{\gamma}_j^{(1)} \leq \hbar_j(s) \leq \tilde{\gamma}_j^{(1)}$, $-\tilde{\gamma}_i^{(2)} \leq \tilde{\hbar}_i(s) \leq \tilde{\gamma}_i^{(2)}$ for any $t \geq t_0$, $s \in \mathbb{R}$, $i \in \mathbb{Z}_n$, $j \in \mathbb{Z}_m$, where $\tilde{\gamma}_j^{(1)}$ and $\tilde{\gamma}_i^{(2)}$ are positive scalars.*

We regard higher-order BAMNN (1) as a master drive system and consider the following form of slave matching response systems:

$$
\begin{aligned}
\dot{\hat{\zeta}}_i(t) = & -\mathfrak{a}_i \hat{\zeta}_i(t) + \sum_{j \in \mathbb{Z}_m} \left[\mathfrak{b}_{ij} h_j(\hat{\vartheta}_j(t)) + \mathfrak{c}_{ij} l_j(\hat{\vartheta}_j(p_{ij} t)) \right] \\
& + \sum_{j \in \mathbb{Z}_m} \sum_{l \in \mathbb{Z}_m} \mathfrak{d}_{ijl} \hbar_j(\hat{\vartheta}_j(p_{ijl} t)) \hbar_l(\hat{\vartheta}_l(p_{ijl} t)) \\
& + I_i(t) + U_i(t), i \in \mathbb{Z}_n, t \in [t_0, \infty),
\end{aligned}
\tag{2a}
$$

$$
\begin{aligned}
\dot{\hat{\vartheta}}_j(t) = & -\hat{\mathfrak{a}}_j \hat{\vartheta}_j(t) + \sum_{i \in \mathbb{Z}_n} \left[\hat{\mathfrak{b}}_{ji} \tilde{h}_i(\hat{\zeta}_i(t)) + \hat{\mathfrak{c}}_{ji} \tilde{l}_i(\hat{\zeta}_i(\hat{p}_{ji} t)) \right] \\
& + \sum_{i \in \mathbb{Z}_n} \sum_{r \in \mathbb{Z}_n} \hat{\mathfrak{d}}_{jir} \tilde{\hbar}_i(\hat{\zeta}_i(\hat{p}_{jir} t)) \tilde{\hbar}_r(\hat{\zeta}_r(\hat{p}_{jir} t)) \\
& + \tilde{I}_j(t) + V_j(t), j \in \mathbb{Z}_m, t \in [t_0, \infty),
\end{aligned}
\tag{2b}
$$

$$
\hat{\zeta}_i(s) = \hat{\varphi}_i(s), \hat{\vartheta}_j(s) = \hat{\psi}_j(s), \delta t_0 \leq s \leq t_0, i \in \mathbb{Z}_n, j \in \mathbb{Z}_m,
\tag{2c}
$$

where $U_i(t)$ and $V_j(t)$ are the controllers for realizing the SGPS.

Let $\epsilon_i(t) = \zeta_i(t) - \hat{\zeta}_i(t)$ and $\tilde{\epsilon}_j(t) = \vartheta_j(t) - \hat{\vartheta}_j(t)$. Take $\epsilon_i(t)$ and $\tilde{\epsilon}_j(t)$ as the synchronization error variables. Then, from Equations (1) and (2), we can obtain the error dynamical system:

$$
\begin{aligned}
\dot{\epsilon}_i(t) = & -\mathfrak{a}_i \epsilon_i(t) + \sum_{j \in \mathbb{Z}_m} \left[\mathfrak{b}_{ij} h_j^*(\tilde{\epsilon}_j(t)) + \mathfrak{c}_{ij} l_j^*(\tilde{\epsilon}_j(p_{ij} t)) \right] \\
& + \sum_{j \in \mathbb{Z}_m} \sum_{l \in \mathbb{Z}_m} \mathfrak{d}_{ijl} \Big[\hbar_j(\vartheta_j(p_{ijl} t)) \hbar_l^*(\tilde{\epsilon}_l(p_{ijl} t)) \\
& + \hbar_j^*(\tilde{\epsilon}_j(p_{ijl} t)) \hbar_l(\hat{\vartheta}_l(p_{ijl} t)) \Big] \\
& - U_i(t), i \in \mathbb{Z}_n, t \in [t_0, \infty),
\end{aligned}
\tag{3a}
$$

$$
\begin{aligned}
\dot{\tilde{\epsilon}}_j(t) = & -\hat{\mathfrak{a}}_j\tilde{\epsilon}_j(t) + \sum_{i\in\mathbb{Z}_n}\left[\hat{\mathfrak{b}}_{ji}\tilde{h}_i^*(\epsilon_i(t)) + \hat{\mathfrak{c}}_{ji}\tilde{l}_i^*(\epsilon_i(\hat{p}_{ji}t))\right] \\
& + \sum_{i\in\mathbb{Z}_n}\sum_{r\in\mathbb{Z}_n}\hat{\mathfrak{d}}_{jir}\Big[\tilde{\hbar}_i(\zeta_i(\hat{p}_{jir}t))\tilde{\hbar}_r^*(\epsilon_r(\hat{p}_{jir}t)) \\
& + \tilde{\hbar}_i^*(\epsilon_i(\hat{p}_{jir}t))\tilde{\hbar}_r(\hat{\zeta}_r(\hat{p}_{jir}t))\Big] \\
& - V_j(t), j \in \mathbb{Z}_m, t \in [t_0, \infty),
\end{aligned} \tag{3b}
$$

$$
\epsilon_i(s) = \rho_i(s), \tilde{\epsilon}_j(s) = \varrho_j(s), \delta t_0 \le s \le t_0, i \in \mathbb{Z}_n, j \in \mathbb{Z}_m, \tag{3c}
$$

where

$$
\begin{aligned}
h_j^*(\tilde{\epsilon}_j(\cdot)) &= h_j(\tilde{\epsilon}_j(\cdot) + \hat{\vartheta}_j(\cdot)) - h_j(\hat{\vartheta}_j(\cdot)), \\
\tilde{h}_i^*(\epsilon_i(\cdot)) &= \tilde{h}_i(\epsilon_i(\cdot) + \hat{\zeta}_i(\cdot)) - \tilde{h}_i(\hat{\zeta}_i(\cdot)), \\
l_j^*(\tilde{\epsilon}_j(\cdot)) &= l_j(\tilde{\epsilon}_j(\cdot) + \hat{\vartheta}_j(\cdot)) - l_j(\hat{\vartheta}_j(\cdot)), \\
\tilde{l}_i^*(\epsilon_i(\cdot)) &= \tilde{l}_i(\epsilon_i(\cdot) + \hat{\zeta}_i(\cdot)) - \tilde{l}_i(\hat{\zeta}_i(\cdot)), \\
\hbar_j^*(\tilde{\epsilon}_j(\cdot)) &= \hbar_j(\tilde{\epsilon}_j(\cdot) + \hat{\vartheta}_j(\cdot)) - \hbar_j(\hat{\vartheta}_j(\cdot)), \\
\tilde{\hbar}_i^*(\epsilon_i(\cdot)) &= \tilde{\hbar}_i(\epsilon_i(\cdot) + \hat{\zeta}_i(\cdot)) - \tilde{\hbar}_i(\hat{\zeta}_i(\cdot)). \\
\rho_i(s) &= \varphi_i(s) - \hat{\varphi}_i(s), \varrho_j(s) = \psi_j(s) - \hat{\psi}_j(s)
\end{aligned}
$$

Due to Assumptions 1–3, we deduce that

$$
\begin{aligned}
& |h_j^*(\omega)| \le \bar{h}_j|\omega|,\ |\tilde{h}_i^*(\omega)| \le \bar{\tilde{h}}_i|\omega|, \\
& |l_j^*(\omega)| \le \bar{l}_j|\omega|,\ |\tilde{l}_i^*(\omega)| \le \bar{\tilde{l}}_i|\omega|, \\
& |\hbar_j^*(\omega)| \le \bar{\hbar}_j|\omega|,\ |\tilde{\hbar}_i^*(\omega)| \le \bar{\tilde{\hbar}}_i|\omega|, \omega \in \mathbb{R},\ i \in \mathbb{Z}_n, j \in \mathbb{Z}_m.
\end{aligned} \tag{4}
$$

Remark 1. *Assumptions 1–4 guarantee the existence and uniqueness of the solutions to the considered differential equations, ensuring that the solutions of the system will not diverge within a finite time, thus guaranteeing the effectiveness of the stability analysis. The assumptions about the activation functions prevent the nonlinear terms from causing system instability due to excessive amplification in the state space. In the analysis of the synchronization error dynamics, these assumptions help simplify the estimation of the coupling terms and interaction terms.*

Let

$$
\epsilon_i(t) = \zeta_i(t) - \hat{\zeta}_i(t), \tilde{\epsilon}_j(t) = \vartheta_j(t) - \hat{\vartheta}_j(t).
$$

Definition 1 ([18]). *The HOBAMNN* (1) *is said to be semi-globally polynomially stable, if there exist scalars $\mathfrak{R} > 0$, $K > 0$, and $\beta > 0$ such that*

$$
\left(\|\zeta(t)\|_2^2 + \|\vartheta(t)\|_2^2\right)^{1/2} \le K\|(\varphi, \psi)\|_\infty \left(\frac{1+t}{1+t_0}\right)^{-\beta}
$$

for any $t \ge t_0$, $\varphi \in \mathbb{C}([\delta t_0, t_0], \mathbb{R}^n)$ and $\psi \in \mathbb{C}([\delta t_0, t_0], \mathbb{R}^m)$ subject to $\|(\varphi, \psi)\|_\infty < \mathfrak{R}$, where

$$
\zeta(t) = \mathrm{col}(\zeta_1(t), \zeta_2(t), \dots, \zeta_n(t)),\ \vartheta(t) = \mathrm{col}(\vartheta_1(t), \vartheta_2(t), \dots, \vartheta_m(t)),
$$

$$
\|(\varphi, \psi)\|_\infty = \sup_{s\in[\delta t_0, t_0]} \max\{\|\varphi(s)\|_\infty, \|\psi(s)\|_\infty\},
$$

$$\varphi(s) = \mathrm{col}(\varphi_1(s), \varphi_2(s), \ldots, \varphi_n(s)),\ \psi(s) = \mathrm{col}(\psi_1(s), \psi_2(s), \ldots, \psi_m(s)).$$

Specifically, when $\mathfrak{R} = +\infty$, HOBAMNN (1) is defined as globally polynomially stable.

Remark 2. *Global polynomial stability requires that the system polynomially converges to the equilibrium state under all initial conditions in the entire state space. In contrast, semi-global polynomial stability requires that the system polynomially converges to the equilibrium state corresponding to the initial conditions within some fixed bounded set. In the case of global polynomial stability, the polynomial decay rate is consistent for any initial state, but for semi-global polynomial stability, the decay rate depends on the selected set.*

Definition 2. *The response HOBAMNN* (2) *and HOBAMNN* (1) *are said to achieve SGPS, if there exist scalars $\mathfrak{R} > 0$, $K > 0$, and $\lambda > 0$ such that any solution $(\epsilon(t), \tilde{\epsilon}(t))$ of error dynamical system* (3) *satisfies*

$$\left(\|\epsilon(t)\|_2^2 + \|\tilde{\epsilon}(t)\|_2^2\right)^{1/2} \leq K\|(\varpi, \tilde{\varpi})\|_\infty \left(\frac{1+t}{1+t_0}\right)^{-\lambda}$$

for any $t \geq t_0$, $\varpi \in \mathbb{C}([\delta t_0, t_0], \mathbb{R}^n)$ and $\tilde{\varpi} \in \mathbb{C}([\delta t_0, t_0], \mathbb{R}^m)$ subject to $\|(\varpi, \tilde{\varpi})\|_\infty < \mathfrak{R}$, where

$$\epsilon(t) = \mathrm{col}(\epsilon_1(t), \epsilon_2(t), \ldots, \epsilon_n(t)),\ \tilde{\epsilon}(t) = \mathrm{col}(\tilde{\epsilon}_1(t), \tilde{\epsilon}_2(t), \ldots, \tilde{\epsilon}_m(t)),$$

$$\|(\varpi, \tilde{\varpi})\|_\infty = \sup_{s \in [\delta t_0, t_0]} \max\{\|\varpi(s)\|_\infty, \|\tilde{\varpi}(s)\|_\infty\},$$

$$\varpi(s) = \mathrm{col}(\varpi_1(s), \varpi_2(s), \ldots, \varpi_n(s)),\ \tilde{\varpi}(s) = \mathrm{col}(\tilde{\varpi}_1(s), \tilde{\varpi}_2(s), \ldots, \tilde{\varpi}_m(s)).$$

That is, the error system (3) *controlled by the controllers $U_i(t)$ and $V_j(t)$ is semi-globally polynomially stable.*

The objective of this paper is to design a state feedback controller of the following form:

$$\begin{aligned} U_i(t) &= (\mu_i - \mathfrak{a}_i)\epsilon_i(t),\ i \in \mathbb{Z}_n, t \geq t_0, \\ V_j(t) &= (\tilde{\mu}_j - \hat{\mathfrak{a}}_j)\tilde{\epsilon}_j(t), j \in \mathbb{Z}_m, t \geq t_0, \end{aligned} \tag{5}$$

which allows HOBAMNNs (1) and (2) achieve SGPS, where $\mu_i > 0$ and $\tilde{\mu}_j > 0$ are the controller gains to be determined. In other words, the goal is to derive new sufficient conditions that ensure that the error dynamical system (3) exhibits semi-global polynomial stability.

3. Main Results

Lemma 1 ([18]). *Let $\kappa(x) = (\bar{\tau} - \gamma)(x - T) - \tau \ln(\frac{1+x}{1+T})$, $x \in (-1, T]$, where γ, $\bar{\tau}$, τ, and T are positive scalars such that $\bar{\tau} - \gamma \geq \tau$ and $T > t_0$. Then, for all $x \in [t_0, T]$, the following inequality holds: $\kappa(x) \leq 0$; that is, $\bar{\tau}(x - T) - \tau \ln(\frac{1+x}{1+T}) \leq \gamma(x - T)$ for any $x \in [t_0, T]$.*

Theorem 1. *Under Assumptions 1–4, let known positive scalars ζ, ϑ, λ, μ_i, $\tilde{\mu}_j$, η_i, and $\tilde{\eta}_j$ be subject to*

$$\lambda < \min\left(\min_{i \in \mathbb{Z}_n}(\mu_i - \eta_i), \min_{j \in \mathbb{Z}_m}(\tilde{\mu}_j - \tilde{\eta}_j)\right) \tag{6}$$

if there are $\tilde{\zeta}_i > 0$ and $\tilde{\vartheta}_j > 0$ such that

$$1 + \tilde{\Lambda}_i \prec \tilde{\zeta}_i, \tag{7a}$$

$$1 + \tilde{\aleph}_j \prec \tilde{\vartheta}_j, \tag{7b}$$

where

$$\tilde{\Delta}_i = \sum_{j\in\mathbb{Z}_m} \tilde{\Delta}_{ij}\tilde{\vartheta}_j, \tilde{\Delta}_{ij} = \Theta_{ij} + \Xi_{ij},$$

$$\tilde{\aleph}_j = \sum_{i\in\mathbb{Z}_n} \tilde{\aleph}_{ji}\tilde{\zeta}_i, \tilde{\aleph}_{ji} = \overline{\Theta}_{ji} + \overline{\Xi}_{ji},$$

$$\Theta_{ij} = \frac{|\mathfrak{b}_{ij}|\bar{h}_j + |\mathfrak{c}_{ij}|\bar{l}_j p_{ij}^{-\lambda}}{\eta_i}, \overline{\Theta}_{ji} = \frac{|\hat{\mathfrak{b}}_{ji}|\bar{\bar{h}}_i + |\hat{\mathfrak{c}}_{ji}|\bar{\bar{l}}_i \hat{p}_{ji}^{-\lambda}}{\tilde{\eta}_j},$$

$$\Xi_{ij} = \frac{\sum_{l\in\mathbb{Z}_m} \tilde{\gamma}_l^{(1)}\left(|\mathfrak{d}_{ilj}|p_{ilj}^{-\lambda} + |\mathfrak{d}_{ijl}|p_{ijl}^{-\lambda}\right)\bar{\hbar}_j}{\eta_i},$$

$$\overline{\Xi}_{ji} = \frac{\sum_{r\in\mathbb{Z}_n} \tilde{\gamma}_r^{(2)}\left(|\hat{\mathfrak{d}}_{jri}|\hat{p}_{jri}^{-\lambda} + |\hat{\mathfrak{d}}_{jir}|\hat{p}_{jir}^{-\lambda}\right)\bar{\bar{\hbar}}_i}{\tilde{\eta}_j},$$

Then, error system (3) is semi-globally polynomially stable; that is, the drive system HOBAMNN (1) and response system HOBAMNN (2) achieve SGPS.

Proof. Choose $\Upsilon > 1$ such that

$$\Upsilon\tilde{\zeta} \succ \mathrm{col}(1 \ \cdots \ 1), \ \Upsilon\tilde{\vartheta} \succ \mathrm{col}(1 \ \cdots \ 1).$$

where

$$\tilde{\zeta} = \mathrm{col}(\tilde{\zeta}_1 \ \cdots \ \tilde{\zeta}_n), \ \tilde{\vartheta} = \mathrm{col}(\tilde{\vartheta}_1 \ \cdots \ \tilde{\vartheta}_m).$$

For any fixed initial functions $\varpi \in C([\delta t_0, t_0], \mathbb{R}^n)$ and $\tilde{\varpi} \in C([\delta t_0, t_0], \mathbb{R}^m)$, define

$$\hat{\epsilon}(t) = \Upsilon\|(\varpi,\tilde{\varpi})\|_\infty\left(\frac{1+t}{1+t_0}\right)^{-\lambda}\tilde{\zeta}, \ t \geq \delta t_0, \tag{8}$$

$$\hat{\tilde{\epsilon}}(t) = \Upsilon\|(\rho,\varrho)\|_\infty\left(\frac{1+t}{1+t_0}\right)^{-\lambda}\tilde{\vartheta}, \ \ t \geq \delta t_0. \tag{9}$$

Suppose that $(\epsilon(t),\tilde{\epsilon}(t))$ is a solution of the error system (3). Next, the following expression will be proven:

$$|\epsilon(t)| \preceq \hat{\epsilon}(t), \ |\tilde{\epsilon}(t)| \preceq \hat{\tilde{\epsilon}}(t), t \geq \delta t_0, \tag{10}$$

i.e.,

$$|\epsilon(t)| \preceq \Upsilon\|(\varpi,\tilde{\varpi})\|_\infty\left(\frac{1+t}{1+t_0}\right)^{-\lambda}\tilde{\zeta}, \ t \geq \delta t_0, \tag{11a}$$

$$|\tilde{\epsilon}(t)| \preceq \Upsilon\|(\varpi,\tilde{\varpi})\|_\infty\left(\frac{1+t}{1+t_0}\right)^{-\lambda}\tilde{\vartheta}, \ \ t \geq \delta t_0. \tag{11b}$$

Based on (5), it is obtained that

$$\begin{aligned}\dot{\epsilon}_i(t) &= -\mu_i\epsilon_i(t) + \sum_{j\in\mathbb{Z}_m}\Big[\mathfrak{b}_{ij}h_j^*(\tilde{\epsilon}_j(t)) + \mathfrak{c}_{ij}l_j^*(\tilde{\epsilon}_j(p_{ij}t))\Big] \\ &\quad + \sum_{j\in\mathbb{Z}_m}\sum_{l\in\mathbb{Z}_m}\mathfrak{d}_{ijl}\Big[\hbar_j(\vartheta_j(p_{ijl}t))\hbar_l^*(\tilde{\epsilon}_l(p_{ijl}t)) \\ &\quad + \hbar_j^*(\tilde{\epsilon}_j(p_{ijl}t))\hbar_l(\hat{\vartheta}_l(p_{ijl}t))\Big], i\in\mathbb{Z}_n, t\in[t_0,\infty). \end{aligned} \tag{12}$$

By multiplying both sides of Equation (12) by $e^{\mu_i(t-t_0)}$ and then taking the integration from t_0 to t, we have

$$\begin{aligned}\epsilon_i(t) &= e^{-\mu_i(t-t_0)}\epsilon_i(t_0) \\ &\quad + \sum_{j\in\mathbb{Z}_m}\mathfrak{b}_{ij}\int_{t_0}^t e^{\mu_i(\omega-t)}h_j^*(\tilde{\epsilon}_j(\omega))d\omega \\ &\quad + \sum_{j\in\mathbb{Z}_m}\mathfrak{c}_{ij}\int_{t_0}^t e^{\mu_i(\omega-t)}l_j^*(\tilde{\epsilon}_j(p_{ij}\omega))d\omega \\ &\quad + \sum_{j\in\mathbb{Z}_m}\sum_{l\in\mathbb{Z}_m}\mathfrak{d}_{ijl}\int_{t_0}^t e^{\mu_i(\omega-t)}\Big[\hbar_j(\vartheta_j(p_{ijl}\omega))\hbar_l^*(\tilde{\epsilon}_l(p_{ijl}\omega))| \\ &\quad + \hbar_j^*(\tilde{\epsilon}_j(p_{ijl}\omega))\hbar_l(\hat{\vartheta}_l(p_{ijl}\omega))\Big]d\omega, \\ &\quad i\in\mathbb{Z}_n, t\in[t_0,\infty). \end{aligned} \tag{13}$$

According to Assumptions 1–3 and 4, one can derive

$$\begin{aligned}|\epsilon_i(t)| &\le e^{-\mu_i(t-t_0)}|\rho_i(t_0)| \\ &\quad + \sum_{j\in\mathbb{Z}_m}|\mathfrak{b}_{ij}|\bar{h}_j\int_{t_0}^t e^{\mu_i(\omega-t)}|\tilde{\epsilon}_j(\omega)|d\omega \\ &\quad + \sum_{j\in\mathbb{Z}_m}|\mathfrak{c}_{ij}|\bar{l}_j\int_{t_0}^t e^{\mu_i(\omega-t)}|\tilde{\epsilon}_j(p_{ij}\omega)|d\omega \\ &\quad + \sum_{j\in\mathbb{Z}_m}\sum_{l\in\mathbb{Z}_m}|\mathfrak{d}_{ijl}|\int_{t_0}^t e^{\mu_i(\omega-t)}\Big[\gamma_j^{(1)}\bar{\hbar}_l|\tilde{\epsilon}_l(p_{ijl}\omega)| \\ &\quad + \bar{\hbar}_j\gamma_l^{(1)}|\tilde{\epsilon}_j(p_{ijl}\omega)|\Big]d\omega, i\in\mathbb{Z}_n, t\in[t_0,\infty). \end{aligned} \tag{14}$$

Analogously, we can obtain

$$\begin{aligned}|\tilde{\epsilon}_j(t)| &\le e^{-\tilde{\mu}_j(t-t_0)}|\varrho_j(t_0)| \\ &\quad + \sum_{i\in\mathbb{Z}_n}|\hat{\mathfrak{b}}_{ji}|\bar{\tilde{h}}_i\int_{t_0}^t e^{\tilde{\mu}_j(\omega-t)}|\epsilon_i(\omega)|d\omega \\ &\quad + \sum_{i\in\mathbb{Z}_n}|\hat{\mathfrak{c}}_{ji}|\bar{\tilde{l}}_i\int_{t_0}^t e^{\tilde{\mu}_j(\omega-t)}|\epsilon_i(\hat{p}_{ji}\omega)|d\omega \\ &\quad + \sum_{i\in\mathbb{Z}_n}\sum_{r\in\mathbb{Z}_n}|\hat{\mathfrak{d}}_{jir}|\int_{t_0}^t e^{\tilde{\mu}_j(\omega-t)}\Big[\tilde{\gamma}_i^{(2)}\bar{\tilde{\hbar}}_r|\epsilon_r(\hat{p}_{jir}\omega)| \\ &\quad + \bar{\tilde{\hbar}}_i\tilde{\gamma}_r^{(2)}|\epsilon_i(\hat{p}_{jir}\omega)|\Big]d\omega, j\in\mathbb{Z}_m, t\in[t_0,\infty). \end{aligned} \tag{15}$$

Clearly, (11) holds for any $t\in[\delta t_0, t_0]$. Assume that (11) is not true for all $t\in(t_0,+\infty)$. Then, the following (i) or (ii) is true:

(i) When $t_0 < t \leq T$, there is T and $i^* \in \mathbb{Z}_n$ such that (11) is true, and

$$|\epsilon_{i^*}(T)| = \Upsilon\|(\varpi,\tilde{\varpi})\|_\infty\left(\frac{1+T}{1+t_0}\right)^{-\lambda}\tilde{\zeta}_{i^*}, \tag{16}$$

(ii) When $t_0 < t \leq T$, there is T and $j^* \in \mathbb{Z}_m$ such that (11) is true, and

$$|\tilde{\epsilon}_{j^*}(T)| = \Upsilon\|(\varpi,\tilde{\varpi})\|_\infty\left(\frac{1+T}{1+t_0}\right)^{-\lambda}\tilde{\vartheta}_{j^*}. \tag{17}$$

Case 1: (i) holds. From (14) and (11b), we derive

$$\begin{aligned}
|\epsilon_{i^*}(T)| \leq\ & \Upsilon\|(\varpi,\tilde{\varpi})\|_\infty e^{-\mu_{i^*}(T-t_0)} \\
&+ \sum_{j\in\mathbb{Z}_m}|\mathfrak{b}_{i^*j}|\bar{h}_j\tilde{\vartheta}_j\Upsilon\|(\varpi,\tilde{\varpi})\|_\infty\int_{t_0}^{T}e^{\mu_{i^*}(\omega-T)}\left(\frac{1+\omega}{1+t_0}\right)^{-\lambda}d\omega \\
&+ \sum_{j\in\mathbb{Z}_m}|\mathfrak{c}_{i^*j}|\bar{l}_j p_{i^*j}^{-\lambda}\tilde{\vartheta}_j\Upsilon\|(\varpi,\tilde{\varpi})\|_\infty\int_{t_0}^{T}e^{\mu_{i^*}(\omega-T)}\left(\frac{1+\omega}{1+t_0}\right)^{-\lambda}d\omega \\
&+ \sum_{j\in\mathbb{Z}_m}\sum_{l\in\mathbb{Z}_m}|\mathfrak{d}_{i^*jl}|\int_{t_0}^{T}e^{\mu_{i^*}(\omega-T)}\Bigg[\tilde{\gamma}_j^{(1)}\bar{h}_l p_{i^*jl}^{-\lambda}\tilde{\vartheta}_l\Upsilon\|(\varpi,\tilde{\varpi})\|_\infty\left(\frac{1+\omega}{1+t_0}\right)^{-\lambda} \\
&+\bar{h}_j\tilde{\gamma}_l^{(1)}p_{i^*jl}^{-\lambda}\tilde{\vartheta}_j\Upsilon\|(\varpi,\tilde{\varpi})\|_\infty\left(\frac{1+\omega}{1+t_0}\right)^{-\lambda}\Bigg]d\omega \\
=\ & \Upsilon\|(\varpi,\tilde{\varpi})\|_\infty\left(\frac{1+T}{1+t_0}\right)^{-\lambda}\Bigg\{e^{-\mu_{i^*}(T-t_0)}\left(\frac{1+T}{1+t_0}\right)^{\lambda} \\
&+ \sum_{j\in\mathbb{Z}_m}|\mathfrak{b}_{i^*j}|\bar{h}_j\tilde{\vartheta}_j\int_{t_0}^{T}e^{\mu_{i^*}(\omega-T)}\left(\frac{1+\omega}{1+T}\right)^{-\lambda}d\omega \\
&+ \sum_{j\in\mathbb{Z}_m}|\mathfrak{c}_{i^*j}|\bar{l}_j p_{i^*j}^{-\lambda}\tilde{\vartheta}_j\int_{t_0}^{T}e^{\mu_{i^*}(\omega-T)}\left(\frac{1+\omega}{1+T}\right)^{-\lambda}d\omega \\
&+ \sum_{j\in\mathbb{Z}_m}\sum_{l\in\mathbb{Z}_m}|\mathfrak{d}_{i^*jl}|\left[\tilde{\gamma}_j^{(1)}\bar{h}_l p_{i^*jl}^{-\lambda}\tilde{\vartheta}_l+\bar{h}_j\tilde{\gamma}_l^{(1)}p_{i^*jl}^{-\lambda}\tilde{\vartheta}_j\right] \\
&\times\int_{t_0}^{T}e^{\mu_{i^*}(\omega-T)}\left(\frac{1+\omega}{1+T}\right)^{-\lambda}d\omega\Bigg\}
\end{aligned}$$

$$\begin{aligned}
=\ & \Upsilon\|(\varpi,\tilde{\varpi})\|_\infty\left(\frac{1+T}{1+t_0}\right)^{-\lambda}\Bigg\{e^{-\mu_{i^*}(T-t_0)}\left(\frac{1+T}{1+t_0}\right)^{\lambda} \\
&+\Bigg[\sum_{j\in\mathbb{Z}_m}\left(|\mathfrak{b}_{i^*j}|\bar{h}_j+|\mathfrak{c}_{i^*j}|\bar{l}_j p_{i^*j}^{-\lambda}\right)\tilde{\vartheta}_j \\
&+\sum_{j\in\mathbb{Z}_m}\sum_{l\in\mathbb{Z}_m}\left(|\mathfrak{d}_{i^*lj}|\tilde{\gamma}_l^{(1)}\bar{h}_j p_{i^*lj}^{-\lambda}+|\mathfrak{d}_{i^*jl}|\bar{h}_j\tilde{\gamma}_l^{(1)}p_{i^*jl}^{-\lambda}\right)\tilde{\vartheta}_j\Bigg] \\
&\times\int_{t_0}^{T}e^{\mu_{i^*}(\omega-T)}\left(\frac{1+\omega}{1+T}\right)^{-\lambda}d\omega\Bigg\} \\
=\ & \Upsilon\|(\varpi,\tilde{\varpi})\|_\infty\left(\frac{1+T}{1+t_0}\right)^{-\lambda}\Bigg[e^{-\mu_{i^*}(T-t_0)}\left(\frac{1+T}{1+t_0}\right)^{\lambda} \\
&+\eta_{i^*}\tilde{\Delta}_{i^*}\int_{t_0}^{T}e^{\mu_{i^*}(\omega-T)}\left(\frac{1+\omega}{1+T}\right)^{-\lambda}d\omega\Bigg],
\end{aligned}$$

where

$$\tilde{\Delta}_{i^*} = \sum_{j\in\mathbb{Z}_m} \tilde{\Delta}_{i^*j}\tilde{\vartheta}_j.\tilde{\Delta}_{i^*j} = \Theta_{i^*j} + \Xi_{i^*j},$$

Noting that $e^{\mu_{i^*}(\omega-T)-\lambda\ln\left(\frac{1+\omega}{1+T}\right)} \leq e^{\eta_{i^*}(\omega-T)}$ for any $\omega \in [t_0, T]$ from Lemma 1, we have from (7a) that

$$\begin{aligned}
|\epsilon_{i^*}(T)| &\leq \Upsilon\|(\varpi,\tilde{\varpi})\|_\infty\left(\frac{1+T}{1+t_0}\right)^{-\lambda}\left[e^{\eta_{i^*}(t_0-T)} + \eta_{i^*}\tilde{\Delta}_{i^*}\int_{t_0}^{T} e^{\eta_{i^*}(\omega-T)}d\omega\right] \\
&\leq \Upsilon\|(\varpi,\tilde{\varpi})\|_\infty\left(\frac{1+T}{1+t_0}\right)^{-\lambda}(1+\tilde{\Delta}_{i^*}),
\end{aligned} \quad (18)$$

We have $|\epsilon_{i^*}(T)| < \Upsilon\|(\varpi,\tilde{\varpi})\|_\infty\left(\frac{1+T}{1+t_0}\right)^{-\lambda}\tilde{\zeta}_{i^*}$, which contradicts (16).
Case 2: (ii) holds. Using (15) and (11a), we derive

$$\begin{aligned}
|\tilde{\epsilon}_{j^*}(T)| \leq\ & \Upsilon\|(\varpi,\tilde{\varpi})\|_\infty e^{-\tilde{\mu}_{j^*}(T-t_0)} \\
&+ \sum_{i\in\mathbb{Z}_n}|\hat{\mathfrak{b}}_{j^*i}|\bar{\bar{h}}_i\tilde{\zeta}_i\Upsilon\|(\varpi,\tilde{\varpi})\|_\infty\int_{t_0}^{T} e^{\tilde{\mu}_{j^*}(\omega-T)}\left(\frac{1+\omega}{1+t_0}\right)^{-\lambda}d\omega \\
&+ \sum_{i\in\mathbb{Z}_n}|\hat{\mathfrak{c}}_{j^*i}|\bar{\bar{l}}_i\hat{p}_{j^*i}^{-\lambda}\tilde{\zeta}_i\Upsilon\|(\varpi,\tilde{\varpi})\|_\infty\int_{t_0}^{T} e^{\tilde{\mu}_{j^*}(\omega-T)}\left(\frac{1+\omega}{1+t_0}\right)^{-\lambda}d\omega \\
&+ \sum_{i\in\mathbb{Z}_n}\sum_{r\in\mathbb{Z}_n}|\hat{\mathfrak{d}}_{j^*ir}|\int_{t_0}^{T} e^{\tilde{\mu}_{j^*}(\omega-T)}\left[\tilde{\gamma}_i^{(2)}\bar{\bar{\hbar}}_r\hat{p}_{j^*ir}^{-\lambda}\tilde{\zeta}_r\Upsilon\|(\varpi,\tilde{\varpi})\|_\infty\left(\frac{1+\omega}{1+t_0}\right)^{-\lambda}\right. \\
&\left.+\bar{\bar{\hbar}}_i\tilde{\gamma}_r^{(2)}\hat{p}_{j^*ir}^{-\lambda}\tilde{\zeta}_i\Upsilon\|(\varpi,\tilde{\varpi})\|_\infty\left(\frac{1+\omega}{1+t_0}\right)^{-\lambda}\right]d\omega \\
=\ & \Upsilon\|(\varpi,\tilde{\varpi})\|_\infty\left(\frac{1+T}{1+t_0}\right)^{-\lambda}\left\{e^{-\tilde{\mu}_{j^*}(T-t_0)}\left(\frac{1+T}{1+t_0}\right)^{\lambda}\right. \\
&+ \sum_{i\in\mathbb{Z}_n}|\hat{\mathfrak{b}}_{j^*i}|\bar{\bar{h}}_i\tilde{\zeta}_i\int_{t_0}^{T} e^{\tilde{\mu}_{j^*}(\omega-T)}\left(\frac{1+\omega}{1+T}\right)^{-\lambda}d\omega \\
&+ \sum_{i\in\mathbb{Z}_n}|\hat{\mathfrak{c}}_{j^*i}|\bar{\bar{l}}_i\hat{p}_{j^*i}^{-\lambda}\tilde{\zeta}_i\int_{t_0}^{T} e^{\tilde{\mu}_{j^*}(\omega-T)}\left(\frac{1+\omega}{1+T}\right)^{-\lambda}d\omega \\
&+ \sum_{i\in\mathbb{Z}_n}\sum_{r\in\mathbb{Z}_n}\left[|\hat{\mathfrak{d}}_{j^*ir}|\tilde{\gamma}_i^{(2)}\bar{\bar{\hbar}}_r\hat{p}_{j^*ir}^{-\lambda}\tilde{\zeta}_r\right. \\
&\left.\left.+|\hat{\mathfrak{d}}_{j^*ir}|\bar{\bar{\hbar}}_i\tilde{\gamma}_r^{(2)}\hat{p}_{j^*ir}^{-\lambda}\tilde{\zeta}_i\right]\int_{t_0}^{T} e^{\tilde{\mu}_{j^*}(\omega-T)}\left(\frac{1+\omega}{1+T}\right)^{-\lambda}d\omega\right\}
\end{aligned}$$

$$
\begin{aligned}
&= \Upsilon\|(\varpi,\tilde{\varpi})\|_\infty\left(\frac{1+T}{1+t_0}\right)^{-\lambda}\Bigg\{e^{-\tilde{\mu}_{j^*}(T-t_0)}\left(\frac{1+T}{1+t_0}\right)^{\lambda} \\
&+\sum_{i\in\mathbb{Z}_n}|\hat{\mathfrak{b}}_{j^*i}|\bar{\bar{h}}_i\zeta_i\int_{t_0}^{T}e^{\tilde{\mu}_{j^*}(\omega-T)}\left(\frac{1+\omega}{1+T}\right)^{-\lambda}d\omega \\
&+\sum_{i\in\mathbb{Z}_n}|\hat{\mathfrak{c}}_{j^*i}|\bar{\bar{l}}_i\rho_{j^*i}^{-\lambda}\tilde{\zeta}_i\int_{t_0}^{T}e^{\tilde{\mu}_{j^*}(\omega-T)}\left(\frac{1+\omega}{1+T}\right)^{-\lambda}d\omega \\
&+\sum_{i\in\mathbb{Z}_n}\sum_{r\in\mathbb{Z}_n}\Big[|\hat{\mathfrak{d}}_{j^*ri}|\tilde{\gamma}_r^{(2)}\bar{\bar{\hbar}}_i\rho_{j^*ri}^{-\lambda}\tilde{\zeta}_i \\
&+|\hat{\mathfrak{d}}_{j^*ir}|\bar{\bar{\hbar}}_i\tilde{\gamma}_r^{(2)}\rho_{j^*ir}^{-\lambda}\tilde{\zeta}_i\Big]\int_{t_0}^{T}e^{\tilde{\mu}_{j^*}(\omega-T)}\left(\frac{1+\omega}{1+T}\right)^{-\lambda}d\omega\Bigg\} \\
&= \Upsilon\|(\varpi,\tilde{\varpi})\|_\infty\left(\frac{1+T}{1+t_0}\right)^{-\lambda}\Bigg\{e^{-\tilde{\mu}_{j^*}(T-t_0)}\left(\frac{1+T}{1+t_0}\right)^{\lambda} \\
&+\Bigg[\sum_{i\in\mathbb{Z}_n}\left(|\hat{\mathfrak{b}}_{j^*i}|\bar{\bar{h}}_i+|\hat{\mathfrak{c}}_{j^*i}|\bar{\bar{l}}_i\rho_{j^*i}^{-\lambda}\right)\tilde{\zeta}_i \\
&+\sum_{i\in\mathbb{Z}_n}\sum_{r\in\mathbb{Z}_n}\left(|\hat{\mathfrak{d}}_{j^*ri}|\tilde{\gamma}_r^{(2)}\bar{\bar{\hbar}}_i\rho_{j^*ri}^{-\lambda}+|\hat{\mathfrak{d}}_{j^*ir}|\bar{\bar{\hbar}}_i\tilde{\gamma}_r^{(2)}\rho_{j^*ir}^{-\lambda}\right)\tilde{\zeta}_i\Bigg] \\
&\times\int_{t_0}^{T}e^{\tilde{\mu}_{j^*}(\omega-T)}\left(\frac{1+\omega}{1+T}\right)^{-\lambda}d\omega\Bigg\}
\end{aligned}
$$

$$
\begin{aligned}
&= \Upsilon\|(\varpi,\tilde{\varpi})\|_\infty\left(\frac{1+T}{1+t_0}\right)^{-\lambda}\Bigg[e^{-\tilde{\mu}_{j^*}(T-t_0)}\left(\frac{1+T}{1+t_0}\right)^{\lambda} \\
&+\tilde{\eta}_{j^*}\tilde{\aleph}_{j^*}\int_{t_0}^{T}e^{\tilde{\mu}_{j^*}(\omega-T)}\left(\frac{1+\omega}{1+T}\right)^{-\lambda}d\omega\Bigg],
\end{aligned}
\tag{19}
$$

where

$$
\tilde{\aleph}_{j^*}=\sum_{i\in\mathbb{Z}_n}\tilde{\aleph}_{j^*i}\tilde{\zeta}_i,\ \tilde{\aleph}_{j^*i}=\overline{\Theta}_{j^*i}+\overline{\Xi}_{j^*i}.
$$

Noting that $e^{\tilde{\mu}_{j^*}(\omega-T)-\lambda\ln\left(\frac{1+\omega}{1+T}\right)}\le e^{\tilde{\eta}_{j^*}(\omega-T)}$ for any $\omega\in[t_0,T]$ from Lemma 1, we have from (7b) that

$$
\begin{aligned}
|\tilde{\epsilon}_{j^*}(T)| &\le \Upsilon\|(\varpi,\tilde{\varpi})\|_\infty\left(\frac{1+T}{1+t_0}\right)^{-\lambda}\left[e^{\tilde{\eta}_{j^*}(t_0-T)}+\tilde{\eta}_{j^*}\tilde{\aleph}_{j^*}\int_{t_0}^{T}e^{\tilde{\eta}_{j^*}(\omega-T)}d\omega\right] \\
&\le \Upsilon\|(\varpi,\tilde{\varpi})\|_\infty\left(\frac{1+T}{1+t_0}\right)^{-\lambda}(1+\tilde{\aleph}_{j^*}),
\end{aligned}
\tag{20}
$$

We obtain $|\tilde{\epsilon}_{j^*}(T)|<\Upsilon\|(\varpi,\tilde{\varpi})\|_\infty\left(\frac{1+T}{1+t_0}\right)^{-\lambda}.\tilde{\vartheta}_{j^*}$, which contradicts (16). Consequently, for all $t\in[t_0,+\infty)$, (11) is true. Therefore,

$$
\begin{aligned}
&\sum_{i\in\mathbb{Z}_n}\epsilon_i^2(t)+\sum_{j\in\mathbb{Z}_m}\tilde{\epsilon}_j^2(t) \\
&\le \sum_{i\in\mathbb{Z}_n}\Upsilon^2\tilde{\zeta}_i^2\|(\varpi,\tilde{\varpi})\|_\infty^2\left(\frac{1+t}{1+t_0}\right)^{-2\lambda}+\sum_{j\in\mathbb{Z}_m}\Upsilon^2\tilde{\vartheta}_j^2\|(\varpi,\tilde{\varpi})\|_\infty^2\left(\frac{1+t}{1+t_0}\right)^{-2\lambda} \\
&\le \Gamma^2\|(\varpi,\tilde{\varpi})\|_\infty^2\left(\frac{1+t}{1+t_0}\right)^{-2\lambda},\forall t\ge t_0,
\end{aligned}
$$

where $\Gamma = \left(\sum_{i\in\mathbb{Z}_n} \Upsilon^2\tilde{\zeta}_i^2 + \sum_{j\in\mathbb{Z}_m} \Upsilon^2\tilde{\vartheta}_j^2\right)^{1/2}$.

In accordance with Definition 2, error system (3) is semi-globally polynomially stable; that is, the drive system HOBAMNN (1) and response system HOBAMNN (2) achieve SGPS. □

4. Illustrative Examples

Next, the effectiveness of the results given in this paper will be illustrated through a specific numerical example.

Example 1. *Consider drive and response HOBAMNNs* (1) *and* (2) *with the controllers in* (5)*: let* $n = 2$; $m = 2$; $\mathfrak{a}_1 = 0.4$; $\mathfrak{a}_2 = 0.4$; $\hat{\mathfrak{a}}_1 = 0.3$; $\hat{\mathfrak{a}}_2 = 0.4$; $\mathfrak{b}_{11} = 1.2$; $\mathfrak{b}_{12} = -0.6$; $\mathfrak{b}_{21} = -1.3$; $\mathfrak{b}_{22} = 0.24$; $\hat{\mathfrak{b}}_{11} = 1.2$; $\hat{\mathfrak{b}}_{12} = -0.42$; $\hat{\mathfrak{b}}_{21} = 2.2$; $\hat{\mathfrak{b}}_{22} = 0.22$; $\mathfrak{c}_{11} = -1.3$; $\mathfrak{c}_{12} = 1.5$; $g\ \mathfrak{c}_{21} = 2.4$; $\mathfrak{c}_{22} = 1.1$; $\hat{\mathfrak{c}}_{11} = 0.16$; $\hat{\mathfrak{c}}_{12} = -0.36$; $\hat{\mathfrak{c}}_{21} = -0.12$; $\hat{\mathfrak{c}}_{22} = 0.43$; $\mathfrak{d}_{111} = 1$; $\mathfrak{d}_{112} = 2$; $\mathfrak{d}_{121} = 1$; $\mathfrak{d}_{122} = 1$; $\mathfrak{d}_{211} = 2$; $\mathfrak{d}_{212} = 1$; $\mathfrak{d}_{221} = 1$; $\mathfrak{d}_{222} = 0.5$; $\hat{\mathfrak{d}}_{111} = 0.1$; $\hat{\mathfrak{d}}_{112} = 0.3$; $\hat{\mathfrak{d}}_{121} = 0.1$; $\hat{\mathfrak{d}}_{122} = 0.3$; $\hat{\mathfrak{d}}_{211} = 0.1$; $\hat{\mathfrak{d}}_{212} = 0.21$; $\hat{\mathfrak{d}}_{221} = 0.2$; $\hat{\mathfrak{d}}_{222} = 0.11$; $p_{11} = 0.5$; $p_{12} = 0.4$; $p_{21} = 0.2$; $p_{22} = 0.8$; $\hat{p}_{11} = 0.7$; $\hat{p}_{12} = 0.1$; $\hat{p}_{21} = 0.2$; $\hat{p}_{22} = 0.9$; $\mathfrak{p}_{111} = \mathfrak{p}_{112} = \mathfrak{p}_{121} = \mathfrak{p}_{211} = \mathfrak{p}_{212} = \mathfrak{p}_{221} = \mathfrak{p}_{222} = 0.8$; $\mathfrak{p}_{122} = 0.9$; $\hat{\mathfrak{p}}_{111} = \hat{\mathfrak{p}}_{112} = \hat{\mathfrak{p}}_{121} = \hat{\mathfrak{p}}_{122} = 0.8$; $\hat{\mathfrak{p}}_{211} = 0.4$; $\hat{\mathfrak{p}}_{212} = 0.6$; $\hat{\mathfrak{p}}_{221} = 0.3$; $\hat{\mathfrak{p}}_{222} = 0.7$.

$$h_1(s) = 0.2s\tanh^2(s), h_2(s) = 0.3s\tanh^2(s),$$

$$\tilde{h}_1(s) = 0.03s\tanh^2(s), \tilde{h}_2(s) = 0.2s\tanh^2(s),$$

$$l_1(s) = 0.3s\tanh^2(s), l_2(s) = 0.04s\tanh^2(s),$$

$$\tilde{l}_1(s) = 0.04s\tanh^2(s), \tilde{l}_2(s) = 0.02s\tanh^2(s),$$

$$\hbar_1(s) = \hbar_2(s) = 0.2\tanh(s), \tilde{\hbar}_1(s) = \tilde{\hbar}_2(s) = 0.3\tanh(s), s \in \mathbb{R}.$$

Clearly, set the following: $\bar{h}_1 = 0.2$; $\bar{h}_2 = 0.3$; $\bar{\bar{h}}_1 = 0.03$; $\bar{\bar{h}}_2 = 0.2$; $\bar{l}_1 = 0.3$; $\bar{l}_2 = 0.04$; $\bar{\bar{l}}_1 = 0.04$; $\bar{\bar{l}}_2 = 0.02$; $\bar{\hbar}_1 = \bar{\hbar}_2(s) = 0.2$; $\bar{\bar{\hbar}}_1 = \bar{\bar{\hbar}}_2(s) = 0.3$; $\tilde{\gamma}_1^{(1)} = \tilde{\gamma}_2^{(1)} = 0.2$; $\tilde{\gamma}_1^{(2)} = \tilde{\gamma}_2^{(2)} = 0.3$. *Assumptions 1–4 are satisfied.*

When $\lambda = 0.05$, $\mu_1 = 2.6$, $\mu_1 = 1.6$, $\tilde{\mu}_1 = 2.0$, $\tilde{\mu}_1 = 1.8$, $\eta_1 = 2.54$, $\eta_2 = 1.54$, $\tilde{\eta}_1 = 1.94$, *and* $\tilde{\eta}_2 = 1.74$, *by solving inequalities (7a) and (7b) in Theorem 1, the following feasible solutions are obtained:*

$$\tilde{u} = [3.0386, 4.3666]^T, \tilde{v} = [2.4361, 2.5156]^T.$$

It can be readily verified that the conditions of Theorem 1 in our paper are met. Consequently, based on Theorem 1 in our paper, the drive system given by (1) *and the response system given by* (2) *experience semi-global polynomial synchronization under controllers* (5). *We choose the initial values of the state variables as* $\zeta(s) = [0.4, 0.5]^T$, $\vartheta(s) = [0.2, 0.1]^T$, $\hat{\zeta}(s) = [0.6, 0.3]^T$, *and* $\hat{\vartheta}(s) = [0.4, 0.6]^T$. *We also define the external input as* $I_1 = I_2 = 0$, $J_1 = J_2 = 0$. *The error curves of drive–response systems* $\epsilon_1(t), \epsilon_2(t), \tilde{\epsilon}_1(t)$, *and* $\tilde{\epsilon}_2(t)$ *are shown in Figure 1; the curves of variables* $\zeta_1(t), \zeta_2(t), \vartheta_1(t), \vartheta_2(t), \hat{\zeta}_1(t), \hat{\zeta}_2(t), \hat{\vartheta}_1(t)$, *and* $\hat{\vartheta}_2(t)$ *are shown in Figures 2 and 3.*

Figures 4 and 5, respectively, show the state–response curves corresponding to the time delays of $\mathfrak{p}_{ijl} = \hat{\mathfrak{p}}_{jir} = 0.1$ *and* $\mathfrak{p}_{ijl} = \hat{\mathfrak{p}}_{jir} = 0.5$, $i, j, r, l \in \mathbb{Z}_2$, *indicating that different time delays affect the convergence rate of the error system.*

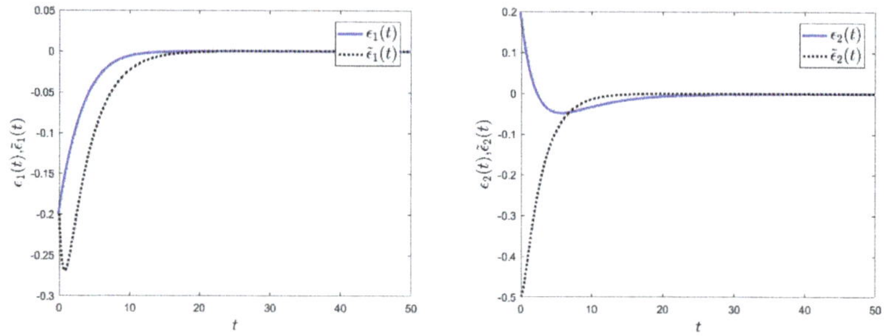

Figure 1. The error curves of $\epsilon(t)$ and $\tilde{\epsilon}(t)$.

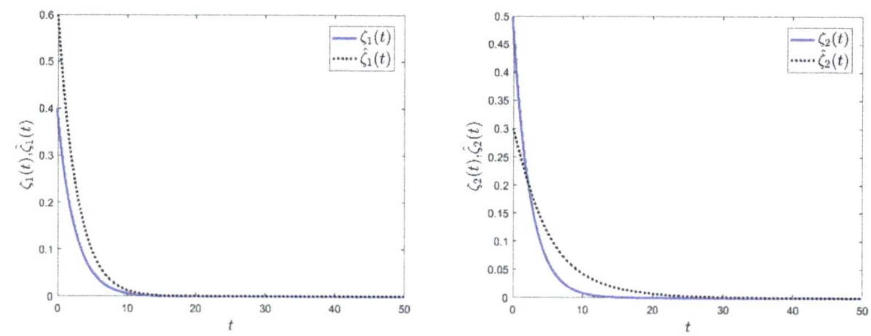

Figure 2. Synchronization curves of $\zeta(t)$ and $\hat{\zeta}(t)$.

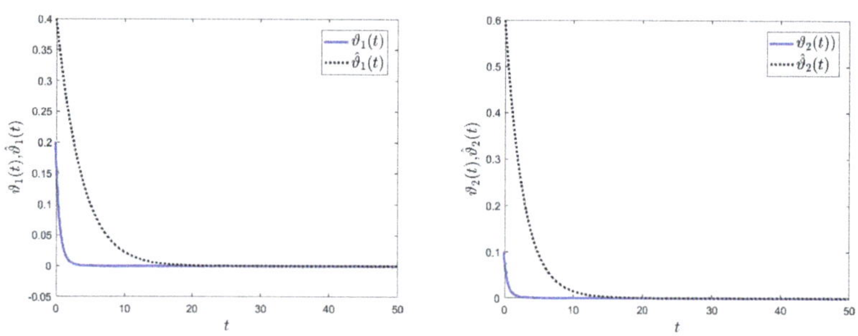

Figure 3. Synchronization curves of $\vartheta(t)$ and $\hat{\vartheta}(t)$.

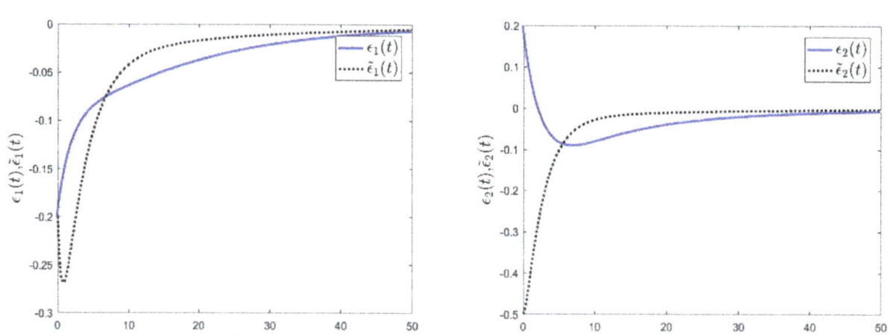

Figure 4. The error curves of $\epsilon(t)$ and $\tilde{\epsilon}(t)$ when $p_{ijl} = \hat{p}_{jir} = 0.1, i, j, r, l \in \mathbb{Z}_2$.

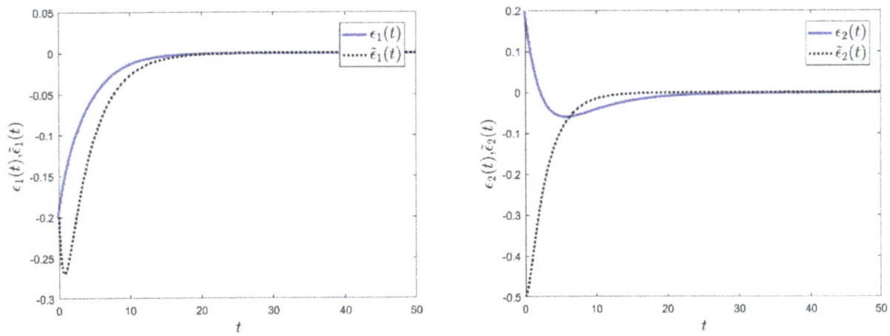

Figure 5. The error curves of $\epsilon(t)$ and $\tilde{\epsilon}(t)$ when $p_{ijl} = \hat{p}_{jir} = 0.5, i, j, r, l \in \mathbb{Z}_2$.

5. Conclusions

This paper addresses the issue of SGPS for HOBAMNNs with multiple proportional delays. Utilizing the definition of SGPS, we initially derive delay-dependent SGPS criteria for the error dynamical system. Subsequently, a controller gain is provided. Finally, we present illustrative examples to demonstrate the applicability of the conclusions. Compared with previous research, the main contribution of this work lies in the first investigation of SGPS for HOBAMNNs with multiple proportional delays. By directly deriving easily implementable sufficient criteria based on the definition of SGPS, our approach is applicable to a broader class of NN models. In [47], the general decay synchronization concept for the considered network based on ψ-type stability has been given. The general decay synchronization contained polynomial synchronization, exponential synchronization, logarithmic synchronization, and other synchronization as its special cases. We will consider this issue in further research.

Author Contributions: Conceptualization, E.-y.C. and X.Z.; Methodology, E.-y.C., X.Z. and L.Z.; Writing—original draft, E.-y.C., X.Z. and L.Z.; Writing—review & editing, E.-y.C., X.Z. and L.Z. All authors have read and agreed to the published version of the manuscript.

Funding: This work was supported in part by the Natural Science Foundation of Heilongjiang Province (No. LH2022F046 and No. YQ2022F015), the Project for the Research Foundation of Young Doctors of Harbin University (No. HUDF2022112) and Harbin Science and Technology Plan Project (No. 2023ZCZJCG045 and No. 2023ZCZJCG046).

Data Availability Statement: The original contributions presented in this study are included in the article. Further inquiries can be directed to the corresponding author.

Conflicts of Interest: The authors declare no conflicts of interest.

References

1. Townsend, J.; Chaton, T.; Monteiro, J.M. Extracting relational explanations from deep neural networks: A survey from a neural-symbolic perspective. *IEEE Trans. Neural Netw. Learn. Syst.* **2020**, *31*, 3456–3470. [CrossRef] [PubMed]
2. Thangarajan, S.K.; Chokkalingam, A. Integration of optimized neural network and convolutional neural network for automated brain tumor detection. *Sens. Rev.* **2021**, *41*, 16–34. [CrossRef]
3. Lee, Y.; Doolen, G.; Chen, H.H.; Sun, G.Z.; Maxwell, T.; Lee, H.Y. Machine learning using a higher order correlation network. *Phys. D Nonlinear Phenom.* **1986**, *22*, 276–306. [CrossRef]
4. Chen, Y.; Zhang, X.; Xue, Y. Global exponential synchronization of high-order quaternion Hopfield neural networks with unbounded distributed delays and time-varying discrete delays. *Math. Comput. Simul.* **2022**, *193*, 173–189. [CrossRef]
5. Dong, Z.; Wang, X.; Zhang, X.; Hu, M.; Dinh, T.N. Global exponential synchronization of discrete-time high-order switched neural networks and its application to multi-channel audio encryption. *Nonlinear Anal. Hybrid Syst.* **2023**, *47*, 101291. [CrossRef]
6. Kosko, B. Adaptive bidirectional associative memories. *Appl. Opt.* **1987**, *26*, 4947–4960. [CrossRef]
7. Kosko, B. Bi-directional associative memories. *IEEE Trans. Syst. Man Cybern.* **1988**, *18*, 49–60. [CrossRef]

8. Simpson, P.K. Higher-ordered and intraconnected bidirectional associative memories. *IEEE Trans. Syst. Man Cybern. Syst.* **1990**, *20*, 637–653. [CrossRef]
9. Cao, J.; Liang, J.; Lam, J. Exponential stability of high-order bidirectional associative memory neural networks with time delays. *Phys. D Nonlinear Phenom.* **2004**, *199*, 425–436. [CrossRef]
10. Aouiti, C.; Li, X.; Miaadi, F. A new LMI approach to finite and fixed time stabilization of high-order class of BAM neural networks with time-varying delays. *Neural Process. Lett.* **2019**, *50*, 815–838. [CrossRef]
11. Ho, D.W.C.; Liang, J.; Lam, J. Global exponential stability of impulsive high-order BAM neural networks with time-varying delays. *Neural Netw.* **2006**, *19*, 1581–1590. [CrossRef]
12. Wang, F.; Liu, M. Global exponential stability of high-order bidirectional associative memory (BAM) neural networks with time delays in leakage terms. *Neurocomputing* **2016**, *177*, 515–528. [CrossRef]
13. Yang, W.; Yu, W.; Cao, J.; Alsaadi, F.E.; Hayat, T. Almost automorphic solution for neutral type high-order Hopfield BAM neural networks with time-varying leakage delays on time scales. *Neurocomputing* **2017**, *267*, 241–260. [CrossRef]
14. Aouiti, C.; Sakthivel, R.; Touati, F. Global dissipativity of high-order Hopfield bidirectional associative memory neural networks with mixed delays. *Neural Comput. Appl.* **2020**, *32*, 10183–10197. [CrossRef]
15. Zu, J.; Yu, Z.; Meng, Y. Global exponential stability of high-order bidirectional associative memory (BAM) neural networks with proportional delays. *Neural Process. Lett.* **2020**, *51*, 2531–2549. [CrossRef]
16. Xing, L.; Zhou, L. Polynomial dissipativity of proportional delayed BAM neural networks. *Int. J. Biomath.* **2020**, *13*, 2050050. [CrossRef]
17. Zhou, L.; Zhao, Z. Asymptotic stability and polynomial stability of impulsive Cohen–Grossberg neural networks with multi-proportional delays. *Neural Process. Lett.* **2020**, *51*, 2607–2627. [CrossRef]
18. Wang, Y.; Yang, X.; Chen, X.; Liu, C. Positivity and semi-global polynomial stability of high-order Cohen–Grossberg BAM neural networks with multiple proportional delays. *Inf. Sci.* **2025**, *689*, 121512. [CrossRef]
19. Pecora, L.M.; Carroll, T.L. Synchronization in chaotic system. *Phys. Rev. Lett.* **1990**, *64*, 821–824. [CrossRef]
20. Zhou, L. Dissipativity of a class of cellular neural networks with proportional delays. *Nonlinear Dyn.* **2013**, *73*, 1895–1903. [CrossRef]
21. Jia, S.; Hu, C.; Yu, J.; Jiang, H. Asymptotical and adaptive synchronization of Cohen-Grossberg neural networks with heterogeneous proportional delays. *Neurocomputing* **2018**, *275*, 1449–1455. [CrossRef]
22. Yang, X.; Song, Q.; Cao, J.; Lu, J. Synchronization of Coupled Markovian Reaction-Diffusion Neural Networks with Proportional Delays via Quantized Control. *IEEE Trans. Neural Netw. Learn. Syst.* **2019**, *30*, 951–958. [CrossRef]
23. Li, Q.; Zhou, L. Global asymptotic synchronization of inertial memristive Cohen-Grossberg neural networks with proportional delays. *Commun. Nonlinear Sci. Numer. Simul.* **2023**, *123*, 107295. [CrossRef]
24. Zhou, L. Delay-dependent exponential synchronization of recurrent neural networks with multiple proportional delays. *Neural Process. Lett.* **2015**, *42*, 619–632. [CrossRef]
25. Wan, P.; Sun, D.; Chen, D.; Zhao, M.; Zheng, L. Exponential synchronization of inertial reaction-diffusion coupled neural networks with proportional delay via periodically intermittent control. *Neurocomputing* **2019**, *356*, 195–205. [CrossRef]
26. Su, L.; Zhou, L. Exponential synchronization of memristor-based recurrent neural networks with multi-proportional delays. *Neural Comput. Appl.* **2019**, *31*, 7907–7920. [CrossRef]
27. Li, L.; Chen, W.; Wu, X. Global Exponential Stability and Synchronization for Novel Complex-Valued Neural Networks With Proportional Delays and Inhibitory Factors. *IEEE Trans. Cybern.* **2021**, *51*, 2142–2152. [CrossRef]
28. Zhang, W.; Li, C.; Huang, T.; Huang, J. Finite-time Synchronization of Neural Networks with Multiple Proportional Delays via Non-chattering Control. *Int. J. Control Autom. Syst.* **2018**, *16*, 2473–2479. [CrossRef]
29. Xiaolin, X.; Rongqiang, T.; Xinsong, Y. Finite-Time Synchronization of Memristive Neural Networks with Proportional Delay. *Neural Process. Lett.* **2019**, *50*, 1139–1152.
30. Yang, W.; Huang, J.; He, X.; Wen, S.; Huang, T. Finite-Time Synchronization of Neural Networks With Proportional Delays for RGB-D Image Protection. *IEEE Trans. Neural Netw. Learn. Syst.* **2024**, *35*, 8149–8160. [CrossRef]
31. Han, J.; Zhou, L. Finite-time synchronization of proportional delay memristive competitive neural networks. *Neurocomputing* **2024**, *610*, 128612. [CrossRef]
32. Duan, L.; Li, J. Finite-time synchronization for a fully complex-valued BAM inertial neural network with proportional delays via non-reduced order and non-separation approach. *Neurocomputing* **2025**, *611*, 128648. [CrossRef]
33. Aouiti, C.; Assali, E.A.; Chérif, F.; Zeglaoui, A. Fixed-time synchronization of competitive neural networks with proportional delays and impulsive effect. *Neural Comput. Appl.* **2020**, *32*, 13245–13254. [CrossRef]
34. Duan, L.; Li, J. Fixed-time synchronization of fuzzy neutral-type BAM memristive inertial neural networks with proportional delays. *Inf. Sci.* **2021**, *576*, 522–541. [CrossRef]
35. Wan, Y.; Zhou, L. Fixed-time synchronization of discontinuous proportional delay inertial neural networks with uncertain parameters. *Inf. Sci.* **2024**, *678*, 120931. [CrossRef]

36. Liu, Y.; Wan, X.; Wu, E.; Yang, X.; Alsaadi, F.E.; Hayat, T. Finite-time synchronization of Markovian neural networks with proportional delays and discontinuous activations. *Nonlinear Anal. Model. Control* **2018**, *23*, 515–532. [CrossRef]
37. Wang, W. Finite-time synchronization for a class of fuzzy cellular neural networks with time-varying coefficients and proportional delays. *Fuzzy Sets Syst.* **2018**, *338*, 40–49. [CrossRef]
38. Alimi, A.M.; Aouiti, C.; Assali, E.A. Finite-time and fixed-time synchronization of a class of inertial neural networks with multi-proportional delays and its application to secure communication. *Neurocomputing* **2019**, *332*, 29–43. [CrossRef]
39. Zhang, W.; Li, C.; Yang, S.; Yang, X. Synchronization criteria for neural networks with proportional delays via quantized control. *Nonlinear Dyn.* **2018**, *94*, 541–551. [CrossRef]
40. Kinh, C.T.; Hien, L.V.; Ke, T.D. Power-Rate Synchronization of Fractional-Order Nonautonomous Neural Networks with Heterogeneous Proportional Delays. *Neural Process. Lett.* **2018**, *47*, 139–151. [CrossRef]
41. Guan, K. Global power-rate synchronization of chaotic neural networks with proportional delay via impulsive control. *Neurocomputing* **2018**, *283*, 256–265. [CrossRef]
42. Zhou, L.; Zhao, Z. Exponential synchronization and polynomial synchronization of recurrent neural networks with and without proportional delays. *Neurocomputing* **2020**, *372*, 109–116. [CrossRef]
43. Yao, Z.; Zhang, Z.; Wang, Z.; Lin, C.; Chen, J. Polynomial synchronization of complex-valued inertial neural networks with multi-proportional delays. *Commun. Theor. Phys.* **2022**, *74*, 125801. [CrossRef]
44. Zhou, L.; Zhu, Q.; Huang, T. Global Polynomial Synchronization of Proportional Delayed Inertial Neural Networks. *IEEE Trans. Syst. Man Cybern. Syst.* **2023**, *53*, 4487–4497. [CrossRef]
45. Zhang, J.; Li, Z.; Cao, J.; Abdel-Aty, M.; Meng, X. Polynomial synchronization of quaternion-valued fuzzy cellular neural networks with proportional delays. *Nonlinear Dyn.* **2025**, *113*, 3523–3542. [CrossRef]
46. Wan, Y.; Zhou, L.; Han, J. Global polynomial synchronization of proportional delay memristive neural networks with uncertain parameters and its application to image encryption. *Eng. Appl. Artif. Intell.* **2025**, *147*, 110290. [CrossRef]
47. Huang, Y.; Zhao, X. General Decay Synchronization of State and Spatial Diffusion Coupled Delayed Memristive Neural Networks with Reaction-diffusion Terms. *Int. J. Control Autom. Syst.* **2024**, *22*, 2313–2326. [CrossRef]

mathematics

MDPI

Article

On the Evolution Operators of a Class of Time-Delay Systems with Impulsive Parameterizations

Manuel De la Sen [1,*], Asier Ibeas [2], Aitor J. Garrido [3] and Izaskun Garrido [3]

[1] Automatic Control Group–ACG, Institute of Research and Development of Processes, Department of Electricity and Electronics, Faculty of Science and Technology, University of the Basque Country–UPV/EHU, 48940 Leioa, Bizkaia, Spain
[2] Department of Telecommunications and Systems Engineering, Universitat Autònoma de Barcelona, UAB, 08193 Barcelona, Spain; asier.ibeas@uab.cat
[3] Automatic Control Group–ACG, Institute of Research and Development of Processes–IIDP, Department of Automatic Control and Systems Engineering, Faculty of Engineering of Bilbao, University of the Basque Country–UPV/EHU, Po Rafael Moreno no3, 48013 Bilbao, Bizkaia, Spain; aitor.garrido@ehu.eus (A.J.G.); izaskun.garrido@ehu.eus (I.G.)
* Correspondence: manuel.delasen@ehu.eus

Abstract: This paper formalizes the analytic expressions and some properties of the evolution operator that generates the state-trajectory of dynamical systems combining delay-free dynamics with a set of discrete, or point, constant (and not necessarily commensurate) delays, where the parameterizations of both the delay-free and the delayed parts can undergo impulsive changes. Also, particular evolution operators are defined explicitly for the non-impulsive and impulsive time-varying delay-free case, and also for the case of impulsive delayed time-varying systems. In the impulsive cases, in general, the evolution operators are non-unique. The delays are assumed to be a finite number of constant delays that are not necessarily commensurate, that is, all of them being integer multiples of a minimum delay. On the other hand, the impulsive actions through time are assumed to be state-dependent and to take place at certain isolated time instants on the matrix functions that define the delay-free and the delayed dynamics. Some variants are also proposed for the cases when the impulsive actions are state-independent or state- and dynamics-independent. The intervals in-between consecutive impulses can be, in general, time-varying while subject to a minimum threshold. The boundedness of the state-trajectory solutions, which imply the system's global stability, is investigated in the most general case for any given piecewise-continuous bounded function of initial conditions defined on the initial maximum delay interval. Such a solution boundedness property can be achieved, even if the delay-free dynamics is unstable, by an appropriate distribution of the impulsive actions. An illustrative first-order example is developed in detail to illustrate the impulsive stabilization results.

Keywords: delay differential systems; point delays; evolution operator; impulsive actions; global stability

MSC: 34C40; 34D20; 34K12; 37L05

1. Introduction

Systems with delayed effects appear in many real-life problems, such as war and peace models, some biological problems—for instance, the sunflower equation, logistic equations, epidemic models, etc.—electrical transmission lines, economic models, heat exchangers, urban traffic, digital control, remote control, tele-operation processes, integro-differential

Volterra-type equations, neutral equations, etc. [1–14]. See also some of the references therein. Delays often influence the solution trajectory.

Different types of delays are common and these types sometimes appear in a combined manner. In this context, delays can be internal, that is, in the state dynamics, or external, in the sense that they operate either on the forcing inputs, or controls, or in the measurable outputs, or in both of them. Typically, the delays can be either constant or time-dependent point delays or they can also have a distributed nature. On the other hand, point delays can be commensurate, in the sense that all of them are integer multiples of a base delay, or incommensurate, when they do not have the above mutual proportionally nature—see, for instance, [1]. Distributed delays are typical in certain either deterministic or stochastic classes of Volterra-type integro-differential equations. See, for instance, [11–14] and some of the references therein. In particular, in [12], the stability of a class of integro-differential Volterra-type equations, including the dynamics associated with a finite number of point delays and impulsive effects, is analyzed by means of a Karovskii–Lyapunov analysis.

From the point of view of differential systems, time-delay systems are infinite-dimensional because of their time-interval-dependent memory, and so they possess infinitely many characteristic zeros. The initial conditions of time-delay differential systems are defined by any piecewise-continuous bounded function on the time interval $[-h,\ 0]$, where h is the maximum size of all the delays present in the system, which coincides with the delay of the maximum size.

It has been seen that, in the event that there is no time-varying dynamics in the delay-free part, and furthermore, there are no delays in the dynamics, then the solution of the differential system is generated by an evolution operator; this is a C_0-semigroup of a time-invariant infinitesimal generator [15–20], which is a one-parameter semigroup that is both strongly continuous and uniformly continuous. The one-parameter semigroup property of the linear time-invariant undelayed typically becomes lost if the dynamics is time-varying and/or it involves delays [21].

On the other hand, impulsive continuous-time- and discrete-time-controlled systems and their stability, asymptotic stability, and stabilization properties under appropriate controls have been studied in the background literature in both delay-free and delayed cases. See, for instance, Refs. [22–28] and some of the references therein. In particular, the global exponential stability of a type of system with control impulses and time-varying delays is studied in [22] by means of an impulsive delay differential inequality. Also, an "ad hoc" impulsive stabilizing controller was synthesized. In [23], an inequality of Razumikhin-type with delays in the impulses is addressed, while the information on the time delay in the impulses is used for stabilization of the delayed systems. In [27], a sliding-mode controller is designed for impulsive stabilization of a class of time-delay systems in the presence of input disturbances. The designed control allows for counteracting the unsuitable perturbation effects. In [28], sufficiency-type conditions for exponential stability are developed for delayed systems where the delay size is not limited by the distribution of the impulsive intervals. Related studies have also been extended to some nonlinear problems involving delays such as Cohen–Grossberg neural networks or actuator-saturated dynamics and to some stochastic control problems involving delays [29–31]. The distribution of the impulses through time is not necessarily periodic since the aperiodicity, and eventual sampling adaptation to the signal profiles, allows for the improvement of the data acquisition performance [32]; improvement of the system dynamics in discrete-time systems [33]; to better fit certain optimization processes [34]; the improvement of the signal filtering and attenuation of the noise effects [35]; or the improvement of behavior prediction [36]. Some strategies of non-periodic sampling are described and discussed in [37–40]. In [41], non-uniform sampling is proposed for the improvement of tracking control against stochastic actuator faults. On the other hand, the adaptation transients can be improved by using adaptive sampling that is, by nature, non-uniform and adapts itself to the signal variations. This allows for reducing the signal overshoot peaks, especially at the beginning of the state and the output responses. See, for instance, Refs. [42–47] and some of the references therein. In particular, non-periodic sampled-data controllers have been proposed for distributed networked control against potential cyber-attacks of a stochastic type [46]. In [48,49], impulsive controls are proposed and synthesized for certain epidemic models in such a way that the controls are not uniformly distributed through time. Typically, the impulsive effects are characterized through Dirac distributions in the differential system, which generate finite jumps in the solution trajectory at the time instants where such impulsive effects take place. Some classical books of systems theory and physics explain both the intuitive ideas behind and the mathematical description of the impulsive effects. See, for instance, [50–52]. Some recent results in the field of time-delay systems are given in [53–56] as follows: In [53], the solvability of a state-dependent integro-differential inclusion is studied together with the existence and uniqueness of solutions of these types of equations when subject to delay nonlocal conditions. In [54], new sufficient and necessary conditions are derived regarding the oscillatory behavior of second-order differential equations with mixed and multiple delays under a canonical operator. In [55], oscillation conditions are presented for fourth-order neutral differential equations. On the other hand, the purpose of the investigation performed in [56] is the study of the asymptotic properties and oscillation regime of neutral differential equations with delays of even order. The given results are based on the Riccati transformation together with a comparison with first- and second-order delay equations.

This paper relies on the analytic forms and some relevant properties of the evolution operators that generate the state-trajectory solutions of a class of eventually impulsive linear time-delay with linear time-varying mixed delay-free dynamics and delayed dynamics. The analysis of the impulsive effects is a main novelty compared with the results given in [21]. It should be pointed out that impulses translate into finite jumps in the solution trajectory. In this article, the impulsive actions are assumed to take place inside the parameterization instead of influencing the forcing terms as is usual in the related previous background literature. The eventual impulses directly influence the parameterization of the undelayed dynamics and, eventually, that of the delayed dynamics in the differential system at the impulsive time instants. The various combined delayed dynamics correspond to a finite number of known constant point delays. In more detail, the evolution operators are made explicit for both the non-impulsive and the impulsive time-varying delay-free cases and also for the impulsive time-varying systems with eventual delayed dynamics. The delays are assumed to be constant and, in general, multiple and arising in a finite number but they are not necessarily commensurate in the sense that they are not required to be an integer multiple of a minimum or base-minimum delay. The impulsive actions are assumed to be state-dependent and to take place at certain isolated time instants on the matrix functions, which define the delay-free and the delayed dynamics. Some variants of the above model are also briefly discussed for the cases when the impulsive actions are either state-independent or both state- and dynamics-independent. It is assumed that the inter-impulse intervals, that is, the time intervals in-between consecutive impulses, can be, in general, time-varying while being subject to a minimum threshold. The boundedness and the associated global stabilization of the state-trajectory solutions for any given piecewise-continuous bounded function of the initial conditions (defined on the initial maximum delay interval) are investigated in the most general case of the proposed time-varying impulsive system with delays. Such a boundedness property can be achieved, even if the delay-free dynamics is unstable, by an appropriate distribution of the impulsive actions.

An illustrative first-order example with impulsive parametrization changes is developed in detail to illustrate the boundedness and stabilization results.

The impulsive system under study could be interpreted as a limit case of a switched delay system with instantaneous switching actions from one parameterization to another, and then immediately returning to the former parameterization in the configuration previous to the impulsive action. In that context, the parameterizations are impulsive and seen as instantaneous switching actions occurring at the impulsive time instants.

The paper is organized as follows. Section 2 presents expressions of the evolution operator that generate the state-trajectory solution of a class of linear time-varying differential delay-free systems. The evolution operators used in this article are based on the analysis of the solution of the differential systems with time delays taking into account the impulses in the parameterization of the dynamics that are, in general, state-dependent and lead to finite jumps in the solution of the differential system at the impulsive time instants. In that context, the impulsive time instants might be either effective or ineffective according to their validity to produce, or not, parameterization changes in the dynamics. Intuitively, an impulsive time instant is considered to be ineffective if it is not able to generate a jump in the state being valid to modify the parameterization of the dynamics. The simplest case (but not the only one) of impulsive ineffectiveness happens when the left limit of the trajectory solution is null at the "a priori" claimed impulsive time instant. In such a case, another closely allocated impulsive time instant candidate should be tried. To establish the main results, the impulsive-free part of the matrix function of dynamics of such systems is supposed to be bounded, piecewise-continuous, and Lebesgue-integrable on $[0, \infty)$. The cases of absence and presence of Dirac-type impulses in the system matrix of dynamics are described. In the impulsive case, the evolution operator is seen to be, in general, non-unique. The efficiency of the impulsive time instants in the generation of relevant impulsive actions depends on the particular evolution of the matrix function that describes the dynamics. In that sense, the potential impulsive time instants might be effective or ineffective. Section 3 extends the above results to the presence of delayed dynamics associated with, in general, multiple constant point delays. The impulsive actions at certain time instants can take place both in the delay-free dynamics and in the various matrices of delayed dynamics. The boundedness of the solution trajectory leading, as a result, to the global stability of the system for any bounded initial conditions is also investigated. An appropriate distribution of the impulsive time instants, subject to a minimum inter-impulsive threshold, is proved to be essential for the potential stabilization of the differential system. An illustrative first-order example is discussed in detail to visualize the theoretical results of Section 3. Finally, some conclusions end the paper.

Nomenclature

$$\overline{p} = \{1, 2, \cdots, p\}$$

Commensurate point delays $h_m = h_1 < h_2 < \cdots < h_p = h$ are those that are the integer multiple of a minimum common multiple, which is the minimum, or base, delay $h_m = h_1$, namely, $h_i = ih_m$ for $i \in \overline{p}$, then $h = h_p = ph_m$.

Incommensurate point delays $h_m = h_1 < h_2 < \cdots < h_p = h$ are those that are not the integer multiple of a minimum common multiple.

$\overline{f}_{ta}$ denotes the strip of the function $f : \mathbf{R} \to \mathbf{R}^n$ on $[t-a, t]$, defined as a function from $\mathbf{R}$ to $\mathbf{R}^n$ by $\overline{f}_{ta}(\tau) = f(\tau); \tau \in [t-a, t]$, $\overline{f}_{ta}(\tau) = 0;\ \tau \in \mathbf{R} \backslash [t-a, t];\ t \in \mathbf{R}$ in such a way that the support of $\overline{f}_{ta}$ is a proper or improper subset of $[t-a, t]$. Thus, $\overline{x}_{th}$ is the strip of the solution $x(t)$ on $[t-h, t]$ of an n-th-order time delay system on a maximum delay period of size h. To abbreviate the notation, it is referred to simply as $\overline{x}_t$ to avoid confusion.

I_n is the n-th identity matrix;

0_n is the n-th zero matrix.

$$\boldsymbol{R}_{0+} = \boldsymbol{R}_+ \cup \{0\} = \{r \in \boldsymbol{R} : r \geq 0\};\ \boldsymbol{R}_+ = \{r \in \boldsymbol{C} : r > 0\},$$

$$\boldsymbol{R}_{-0} = \boldsymbol{R}_- \cup \{0\} = \{r \in \boldsymbol{R} : r \leq 0\};\ \boldsymbol{R}_- = \{r \in \boldsymbol{R} : r < 0\},$$

where $\boldsymbol{R}$ is the set of real numbers, and

$$\boldsymbol{C}_{0+} = \boldsymbol{C}_+ \cup \{0\} = \{z \in \boldsymbol{C} : Rez \geq 0\};\ \boldsymbol{C}_+ = \{z \in \boldsymbol{C} : Rez > 0\},$$

$$\boldsymbol{C}_{-0} = \boldsymbol{C}_- \cup \{0\} = \{z \in \boldsymbol{C} : Rez \leq 0\};\ \boldsymbol{C}_- = \{z \in \boldsymbol{C} : Rez < 0\},$$

where $\boldsymbol{C}$ is the set of complex numbers.

In the same way, we can define "mutatis mutandis" the respective subsets $\boldsymbol{Z}_{0+}$, $\boldsymbol{Z}_+$, $\boldsymbol{Z}_{-0}$, and $\boldsymbol{Z}_-$ of the set $\boldsymbol{Z}$ of integer numbers.

The closures of the real set and subsets are $cl\boldsymbol{R} = \boldsymbol{R} \cup \{\pm\infty\}$,

$$cl\boldsymbol{R}_{0+} = \boldsymbol{R}_{0+} \cup \{+\infty\};\ cl\boldsymbol{R}_+ = \boldsymbol{R}_+ \cup \{0, +\infty\},$$

$$cl\boldsymbol{R}_{-0} = \boldsymbol{R}_{-0} \cup \{-\infty\};\ cl\boldsymbol{R}_- = \boldsymbol{R}_- \cup \{0, -\infty\},$$

where $BPC([-h, 0]; \boldsymbol{R}^n)$ denotes the set of bounded piecewise-continuous functions from $[-h, 0]$ to $\boldsymbol{R}^n$.

$PC^1(\boldsymbol{R}_+; \boldsymbol{R}^n)$ is the continuous differentiable class of n-real vector functions on $\boldsymbol{R}_+$, whose first-derivative is piecewise-continuous but not necessarily continuous. Note that $C^1(\boldsymbol{R}_+; \boldsymbol{R}^n) \subset PC^1(\boldsymbol{R}_+; \boldsymbol{R}^n)$.

$\boldsymbol{R}_{0+h}(t) = \{[t-h, t] : t \in \boldsymbol{R}_{0+}\} \subset \boldsymbol{R};\ \boldsymbol{R}_{+h}(t) = \{[t-h, t] : t \in \boldsymbol{R}_+\} \subset \boldsymbol{R}$ are, respectively, non-negative and positive strips of real intervals of the Lebesgue measure h relative to the time instant "t".

An impulsive real function $f : \boldsymbol{R}_{0+} \to \boldsymbol{R}$ is that which has a non-zero set of Dirac-distribution-type impulses $K\delta(\tau - t_i)$ on a finite set of impulsive points $\tau = t_i$ such that there is an impulsive jump $f(t_i^+) - f(t_i^-) = K(t_i^-)\delta(0)$ at $t = t_i$ of size $K(t_i^-)(\neq 0) \in \boldsymbol{R}$. The same idea applies for a vector function $f : \boldsymbol{R}_{0+} \to \boldsymbol{R}^n$ in the sense that $t = t_i \in \boldsymbol{R}_{0+}$ is impulsive if there is at least a component $j \in \overline{n}$ of $f(t_i)$ such that $f_j(t_i^+) - f_j(t_i^-) = K_j(t_i^-)\delta(0)$ with $K_j(t_i^-) \neq 0$. Thus, t_i is an impulsive point of $f(t)$ if $f(t_i^+) - f(t_i^-) = (K_1(t_i^-)\delta(0), K_2(t_i^-)\delta(0), \cdots, K_2(t_i^-)\delta(0))^T$ is non-zero, that is, if there is at least one non-zero $K_j(t_i^-)$ for $j \in \overline{n}$. An abbreviated notation for that is $f(t_i^+) - f(t_i^-) = (K_j(t_i^-)\delta(0))$. Again, a generalization for the real matrix functions $F : \boldsymbol{R}_{0+} \to \boldsymbol{R}^{n\times n}$ is direct in the sense that t_k is an impulsive point of $F(t) = (F_{ij}(t))$ if $F(t_k) - F(t_k^-) = (K_{ij}(t_k^-)\delta(0))$ with at least one entry of $K(t_k^-) = (K_{ij}(t_k^-))$ being non-zero. Note that if t is non-impulsive, then the impulsive jump amplitude is null. To keep the notation less involved, the right limit t^+ of t is simply denoted by t so that $F(t)$ stands as the notation for $F(t^+)$.

The spectral radius of a matrix function of time $A : \boldsymbol{R}_{0+} \to \boldsymbol{R}^{n\times n}$ is denoted by $\rho(A(t))$;

$e_i \in \boldsymbol{R}^n$ is the unit's i-th Euclidean vector whose unique non-zero component is the i-th one that equalizes unity;

"iff" is the usual equivalent abbreviation of the claim "if and only if";

χ_0 denotes the infinity cardinal of a numerable set;

The entry-to-entry definition of a matrix $K \in \boldsymbol{R}^{n\times m}$ is denoted as $K = (K_{ij});\ i \in \overline{n}$, $j \in \overline{m}$.

$RH_{\infty}^{n\times n}$ is the Hardy space of real–rational complex-valued proper transfer matrices $G(s)$ from C to $C^{n\times m}$, analytic in C_{0+}, and of finite norm $\|G(s)\|_{\infty} = \underset{\omega\in R_{0+}}{max}\ \overline{\sigma}(G(i\omega))$, where $\overline{\sigma}(G(i\omega))$ is the maximum singular value of $G(s)$ for $s = i\omega$; and $i = \sqrt{-1}$ is the complex imaginary unit.

2. Time-Varying Linear Delay-Free Differential Systems and Their Evolution Operators for the Non-Impulsive and Impulsive Cases

This section studies the analytic expressions of the evolution operator that generate the state-trajectory solution of a class of linear time-varying differential delay-free systems. The impulsive-free part of the system matrix function is assumed to be bounded, piecewise-continuous, and Lebesgue-integrable for all time. The cases of absence and presence of Dirac-distribution-type impulses in the entries of the system matrix of dynamics are described and the corresponding expressions of the evolution operators [15,21], which generate the solution trajectories for given initial conditions, are given explicitly. In the impulsive case, the evolution operator is seen to be, in general, non-unique. The efficiency of the impulsive time instants to generate relevant impulsive actions depends on the particular evolution of the matrix function that describes the dynamics. In this sense, the impulsive time instants might be either effective or ineffective. A discussion is also provided for the case when the impulses do not affect the parameterization of the matrix of dynamics while they produce finite state-independent jumps in the solution trajectory at the impulsive time instants.

Consider the subsequent linear time-varying differential system of order n:

$$\dot{x}(t) = A(t)x(t);\ x(0) = x_0 \tag{1}$$

where $A : R_{0+} \to R^{n\times n}$ is bounded and piecewise-continuous Lebesgue-integrable on R_{0+}; and $A(t)$ and $\int_0^t A(\tau)d\tau$ are assumed to commute for all $t \geq 0$.

Theorem 1. *The following properties hold:*

(i) *The unique solution of (1) is given below:*

$$x(t) = e^{\int_0^t A(\tau)d\tau}x_0; t \in R_{0+} \tag{2}$$

so that the unique evolution operator of (1) from R_{0+} to $R^{n\times n}$ is $\Psi(t) = e^{\int_0^t A(\tau)d\tau}$ for any $t \in R_{0+}$.

(ii) *The evolution operator $\Psi(t) = e^{\int_0^t A(\tau)d\tau}$ for any $t \in R_{0+}$ satisfies the integral equation*

$$\Psi(t) = I_n + \int_0^t A(\tau)\Psi(\tau)d\tau = I_n + \int_0^t A(\tau)e^{\int_0^\tau A(\sigma)d\sigma}d\tau; t \in R_{0+}. \tag{3}$$

Proof. It turns out that if (2) holds then (1) holds. Assume that there exists another solution for the same initial conditions of the following form:

$$x(t) = \Phi(t)x_0;\ t \in R_{0+} \tag{4}$$

so that

$$\dot{x}(t) = \dot{\Phi}(t)x_0 = A(t)\Phi(t)x_0 = A(t)x(t) = A(t)e^{\int_0^t A(\tau)d\tau}x_0;\ t \in R_{0+} \tag{5}$$

for $t \in \mathbf{R}_{0+}$, and

$$\dot{\Phi}(t) = A(t)e^{\int_0^t A(\tau)d\tau} = \frac{d}{dt}\left(e^{\int_0^t A(\tau)d\tau}\right);\ t \in \mathbf{R}_{0+} \tag{6}$$

Note from (2) and (4) that $e^{\int_0^0 A(\tau)d\tau} = \Phi(0) = I_n$ since $x(0) = x_0$ for any given arbitrary finite x_0. Since $\Psi(0) = e^{\int_0^0 A(\tau)d\tau} = I_n = \Phi(0)$, and

$$\dot{\Phi}(t) = \frac{d}{dt}\left(e^{\int_0^t A(\tau)d\tau}\right) \tag{7}$$

for all $t \in \mathbf{R}_{0+}$ from (6), then $\Phi(t) = e^{\int_0^t A(\tau)d\tau}$ for all $t \in \mathbf{R}_{0+}$. Thus, the evolution operator $\Psi(t) \equiv \Phi(t) = e^{\int_0^t A(\tau)d\tau}$ of (1) is unique for all $t \in \mathbf{R}_{0+}$. Property (i) has been proved. Since $\Psi(t) = e^{\int_0^t A(\tau)d\tau}$ is the unique evolution operator of (1) for all $t \in \mathbf{R}_{0+}$, then

$$\Psi(t) = \Psi(0) + \int_0^t \dot{\Psi}(\tau)d\tau = I_n + \int_0^t \frac{d}{d\tau}\left(e^{\int_0^\tau A(\sigma)d\sigma}\right)d\tau = I_n + \int_0^t A(\tau)\Psi(\tau)d\tau;\ t \in \mathbf{R}_{0+} \tag{8}$$

and Property (ii) has been proved. □

Define $< A >_t = (1/t)\int_0^t A(\tau)d\tau$ as the average of $A : [0, t) \to \mathbf{R}^{n\times n}$, which exists for all $t \in \mathbf{R}_{0+}$ since $\left\|\int_0^t A(\tau)d\tau\right\| < +\infty$ for all $t \in \mathbf{R}_{0+}$. Note that

$$\Psi(t) = e^{\int_0^t A(\tau)d\tau} = e^{((1/t)\int_0^t A(\tau)d\tau)t} = e^{\overline{A}_t t};\ t \in \mathbf{R}_{0+} \tag{9}$$

Thus, the explicit computation of $\Psi(t) = e^{\int_0^t A(\tau)d\tau}$ can be performed by direct or numerical integration from (8) and also as $\Psi(t) = L^{-1}\left\{(s, I_n, -, <, A, >_t)^{-1}\right\}$ via the Laplace inverse transform of $(sI_n - < A >_t)^{-1}$ for each fixed $t \in \mathbf{R}_{0+}$ and its associated (constant for such fixed $t \in \mathbf{R}_{0+}$) averaged n-matrix $< A >_t = (1/t)\int_0^t A(\tau)d\tau$.

The above considerations may be extended for more general Lebesgue integrals, which eventually include Dirac-distribution-type jumps in the integrand, that is, infinite point jumps at isolated sampling instants in the dynamics of the differential system, as is now discussed.

Note from Theorem 1 that, under the simplifying notation convention $\Psi(t, 0) = \Psi(t)$, we can write the following:

$$x(t) = \Psi(t, 0)x_0 = \Psi(t, t_0)x(t_0) = \Psi(t, t_0)\Psi(t_0, 0)x_0 \text{for any } t \geq t_0 \geq 0 \tag{10}$$

Note that the evolution operator of Theorem 1 is not a C_0-semigroup—which is essentially one-parametric—since, if $t \neq t_0 (\neq 0)$ in (10), then the state-solution cannot be expressed, in general, with one parameter $(t - t_0)$ for any t_0 and t because $A(t)$ is time-variant. Consider now the modification of (1) that follows to include impulsive effects in the time derivative of the solution trajectory, which produces proportional instantaneous finite jumps at the impulsive time instants in such a solution trajectory:

$$\dot{x}(t) = (A(t) + \Delta(t))x(t);\ x(0^-) = x_0 \tag{11}$$

$$\Delta(t) = \sum\nolimits_{t_i \in IMP(t)} K(t^-)\hat{A}(t^-)\delta(t - t_i) \tag{12}$$

where $A : \mathbf{R}_{0+} \to \mathbf{R}^{n\times n}$ is bounded and piecewise-continuous Lebesgue-integrable on $[0, t]$ for any $t \in \mathbf{R}_{0+}$; $\hat{A}_{ij}(t^-) = A_{ij}(t^-)$ if the (i, j)-entry of $A(t^-)$ is impulsive, and $\hat{A}_{ij}(t^-) = 0$, otherwise, for $i, j \in \overline{n}$; $\Delta(t)$ is a Lebesgue-integrable impulsive real square n-matrix on

$[0,t]$ for any $t \in \boldsymbol{R}_{0+}$ such that at least one entry of the real non-continuous bounded n-matrix function $K(t^-)$ is non-zero if, and only if, the time instant t is impulsive—that is, $t \in IMP(=\cup_{\tau\in \boldsymbol{R}_{0+}} IMP(\tau))$, where IMP is the total set of impulsive time instants and $IMP(t) = \{\tau(\le t) \in \boldsymbol{R}_{0+} : K(\tau^-)\hat{A}(\tau^-) \neq 0\}$ is the set of impulsive sampling instants up to the time instant t, which has a cardinal $N(t)$, i.e., the set of impulses on $[0,t]$. Note that the support of the impulsive matrix function is, by definition, a set of isolated time instants in $\boldsymbol{R}_{0+}$. We also define by convenience the impulsive set of time instants $IMP(t^-) = \{\tau(< t) \in \boldsymbol{R}_{0+} : K(\tau) \neq 0\}$, of cardinal $N(t^-)$ (i.e., the set of impulses on $[0,t)$) so that $IMP(t) = IMP(t^-)$ if and only if $t \notin IMP$. The total finite or (denumerable) infinite number of impulsive time instants is $card(IMP) = N_{imp} \le \chi_0$, where χ_0 denotes the infinity numerable cardinality. Note from (11)–(12) that $x(t) - x(t^-) = K(t^-)\hat{A}(t^-)x(t^-)$ if $t \in IMP$ and $K(t) = 0$ so that $x(t) = x(t^-)$ if $t \notin IMP$ and also its right limit is zero if $t \in IMP$. Note that $\hat{A}(t) = A(t)$ and $x(t) - x(t^-) = K(t^-)\hat{A}(t^-)x(t^-)$ if, and only if, all the entries of $A(t)$ are impulsive. It can be noticed that if $x(t^-) \in Ker(K(t^-)\hat{A}(t^-))$ then $x(t) = x(t^-)$ and such a time instant t does not have a real, effective impulsive effect in the solution for such an impulsive gain $K(t)$. If, in addition, $x(t^-) \in Ker(\hat{A}(t^-))A(t^-) = 0$, and in particular, if $x(t^-) \in Ker(\hat{A}(t^-))$, then t does not have a real, effective impulsive effect in the solution irrespective of the impulsive gain $K(t)$. Then, such a time instant "t" is non-effective or ineffective versus the case when it is effective. Related to these ideas, the following definitions are pertinent:

Definition 1. *If* $x(t^-) \in Ker(K(t^-)\hat{A}(t^-))$ *for* $t \in IMP$, *then* t *is an ineffective impulsive time instant for the impulsive gain* $K : \boldsymbol{R}_{0+} \to \boldsymbol{R}^{n\times n}$.

Definition 2. *If* $x(t^-) \notin Ker(K(t^-)\hat{A}(t^-))$ *for* $t \in IMP$, *then* t *is an effective impulsive time instant for the impulsive gain* $K : \boldsymbol{R}_{0+} \to \boldsymbol{R}^{n\times n}$.

Definition 3. *The impulsive set of time instants* IMP *is effective for the impulsive matrix function gain* $K : \boldsymbol{R}_{0+} \to \boldsymbol{R}^{n\times n}$ *if* $K(t^-)\hat{A}(t^-)x(t^-) \neq 0$ *for any* $t \in IMP$.

Note also that if $\hat{A}(t^-)x(t^-) \neq 0$, then there always exists some impulsive matrix function gain of $K : \boldsymbol{R}_{0+} \to \boldsymbol{R}^{n\times n}$ for which $t \in IMP$ is effective. It suffices for this concern that $\hat{A}(t^-)x(t^-) \notin KerK(t^-)$. The following simple result holds:

Proposition 1. ***(i)*** *A time instant* $t \in IMP$ *is effective for some impulsive matrix function gain* $K : \boldsymbol{R}_{0+} \to \boldsymbol{R}^{n\times n}$ *iff* $e_i^T \hat{A}(t^-)x(t^-) \neq 0$ *for some* $i = i(t) \in \overline{n}$.

(ii) $e_i^T \hat{A}(t^-)x(t^-) \neq 0$ *for some (unique or non-unique)* $i = i(t) \in \overline{n}$ *implies and it is implied by* $\hat{A}(t^-)x(t^-) \neq 0$ *(the converse implication does not imply the uniqueness of* $i = i(t) \in \overline{n}$ *such that* $e_i^T \hat{A}(t^-)x(t^-) \neq 0$. *Then, Property (i) is fully equivalent to the following assertion: a time instant* $t \in IMP$ *is effective for some impulsive matrix function gain* $K : \boldsymbol{R}_{0+} \to \boldsymbol{R}^{n\times n}$ *iff* $e_i^T \hat{A}(t^-)x(t^-) \neq 0$ *for some* $i = i(t) \in \overline{n}$.

(iii) *A time instant* $t \in IMP$ *is ineffective for any impulsive matrix function gain* $K : \boldsymbol{R}_{0+} \to \boldsymbol{R}^{n\times n}$ *iff* $e_i^T \hat{A}(t^-)x(t^-) = 0$ *for all* $i \in \overline{n}$, *equivalently, iff* $\hat{A}(t^-)x(t^-) = 0$.

Proof: If $e_i^T \hat{A}(t^-)x(t^-) \neq 0$ for $t \in IMP$ and some $i = i(t) \in \overline{n}$, then the i-th component of $\hat{A}(t^-)x(t^-)$ is non-zero. Then, it suffices that the i-th column of $K(t)$ has all its components non-zero in order that $x_j(t) \neq x_j(t^-)$ for all $j \in \overline{n}$. This ensures the existence of a (non-unique) $K : \boldsymbol{R}_{0+} \to \boldsymbol{R}^{n\times n}$ such that $t \in IMP$ is effective. The sufficiency part of Property (i) has been proved. The necessity part is followed by contradiction arguments. Assume that $e_i^T \hat{A}(t^-)x(t^-) = 0$ for $t \in IMP$ and all $i = i(t) \in \overline{n}$. Thus, $v(t) = \ddot{A}(t^-)x(t^-) = 0$ so that $x(t) = x(t^-)$ irrespective of $K : \boldsymbol{R}_{0+} \to \boldsymbol{R}^{n\times n}$. Property (i) has been fully proved. The implication parts " $\Rightarrow$ " and " $\Leftarrow$ " of Property (ii) follow directly from Property (i) so that Property (ii) is proved as equivalent to Property (i). Property (iii) is the dual of Property (i) so its proof is direct under close "ad hoc" arguments. □

The relevance of extending Theorem 1 of the impulsive case relies on keeping the Lebesgue-integrability of $(A(t)+\Delta(t))$ through time when the impulsive contribution $\Delta(t)$ is non-null. In particular, the following cases are of interest:

(a) $card(IMP)<\infty$, that is, there is a finite number of impulsive time instants;
(b) there are infinitely many impulsive time instants but their influences are mutually compensated so that their total contribution to the solution of (11) is bounded for all time;
(c) there are infinitely many impulsive time instants but their respective jumps collapse asymptotically so that $(A(t)+\Delta(t))$ is Lebesgue-integrable on $[0,t]$ for any $t\in \mathbf{R}_{0+}$. Because of its modus operandi, its way of operating, at the impulsive time instants, the system (11)–(12) is said to be a proportional instantaneous finite-jumps system.

The uniqueness of the evolution operator is guaranteed along the inter-switching time intervals but such uniqueness is not guaranteed in the general case, at the right limits of the impulsive time instants, since different impulsive gains can generate the same right limit value of the solution trajectory for a given left limit value. This property is formalized in the subsequent results:

Theorem 2. *The following properties hold:*

(i) *The unique solution of the proportional instantaneous finite-jumps system (11)–(12) is given by the expression below:*

$$\begin{aligned} x(t) &= (I_n+K(t^-)\hat{A}(t^-))\left(e^{\int_{t_{N(t^-)-1}}^{t^-}A(\tau)d\tau}\right)\left(\Pi_{i=1}^{N(t^-)-1}\left[e^{\int_{t_i}^{t_{i+1}^-}A(\tau)d\tau}(I_n+K(t_i^-)\hat{A}(t_i^-))\right]\right)\left(e^{\int_0^{t_1^-}A(\tau)d\tau}\right)x_0 \\ &= (I_n+K(t^-)\hat{A}(t^-))x(t^-);t\in \mathbf{R}_{0+} \end{aligned} \tag{13}$$

where the product of matrices operates from the left to the right in the order of the increasing sequence $\{t_i\}_{i\in \mathbf{Z}_+}$*; and* $IMP(t^-)=\left\{t_1,t_2,\cdots,t_{N(t^-)}\right\}$ *is the impulsive set of time instants on* $[0,t)$ *whose cardinal is* $N(t^-)$*. Thus, the solution of (11)–(12) is given by* $x(t)=\Omega(t)x_0;t\in \mathbf{R}_{0+}$*, where, in general, its non-unique evolution operator is as follows:*

$$\begin{aligned} &\Omega(t)=(I_n+K(t^-)\hat{A}(t^-))\Omega(t^-) \\ &=(I_n+K(t^-)\hat{A}(t^-))\left(e^{\int_{t_{N(t^-)-1}}^{t^-}A(\tau)d\tau}\right)\left(\Pi_{i=1}^{N(t^-)-1}\left[e^{\int_{t_i}^{t_{i+1}^-}A(\tau)d\tau}(I_n+K(t_i^-)\hat{A}(t_i^-))\right]\right)\left(e^{\int_0^{t_1^-}A(\tau)d\tau}\right);t\in \mathbf{R}_{0+} \end{aligned} \tag{14}$$

The evolution operator $\Omega:\mathbf{R}_{0+}\to \mathbf{R}^{n\times n}$ *is unique on* $[0,+\infty)$ *if and only if there is no sequence of impulsive gains of the matrix of dynamics* $\{K'(t_i^-)\}_{t_i\in IMP}\neq\{K(t_i^-)\}_{t_i\in IMP}$ *such that* $x(t_i^-)\in Ker\{(K(t_i^-)-K'(t_i^-))\hat{A}(t_i^-)\}$ *for at least one* $t_i\in IMP$*; equivalently, it is unique if and only if* $x(t_i^-)\notin Ker\{(K(t_i^-)-K'(t_i^-))\hat{A}(t_i^-)\}$ *for all* $t_i\in IMP$*. As a result, if there is at least one* $t_i\in IMP$ *such that* $x(t_i^-)\in Ker\{(K(t_i^-)-K'(t_i^-))\hat{A}(t_i^-)\}$*, with* $K'(t_i^-)\neq K(t_i^-)$*, then* $\Omega:\mathbf{R}_{0+}\to \mathbf{R}^{n\times n}$ *is non-unique.*

(ii) *If* $t\in IMP$ *then* $t=t_{N(t)}$ *and* $IMP(t)=IMP(t^-)\cup\left\{t_{N(t)}\right\}$ *so that (14) becomes the following:*

$$\begin{aligned} \Omega(t) &= (I_n+K(t^-)\hat{A}(t^-))\Omega(t^-) \\ &= (I_n+K(t^-)\hat{A}(t^-))\left(e^{\int_{t_{N(t^-)-1}}^{t^-}A(\tau)d\tau}\right)\left(\Pi_{i=1}^{N(t^-)-1}\left[e^{\int_{t_i}^{t_{i+1}^-}A(\tau)d\tau}(I_n+K(t_i^-)\hat{A}(t_i^-))\right]\right)\left(e^{\int_0^{t_1^-}A(\tau)d\tau}\right) \end{aligned} \tag{15}$$

and

$$\Omega(t^-)=\left(e^{\int_{t_{N(t^-)-1}}^{t^-}A(\tau)d\tau}\right)\left(\prod_{i=1}^{N(t^-)-1}\left[e^{\int_{t_i}^{t_{i+1}^-}A(\tau)d\tau}(I_n+K(t_i^-)\hat{A}(t_i^-))\right]\right)\left(e^{\int_0^{t_1^-}A(\tau)d\tau}\right) \tag{16}$$

If $0=t_1\in IMP$, *then*

$$\Omega(t)=(I_n+K(t^-)\hat{A}(t^-))\left(e^{\int_{t_{N(t^-)-1}}^{t^-}A(\tau)d\tau}\right)\left(\prod_{i=1}^{N(t^-)-1}\left[e^{\int_{t_i}^{t_{i+1}^-}A(\tau)d\tau}(I_n+K(t_i^-)\hat{A}(t_i^-))\right]\right) \tag{17}$$

If $0=t_1\in IMP$ *and* $t\in IMP$, *then* $t=t_{N(t)}$, $t_{N(t^-)-1}=t_{N(t)-2}$, *and* $t_{N(t^-)}=t_{N(t)-1}$ *so that*

$$\begin{aligned}\Omega(t)&=(I_n+K(t^-)\hat{A}(t^-))\Omega(t^-)\\&=(I_n+K(t^-)\hat{A}(t^-))\left(\prod_{i=1}^{N(t)-1}\left[e^{\int_{t_i}^{t_{i+1}}A(\tau)d\tau}(I_n+K(t_i^-)\hat{A}(t_i^-))\right]\right)\\&=(I_n+K(t^-)\hat{A}(t^-))e^{\int_{t_{N(t^-)-1}}^{t}A(\tau)d\tau}\left(\prod_{i=1}^{N(t^-)-1}\left[e^{\int_{t_i}^{t_{i+1}}A(\tau)d\tau}(I_n+K(t_i^-)\hat{A}(t_i^-))\right]\right)\end{aligned} \tag{18}$$

Proof. It turns out from (11)–(12) that

$$x(t)=e^{\int_{t_{i+1}}^{t}A(\tau)d\tau}x(t_{i+1})\text{if } t\in[t_{i+1},t_{i+2})\text{and } t_{i+1},t_{i+2}(>t_{i+1})\in IMP \tag{19}$$

$$\begin{aligned}x(t_{i+1})&=x\left(t_{i+1}^-\right)+\int_{t_{i+1}^-}^{t_{i+1}}\dot{x}(\tau)d\tau\\&=x\left(t_{i+1}^-\right)+\int_{t_{i+1}^-}^{t_{i+1}}K(\tau)\hat{A}\left(t_{i+1}^-\right)x\left(t_{i+1}^-\right)\delta(t_{i+1}-\tau)d\tau\\&=\left(I_n+K\left(t_{i+1}^-\right)\hat{A}\left(t_{i+1}^-\right)\right)x\left(t_{i+1}^-\right)\\&=\left(I_n+K\left(t_{i+1}^-\right)\hat{A}\left(t_{i+1}^-\right)\right)e^{\int_{t_i}^{t_{i+1}}A(\tau)d\tau}x(t_i)\end{aligned} \tag{20}$$

The last identity arising since $A(t)$ is not impulsive; thus, (20) into (19) yields if $t\in[t_{i+1},t_{i+2})$:

$$x(t^-)=e^{\int_{t_{i+1}}^{t}A(\tau)d\tau}x(t_{i+1})=\left(e^{\int_{t_{i+1}}^{t}A(\iota)d\iota}\left(I_n+K\left(t_{i+1}^-\right)\hat{A}\left(t_{i+1}^-\right)\right)\right)e^{\int_{t_i}^{t_{i+1}^-}A(\iota)d\iota}x(t_i) \tag{21}$$

and using recursive calculations for $t\in[t_{i+1},t_{i+2}]$:

$$\begin{aligned}x(t)&=(I_n+K(t^-)\hat{A}(t^-))e^{\int_{t_{i+1}}^{t^-}A(\tau)d\tau}x(t_{i+1})\\&=(I_n+K(t^-)\hat{A}(t^-))\left(e^{\int_{t_{i+1}}^{t^-}A(\tau)d\tau}(I_n+K(t_{i+1}^-)\hat{A}(t_{i+1}^-))\right)\left(e^{\int_{t_i}^{t_{i+1}^-}A(\tau)d\tau}\right)x(t_i)\\&=(I_n+K(t^-)\hat{A}(t^-))\left[\left(e^{\int_{t_{i+1}}^{t^-}A(\tau)d\tau}(I_n+K(t_{i+1}^-)\hat{A}(t_{i+1}^-))\right)\left(e^{\int_{t_i}^{t_{i+1}^-}A(\tau)d\tau}(I_n+K(t_i^-)\hat{A}(t_i^-))\right)\right]\left(e^{\int_{t_{i-1}}^{t_i^-}A(\tau)d\tau}\right)x(t_{i-1})\\&=(I_n+K(t^-)\hat{A}(t^-))\left[\left(e^{\int_{t_{i+1}}^{t}A(\tau)d\tau}(I_n+K(t_{i+1}^-)\hat{A}(t_{i+1}^-))\right)\times\ldots\times\left(e^{\int_{t_1}^{t_2}A(\tau)d\tau}(I_n+K(t_1^-)\hat{A}(t_1^-))\right)\right]\left(e^{\int_0^{t_1^-}A(\tau)d\tau}\right)x_0\end{aligned} \tag{22}$$

which proves (13) for any given finite $x_0=x(0)$ and any $t\in\boldsymbol{R}_{0+}$. This implies that $x(t)=\Omega(t)x_0$; $t\in\boldsymbol{R}_{0+}$ via the evolution operator (14). The solution is unique for given finite initial conditions because (22) is explicit and unique for finite given initial conditions. It turns out from (13) that the evolution operator that generates this solution for any given finite initial conditions is (14). From Theorem 1, this evolution operator is unique at each time interval $[t_i, t_{i+1})$ for any $t_i, t_{i+1} \in IMP$ and any finite initial condition x_0. It turns out that, as outlined below:

(a) the evolution operator is unique on $\cup_{t_i,t_{i+1}\in IMP}[t_i, t_{i+1})$ if $cardIMP = N_{imp} = \chi_0$, i.e., if there are infinitely many impulsive time instants;

(b) the evolution operator is unique on $\left(\cup_{t_i,t_{i+1}\in IMP}[t_i, t_{i+1})\right) \cup \left[t_{N_{imp}}, +\infty\right)$ if $N_{imp} < \chi_0$, i.e., if there is a finite number of impulsive time instants;

(c) the evolution operator is unique on $[0, +\infty)$ if, and only if, there is no sequence of impulsive gains $\{K'(t_i^-)\}_{t_i\in IMP} \neq \{K(t_i^-)\}_{t_i\in IMP}$ such that $x(t_i^-) \in Ker\{(K(t_i^-) - K'(t_i^-))\hat{A}(t_i^-)\}$ for at least a $t_i \in IMP$. Otherwise, assume that there is $t_i \in IMP$ and another impulsive gain matrix $K'(t_i^-) \neq K(t_i^-)$ such that, given $x(t_i^-)$, the right limit of the solution at t_i is $x(t_i) = K(t_i^-)\hat{A}(t_i^-)x(t_i^-) = K'(t_i^-)\hat{A}(t_i^-)x(t_i^-)$. As a result, distinct evolution operators generate an identical solution at t_i and the evolution operator is not unique on $[0, +\infty)$. Then, the evolution operator $\Omega : \mathbf{R}_{0+} \to \mathbf{R}^{n\times n}$ is unique on $[0, +\infty)$ if, and only if, for any sequence of impulsive gains $\{K'(t_i^-)\}_{t_i\in IMP}$ of the matrix of dynamics, such that $\{K'(t_i^-)\}_{t_i\in IMP} \neq \{K(t_i^-)\}_{t_i\in IMP}$, one has that $x(t_i^-) \in Ker\{(K(t_i^-) - K'(t_i^-))\hat{A}(t_i^-)\}$ for all $t_i \in IMP$.

Then, Property (i) has been proved. Property (ii) follows directly for the mentioned particular cases of the evolution operator (14). □

Note that the global non-uniqueness of the evolution operator in Theorem 2 (i) on $[0, +\infty)$ is lost when there is one $t_i \in IMP$ for which there is some impulsive gain $K'(t_i^-) \neq K(t_i^-)$ such that $x(t_i) = K(t_i^-)\hat{A}(t_i^-)x(t_i^-) = K'(t_i^-)\hat{A}(t_i^-)x(t_i^-)$. In this case, the same solution is achieved for distinct impulsive gain matrices. Equivalently, the evolution operator is unique if, and only if, $K'(t_i^-) \neq K(t_i^-)$, one has that $x(t_i^-) \notin Ker\{(K(t_i^-) - K'(t_i^-))\hat{A}(t_i^-)\}$ for each $x(t_i^-)$ for $t_i \in IMP$. We can easily see that, except in some particular cases, the global uniqueness of the evolution operator over time becomes lost.

Note also that the above impulsively parameterized system can be considered as a limit case of a switched system where switches are instantaneous at the switching time instants and the former configuration is re-established immediately after the impulsive actions. In this context, a switched differential system would be of the form $\dot{x}(t) = A_{\sigma(t)}x(t)$. Assume that $t_i \in IMP$, then, for $t \to t_i^-$, one has $\dot{x}(t_i^-) = A_{\sigma(t_i^-)}x(t_i^-)$ and for $t \to t_i^+ (say t_i)$, one has $\dot{x}(t_i) = A_{\sigma(t_i)}x(t_i) = \left[A_{\sigma(t_i^-)} + \Delta(A(t_i^-, K(t_i^-)))\right]x(t_i)$.

Remark 1. *Some examples that visualize that the evolution operator of the proportional instantaneous finite-jumps system (11)–(12) is not always unique for all time are as follows:*

(a) There is some $t_i \in IMP$ such that $x(t_i^-) = 0$, then $x(t_i) = 0$ for the scheduled impulsive gain $K(t_i)$ but also for any other impulsive gain $K'(t_i^-) \neq K(t_i^-)$;

(b) The order of the system is $n \geq 2$, the impulsive gain matrix sequence consists of diagonal matrices and there is one impulsive time instant t_i such that the first component is $x_1(t_i^-) = 0$. Then, any other diagonal gain matrix $K'(t_i^-)$ that coincides with the given one in all the diagonal entries except in the first one generates the same $x(t_i)$ with $x_1(t_i) = 0$ under all such gains, including for $K(t_i^-)$.

Now, consider the following alternative impulsive system to (11)–(12), which is a non-proportional instantaneous finite-jumps system depending on the left values of the matrix of dynamics $A(t)$ for $t \in IMP$, while the impulsive actions are, instead, additive to $A(t^-)$ in the differential system:

$$\dot{x}(t) = (A(t) + \Delta(t))x(t);\ x(0) = x_0 \tag{23}$$

$$\Delta(t) = \sum\nolimits_{t_i \in IMP(t)} K(t^-)\delta(t - t_i) \tag{24}$$

Note that $x(t_i) - x(t_i^-) = K(t_i)x(t_i^-)$ (instead of $K(t_i)\hat{A}(t_i^-)x(t_i^-)$ as it happened in (11)–(12)) if $t_i \in IMP$ and $x(t) = x(t^-)$ if $t \notin IMP$. Note that the increments between the right and the left values of the matrix of dynamics $A(t)$ at impulsive time instants are not proportional to its left value, in contrary to (11)–(12). This implies, in fact, that the feedback solution information from the left limit value of the matrix of the dynamics $A(t)$ value to its right limit value disappears in (23)–(24) with respect to (11)–(12). Thus, the following result is the direct counterpart one for the impulsive system (23)–(24) of Theorem 2:

Theorem 3. *The following properties hold:*

(i) *The unique solution of the instantaneous finite-jumps system (23)–(24) is given by the expression below:*

$$\begin{aligned} x(t) &= (I_n + K(t^-))\left(e^{\int_{t_{N(t^-)-1}}^{t^-} A(\tau)d\tau}\right)\left(\prod\nolimits_{i=1}^{N(t^-)-1}\left[e^{\int_{t_i}^{t_{i+1}^-} A(\tau)d\tau}(I_n + K(t_i^-))\right]\right)\left(e^{\int_0^{t_1^-} A(\tau)d\tau}\right)x_0 \\ &= (I_n + K(t^-))x(t^-);\ t \in \mathbf{R}_{0+} \end{aligned} \tag{25}$$

where $t_0 = 0$; $K(t_0^-) = K(0^-)$; $x_0 = x(0)$; $\{t_i\}_{i \in \mathbf{Z}_+}$; $IMP(t^-) = \left\{t_1, t_2, \cdots, t_{N(t^-)}\right\}$ if $K(0^-) = 0$; and $IMP(t^-) = \left\{t_0 = 0, t_1, \cdots, t_{N(t^-)}\right\}$ if $K(0^-) \neq 0$ is the impulsive set of time instants on $[0, t)$ whose cardinal is $N(t^-)$. Thus, the solution of (23)–(24) is given by $x(t) = \Omega_a(t)x_0; t \in \mathbf{R}_{0+}$, where, in general, the non-unique evolution operator is now redefined as follows, with respect to its definition $\Omega(t)$ of Theorem 2:

$$\begin{aligned} \Omega_a(t) &= (I_n + K(t^-))\Omega_a(t^-) \\ &= (I_n + K(t^-))\left(e^{\int_{t_{N(t^-)-1}}^{t^-} A(\tau)d\tau}\right)\left(\prod\nolimits_{i=1}^{N(t^-)-1}\left[e^{\int_{t_i}^{t_{i+1}^-} A(\tau)d\tau}(I_n + K(t_i^-))\right]\right)\left(e^{\int_0^{t_1^-} A(\tau)d\tau}\right) \end{aligned} \tag{26}$$

The evolution operator $\Omega_a : \mathbf{R}_{0+} \to \mathbf{R}^{n \times n}$ is unique on $[0, +\infty)$ if, and only if, there is no sequence of impulsive gains $\{K'(t_i^-)\}_{t_i \in IMP} \neq \{K(t_i^-)\}_{t_i \in IMP}$ of the matrix of dynamics such that $x(t_i^-) \in Ker\{(K(t_i^-) - K'(t_i^-))\}$ for at least a $t_i \in IMP$. Equivalently, if there is at least a $t_i \in IMP$ such that $x(t_i^-) \in Ker\{(K(t_i^-) - K'(t_i^-))\}$, with $K'(t_i^-) \neq K(t_i^-)$, then $\Omega_a : \mathbf{R}_{0+} \to \mathbf{R}^{n \times n}$ is non-unique.

(ii) *If $t \in IMP$, then $t = t_{N(t)}$ and $IMP(t) = IMP(t^-) \cup \left\{t_{N(t)}\right\}$ so that (26) becomes the following:*

$$\Omega_a(t) = \left(\prod\nolimits_{i=1}^{N(t)-1}\left[e^{\int_{t_i}^{t_{i+1}^-} A(\tau)d\tau}(I_n + K(t_i^-))\right]\right)\left(e^{\int_0^{t_1^-} A(\tau)d\tau}\right) \tag{27}$$

and

$$\Omega_a(t^-) = \left(e^{\int_{t_{N(t^-)-1}}^{t^-} A(\tau)d\tau}\right)\left(\prod\nolimits_{i=1}^{N(t^-)-1}\left[e^{\int_{t_i}^{t_{i+1}^-} A(\tau)d\tau}(I_n + K(t_i^-))\right]\right)\left(e^{\int_0^{t_1^-} A(\tau)d\tau}\right) \tag{28}$$

If $0 = t_1 \in IMP$, *then*

$$\Omega_a(t) = \left(I_n + K\left(t^-\right)\right)e^{\int_{t_{i+1}}^{t^-} A(\tau)d\tau}\left(\prod_{i=1}^{N(t^-)-1}\left[e^{\int_{t_i}^{t_{i+1}^-} A(\tau)d\tau}\left(I_n + K\left(t_i^-\right)\right)\right]\right) \tag{29}$$

If $0 = t_1 \in IMP$ *and* $t = t_{N(t)} \in IMP$, *then*

$$\begin{aligned}\Omega_a(t) &= \left(I_n + K\left(t^-\right)\right)\Omega_a\left(t^-\right) \\ &= \left(I_n + K\left(t^-\right)\right)\left(\prod_{i=1}^{N(t)-1}\left[e^{\int_{t_i}^{t_{i+1}} A(\tau)d\tau}\left(I_n + K\left(t_i^-\right)\right)\right]\right) \\ &= \left(I_n + K\left(t^-\right)\right)e^{\int_{t_{N(t^-)-1}}^{t} A(\tau)d\tau}\left(\prod_{i=1}^{N(t^-)-1}\left[e^{\int_{t_i}^{t_{i+1}} A(\tau)d\tau}\left(I_n + K\left(t_i^-\right)\right)\right]\right)\end{aligned} \tag{30}$$

3. Impulsive Time-Varying Differential Systems with Constant Point Delays and Their Evolution Operator

The results of Section 2 are reformulated for the case where the dynamics include a finite number of constant point delays, with the associated dynamic matrices being bounded and piecewise-continuous on $\mathbf{R}_{0+}$ in the more general setting. The impulsive actions can take place in both the delay-free dynamics and in all or some of the delayed dynamics.

Consider the following impulsive differential system of order n with proportional instantaneous finite jumps and with p, in general, incommensurate constant point delays $h_i; i \in \overline{p}$, subject to $h_i < h_j$ if $j, i(< j) \in \overline{p}$:

$$\dot{x}(t) = (A(t) + \Delta(t))x(t) + \sum_{i=1}^{p}(A_i(t) + \Delta_i(t))x(t - h_i) \tag{31}$$

$$\Delta(t) = \sum_{t_i \in IMPA(t)} K\left(t^-\right)\hat{A}\left(t^-\right)\delta(t - t_i) \tag{32}$$

$$\Delta_i(t) = \sum_{t_i \in IMPA_i(t)} K_i\left(t^-\right)\hat{A}_i\left(t^-\right)\delta(t - t_i) \tag{33}$$

for $i \in \overline{p}$, where the admissible function of the initial conditions $\varphi : \left[-h_p, 0\right] \to \mathbf{R}^n$, with $x(0) = \varphi(0) = x_0$, is bounded piecewise-continuous on $\left[-h_p, 0\right]$. The matrix function $A : \mathbf{R}_{0+} \to \mathbf{R}^{n \times n}$ of delay-free dynamics is bounded, piecewise-continuous, and Lebesgue-integrable on $\mathbf{R}_{0+}$ and the matrix functions $A_i : \mathbf{R}_{0+} \to \mathbf{R}^{n \times n}; i \in \overline{p}$ associated with the delayed dynamics of the various delays are bounded piecewise-continuous. The matrix function $\hat{A} : \mathbf{R}_{0+} \to \mathbf{R}^{n \times n}$ is defined in such a way that $\hat{A}_{ij}\left(t^-\right) = A_{ij}\left(t^-\right)$ if the (i, j)-entry of $A\left(t^-\right)$ is impulsive and $\hat{A}_{ij}\left(t^-\right) = 0$, otherwise, for $i, j \in \overline{n}$. In the same way, $\hat{A}_{kij}\left(t^-\right) = A_{kij}\left(t^-\right)$ if the (i, j)-entry of $A_k\left(t^-\right)$ is impulsive and $\hat{A}_{kij}\left(t^-\right) = 0$, otherwise, for $i, j \in \overline{n}$ and $k \in \overline{p}$.

The above Equations (31)–(33) reflect that impulses also occur for the delayed terms.

It turns out that $K\left(t^-\right)\left(\in \mathbf{R}^{n \times n}\right) \neq 0$ iff $t \in IMPA$, and $K_i\left(t^-\right)\left(\in \mathbf{R}^{n \times n}\right) \neq 0$ iff $t \in IMPA_i$, where $IMPA = \left\{t \in \mathbf{R}_{0+} : K\left(t^-\right)\hat{A}\left(t^-\right) \neq 0\right\}$ is the impulsive set of time instants of $A : \mathbf{R}_{0+} \to \mathbf{R}^{n \times n}$, and $IMPA_i = \left\{t \in \mathbf{R}_{0+} : K_i\left(t^-\right)\hat{A}_i\left(t^-\right) \neq 0\right\}$ is the impulsive set of time instants of $A_i : \mathbf{R}_{0+} \to \mathbf{R}^{n \times n}$ for $i \in \overline{p}$, and $IMPA(t) = \{\tau(\leq t) \in IMPA\}$, $IMPA\left(t^-\right) = \{\tau(< t) \in IMPA\}$, $IMPA_i(t) = \{\tau(\leq t) \in IMPA_i\}$, and $IMPA_i\left(t^-\right) = \{\tau(< t) \in IMPA_i\}$ for $i \in \overline{p}$.

The impulsive sets on time intervals $[t - \sigma, t]$, $[t - \sigma, t)$, and $(t - \sigma, t)$ of $A(t)$ are denoted, respectively, as $IMPA[t - \sigma, t]$, $IMPA[t - \sigma, t)$, $IMPA(t - \sigma, t]$, and $IMPA(t - \sigma, t)$ such that $IMPA[t - \sigma, t] = IMPA[t - \sigma, t) \cup \{t\}$ if $t \in IMPA$, $IMPA[t - \sigma, t] = IMPA(t - \sigma, t] \cup \{t - \sigma\}$ if $(t - \sigma) \in IMPA$, and $IMPA[t - \sigma, t] = IMPA(t - \sigma, t) \cup \{t - \sigma\} \cup \{t\}$ if $(t - \sigma), t \in IMPA$.

Close definitions apply "mutatis mutandis" for the impulsive set of time instants of $A_i(t)$ for $i \in \overline{p}$. The whole impulsive set for impulses in any matrix of dynamics is $IMP = \{t_k\}_{k \in \overline{cardIMP}} = IMPA \cup (\cup_{i \in \overline{p}} IMPA_i)$.

3.1. Trajectory Solution of the Differential Impulsive System with Delays

The following result is immediate from (31)–(33):

Proposition 2. *Assume that* $IMP = \{t_k\}_{k \in \overline{cardIMP}} = IMPA \cup (\cup_{i \in \overline{p}} IMPA_i)$ *with* IMP *can be either finite (i.e., the number of impulses is finite) or infinity numerable (i.e., the number of impulses is infinite but they are located through time) so that* $cardIMP \leq \chi_0$. *Then, the unique solution of (31)–(33) for any given admissible function of the initial conditions* $\varphi : [-h_p, 0] \to \mathbf{R}^n$ *with* $x(0) = \varphi(0) = x_0$ *is as follows:*

$$x(t^-) = e^{\int_{t_k}^{t^-} A(\tau)d\tau} x(t_k) + \sum_{i=1}^{p} \int_{t_k}^{t^-} e^{\int_{\tau}^{t^-} A(\sigma)d\sigma} A_i(\tau)x(\tau - h_i)d\tau \tag{34}$$

$$x(t) = (I_n + K(t^-)\hat{A}(t^-))x(t^-) + \sum_{i=1}^{p} K_i(t^-)\hat{A}_i(t^-)x(t^- - h_i) \tag{35}$$

for any $t \in [t_k, t_{k+1}]$, *provided that* $t_k, t_{k+1} \in IMPA \cup IMPA_i$.

In particular, if $t \in IMPA$ *and* $t \notin IMPA_i$ *for some* $i \in \overline{p}$ *then, one has, from (35)*

$$x(t) = (I_n + K(t^-)\hat{A}(t^-))x(t^-)$$

If $t \in IMPA \cup (\cup_{i \in \Pi} IMPA_i)$ *for* $\Pi (\subseteq \overline{p})$, *then*

$$x(t) = (I_n + K(t^-)\hat{A}(t^-))x(t^-) + \sum_{i \in \Pi} K_i(t^-)\hat{A}_i(t^-)x(t^- - h_i)$$

If $t \in \cup_{i \in \Pi} IMPA_i$ *for* $\Pi (\subseteq \overline{p})$ *and* $t \notin IMPA$, *then from (35),*

$$x(t) = x(t^-) + \sum_{i \in \Pi} K_i(t^-)\hat{A}_i(t^-)x(t^- - h_i).$$

Note that, since the impulsive matrix of any (delayed or not) particular matrix of dynamics is zero if the impulse does not affect such a matrix $A(.)$ and $A_{(.)}(.)$, then (35) is also valid for all the particular cases of Proposition 2.

The last additive term in (34) reflects the contribution of all the delayed impulsive terms of the form $x(t - h_i)$ on the time interval $[t_k - h_i, t - h_i]$ for all $i \in \overline{p}$. Each of them can be empty, for instance, if there is no impulse associated with $x(\tau)$ in such an interval.

A particular case of the above result is direct under the following assumption of constant time intervals of size in-between consecutive impulsive time instants:

Assumption 1. *Assume that* $IMP = \{t_i = iT : x(t_i) \neq x(t_i^-)\}$ *if* $0 \notin IMP$ *, and* $IMP = \{t_i\}_{i \in \mathbf{Z}_+} = \{(i-1)T\}_{i \in \mathbf{Z}_+}$ *if* $0 \in IMP$, *i.e., there are infinitely many impulses through time with a constant time interval* T *in-between each two consecutive impulses.*

Define $j_i(t) = max(j \in \mathbf{Z}_{0+} : jT \leq t - h_i)$ for $i \in \overline{p} \cup \{0\}$ with $h_0 = 0$. Then, $t - h_i = j_i(t)T$ iff $(t - h_i) \in IMP$ so that $K(t^- - h_i) = K(j_i(t)T^-)(\neq 0)$ iff $(t - h_i) \in IMP$ and $j_i(t) < j_{i-1}(t)$ for $i \in \overline{p}$ and $t \in \mathbf{R}_{0+}$.

Define also for each $t \in \mathbf{R}_{0+}$ a proper, improper—which can be empty (if the impulsive set in $[t - h_p, t]$ is empty)—subset $\overline{p}(t)$ of $\overline{p} \cup \{0\}$ by the following:

$\overline{p}(t) = \{z \in \overline{p} \cup \{0\} : (t - h_z) \in IMP\}$ for $t \in \mathbf{R}_{0+}$, which is the indexing set of the impulsive time instants that occurred on $[t - h_p, t]$. As a result, $K(t^- - h_i) = K(j_i(t)T^-)$ is non-zero iff $i \in \overline{p}(t)$. As a result, $i \in \overline{p}(t)$ $(t - h_i) \in IMP$, implying that $t - h_i = j_i(t)T$.

The following result is an immediate consequence of Proposition 2 and Assumption 1:

Proposition 3. *Assume that* $IMP = \{t_i\}_{i \in \mathbf{Z}_+} = \{iT\}_{i \in \mathbf{Z}_+}$ *(Assumption 1), the unique solution of (31)–(33) for any given admissible function of the initial conditions* $\varphi : [-h_p, 0] \to \mathbf{R}^n$ *with* $x(0) = \varphi(0) = x_0$ *is as follows:*

$$x(t^-) = e^{\int_{kT}^{t^-} A(\tau)d\tau} x(kT) + \sum_{i=1}^{p} \int_{kT}^{t^-} e^{\int_{\tau}^{t^-} A(\sigma)d\sigma} A_i(\tau) x(\tau - h_i) d\tau \quad (36)$$

$$\begin{aligned} x(t) &= (I_n + K(t^-)\hat{A}(t^-))x(t^-) + \textstyle\sum_{i=1}^{p} K_i(t^-)\hat{A}_i(t^-)x(t^- - h_i) \\ &= (I_n + K(t^-)\hat{A}(t^-))\left[e^{\int_{kT}^{t^-} A(\tau)d\tau} x(kT) + \textstyle\sum_{i=1}^{p} \int_{kT}^{t^-} e^{\int_{\tau}^{t^-} A(\sigma)d\sigma} A_i(\tau)x(\tau - h_i)d\tau\right] + \textstyle\sum_{i=1}^{p} K_i(t^-)\hat{A}_i(t^-)x(t^- - h_i) \end{aligned} \quad (37)$$

forany $t \in [kT, (k+1)T]$

The next assumption relaxes the constraint that the time interval between consecutive impulsive time instants is constant but is still assumed to be an integer multiple of a positive real constant.

Assumption 2. *If* $IMP \ni t_i = j_i T$ *for some positive integer* $j_i = j(i) \le i$ *, then all the impulses on the interval* $[t - h_p, t]$ *take place at time instants* $t_k = j_k T$ *subject to* $t - h_i \le t_k = j_k T \le t$.

Note from Assumption 2 the following:

(1) If $t \in IMP$, then all the impulsive time instants in $[t - h_p, t]$ are in a non-empty set $IMP[t - h_p, t]$ of cardinal $m = m(t) \ge 1$ and the impulsive time instants are of the form

$$\left\{t_i^1 = i_1 T = t_{i_1}, t_i^2 = i_2 T = t_{i_2}, \cdots, t = t_i = i_m T\right\}, \text{ where} i_k, i_j (< i_k) \in \mathbf{Z}_+ \text{for} j < k$$

(2) The impulsive sets in $[t - h_p, t]$ and $[t - h_p, t)$ can be empty and they verify the relations $IMP[t - h_p, t] = \begin{cases} IMP[t - h_p, t) \text{ if } t \notin IMP \\ IMP[t - h_p, t) \cup \{t\} \text{ if } t \in IMP \end{cases}$.

Note that the above impulsive sets are identical iff $t \notin IMP$ and that they are jointly empty iff there are no impulses in the time interval $[t - h_p, t)$ and $t \notin IMP$.

Assumption 2 implies that the impulsive time instants are (in general, non-consecutive) integer multiples of a constant time interval T rather than aperiodic [42–44]. The delays in that case are still, in general, incommensurate since they are not necessarily integer multiples of a minimum base delay h. However, the case of commensurate delays can be dealt with simply as a particular case with $h_i = ih$ for $i \in \overline{p}$. The following result follows directly from Proposition 2 and Assumption 2:

Proposition 4. *If Assumption 2 holds, then one has for any two consecutive* $t_k (= j_k T)$ *,* $t_{k+1} (= j_{k+1} T) \in IMP$ *that*

$$\begin{aligned} x(j_{k+1}T) &= (I_n + K(j_{k+1}T^-)\hat{A}(j_{k+1}{}^-))x(j_{k+1}T^-) + \textstyle\sum_{i=1}^{p} K_i(j_{k+1}T^-)\hat{A}_i(j_{k+1}T^-)x(j_{k+1}T^- - h_i) \\ &= (I_n + K(j_{k+1}T^-)\hat{A}(j_{k+1}{}^-)) \\ &\times \left[e^{\int_{j_kT}^{j_{k+1}T^-} A(\tau)d\tau} x(j_kT) + \textstyle\sum_{i=1}^{p} \int_{j_kT}^{j_{k+1}T^-} e^{\int_{\tau}^{j_{k+1}T^-} A(\sigma)d\sigma} A_i(\tau)x(\tau - h_i)d\tau\right] + \textstyle\sum_{i=1}^{p} K_i(j_{k+1}T^-)\hat{A}_i(j_{k+1}T^-)x(j_{k+1}T^- - h_i) \end{aligned} \quad (38)$$

And, if $t \in [t_k, t_{k+1})$*, then*

$$x(t) = e^{\int_{j_kT}^{t} A(\tau)d\tau} x(j_kT) + \sum_{i=1}^{p} \int_{j_kT}^{t} e^{\int_{\tau}^{t} A(\sigma)d\sigma} A_i(\tau)x(\tau - h_i)d\tau \quad (39)$$

The evolution operator, which gives the solution for any given function of the initial conditions, follows directly from Proposition 2:

Proposition 5. *Assume that $IMP = \{t_k\}_{k\in \mathbf{Z}_+}$. Then, in general, the non-unique evolution operator that generates the solution (34)–(35) of the differential system (31)–(32) on $[t_k, t]$, with $t_k, t_{k+1} \in IMP$ being consecutive impulsive time instants and $t \in [t_k, t_{k+1}] \in \mathbf{R}_{0+}$, is defined recursively as follows:*

$$Z(t^-, t_k) = e^{\int_{t_k}^{t^-} A(\tau)d\tau} Z(t_k, 0) + \sum_{i=1}^{p} \int_{t_k}^{t^-} e^{\int_{\tau}^{t^-} A(\sigma)d\sigma} A_i(\tau) Z(\tau - h_i, 0) d\tau \tag{40}$$

$$Z(t, t^-) = \left(I_n + K(t^-)\hat{A}(t^-)\right) Z(t^-, t_k) + \sum_{i=1}^{p} K_i(t^-)\hat{A}_i(t^-) Z(t^- - h_i, 0) \tag{41}$$

and $Z(t,t) = I_n$, $Z(t,\tau) = 0_n$ for $t \in \mathbf{R}_{0+}$, and $Z(t,t^-) = I_n$ if $t \notin IMP$ for any $t, (\tau > t) \in \mathbf{R}_{0+}$. The evolution operator is, in general, clearly non-unique and time-differentiable in the open real interval $\cup_{t_i \in IMP}(t_i, t_{i+1})$. If the impulsive set of time instants is finite such that $t_M = \{max t : t \in IMP\} < +\infty$, then the evolution operator is time-differentiable in the open real interval $\left(\cup_{t_i \in IMP}(t_i, t_{i+1})\right) \cup (t_M, +\infty)$.

The non-uniqueness of the evolution operator can be addressed under similar considerations as those used in the proof of Theorem 2 based on the fact that, except for particular cases of the choices of the impulsive gains, the right limits of the solution at impulsive time instants are achievable for more than one impulsive gain from the given reached values of the solution of their left limits. Particular versions of the evolution operator of Proposition 2 follow directly from Propositions 3 and 4 under Assumptions 1 and 2. The particular evolution operators arising for the particular cases discussed in Proposition 2 follow directly from such a result and they are then not displayed explicitly in Proposition 5.

3.2. Some Results on the Solution Boundedness and the Global Stability

The subsequent result relies on the global boundedness of the solution of the impulsive time-delay system in the event that the matrix $A(t)$ is a stability matrix for all time, provided that a minimum threshold in-between consecutive impulsive time instants is respected under sufficient smallness in the norm terms of the matrices of dynamics and that of the impulsive matrix gain. A second part of the result relies on the global stabilization of the differential system by the appropriate choice of the impulsive matrix gain and the set of impulsive time instants, even if the matrix of delay-free dynamics is not stable for any time. The mechanism to achieve stabilization is that the impulses occur at a sufficiently fast rate with the impulsive gain entries being of appropriate signs and of sufficiently large amplitudes. For simplicity of the subsequent exposition, it is assumed that $IMPA_i = \varnothing$ for $i \in \overline{p}$ so that $IMP = IMPA$. This simplification does not imply an essential loss in generality since the resulting most general result could be easily reformulated.

Theorem 4. *The following properties hold:*

(i) *Assume the following:*

  (1) $IMP = IMPA$;

  (2) *for any $t \in \mathbf{R}_{0+}$, $T_{impt} = \sup_{t_k, t_{k+1}(\leq t) \in IMP} (t_{k+1} - t_k) \leq +\infty$ is the largest interval between consecutive impulsive time instants, $t_{k+1} \geq t_k + T_{km}$ up until the time instant "t" for some minimum k-inter-impulsive time interval threshold $T_{km}(\geq T_m) \in \mathbf{R}^+$ for any consecutive $t_k, t_{k+1}(> t_k) \in IMP$ with k-inter-impulse time interval $T_k = t_{k+1} - t_k$;*

(3) $a_t = \sup_{0 \le \tau < +\infty} \|A(\tau)\| < +\infty$, *with the supremum spectral radius of* $A(t)$ *satisfying* $\sup_{0 \le \tau < +\infty} \rho(A(\tau)) < 1$, *that is, all the eigenvalues of* $A(t)$ *have a negative real part for any* $t \in \mathbf{R}_{0+}$, $a_{dt} = \max_{i \in \overline{p}} \sup_{0 \le \tau \le t} \|A_i(\tau)\| < +\infty$, $k_t = \sup_{0 \le \tau \le t} \|K(\tau)\| < +\infty$, *and*

$$\underline{\theta}_k(t) = \left\| e^{\int_{t_k}^{t_k+T_{km}} A(\tau)d\tau} \right\| \le \theta_t = \sup_{t_k,(t_k<t_{k+1}\le t)\in IMP} \left(\left\| e^{\int_{t_k}^{t_{k+1}} A(\tau)d\tau} \right\| \right) < +\infty \tag{42}$$

Then, a sufficient condition for $\sup_{t \in \mathbf{R}_{0+}} \|x(t)\| < +\infty$ *for any given finite admissible function of the initial conditions is outlined below:*

$$\limsup_{t \to \infty} \left[\theta_t (1 + k_t a_t) \left(1 + p a_{dt} T_{impt} (1 + k_t) \right) \right] \le 1, \tag{43}$$

In addition, (43) holds under the stronger sufficiency-type condition

$$\theta_t \le \frac{1}{(1 + k_t a_t)\left(1 + p a_{dt} T_{impt}(1 + k_t)\right)} \tag{44}$$

for all $t \ge t_0$ *and some finite* $t_0 \in \mathbf{R}_+$.

In order for (44) to hold, a necessary condition is that $t_{k+1} \ge t_k + T_{km}$ *with the inter-impulsive minimum time-interval threshold* T_{km} *being sufficiently small, satisfying:*

$$\left\| e^{\int_{t_k}^{t_k+T_{km}} A(\tau)d\tau} \right\| (1 + k_t a_t)(1 + p a_{dt} T_{km}(1 + k_t)) < 1 \tag{45}$$

$$t_k, t_{k+1}(> t_k) \in IMP \text{ with } t_{k+1} = \max(\tau(< t) \in IMP)$$

(ii) *Assume that the conditions of Property (i) hold, except the one invoking that the constraint* $\sup_{0 \le \tau < +\infty} \rho(A(\tau)) < 1$ *holds; furthermore, assume, that for each* $t \in \mathbf{R}_{0+}$, *there exists at least a time instant* $\xi_{t_k} \in [t_k + T_{km}, t_k + T_{km} + h_p]$ *such that* $\hat{A}\left(\xi_{t_k}^-\right)$ *is non-singular and the maximum inter-impulse time interval* $(T_{km} + h_p)$ *is sufficiently small. The set of impulsive time instants is effective for an admissible impulsive matrix function gain, that is, if* $t_k \in IMP$, *then* $\hat{A}\left(\xi_{t_k}^-\right) x\left(\xi_{t_k}^-\right) \ne 0$. *Then, the solution can be made globally bounded for all time for any given admissible function of the initial condition—so that the differential system is globally stable—by means of appropriate choices of a sufficiently short choice of the impulsive set of time instants and the sign and amplitudes of the entries of the impulsive matrix function gain* $K : \mathbf{R}_{0+} \to \mathbf{R}^{n \times n}$. *It can also be achieved under more stringent conditions that* $\lim_{t_k(\in IMP)} x(t_k) = \lim_{t_k(\in IMP)} x\left(t_k^-\right) = 0$.

Proof. For any finite time instant $t \in \mathbf{R}_+$, define $x_t^- = \sup_{0 \le \tau \le t^-} \|x(\tau)\|$ and $x_t = \sup_{0 \le \tau \le t} \|x(\tau)\|$, and also define $x^- = \sup_{0 \le t \le +\infty} |x_t^-|$ and $x = \sup_{0 \le \tau \le +\infty} |x_t|$. Those four amounts depend on the parameterization, impulses, and initial conditions. One has from Proposition 2, and Equations (35) and (34) that

$$x_t \le (1 + k_t a_t) x_t^- \le (1 + k_t a_t) \theta_t \left(1 + p a_{dt} T_{impt}(1 + k_t)\right) x_{\alpha_k(t)} \tag{46}$$

$$x_t^- \le \theta_t \left(1 + p a_{dt} T_{impt}(1 + k_t)\right) x_{\alpha_k(t)} \le \theta_t \left(1 + p a_{dt} T_{impt}(1 + k_t)\right)(1 + k_t a_t) x_{\alpha_k(t)}^- \tag{47}$$

where $\alpha_k(t) = min(t - h_1, t_k(t))$ with $t_k(t) = max(t_k(< t) \in IMP)$. Note that $x_t \geq x_{\alpha_k(t)}$ and that $x_t^- \geq x_{\alpha_k(t)}^-$ by construction of the supremum since $0 < (t - \alpha_k(t)) \leq \gamma$ for all $t \in \mathbf{R}_{0+}$. It turns out from (46)–(47) that $\mathbf{x}^- < +\infty$ and $\mathbf{x} < +\infty$ if (43) holds, guaranteed by (44) for some finite $t_0 \in \mathbf{R}_+$, for which a necessary condition is that T_{km} should be sufficiently small according to (45) since $\theta_t \geq \underline{\theta}_k(t)$ and $T_{impt} \geq T_{km}$ since

$$\begin{aligned} \left\| e^{\int_{t_k}^{t_k+T_{km}} A(\tau)d\tau} \right\| &= \underline{\theta}_k(t) \leq \theta_t = \sup_{t_k,(t_{k+1} \leq t) \in IMP} \left(\left\| e^{\int_{t_k}^{t_{k+1}} A(\tau)d\tau} \right\| \right) \\ &< \frac{1}{(1+k_t a_t)(1+pa_{dt}T_{impt}(1+k_t))} \leq \frac{1}{(1+k_t a_t)(1+pa_{dt}T_{km}(1+k_t))} \end{aligned} \quad (48)$$

that is, only if (45) holds. Property (i) has been proved.

Now, Property (iii) is proved. For the entry-to-entry definition of the matrices $K(t) = (K_{ij}(t))$ and $\hat{A}(t^-) = (\hat{A}_{ij}(t^-))$, rewrite (35) equivalently, as follows, provided that $\sum_{k=1}^{n} \hat{A}_{\updownarrow k}(t^-)x_k(t^-)$ is non-zero for some $\updownarrow = \updownarrow(t) \in \overline{n}$ and each $t \in IMP$ so that

$$\begin{aligned} x_i(t) &= x_i(t^-) + \sum_{j=1}^{n} \sum_{k=1}^{n} K_{ij}(t^-)\hat{A}_{jk}(t^-)x_k(t^-) \\ &= x_i(t^-) + K_{i\updownarrow}(t^-)\sum_{k=1}^{n} \hat{A}_{\updownarrow k}(t^-)x_k(t^-) + \sum_{j(\neq\updownarrow)=1}^{n} \sum_{k=1}^{n} K_{ij}(t^-)\hat{A}_{jk}(t^-)x_k(t^-) \end{aligned} \quad (49)$$

that $x_i(t) = \lambda_i(t)x_i(t^-)$ with

$$\lambda_i(t) = 1 + K_{i\updownarrow}(t^-)\sum_{k=1}^{n} \hat{A}_{\updownarrow k}(t^-)x_k(t^-) + \sum_{j(\neq\updownarrow)=1}^{n} \sum_{k=1}^{n} K_{ij}(t^-)\hat{A}_{jk}(t^-)x_k(t^-) \quad (50)$$

and $0 < |\lambda_i(t)| \leq \varsigma_i(t) \leq 1$ if

$$\begin{aligned} &-\left(\varsigma_i(t) + 1 + \sum_{j(\neq\updownarrow)=1}^{n} \sum_{k=1}^{n} K_{ij}(t^-)\hat{A}_{jk}(t^-)x_k(t^-)\right) \\ &\quad \leq K_{i\updownarrow}(t^-)\sum_{k=1}^{n} \hat{A}_{\updownarrow k}(t^-)x_k(t^-) \\ &\leq \varsigma_i(t) - 1 - \sum_{j(\neq\updownarrow)=1}^{n} \sum_{k=1}^{n} K_{ij}(t^-)\hat{A}_{jk}(t^-)x_k(t^-) \end{aligned} \quad (51)$$

that is,

$$\begin{aligned} &-\frac{\varsigma_i(t) + 1 + \sum_{j(\neq\updownarrow)=1}^{n} \sum_{k=1}^{n} K_{ij}(t^-)\hat{A}_{jk}(t^-)x_k(t^-)}{\sum_{k=1}^{n} \hat{A}_{\updownarrow k}(t^-)x_k(t^-)} \leq K_{i\updownarrow}(t) \\ &\leq \frac{\varsigma_i(t) - 1 - \sum_{j(\neq\updownarrow)=1}^{n} \sum_{k=1}^{n} K_{ij}(t^-)\hat{A}_{jk}(t^-)x_k(t^-)}{\sum_{k=1}^{n} \hat{A}_{\updownarrow k}(t^-)x_k(t^-)} \end{aligned} \quad (52)$$

Now, note the following:

(1) In the event that $\sum_{k=1}^{n} \hat{A}_{\updownarrow k}(t^-)x_k(t^-) = 0$ for some $t \in IMP$ and all $\updownarrow = \updownarrow(t) \in \overline{n}$, then the formula (52) has division by zero and one has, equivalently, $\hat{A}(t^-)x(t^-) = 0$ and $x(t) = x(t^-)$ so that t is then an ineffective impulsive time instant (Definition 1, Proposition 1) irrespective of the value of the impulsive matrix gain;

(2) If the impulsive set IMP is effective irrespective of any non-zero matrix function gain $K(t)$, then $\hat{A}(t^-)x(t^-) \neq 0$ for all $t \in IMP$ (Definition 2, Definition 3, and Proposition 1). Thus, by virtue of the given hypothesis, $\hat{A}(t^-)x(t^-) \neq 0$ for all $t \in IMP$, equivalently $\sum_{k=1}^{n} \hat{A}_{\updownarrow k}(t^-)x_k(t^-) \neq 0$ so that (52) is well-posed without division by zero;

(3) Since $+\infty \geq T_{kM} = t_{k+1} - t_k \geq h_p$ and then

$$h_p \leq T_M = \sup_{t \in \mathbf{R}_{0+}} T_{impt} = \sup_{t \in \mathbf{R}_{0+}} \sup_{t_k, t_{k+1}(\leq t) \in IMP} (t_{k+1} - t_k) \leq +\infty$$

Thus, it follows as a result that if $x(\tau)=0$ for $\tau\in[t,t+T_M]$, then $x(t)=0$ for $t>T_M$, and the differential system has then been stabilized in finite time;

(4) If $x(\tau)$ is not identically zero on $[t_k+T_{km},t_k+T_{km}+h_p]$ for any $t_k\in IMP$, then there is always (at least) an eligible effective impulsive time instant $\xi_{t_k}(=t_{k+1})\in[t_k+T_{km},t+T_{km}+h_p]\cap IMP$ subsequent to "t_k" by hypothesis and provided that $x\left(\xi_{t_k}^-\right)\neq 0$ since for each $t\in \mathbf{R}_{0+}$, there exists at least one such a time instant ξ_{t_k}, such that $\hat{A}\left(\xi_{t_k}^-\right)$ is non-singular and then $\hat{A}\left(\xi_{t_k}^-\right)x\left(\xi_{t_k}^-\right)\neq 0$ if $x(\xi_t^-)\neq 0$. Then, $K(t)$ can be defined so that at ξ_{t_k}, $K(\xi_t^-)\hat{A}(\xi_t^-)x(\xi_t^-)\neq 0$ with $\xi_{t_k}\in IMP$ being an effective impulsive time instant (see Definition 3 and Proposition 1) under the impulsive matrix gain $K(t)$ fulfilling the constraint (52) with the replacement $t\to\xi_{t_k}$. Thus, given an effective $t_k\in IMP$, the next $t_{k+1}\in IMP$ can be fixed as $t_{k+1}=t_k+T_k$ such that $T_k\geq T_{km}$ fulfils the following constraint:

$$\begin{aligned}&\max_{1\leq i\leq \overline{p}}\left|x_i\left(t_{k+1}^-\right)\right|=\left\|x\left(t_{k+1}^-\right)\right\|_\infty\leq\\ &\max_{1\leq i\leq \overline{p}}\left(\left(\lambda_{ki}-\varsigma_i\left\|e_i^T e^{\int_{t_k}^{t_k^-+T_k}A(\tau)d\tau}\right\|_\infty\right)\|x(t_k^-)\|_\infty+\left\|\sum_{i=1}^p e_i^T\int_{t_k}^{t_k^-+T_k}e^{\int_\tau^{t_k^-+T_k}A(\sigma)d\sigma}A_i(\tau)x(\tau-h_i)d\tau\right\|_\infty\right)\end{aligned}\tag{53}$$

provided that $0<\varsigma_i<min\left(1,\lambda_{ki}/\left\|e_i^T e^{\int_{t_k}^{t_k^-+T_k}A(\tau)d\tau}\right\|_\infty\right)$ for $i\in\overline{p}$, from (34)–(35) with $K_i\equiv 0$, since $IMPA_i=\varnothing$; $i\in\overline{p}$, by hypothesis, and provided that $K(t_k^-)$ fulfils the constraint (52). It turns out that (53) implies $\left\|x\left(t_{k+1}^-\right)\right\|_\infty\leq\left(\max_{1\leq i\leq\overline{p}}\lambda_{ki}\right)\|x(t_k^-)\|_\infty$. Then, one has the following features:

(1) If the real sequence $\left\{\max_{1\leq i\leq\overline{p}}\lambda_{ki}\right\}_{k=1}^\infty\subset(0,1]$, then the sequence $\{\|x(t_k^-)\|_\infty\}$ is bounded for any admissible function of the initial conditions. Since $\{\|K(t_k^-)\|\}_{k=1}^\infty$ is bounded, the sequence $\{\|x(t_k)\|_\infty\}$ is also bounded. Since the parameterization of the differential system is bounded on each inter-impulse time interval $[t_k,t_{k+1})$, then $\|x(t)\|_\infty$ is bounded in $\cup_{t_{k,}t_{k+1}\in IMP}[t_k,t_{k+1}]$ and then also in $cl\mathbf{R}_{0+}$. This proves Property (ii);

(2) If the real sequence $\left\{\max_{1\leq i\leq\overline{p}}\lambda_{ki}\right\}_{k=1}^\infty$ satisfies $\limsup_{k\to\infty}\left(\max_{1\leq i\leq\overline{p}}\lambda_{ki}\right)\leq\lambda$ for some $\lambda\in(0,1)$, then the sequence $\{\|x(t_k^-)\|_\infty\}$ is bounded for any admissible function of the initial conditions and it converges asymptotically to zero. Since $\{\|K(t_k^-)\|\}_{k=1}^\infty$ is bounded, then the sequence $\{\|x(t_k)\|_\infty\}$ is also bounded and it converges asymptotically to zero. Since the parameterization matrices of the differential system are bounded on each inter-impulse interval $[t_k,t_{k+1})$, which is finite unless the impulsive parameterization ends in finite time, then $\|x(t)\|_\infty$ is bounded in $\cup_{t_{k,}t_{k+1}\in IMP}[t_k,t_{k+1}]$ and then also in $cl\mathbf{R}_{0+}$. □

Theorem 4 can be directly extended to the general case when $\cup_{i\in\overline{p}}IMPA_i\neq\varnothing$ by an "ad hoc" re-statement of its proof by considering in (35) a non-null impulsive contribution $\sum_{i=1}^p K_i(t^-)\hat{A}_i(t^-)x(t^--h_i)$ for $t\in IMP$ with $IMP=IMPA\cup\left(\cup_{i\in\overline{p}}IMPA_i\right)$.

Remark 2. *Assume for simplicity of the subsequent explanation that $IMP=IMPA$. It turns out that the impulsive system (31)–(33) provides relative jumps at the right-hand-side of impulsive time instants, related to its value at the left limit of the time instant, according to $x(t)=x(t^-)+K(t^-)\hat{A}(t^-)x(t^-)$ defined by the matrix $(I_n+K(t^-)\hat{A}(t^-))$ but $t\in IMP$ is* *ineffective if $K(t^-)\hat{A}(t^-)x(t^-)$ and this concern depends on the solution itself. A way to be able to choose effective impulsive time instants in any case is the implementation of absolute jumps at the impulsive time instants independent of the values at the left limits as follows. If $t \in IMP$, then $x(t) = x(t^-) + K(t^-)\hat{A}(t^-)$ with the impulsive gain being a bounded real vector function $K : \mathbf{R}_{0+} \to \mathbf{R}^n$ with a support set consisting of isolated real points. In this case, any component of $x(t)$ can differ from its counterpart $x(t^-)$ by choosing to be non-zero for all the components of $K(t^-)$ provided that $\hat{A}(t^-)$ is not identically zero. This also facilitates the stabilization by an impulsive action through time by relaxing some of the conditions of Theorem 4. The finite jumps $x(t) = x(t^-) + K(t^-)\hat{A}(t^-)$ in the solution come from the subsequent modification of the impulsive differential system (31)–(33) with $IMP = IMPA$:*

$$\dot{x}(t) = A(t)x(t) + \sum_{i=1}^{p} A_i(t)x(t-h_i) + u(t);\ u(t) = \sum_{t_i \in IMPA(t)} \hat{A}(t^-)K(t^-)\delta(t-t_i)$$

where $u(t)$ is an impulsive open-loop (i.e., without using feedback) control, contrarily to (31)–(33) [50], where, again, if $IMP = IMPA$, it can be rewritten as follows:

$$\dot{x}(t) = A(t)x(t) + \sum_{i=1}^{p} A_i(t)x(t-h_i) + u(t); u(t) = \sum_{t_i \in IMPA(t)} K(t^-)\hat{A}(t^-)\delta(t-t_i)x(t^-)$$

where now $u(t)$ is an impulsive state-feedback control.

Remark 3. *Note that the extension of the impulsive delay-free differential system (23)–(24) to its delayed version might be viewed also as an impulsive open-loop controlled system of the form:*

$$\dot{x}(t) = A(t)x(t) + \sum_{i=1}^{p} A_i(t)x(t-h_i) + u(t); u(t) = \sum_{t_i \in IMPA(t)} K(t^-)\delta(t-t_i)$$

Note that the impulses are not state-dependent and are not related to abrupt modifications in the matrix of delay-free dynamics at the impulsive time instants.

Remark 4. *In the event that the system becomes time-invariant in a finite time t_f, then the impulsive actions can be removed in a finite time while keeping the stability as it is well-known. Assume that for $t \geq t_f$ the differential system is time-invariant as follows:*

$$\dot{x}(t) = Ax(t) + \sum_{i=1}^{p} A_i x(t-h_i) + u(t) = \left(A + \sum_{i=1}^{p} A_i\right)x(t) + \sum_{i=1}^{p} A_i(x(t-h_i) - x(t)) + u(t)$$

It follows that it is globally asymptotically stable for any given finite admissible function of the initial conditions if there are no impulses for $t \geq t_f$, i.e., *$u(t) = 0$ for $t \geq t_f$, and, furthermore,*

(a) A is a stability matrix and $\sum_{i=1}^{p} \sup_{\omega \in \mathbf{R}_{0+}} \left\| \frac{A_i}{i\omega I_n - A} \right\|_2 < 1$ (guaranteed if $\max_{i \in \bar{p}} \sup_{\omega \in \mathbf{R}_{0+}} \left\| \frac{A_i}{i\omega I_n - A} \right\|_2 < p^{-1}$);

(b) Or $\left(A + \sum_{i=1}^{p} A_i\right)$ is a stability matrix and $\sum_{i=1}^{p} \sup_{\omega \in \mathbf{R}_{0+}} \left\| \frac{A_i}{i\omega I_n - A - \sum_{i=1}^{p} A_i} \right\|_2 < \frac{1}{2}$ (guaranteed if $\max_{i \in \bar{p}} \sup_{\omega \in \mathbf{R}_{0+}} \left\| \frac{A_i}{i\omega I_n - A - \sum_{i=1}^{p} A_i} \right\|_2 < \frac{1}{2p}$).

The above conditions guarantee that all the zeros of the characteristic equation $\det\left(sI_n - A - \sum_{i=1}^{p} A_i e^{-h_i s}\right) = 0$ are in $\mathrm{Re}\, s < 0$—that is, equivalently, that $\left(sI_n - A - \sum_{i=1}^{p} A_i e^{-h_i s}\right)^{-1}$ exists for $\mathrm{Re}\, s \geq 0$. As a result, the transfer matrix $G(s) = \left(sI_n - A - \sum_{i=1}^{p} A_i e^{-h_i s}\right)^{-1} \in \mathbf{RH}_\infty^{n \times n}$—that is, it is strictly stable. See, for instance, [1,4].

The above remark is induced to guess that the global asymptotic stability of the time-varying differential system can be achieved in the absence of impulsive monitored parameterizations, or under a finite number of them, if a nominal time-invariant limit differential system of reference is globally asymptotically stable and the parametrical deviations from it of the current differential system are sufficiently small through time. The subsequent result relies on this feature.

Theorem 5. *Assume that the three hypotheses below hold:*

(1) $\widetilde{A}_i(t) = A_i(t) - A_i;\ i \in \overline{p} \cup \{0\}$ *are bounded piecewise-continuous for* $t \in \mathbf{R}_{0+}$, *where* $A_0 = A$, $\widetilde{A}_0(t) = \widetilde{A}(t) = A(t) - A = A_0(t) - A_0$ *for* $t \in \mathbf{R}_{0+}$ *and some given constant matrices* $A_i \in \mathbf{R}^{n \times n};\ i \in \overline{p} \cup \{0\}$;

(2) *For some finite* $t_f \in \mathbf{R}_{0+}$ *and all* $t \geq t_f$, $\sup_{t \geq t_f} \left| \widetilde{A}_{i_{jk}}(t) \right| \leq E_{i_{jk}};\ i \in \overline{p} \cup \{0\};\ j,k \in \overline{n}$ *and* $E_i = \left(E_{i_{jk}} \right)$ *for* $i \in \overline{p} \cup \{0\};\ j,k \in \overline{n}$;

(3) *Any of the two conditions below holds:*

(3.1) *A is a stability matrix and* $\sum_{i=0}^{p} \sup_{\omega \in \mathbf{R}_{0+}} \left\| \frac{A_i + E_i}{i\omega I_n - A} \right\|_2 < 1$, *or if* $\max_{i \in \overline{p}} \sup_{\omega \in \mathbf{R}_{0+}} \left\| \frac{A_i + E_i}{i\omega I_n - A} \right\|_2 < p^{-1}$;

(3.2) $\left(A + \sum_{i=1}^{p} A_i \right)$ *is a stability matrix and* $\sum_{i=0}^{p} \sup_{\omega \in \mathbf{R}_{0+}} \left\| \frac{A_i + E_i}{i\omega I_n - \sum_{i=0}^{p} (A_i + E_i)} \right\|_2 < \frac{1}{2}$ *or if* $\max_{i \in \overline{p}} \sup_{\omega \in \mathbf{R}_{0+}} \left\| \frac{A_i + E_i}{i\omega I_n - A - \sum_{i=1}^{p} A_i} \right\|_2 < \frac{1}{2p}$

where $E_i = \left(E_{i_{jk}} \right)$ *for* $i \in \overline{p} \cup \{0\}$.

Then, the following properties hold:

(i) *The nominal time-invariant differential system is globally asymptotically stable.*

$$\dot{x}_L(t) = A x_L(t) + \sum_{i=1}^{p} A_i x_L(t - h_i);\ x_L(t) = \varphi(t)$$

with bounded piecewise-continuous initial conditions $x(t) = \varphi(t)$ *for* $t \in [-h_p, 0]$. *Also, the auxiliary differential system is as follows:*

$$\dot{\overline{x}}(t) = A\overline{x}(t) + \sum_{i=0}^{p} (A_i + E_i)\overline{x}(t - h_i) = A\overline{x}(t) + \sum_{i=1}^{p} A_i \overline{x}(t - h_i) + \sum_{i=0}^{p} E_i \overline{x}(t - h_i)$$

with bounded piecewise-continuous initial conditions $x(t) = \varphi(t)$ *for* $t \in [-h_p, 0]$, $h_0 = 0$, $A_0 = 0$, $\widetilde{A}_0(t) = \widetilde{A}(t)$, *and* $E_i = \left(E_{i_{jk}} \right)$ *for* $i \in \overline{p} \cup \{0\};\ j,k \in \overline{n}$ *is globally asymptotically stable;*

(ii) *The current differential system*

$$\dot{x}(t) = Ax(t) + \sum_{i=0}^{p} \left(A_i + \widetilde{A}_i(t) \right) x(t - h_i)$$

is globally asymptotically stable;

(iii) *Assume that* $E_i = \lambda_i \|A_i\|_2 I_n$ *for some constants* $\lambda_i \in \mathbf{R}_{0+};\ i \in \overline{p} \cup \{0\}$ *with* $\lambda = \max_{i \in \overline{p} \cup \{0\}} \lambda_i$. *Then, Properties (i)–(ii) hold if any of the conditions below hold:*

(3.1′) *A is a stability matrix and* $\sum_{i=0}^{p} \sup_{\omega \in \mathbf{R}_{0+}} \left\| \frac{A_i}{i\omega I_n - A} \right\|_2 < \frac{1}{1 + \lambda}$ *(which is guaranteed under the sufficient condition* $\max_{i \in \overline{p}} \sup_{\omega \in \mathbf{R}_{0+}} \left\| \frac{A_i}{i\omega I_n - A} \right\|_2 < \frac{1}{p(1+\lambda)}$*)*;

(3.2′) $\left(A+\sum_{i=1}^{p}A_i\right)$ *is a stability matrix and* $\sum_{i=0}^{p}\sup_{\omega\in\mathbf{R}_{0+}}\left\|\frac{A_i}{i\omega I_n-\sum_{i=0}^{p}(A_i+E_i)}\right\|_2<\frac{1}{2(1+\lambda)}$ *(which is guaranteed if* $\max_{i\in\overline{p}}\sup_{\omega\in\mathbf{R}_{0+}}\left\|\frac{A_i}{i\omega I_n-A-\sum_{i=1}^{p}A_i}\right\|_2<\frac{1}{2p(1+\lambda)}$*).*

Proof. Property (i) follows since any of the conditions (3.1) or (3.2) guarantee: (a) the global asymptotic stability of the auxiliary system; and (b) the global stability of the time-invariant nominal system since it satisfies the constraints $0=\sup_{t\geq t_f}\left|\widetilde{A}_{i_{jk}}(t)\right|\leq E_{i_{jk}};\,i\in\overline{p}\cup\{0\},\,j,k\in\overline{n}$ included in any of the conditions (3.1) or (3.2). Property (i) has been proved.

To prove Property (ii), note that for $t\geq t_f$, one has, for any vector norm and corresponding induced matrix norm,

$$\left\|\dot{\overline{x}}(t)\right\|\leq\|A\|\|\overline{x}(t)\|+\sum_{i=1}^{p}\|A_i\|\|\overline{x}(t-h_i)\|+\sum_{i=0}^{p}\|E_i\|\|\overline{x}(t-h_i)\|$$

$$\begin{aligned}\|\dot{x}(t)\| &\leq\|A\|\|x(t)\|+\sum_{i=1}^{p}\|A_i\|\|x(t-h_i)\|+\sum_{i=0}^{p}\left\|\widetilde{A}_i(t)\right\|\|x(t-h_i)\|\\ &\leq\|A\|\|x(t)\|+\sum_{i=1}^{p}\|A_i\|\|x(t-h_i)\|+\sum_{i=0}^{p}\|E_i\|\|x(t-h_i)\|\end{aligned}$$

Since the function of the initial conditions is the same for the current differential system and the auxiliary differential system, i.e., $x(t)=\overline{x}(t)=\varphi(t)$ for $t\in[-h_p,0]$, then

$$\|\dot{x}(t)\|\leq\left\|\dot{\overline{x}}(t)\right\|=\|A\|\|\overline{x}(t)\|+\sum_{i=1}^{p}\|A_i\|\|\overline{x}(t-h_i)\|+\sum_{i=0}^{p}\|E_i\|\|\overline{x}(t-h_i)\|\text{for} t\in[-h_p,0]$$

and by complete induction based on the above differential inequality, one has the following:

$$\left[(x(t)=\overline{x}(t))\wedge\left(\|\dot{x}(t)\|\leq\left\|\dot{\overline{x}}(t)\right\|\right);t\in[-h_p,0]\right]\Rightarrow(\|x(t)\|\leq\|\overline{x}(t)\|;t\geq-h_p)$$

Since from Property (i) $\overline{x}(t)\to0$ and $\dot{\overline{x}}(t)\to0$ as $t\to\infty$, and both the trajectory solution and its time first-derivative are bounded for all time, then the current differential system is also globally asymptotically stable—that is, the solution trajectory and its first time-derivative are bounded for all time and converge asymptotically to zero as time tends to infinity. Property (ii) has been proved. Property (iii) is a direct conclusion as a particular case of Properties [(i)–(ii)] under any of the conditions (3.1′) or (3.2′), which are "ad hoc" modifications of the conditions (3.1)–(3.2). □

A particular interest of the above result is when $A_i(t)\to A_i$ as $t\to\infty$ for $i\in\overline{p}\cup\{0\}$, that is, when the nominal differential system of reference is a limiting system of the current time-varying one.

A simple first-order example with a single point delay is described in detail to illustrate the mechanism of stabilization under impulsive monitored parameterizations. The example is illustrative to see, in an analytic way, the effects of the impulsive parameterization in the solution with the main focus on the stability context and how closed-loop stabilization can be achievable by an appropriate selection of the sign and amplitude of the impulsive gains at suitable chosen effective impulsive time instants. The role in the stabilization of the involvement of a finite or infinite number of impulsive time instants is also seen.

Example 1. *Consider the subsequent differential equation:*

$$\dot{x}(t)=a(t)x(t)+a_d(t)x(t-h)\tag{54}$$

With a finite delay h and impulsive effects in the function of delay-free dynamics, the impulsive set of time instants is $IMP = \{t_k\}_{k=1}^{\infty}$, $a : \mathbf{R}_{0+} \to \mathbf{R}$ *is bounded piecewise-continuous in all the inter-impulsive intervals* (t_k, t_{k+1})*—with* $t_{k+1} = t_k + T_k$*—and* $a_d : \mathbf{R}_{0+} \to \mathbf{R}$ *is bounded piecewise-continuous. The function of the initial conditions* $\varphi : [-h, 0] \to \mathbf{R}$ *is bounded piecewise-continuous with* $\varphi(0) = x(0) = x_0$*. The solution is the following one for* $t \in [t_k, t_{k+1})$ *is given by the following:*

$$\begin{aligned} x(t^-) &= e^{\int_{t_k}^{t^-} a(\tau)d(\tau)} x(t_k) + \int_{t_k}^{t^-} e^{\int_\tau^{t^-} a(\sigma)d\sigma} a_d(\tau)x(\tau-h)d\tau \\ &= \left(1 + k(t_k^-)a(t_k^-)\right) e^{\int_{t_k}^{t^-} a(\tau)d(\tau)} x(t_k^-) + \int_{t_k}^{t^-} e^{\int_\tau^{t^-} a(\sigma)d\sigma} a_d(\tau)x(\tau-h)d\tau \end{aligned} \tag{55}$$

Thus,

$$x\left(t_{k+1}^-\right) = \left(1 + k(t_k^-)a(t_k^-)\right) e^{\int_{t_k}^{t_{k+1}^-} a(\tau)d(\tau)} x(t_k^-) + \int_{t_k}^{t_{k+1}^-} e^{\int_\tau^{t_{k+1}^-} a(\sigma)d\sigma} a_d(\tau)x(\tau-h)d\tau \tag{56}$$

Assume that the impulsive sequence of gains is claimed to guarantee that the matching objective $x\left(t_{k+1}^-\right) = \rho(t_k, t_{k+1})x(t_k^-)$ *at the left limits of the impulsive time instant holds, where* $\{\rho(t_k, t_{k+1})\}_{k=1}^{\infty}$ *is bounded and* $\limsup_{t_k\to\infty} \rho(t_k, t_{k+1}) \le \rho, \liminf_{t_k\to\infty} \rho(t_k, t_{k+1}) \ge -\rho$ *where* $\rho(\le 1) \in \mathbf{R}_+$*. Note that if* $\rho = 1$*, then there exists a finite* $\lim_{t_k\to\infty} \left|x(t_k^-)\right|$*. Then,*

$$\left(\rho(t_k, t_{k+1}) - \left(1 + k(t_k^-)a(t_k^-)\right) e^{\int_{t_k}^{t_{k+1}^-} a(\tau)d(\tau)}\right) x(t_k^-) = \int_{t_k}^{t_{k+1}^-} e^{\int_\tau^{t_{k+1}^-} a(\sigma)d\sigma} a_d(\tau)x(\tau-h)d\tau \tag{57}$$

equivalently,

$$k(t_k^-)a(t_k^-) e^{\int_{t_k}^{t_{k+1}^-} a(\tau)d(\tau)} x(t_k^-) = \left(\rho(t_k, t_{k+1}) - e^{\int_{t_k}^{t_{k+1}^-} a(\tau)d(\tau)}\right) x(t_k^-) - \int_{t_k}^{t_{k+1}^-} e^{\int_\tau^{t_{k+1}^-} a(\sigma)d\sigma} a_d(\tau)x(\tau-h)d\tau \tag{58}$$

and equivalently, if $t_k \in IMP$*, is effective, then*

$$\begin{aligned} k(t_k^-) &= k(t_k^-, T_k) \\ &= a^{-1}(t_k^-)\left(\left(\rho(t_k, T_k) e^{-\int_{t_k}^{t_k^- + T_k} a(\tau)d(\tau)} - 1\right) - x^{-1}(t_k^-) e^{-\int_{t_k}^{t_k^- + T_k} a(\tau)d(\tau)} \int_{t_k}^{t_{k+1}^-} e^{\int_\tau^{t_k^- + T_k} a(\sigma)d(\sigma)} a_d(\tau)x(\tau-h)d\tau\right) \end{aligned} \tag{59}$$

Claim 1: $\left\{\left|x(t_k^-)\right|\right\}_{k=1}^{\infty}$ *is bounded.*

Proof. Assume, on the contrary, that $\left\{\left|x(t_k^-)\right|\right\}_{k=1}^{\infty}$ is unbounded. Then, for some large $M \in \mathbf{R}_+$, there exists a strictly increasing subsequence $\left\{\left|x\left(t_{k_j}^-\right)\right|\right\}_{j=1}^{\infty}$ of $\left\{\left|x(t_k^-)\right|\right\}_{k=1}^{\infty}$ with $\left|x\left(t_{k_j}^-\right)\right| \le cM$ for $c(\ge 1) \in \mathbf{R}_+$ but then $\left|x\left(t_{k_{j+1}}^-\right)\right| \le \rho^{k_{j+1}-k_1}\left|x\left(t_{k_j}^-\right) \le cM\right|\rho^{k_{j+1}-k_1}$ and $\limsup_{j\to\infty}\left|x\left(t_{k_{j+1}}^-\right)\right| \le cM \lim_{j\to+\infty} \rho^{k_{j+1}-k_1} (\in [0, cM])$ since $\rho \le 1$ is a contradiction. Then, $\left\{\left|x(t_k^-)\right|\right\}_{k=1}^{\infty}$ is bounded. □

Claim 2: *If* $\rho = 1$, $\left\{\left|x(t_k^-)\right|\right\}_{k=1}^{\infty}$ *is bounded and it does not converge to zero. Furthermore,* $\left\{\left|k(t_k^-)\right|\right\}_{k=1}^{\infty}$ *is bounded,* $\{|x(t_k)|\}_{k=1}^{\infty}$ *is bounded, and* $x : [-h, +\infty) \to \mathbf{R}$ *is bounded if* $cardIMP = \chi_0$ *(i.e., if there are infinitely many impulses) and* $0 < T_m < T_M = \sup_{t_k, t_{k+1} \in IMP}(t_{k+1} - t_k) < +\infty$*. Then, the differential Equation (54) is globally stable for any given admissible function of the initial conditions.*

Proof. The following $\{|x(t_k^-)|\}_{k=1}^{\infty}$ is bounded if $\rho = 1$ since it is bounded for $\rho \leq 1$ (Claim 1). Furthermore, since each $t_k \in IMP$ is effective, $\{|x(t_k^-)|\}_{k=1}^{\infty}$ neither converges to zero nor has some null element. On the other hand, $\{|k(t_k^-)|\}_{k=1}^{\infty}$ is bounded from (59), $\{|x(t_k)|\}_{k=1}^{\infty}$ is bounded since $\{|k(t_k^-)|\}_{k=1}^{\infty}$ and $\{|x(t_k^-)|\}_{k=1}^{\infty}$ are bounded. Finally, since there are infinitely many impulses, and the time interval in-between any two consecutive impulses is finite by the hypotheses, then $x : [-h, +\infty) \to \mathbf{R}$ is bounded in $\cup_{t_k, t_{k+1} \in IMP}(t_k, t_{k+1})$ since $\{|x(t_k^-)|\}_{k=1}^{\infty}$ and $\{|x(t_k)|\}_{k=1}^{\infty}$ are bounded from the boundedness and piecewise-continuity of $a, a_d : \mathbf{R}_{0+} \to \mathbf{R}$ in $\cup_{t_k, t_{k+1} \in IMP}(t_k, t_{k+1})$. The global stability of (54) follows as a result. □

Remark 5. *Note that if $cardIMP = \chi_0$ and the objective $x\left(t_{k+1}^-\right) = \rho(t_k, t_{k+1})x(t_k^-)$, where $\{\rho(t_k, t_{k+1})\}_{k=1}^{\infty}$ is bounded with $\limsup_{t_k \to \infty} \rho(t_k, t_{k+1}) \leq \rho$, $\liminf_{t_k \to \infty} \rho(t_k, t_{k+1}) \geq -\rho$ is fixed with $\rho < 1$, then $\{|x(t_k^-)|\}_{k=1}^{\infty} \to 0$ and $\{|k(t_k^-)|\}_{k=1}^{\infty} \to +\infty$ from (59) since $\{|x(t_k^-)|\}_{k=1}^{\infty} \to 0$. This also implies that the members of IMP lose effectiveness as they tend to infinity (that is, the impulsive time instants tending to infinity are not effective). One then concludes that, in the case of injecting infinitely many impulses, the matching objective $x\left(t_{k+1}^-\right) = \rho(t_k, t_{k+1})x(t_k^-)$ with $\rho < 1$ is not appropriate in practice since the sequence of impulsive gains diverges.*

Claim 3: *Assume that either*

(1) $cardIMP = \chi_0$ (there are infinitely many impulses) and either the matching objective $x\left(t_{k+1}^-\right) = \rho(t_k, t_{k+1})x(t_k^-)$, where $\{\rho(t_k, t_{k+1})\}_{k=1}^{\infty}$ is bounded, $\limsup_{t_k \to \infty} \rho(t_k, t_{k+1}) = -\liminf_{t_k \to \infty} \rho(t_k, t_{k+1}) = 1$ and the inter-impulses intervals are subject to finite lower-bounds and upper-bounds;

(2) Or the above matching objective is not fixed, $cardIMP < \chi_0$ (there is a finite number of impulses), there is a finite time instant T for which $\max(t \in \mathbf{R}_{0+} : t \in IMP) \leq T$.

Then, the set IMP can be defined with all the impulsive time instants being effective provided that there is no $t \in \mathbf{R}_{0+}$ such that $x(\tau) \equiv 0$ in the time interval $[t, t+h]$.

Proof. Assume that $t_k \in IMP$ and take $\vartheta \geq T_m$ such that

$$x(t_k^- + \vartheta) = e^{\int_0^{\vartheta} e^{a(t_k+\tau)} d\tau} x(t_k) + \int_0^{\vartheta} e^{\int_{\tau}^{\vartheta} e^{a(t_k+\vartheta-\sigma)} d\sigma} a_d(t_k+\tau)x(t_k+\tau-h)d\tau = 0 \tag{60}$$

so that $t_{k+1}^0 = t_k + \vartheta$ is not an effective impulsive time instant. Now, if $T_M = T_m + h$, then the above constraint holds for all $\theta \in [T_m, T_m + h]$ and there is no impulsive action on $[t_k, t_k + T_m + h]$, and then $x(t) \equiv 0$ for $t \geq t_k + T_m$. Thus, if there is no $t \in [t_k + T_m, t_k + T_m + h]$ such that $x(t) \equiv 0$ for $t \in [t_k, t_k + T_m + h]$, then it is guaranteed that there is some $t_{k+1} \in [t_k + T_m, t_k + T_m + h]$ such that $x\left(t_{k+1}^-\right) \neq 0$. Such a t_{k+1} is eligible as the next impulsive time instant to $t_k \in IMP$ since $T_M = T_m + h$ is finite and $t_{k+1} \in [T_m, T_M]$ and it is compatible with the matching objective for $\rho = 1$ (see Claim 2). □

Remark 6. *Note that Claim 3 relies on the fact that, if there are infinitely many impulses, then all of them can be chosen to be effective under the first set of constraints of the claim. In the case of a finite number of impulses, they can be chosen to be effective.*

It has been seen that, if $\rho < 1$, then $|x(t_k^-)| \to 0$ as $k \to +\infty$ asymptotically at an exponential rate. Then, $\{x(t_k^-)\}_{k=1}^{\infty}$ and $\{x(t_k)\}_{k=1}^{\infty}$ are bounded but the boundedness of the sequence of impulsive gains $\{k(t_k^-)\}_{k=1}^{\infty}$ fails. This problem is avoided in the case of absolute jumps at impulsive time instants of the form $x(t_k) = x(t_k^-) + k(t_k^-)a(t_k^-)$ in the solution generated from absolute impulses in the parameterization of $a(t)$ (see Remark 2). In this case, (59) is replaced with

$$k(t_k^-) = a^{-1}(t_k^-)\left(\left(\rho(t_k, T_k)e^{-\int_{t_k}^{t_k^-+T_k} a(\tau)d(\tau)} - 1\right) - e^{-\int_{t_k}^{t_k^-+T_k} a(\tau)d(\tau)} \int_{t_k}^{t_{k+1}^-} e^{\int_{\tau}^{t_k^-+T_k} a(\sigma)d(\sigma)} a_d(\tau)x(\tau-h)d\tau\right) \quad (61)$$

and the reasoning on the boundedness of the sequences $\{x(t_k^-)\}_{k=1}^{\infty}$, $\{x(t_k)\}_{k=1}^{\infty}$, and $\{k(t_k^-)\}_{k=1}^{\infty}$ of Claim 2 remain valid even if $\rho < 1$ since the requirement for the impulsive time instants to be effective is no longer needed.

The solution of (54) might be re-stated in an equivalent form to (55) on the right limits of the time instants as follows. If $t_k \in IMP$ and $t \in [t_k, t_{k+1}]$, then $t_{k+1} \in IMP$ is the next consecutive time instant to t_k. Then, one has that

$$\begin{aligned} x(t_{k+1}) &= \left(1 + k\left(t_{k+1}^-\right)a\left(t_{k+1}^-\right)\right)x\left(t_{k+1}^-\right) = \left(1 + \left|k\left(t_{k+1}^-\right)\right|\left|a\left(t_{k+1}^-\right)\right| sgnk\left(t_{k+1}^-\right) sgna\left(t_{k+1}^-\right)\right)x\left(t_{k+1}^-\right) \\ &= \left(1 + k\left(t_{k+1}^-\right)a\left(t_{k+1}^-\right)\right)\left[e^{\int_{t_k}^{t_{k+1}^-} a(\tau)d(\tau)} x(t_k) + \int_{t_k}^{t_{k+1}^-} e^{\int_{\tau}^{t_{k+1}^-} a(\sigma)d\sigma} a_d(\tau)x(\tau-h)d\tau\right] \end{aligned} \quad (62)$$

with sgn(0) defined as zero and $sgn(x) = x/|x|$ if $x \neq 0$. It is direct to see that if $a\left(t_{k+1}^-\right) \neq 0$ and $k\left(t_{k+1}^-\right)$ is chosen with $sgnk\left(t_{k+1}^-\right) = sgna\left(t_{k+1}^-\right)$, then $|x(t_{k+1})| > \left|x\left(t_{k+1}^-\right)\right|$ and if $sgnk\left(t_{k+1}^-\right) = -sgna\left(t_{k+1}^-\right)$, and then $|x(t_{k+1})| < \left|x\left(t_{k+1}^-\right)\right|$. Define $T_k = t_{k+1} - t_k \in [T_m, T_{kM}]$ for $t_k, t_{k+1} \in IMP$, and

$$\alpha(t_k, \delta) = (1 + k(t_k+\delta)a(t_k+\delta))$$

$$\beta(t_k, \delta) = \beta(\overline{x}_{t_k}, \delta) = e^{\int_{t_k}^{t_k^-+\delta} a(\tau)d(\tau)} x(t_k) + \int_{t_k}^{t_k^-+\delta} e^{\int_{\tau}^{t_k^-+\delta} a(\sigma)d\sigma} a_d(\tau)x(\tau-h)d\tau$$

for $\delta \in (0, T_k)$. As a result, one has that

$$x(t_k+\delta) = \alpha(t_k, \delta)\beta(t_k, \delta)$$

Note also that

$$\overline{\beta}(t_k, T_k) = \sup_{0<\delta<T_k}\left(\left|e^{\int_{t_k}^{t_k^-+\delta} a(\tau)d(\tau)}\right| + \delta\left|e^{\int_{\tau}^{t_k^-+\delta} a(\sigma)d\sigma}\right| \max_{t_k \le \tau \le t_k+\delta}|a_d(\tau)|\right) \sup_{t_k \le \tau < t_k+\delta}|x(\tau)| \ge \sup_{0<\delta<T_k} \beta(t_k, \delta)$$

Now, given $t_k \in IMP$ and $\zeta_k \in (0, \zeta]$, if one chooses the next impulsive time instant $t_{k+1}(\in IMP) = t_k + T_k$ with $T_k = inf\left(\delta \ge T_m : |\alpha(t_k, \delta)|\left(\overline{\beta}(t_k, T_k)/\sup_{t_k \le \tau < t_k+\delta}|x(\tau)|\right) \le \zeta_k\right)$ and then $|x(t_{k+1})| \le \zeta_k \sup_{0 \le \tau < T_k}|x(t_k+\tau)|$ and also, as a result, if $\limsup_{t_k \to +\infty}\zeta_k \le 1$, then $\sup_{0 \le t < +\infty}(|x(t)|) < +\infty$. The choice of $k\left(t_{k+1}^-\right)$ is made as follows in order to satisfy the constraint:

$$\left|1 + k\left(t_{k+1}^-\right)a\left(t_{k+1}^-\right)\right| \le \zeta_k\left[1/\sup_{0<\delta<T_k}\left(\left|e^{\int_{t_k}^{t_k^-+\delta} a(\tau)d(\tau)}\right| + \delta\left|e^{\int_{\tau}^{t_k^-+\delta} a(\sigma)d\sigma}\right| \max_{t_k \le \tau \le t_k+\delta}|a_d(\tau)|\right)\right]$$

in such a way that

(a) If $\zeta_k \leq \sup_{0<\delta<T_k}\left(\left|e^{\int_{t_k}^{t_k^-+\delta} a(\tau)d(\tau)}\right| + \delta\left|e^{\int_{\tau}^{t_k^-+\delta} a(\sigma)d\sigma}\right| \max_{t_k\leq\tau\leq t_k+\delta}|a_d(\tau)|\right)$, then $k\left(t_{k+1}^-\right)$ is chosen to satisfy the following:

$$sgn\left(k\left(t_{k+1}^-\right)\right) = -sgn\left(a\left(t_{k+1}^-\right)\right) \tag{63}$$

$$\frac{1}{\left|a\left(t_{k+1}^-\right)\right|}\left(1 - \frac{\zeta_k}{\sup_{0<\delta<T_k}\left(\left|e^{\int_{t_k}^{t_k^-+\delta} a(\tau)d(\tau)}\right| + \delta\left|e^{\int_{\tau}^{t_k^-+\delta} a(\sigma)d\sigma}\right| \max_{t_k\leq\tau\leq t_k+\delta}|a_d(\tau)|\right)}\right) \leq \left|k\left(t_{k+1}^-\right)\right| \leq 1 \tag{64}$$

or

(b) If $\zeta_k \geq \sup_{0<\delta<T_k}\left(\left|e^{\int_{t_k}^{t_k^-+\delta} a(\tau)d(\tau)}\right| + \delta\left|e^{\int_{\tau}^{t_k^-+\delta} a(\sigma)d\sigma}\right| \max_{t_k\leq\tau\leq t_k+\delta}|a_d(\tau)|\right)$, then $k\left(t_{k+1}^-\right)$ is chosen to satisfy:

$$sgn\left(k\left(t_{k+1}^-\right)\right) = sgn\left(a\left(t_{k+1}^-\right)\right) \tag{65}$$

$$\left|k\left(t_{k+1}^-\right)\right| \geq \frac{1}{\left|a\left(t_{k+1}^-\right)\right|}\left(\frac{\zeta_k}{\sup_{0<\delta<T_k}\left(\left|e^{\int_{t_k}^{t_k^-+\delta} a(\tau)d(\tau)}\right| + \delta\left|e^{\int_{\tau}^{t_k^-+\delta} a(\sigma)d\sigma}\right| \max_{t_k\leq\tau\leq t_k+\delta}|a_d(\tau)|\right)} - 1\right) \tag{66}$$

Note that the constraint $\limsup_{t_k\to+\infty}\zeta_k \leq 1$ can also be guaranteed with the appropriate choice of the impulsive gain sequence while fixing a sufficiently small inter-impulse minimum threshold interval T_m and the choice of T_k approaching to T_m as k tends to infinity. This threshold can be fixed greater as $a(t)$ becomes negative on relevant intervals of time.

4. Conclusions

The first part of this study has derived explicit expressions for the evolution associated with the state-trajectory solution of a class of linear time-varying differential delay-free systems. The impulsive-free part of its matrix function of dynamics of such systems has been assumed bounded and piecewise-continuous Lebesgue-integrable for all time.

The cases of the absence and the presence of impulsive actions in the system matrix of dynamics are described. In the impulsive case, the evolution operator is seen to be, in general, non-unique. Subsequently, the above obtained results are extended to the presence of delayed dynamics associated with constant point delays, and the evolution operators that generate the trajectory solution are given in an explicit fashion, while they are non-unique, in general, in the impulsive case.

The parameterization impulsive actions at certain time instants can take place in the delay-free dynamics and also in the various matrices of delayed dynamics followed by an immediate return to the previous configuration. The impulsive actions are interpreted as an instantaneous abrupt switching change in the parameterization. Furthermore, the parameterization impulsive actions might be, in general, non-unique in the sense that, depending on the left limits of the solution values at impulsive time instants, the necessary impulsive gains for monitoring the instantaneous switched parameterizations can be non-unique for the achievement of a certain suitable right limit of the solution trajectory.

Next, the boundedness of the solution trajectory of the delayed impulsive differential system is also investigated. It has been seen that an appropriate distribution of the impulsive time instants is relevant for the potential stabilization of the delayed differential system, even in the case when the delay-free dynamics is unstable.

Author Contributions: Conceptualization, M.D.l.S. and A.I.; methodology, M.D.l.S.; validation, A.I., A.J.G. and I.G.; formal analysis, M.D.l.S. and A.I.; investigation, M.D.l.S., A.I., A.J.G. and I.G.; resources, M.D.l.S. and I.G.; writing—original draft preparation, M.D.l.S.; writing—review and editing, M.D.l.S. and A.I.; visualization, A.J.G. and I.G.; supervision, M.D.l.S.; project administration, A.J.G.; funding acquisition, A.J.G. All authors have read and agreed to the published version of the manuscript.

Funding: Basque Government [IT1555-22].

Data Availability Statement: The original contributions presented in the study are included in the article, further inquiries can be directed to the corresponding author.

Acknowledgments: The authors would like to thank the Basque Government for funding this research work through Grant IT1555-22. They also thank MICIU/AEI/ 10.13039/501100011033 and FEDER/UE for partially funding their research work through Grants PID2021-123543OB-C21 and PID2021-123543OB-C22.

Conflicts of Interest: The authors declare that they have no competing interests.

References

1. Niculescu, S.I. *Delay Effects on Stability. A Robust Control Approach*; Springer: Berlin/Heidelberg, Germany, 2001.
2. Michiels, W.; Van Assche, V.; Niculescu, S.-I. Stabilization of time-delay systems with a Controlled time-varying delay and applications. *IEEE Trans. Autom. Control* **2005**, *50*, 493–504. [CrossRef]
3. De la Sen, M. About Robust Stability of Caputo Linear Fractional Dynamic Systems with Time Delays through Fixed Point Theory. *Fixed Point Theory Appl.* **2011**, *2011*, 867932. [CrossRef]
4. Delasen, M. On some structures of stabilizing control laws for linear and time-invariant systems with bounded point delays and unmeasurable states. *Int. J. Control* **1994**, *59*, 5298–5541.
5. Zhang, X.; Han, Q.; Seuret, A.; Gouaisbaut, F.; He, Y. Overview of recent advances in stability of linear systems with time-varying delays. *IET Control. Theory Appl.* **2019**, *13*, 1–16. [CrossRef]
6. Shen, J.; Lam, J. On ℓ_∞ and L_∞ gains for positive systems with bounded time-varying delays. *Int. J. Syst. Sci.* **2015**, *46*, 1953–1960. [CrossRef]
7. Guajardo-Benavides, E.J.; Arteaga, M.A. On the finite time force estimation for bilateral teleoperation of robot manipulators with time varying delays. *Control Eng. Pract* **2023**, *138*, 105622. [CrossRef]
8. Feng, Z.; Zhang, X.; Lam, J.; Fan, C. Estimation of reachable set for switched singular systems with time-varying delay and state jump. *Appl. Math. Comput.* **2023**, *456*, 128132. [CrossRef]
9. Qian, M.; Sun, C.; Wang, C.; Yan, X.; Bo, C. Control of time-delay interconnected nonlinear systems under input saturations: A broad learning system-based approach. *Int. J. Syst. Sci.* **2023**, *55*, 1037–1055. [CrossRef]
10. Zhang, C.-K.; He, Y.; Jiang, L.; Wang, Q.-G.; Wu, M. Stability Analysis of Discrete-Time Neural Networks With Time-Varying Delay via an Extended Reciprocally Convex Matrix Inequality. *IEEE Trans. Cybern.* **2017**, *47*, 3040–3049. [CrossRef]
11. Burton, T.A. *Stability and Periodic Solutions of Ordinary and Functional Differential Equations*; Dover Publications Inc.: Mineola, NY, USA, 1985.
12. De la Sen, M. A study of the stability of integro-differential Volterra-type systems of equations with impulsive effects and point delay dynamics. *Mathematics* **2024**, *12*, 960. [CrossRef]
13. Yeniçerioğlu, A.F. Stability of linear impulsive neutral delay differential equations with constant coefficients. *J. Math. Anal. Appl.* **2019**, *479*, 2196–2213. [CrossRef]
14. Jin, S. Existence and uniqueness of solutions for the stochastic Volterra-Levin equation with variable delays. *Open Math.* **2022**, *20*, 769–782. [CrossRef]
15. Pani, A.K. Semigroup Theory and Evolution Equations, Internet Publication. Available online: https://www.researchgate.net/profile/Amiya-Pani/publication/303569377_Semigroup_Theory_and_Evolution_Equations/links/5748fd8208ae2e0dd30169c3/Semigroup-Theory-and-Evolution-Equations.pdf (accessed on 20 December 2024).

16. Beffa, F. *Weakly Nonlinear Systems with Applications in Communication Systems*; Springer Nature Switzerland AG: Cham, Switzerland, 2024.
17. Engel, K.G.; Nagel, R.; Brendle, S. *One-Parameter Semigroups for Linear Evolution Equations*; Springer: Berlin/Heidelberg, Germany, 2013.
18. Missier, S.P.; Rodrigo, P.A. Strongly α^*-continuous functions in topological spaces. *IOSR J. Math.* **2014**, *10*, 55–60. [CrossRef]
19. Janković, D.S.; Konstadilaki-Savvopoulou, C. On α-continuous functions. *Math. Bohem.* **1992**, *117*, 259–270. [CrossRef]
20. Chang, S.S.; Cho, Y.J.; Zhou, H. Demi-closed principle and weak convergence problems for asymptotically nonexpansive mappings. *J. Korean Math. Soc.* **2001**, *38*, 1245–1260.
21. De la Sen, M. On the evolution operators of a class of linear time-delay systems. *Mathematics* **2024**, *12*, 3575. [CrossRef]
22. Yang, Z.; Xu, D. Stability Analysis and Design of Impulsive Control Systems With Time Delay. *IEEE Trans. Autom. Control* **2007**, *52*, 1448–1454. [CrossRef]
23. Li, X.; Li, P. Stability of time-delay systems with impulsive control involving stabilizing delays. *Automatica* **2021**, *124*, 10933. [CrossRef]
24. Li, X.; Song, S. Stabilization of Delay Systems: Delay-Dependent Impulsive Control. *IEEE Trans. Autom. Control.* **2016**, *62*, 406–411. [CrossRef]
25. Zhang, Y.; Sun, J.; Feng, G. Impulsive Control of Discrete Systems With Time Delay. *IEEE Trans. Autom. Control* **2009**, *54*, 830–834. [CrossRef]
26. Sau, N.H.; Thuan, M.V.; Phuong, N.T. Exponential stability for discrete-time impulsive positive singular system with time delays. *Int. J. Syst. Sci.* **2024**, *55*, 1510–1527. [CrossRef]
27. Chen, W.-H.; Xu, W.; Zheng, W.X. Sliding-mode-based impulsive control for a class of time-delay systems with input disturbance. *Automatica* **2024**, *164*, 111633. [CrossRef]
28. Yu, Z.; Ling, S.; Liu, P.X. Exponential stability of time-delay systems with flexible delayed impulse. *Asian J. Control.* **2024**, *26*, 265–279. [CrossRef]
29. Zhang, J.; Nie, X. Multiple exponential stability for short memory fractional impulsive Cohen-Grossberg neural networks with time delays. *Appl. Math. Comput.* **2024**, *486*, 129066. [CrossRef]
30. Zhu, C.; Han, X.; Li, X. Analysis and Design of Time-Delay Impulsive Systems Subject to Actuator Saturation. *IEEE/CAA J. Autom. Sin.* **2024**, *11*, 196–204. [CrossRef]
31. Xu, J.; Liu, Y.; Meng, Q.; Cao, J.; Abdel-Aty, M. Unified stability criteria for impulsive stochastic delayed systems. *Nonlinear Anal. Hybrid Syst.* **2024**, *52*, 101474. [CrossRef]
32. Elmi, M. Advanced Non-Uniform Sampling Techniques for Energy-Efficient Data Acquisition. Ph.D. Thesis, University of Alberta, Edmonton, AB, Canada, 2024.
33. Wen, Y.; Vanden-Eijnden, E.; Peherstorfer, B. Coupling parameter and particle dynamics for adaptive sampling in Neural Galerkin schemes. *Phys. D Nonlinear Phenom.* **2024**, *462*, 134129. [CrossRef]
34. Xie, Y.; Bollapragada, R.; Byrd, R.; Nocedal, J. Constrained and composite optimization via adaptive sampling methods. *IMA J. Numer. Anal.* **2024**, *44*, 680–709. [CrossRef]
35. Cao, J.; Yang, Z.; Chen, X. Delay Coprime Sampling: A Simplified Sub-Nyquist Sampling for Noisy Multi-Sinusoidal Signals. *IEEE Signal Process. Lett.* **2024**, *31*, 1720–1724. [CrossRef]
36. Desmars, N.; Bonnefoy, F.; Grilli, S.; Ducrozet, G.; Perignon, Y.; Guérin, C.-A.; Ferrant, P. Experimental and numerical assessment of deterministic nonlinear ocean waves prediction algorithms using non-uniformly sampled wave gauges. *Ocean Eng.* **2020**, *212*, 107659. [CrossRef]
37. Zhang, X.-M.; Han, Q.-L.; Ge, X.; Ning, B.; Zhang, B.-L. Sampled-data control systems with non-uniform sampling: A survey of methods and trends. *Annu. Rev. Control* **2023**, *55*, 70–91. [CrossRef]
38. Khan, M.S. Strategies for Non-Uniform Rate Sampling in Digital Control Theory. Doctoral's Dissertation, Loughborough University, Loughborough, UK, 2010.
39. Khan, S.; Goodall, R.M.; Dixon, R. Non-uniform sampling strategies for digital control. *Int. J. Syst. Sci.* **2013**, *44*, 2234–2254. [CrossRef]
40. Albertos, P.; Salt, J. Non-uniform sampled-data control of MIMO systems. *Annu. Rev. Control* **2011**, *35*, 65–76. [CrossRef]
41. Hu, S.; Yue, D.; Du, Z.; Liu, J. Reliable H∞ non-uniform sampling tracking control for continuous-time non-linear systems with stochastic actuator faults. *IET Control Theory Appl.* **2012**, *6*, 120–129. [CrossRef]
42. Delasen, M. A method for improving the adaptation transient using adaptive sampling. *Int. J. Control* **1984**, *40*, 639–665.
43. Delasen, M. Adaptive sampling for improving the adaptation transients in hybrid adaptive-control. *Int. J. Control* **1985**, *41*, 1189–1205. [CrossRef]
44. Delasen, M. Application of the non-periodic sampling to the identifiability and model-matching problems in dynamic-systems. *Int. J. Syst. Sci.* **1983**, *14*, 367–383.

45. Berberich, J.; Wildhagen, S.; Hertneck, M.; Allgöwer, F. Data-driven analysis and control of continuous-time systems under aperiodic sampling. *IFAC-PapersOnLine* **2021**, *54*, 210–215. [CrossRef]
46. Bansal, K.; Mukhija, P. Aperiodic sampled-data control of distributed networked control systems under stochastic cyber-attacks. *IEEE/CAA J. Autom. Sin.* **2020**, *7*, 1064–1073. [CrossRef]
47. Yan, Z.; Huang, X.; Cao, J. Variable-sampling-period dependent global stabilization of delayed memristive neural networks based on refined switching event-triggered control. *Sci. China Inf. Sci.* **2020**, *63*, 1–16. [CrossRef]
48. Rattanakul, C.; Chaiya, I. A mathematical model for predicting and controlling COVID-19 transmission with impulsive vaccination. *AIMS Math.* **2024**, *9*, 6281–6304. [CrossRef]
49. Rao, R.; Zhu, Q. Synchronization for Reaction–Diffusion Switched Delayed Feedback Epidemic Systems via Impulsive Control. *Mathematics* **2024**, *12*, 447. [CrossRef]
50. Kailath, T. *Linear Systems*; Prentice-Hall Ltd.: Englewood Cliffs, NJ, USA, 1980.
51. Zadeh, L.A.; Desoer, C.A. *Linear System Theory: The State Space Approach*; McGraw-Hill: New York, NY, USA, 1963.
52. Messiah, A. *Quantum Mechanics*; North-Holland Publishing Company: Amsterdam, The Netherlands, 1961; Volume I.
53. Hassan, T.S.; Ahmed, R.G.; El-Sayed, A.M.A.; El-Nabulsi, R.A.; Moaaz, O.; Mesmouli, M.B. Solvability of a State–Dependence Functional Integro-Differential Inclusion with Delay Nonlocal Condition. *Mathematics* **2022**, *10*, 2420. [CrossRef]
54. Santra, S.S.; El-Nabulsi, R.A.; Khedher, K.M. Oscillation of Second-Order Differential Equations with Multiple and Mixed Delays under a Canonical Operator. *Mathematics* **2021**, *9*, 1323. [CrossRef]
55. Moaaz, O.; El-Nabulsi, R.A.; Bazighifan, O. Oscillatory behavior of fourt-order differential equations with neutral delay. *Symmetry* **2020**, *12*, 371. [CrossRef]
56. Moaaz, O.; El-Nabulsi, R.A.; Bazighifan, O.; Muhib, A. New Comparison Theorems for the Even-Order Neutral Delay Differential Equation. *Symmetry* **2020**, *12*, 764. [CrossRef]

Σ mathematics

MDPI

Article

Global Well-Posedness and Determining Nodes of Non-Autonomous Navier–Stokes Equations with Infinite Delay on Bounded Domains

Huanzhi Ge [1,2] and Feng Du [2,*]

[1] School of Information and Mathematics, Yangtze University, Jingzhou 434023, China; 2022710188@yangtzeu.edu.cn
[2] School of Mathematics and Physics Science, Jingchu University of Technology, Jingmen 448000, China
* Correspondence: 200708001@jcut.edu.cn

Abstract: The asymptotic behavior of solutions to nonlinear partial differential equations is an important tool for studying their long-term behavior. However, when studying the asymptotic behavior of solutions to nonlinear partial differential equations with delay, the delay factor $u(t+\theta)$ in the delay term may lead to oscillations, hysteresis effects, and other phenomena in the solution, which increases the difficulty of studying the well-posedness and asymptotic behavior of the solution. This study investigates the global well-posedness and asymptotic behavior of solutions to the non-autonomous Navier–Stokes equations incorporating infinite delays. To establish global well-posedness, we first construct several suitable function spaces and then prove them using the Galekin approximation method. Then, by accurately estimating the number of determining nodes, we reveal the asymptotic behavior of the solution. The results indicate that the long-term behavior of a strong solution can be determined by its values at a finite number of nodes.

Keywords: Navier–Stokes equations; infinite delay; global well-posedness; asymptotic behavior; determining nodes; long-time behavior

MSC: 35B40; 35B41; 37G35; 35Q35

1. Introduction

In this paper, we study the non-autonomous Navier–Stokes model with infinite delay in 2D bounded domains, which is given by the following equations:

$$\begin{cases} \dfrac{\partial u}{\partial t} - \nu\Delta u + (u\cdot\nabla)u + \nabla p = f(t) + G(t, u(t+\theta)) \quad \text{in} \quad (x,t) \in \Omega\times(\tau,T), \\ \operatorname{div} u = 0 \quad \text{in} \quad (x,t)\in\Omega\times(\tau,T), \\ u = 0 \qquad \text{on} \quad (x,t)\in\partial\Omega\times(\tau,T), \\ u(x,\tau+\theta) = \phi(x,\theta) \quad x\in\Omega \quad \theta\in(-\infty,0], \end{cases} \tag{1}$$

where the unknown functions $u(x,t) = (u^{(1)}(x,t), u^{(2)}(x,t))$ and $p = p(x,t)$ represent the velocity field and the pressure of the fluid motion, respectively. The function $f(t) = (f^{(1)}(t), f^{(2)}(t))$ is the external force, which is a given vector function that varies with time t. The parameter $\nu > 0$ denotes the viscosity coefficient. The function $u(t+\theta)$ represents the history of the state $u(\cdot)$ at time t, where $\theta\in(-\infty,0]$. The function $G(\cdot,\cdot)$ is a known continuous function, as required by the study.

In addition, $\Omega \subset \mathbb{R}^2$ is an open set with smooth boundaries, and the function $\phi(x,\theta)$ is the initial value of Equation (1) in the delay time$(-\infty,0]$. These assumptions typically serve as the basis for ensuring the well-posedness of the solution to Equation (1) in Ω. They also imply that the boundary has well-defined tangent vectors at each point and that the shape of the boundary does not exhibit sharp points or discontinuous regions. The assumption of regularity in the initial data is to satisfy the requirements of adaptability, regularity, and long-term behavior of the solution to Equation (1) in Ω.

The Navier–Stokes equations describe the motion of fluids, involving multiple factors such as velocity, pressure, and viscosity. Introducing delay factors allows for a more realistic simulation of inertia and time-delay effects in fluid flow, including interactions at fluid–solid interfaces and the impact of temperature variations on fluid states. In many physical phenomena, the response of fluids is not immediate but involves a time delay, which leads to the influence of time delay on the motion state of fluids and indirectly affects the stability of the system. Therefore, studying the Navier–Stokes equations with delay provides insights into flow stability across varying parameters and elucidates how delays influence flow transitions and turbulence onset. Incorporating delay factors enhances model accuracy, improving the prediction and understanding of fluid behavior. The study of Navier–Stokes equations with delay is not limited to traditional fluid mechanics but also involves multiple fields such as control theory, nonlinear dynamics, and mathematical physics, promoting interdisciplinary research and communication.

Owing to their wide applications, the Navier–Stokes equations have been extensively studied by mathematicians and physicists. In particular, the well-posedness and regularity of solutions are the most significant concerns. Several papers have been dedicated to investigating the well-posedness of solutions, including references [1–4]. Foias and Temam, among others, introduced the concepts of definite modules, degrees of freedom, and determining nodes of the system in [5]. These concepts describe how the asymptotic behavior of the system can be determined by a finite number of quantities, revealing the internal structural properties of the attractor. The term "determining nodes" refers to the process of numerically solving partial differential equations, where the solutions at certain specific grid points or nodes are uniquely determined by specific boundary conditions, initial conditions, or solutions at other nodes. In other words, the values of these nodes do not depend on the values of other unknown nodes but are directly calculated based on given conditions, thereby reducing uncertainty in the solving process. This concept is further elaborated in references [6–15]. Kakizawa used the energy method to prove the asymptotic behavior of strong solutions to the initial-boundary value problem for general semilinear parabolic equations in [12]. Additional related research can be found in references [6–9,11,14,16,17].

The phenomenon of time delay is ubiquitous and closely related to real life. For example, when we aim to control or change the original state of a system by applying external forces, we must consider not only the current state of the system but also the impact of its previous states, i.e., the lag factor. Therefore, time delay effects are often incorporated into models when dealing with practical problems. Examples include the delayed Navier–Stokes model (see [16,18]) and wave equations with time delay (see [19]). Hernandez and Wu studied the well-posedness and global attractors of abstract Cauchy problems with state-dependent delay and provided examples of PDEs with state-dependent delay in [20], which offers important insights into the application of state-dependent delay in specific PDEs and the study of their well-posedness and asymptotic solutions. Other related results can be found in references [21,22]. Regarding the Navier–Stokes equations, García-Luengo, Marín-Rubio, and Real investigated the asymptotic behavior of the Navier–Stokes model with finite delay in [8,14], while Chueshov studied the finite-dimensional global attractors for parabolic nonlinear equations with state-dependent delay, using the Galerkin method to prove global well-posedness in [21]. For the study of infinite delay, Fu and Liu investigated the well-posedness of solutions to a class of second-order non-autonomous abstract time-delay functional differential equations with infinite delay and demonstrated the application of their conclusions through examples (see Section 6 in [23]), which can be referenced in [23–25]. However, these articles only studied the well-posedness of solutions for non-autonomous systems with infinite time delay. They did not address the asymptotic behavior and regularity of solutions, and the equations provided in the examples were not specifically applied to several specific differential equations. In this paper, we apply the above research conclusions to the Navier–Stokes equations. Based on the extensive foundational work on well-posedness established by Caraballo et al., we use the theory of determining nodes to characterize the asymptotic behavior of solutions to the non-autonomous Navier–Stokes equations with infinite delay by estimating their number. The most crucial step in studying the process and methods of non-autonomous Navier–Stokes equations with infinite delay is to handle the infinite time delay term $u(t+\theta)$, which is particularly important for studying the well-posedness of nonlinear PDEs with time delay effects. In addition, dealing with the delay term is usually the most critical step in the research process of the well-posedness and asymptotic behavior of nonlinear PDE solutions with other delay effects.

The paper is arranged as follows: In Section 2, we first establish several basic function spaces and several operators, then introduce several relevant theorems and define the weak and strong solutions of Equation (1). In addition, to deal with the infinite delay term $u(t+\theta)$, we refer to descent function space $\mathcal{C}_\gamma(H)$. Unlike the finite delay term, we not only need to consider the influence of the system state at a certain time in the past, but also need to consider the comprehensive influence of the system state at the past time. In Section 3, we investigate the global well-posedness of the strong solutions for Equation (1) by the Galerkin method without considering the pressure term p. In Section 4, we commit our focus to proving Equation (1) has a finite number of determining nodes.

2. Preliminaries

In this section, we introduce several common conclusions that are essential applications that we used in this paper.

2.1. Basic Function Spaces and Conclusions

We introduce several basic function spaces, which are as follows:

$$\begin{aligned}
&\mathcal{V} := \left\{\varphi \in (C_0^\infty(\Omega))^2 : \operatorname{div}\varphi = 0, \varphi = (\varphi^{(1)}, \varphi^{(2)})\right\};\\
&H := \text{closure of } \mathcal{V} \text{ in } (L^2(\Omega))^2, \text{with norm } \|\cdot\|_H;\\
&V := \text{closure of } \mathcal{V} \text{ in } (H_0^1(\Omega))^2, \text{with norm } \|\cdot\|_V;\\
&V' := \text{dual space of } V \text{ with norm } \|\cdot\|_{V'}.
\end{aligned}$$

The definitions of norms $\|\cdot\|_H$ and $\|\cdot\|_V$ are as follows:

$$\|\varphi\|_H = \left(\int_\Omega |\varphi|^2 \mathrm{d}x\right)^{\frac{1}{2}}, \quad \|\varphi\|_V = \left(\int_\Omega \left(|\varphi|^2 + |\nabla\varphi|^2\right)\mathrm{d}x\right)^{\frac{1}{2}};$$

for convenience, we use "$\|\cdot\|$" as "$\|\cdot\|_H$". In addition, we denote the inner product in $L^2(\Omega), H$ by $(\cdot,\cdot)$ and denote the inner product in V by $((\cdot,\cdot))$. In addition, we denote the dual product between V and V' by $\langle\cdot,\cdot\rangle$.

In order to be able to express Equation (1) as an abstract equation, we define several operators. Firstly, we define the Stokes operator A as follows:

$$\langle Au, \varphi \rangle = \nu((u, \varphi)) = \nu \sum_{i,j=1}^{2} \int_{\Omega} \frac{\partial u_i}{\partial x_j} \frac{\partial \varphi_i}{\partial x_j} dx, \tag{2}$$

for any $u = (u^{(1)}, u^{(1)}), \varphi = (\varphi^{(1)}, \varphi^{(2)}) \in V$. Moreover, $D(A) := V \cap (H^2(\Omega))^2$, and the operator A is the linear continuous operator, which both form V to V' and $D(A)$ to H. Then, we denote the linear function

$$b(u, v, w) = \sum_{i,j=1}^{2} \int_{\Omega} u_i \frac{\partial v_j}{\partial x_i} w_j dx, \quad \forall u, v, w \in V.$$

It is obvious that the linear function $b(\cdot, \cdot, \cdot)$ is continuous trilinear on $V \times V \times V$ and it satisfies

$$b(u, v, w) = -b(u, w, v), \quad b(u, v, v) = 0, \quad \forall\, u, v, w \in V.$$

In addition, we use the following lemma to provide estimators of the linear function $b(\cdot, \cdot, \cdot)$, which can be found in references [26,27].

Lemma 1. *There exists a positive constant C_Ω that depends only on Ω, such that*

$$|b(u, v, w)| \leq C_\Omega \|u\|^{\frac{1}{2}} \|Au\|^{\frac{1}{2}} \|v\|_V \|w\|, \quad \forall u \in D(A), v \in V, w \in H. \tag{3}$$

$$|b(u, v, w)| \leq C_\Omega \|Au\| \|v\|_V \|w\|, \quad \forall u \in D(A), v \in V, w \in H. \tag{4}$$

If $u \in L^\infty, v \in V, w \in H$, then the linear function $b(\cdot, \cdot, \cdot)$ satisfies

$$|b(u, v, w)| \leq \|u\|_{L^\infty} \|v\|_V \|w\|. \tag{5}$$

If $u, v, w \in V$, it satisfies

$$|b(u, v, w)| \leq \|u\|^{\frac{1}{2}} \|\nabla u\|^{\frac{1}{2}} \|v\|^{\frac{1}{2}} \|\nabla v\|^{\frac{1}{2}} \|w\|. \tag{6}$$

To handle the infinite delays $G(t, u(t + \theta))$, we define the space $C_\gamma(H)$ with a suitable constant $\gamma > 0$, as follows:

$$C_\gamma(H) = \left\{ \zeta \in C((-\infty, 0); H) | \exists \lim_{s \to -\infty} e^{\gamma s} \zeta(s) \in H \right\},$$

which is a Banach space with the norm

$$\|\zeta\|_{C_\gamma(H)} = \sup_{s \in (-\infty, 0]} e^{\gamma s} \|\zeta(s)\|.$$

The space $C_\gamma(H)$ represents the space of descent functions, where the parameter $\gamma > 0$ is typically used to describe the growth rate of the function in $C_\gamma(H)$. The purpose of introducing $C_\gamma(H)$ is to ensure that the growth property of the function does not affect the long-term behavior of the system and also satisfies the descent conditions required by continuous functions with changing states due to time delay effects.

To establish the well-posedness of Equation (1), the continuous function $G : [\tau, T] \times C_\gamma(H) \mapsto (L^2(\Omega))^2$ is assumed to satisfy the following conditions.

(I) For any η, the mapping $t \mapsto G(t, \eta)$ is measurable;

(II) $G(t, 0) = (0, 0)$;

(III) There exists $L_G > 0$, such that

$$\|G(t,x_1) - G(t,x_2)\| \leq L_G\|x_1 - x_2\|_{\mathcal{C}_\gamma(H)}, \quad \forall x_1, x_2 \in \mathcal{C}_\gamma(H). \tag{7}$$

When studying differential equations with infinite time delay, Lipschitz conditions also help to investigate the asymptotic behavior of solutions. For example, when studying the steady-state or periodic solutions of a system after long-term operation, the Lipschitz condition can ensure that the solutions do not experience explosive growth in time. In addition, the Lipschitz condition ensures understanding of the continuous dependence on the initial conditions, as infinite delay terms may lead to temporal irregularities in the solution. By ensuring that the mapping is Lipschitz, it can be proven that small initial perturbations do not cause significant changes in the solution, thereby ensuring its stability.

Based on the above conclusion, we define the weak and strong solution of Equation (1) as follows.

2.2. The Weak Solution and Strong Solution

Definition 1. *Assume $f \in L^2(\tau, T; V')$ and $u(\tau) = \phi \in \mathcal{C}_\gamma(H)$. A weak solution is any function $u \in \mathcal{C}_\gamma(H)$ of Equation (1) if it satisfies*

(I) $u \in L^\infty(\tau, T; H) \cap L^2(\tau, T; V)$, for all $T > \tau$;

(II) For all $\sigma \in V$, such that

$$\frac{\mathrm{d}}{\mathrm{d}t}(u(t),\sigma) - \nu\langle Au(t),\sigma\rangle + b(u(t),u(t),\sigma) = \langle f(t),\sigma\rangle + \big(G(t,u(t+\theta)),\sigma\big), \tag{8}$$

$$u(\tau+\theta) = \phi(\theta) \in \mathcal{C}_\gamma(H), \quad \theta \in (-\infty, 0] \tag{9}$$

holds in the distribution sense of $\mathcal{D}'(\tau, T)$.

Assume $f \in L^2(\tau, T; H)$; if $u \in \mathcal{C}_\gamma(H)$ is a weak solution of Equations (8) and (9) and $u \in L^\infty(\tau, T; V) \cap L^2(\tau, T; D(A))$ for all $T > \tau$, then $u \in \mathcal{C}_\gamma(H)$ is called a strong solution of Equations (8) and (9). Furthermore, the function $u' \in L^2(\tau, T; H)$.

Remark 1. *If $u \in \mathcal{C}_\gamma(H)$ is a weak solution to Equation (1), then in this case, from Equations (8) and (9), for any $\tau \leq s \leq t$, the following energy equality holds*

$$\begin{aligned}&\|u(t)\|^2 + 2\nu\int_s^t \|u(r)\|_V{}^2\mathrm{d}r\\ &= \|u(\tau)\|^2 + 2\int_s^t \Big(\langle f(r),u(r)\rangle + \big(G(t,u(r+\theta))\big),u(r)\Big)\mathrm{d}r.\end{aligned} \tag{10}$$

In addition, we introduce a useful inequality in the differential equation theory. This will play an important role in making a priori estimates.

Lemma 2. *(Gronwall Inequation) Assume $g, p, q \in C([a,b]; \mathbb{R}^+)$ and for all $t \in [a,b]$ satisfy*

$$g(t) \leq g(a) + \int_a^t (p(s)g(s) + q(s))\mathrm{d}s,$$

then any $t \in [a,b]$, and functions g, p, q satisfy

$$g(t) \leq e^{\int_a^t p(s)\mathrm{d}s}\Big(g(a) + \int_a^t q(s)\mathrm{d}s\Big), \quad \forall t \in [a,b]. \tag{11}$$

3. Global Well-Posedness

In this section, we study the global well-posedness of Equation (1). Therefore, we present the existence and uniqueness theorem for the weak solution of Equation (1). Therefore, we apply the treatment of the infinite delay term $u(t+\theta)$ to the proof of the global well-posedness of the non-autonomous Navier–Stokes equation, that is, adding the infinite delay term $u(t+\theta)$ to the proof of the global well-posedness of the non-autonomous Navier–Stokes equation.

3.1. The Existence of Solutions

Theorem 1. *Suppose $f \in L^2(\tau, T; V')$, and there exist constants $C = C(\nu, \lambda_1, L_G)$ that satisfy*

$$\frac{1}{\nu}\int_\tau^t e^{C(t-r)}\|f(r)\|_{V'}^2 \mathrm{d}r < +\infty,$$

and the function $G(\cdot,\cdot)$ satisfies the conditions (I)-(III). Then for all $T > \tau$ and $u(\tau) = \phi \in C_\gamma(H)$, the function $u \in C_\gamma(H) \cap L^\infty(\tau, T; H) \cap L^2(\tau, T; V)$ is the weak solution of Equation (1).

Proof. For the proof of Theorem 1, we use the Galerkin approximation method. The proof is divided into the following three steps.

Step 1: Construct the approximate solution.

Taking a set of canonical orthonormal basis $\{\xi_i\} \subset V$ on the Hilbert space H, denote

$$V_k = \text{span}[\xi_1, \xi_2, \cdots, \xi_k], \quad k = 1, 2, \cdots;$$

from the Gram–Schmidt theorem, the projection of H onto V_k is defined by

$$P_k u = \sum_{i=1}^{k}(u, \xi_i)\xi_i.$$

Since the Stokes operator A is compact operator on the V space, it satisfies

$$A\xi_i = \lambda_i \xi_i, \quad (\lambda_i > 0, i = 1, 2\cdots, k),$$

where λ_i is the eigenvalue of Stokes operator A. Sort them in ascending order and renumber them as follows:

$$0 < \lambda_1 \le \lambda_2 \le \cdots \le \lambda_n \le \cdots,$$

and they satisfy $\lim_{i\to\infty} \lambda_i = \infty$. We take the minimum eigenvalue λ_1 of Stokes operator A as the first eigenvalue.

From this, we construct the approximate solution of Equation (1) from the space V_k as follows:

$$u_k(x,t) = \sum_{i=1}^{k} a_{ki}(t)\xi_i(x),$$

where $a_{ki}(t) = (u_k, \xi_i)$ and all $t \in (\tau, T)$ satisfy

$$\frac{\mathrm{d}}{\mathrm{d}t}(u_k(t), \xi_i) + \nu\langle Au_k(t), \xi_i\rangle + b(u_k, u_k, \xi_i) = \langle f(t), \xi_i\rangle + \big(G(t, u_k(t+\theta)), \xi_i\big), \tag{12}$$

and initial conditions

$$u_k(\tau+\theta) = P_k\phi(\theta), \quad \theta \in (-\infty, 0]. \tag{13}$$

Therefore, Equations (12) and (13) satisfy the condition of existence and uniqueness of local solutions for the system of ordinary differential equation with infinite delay (e.g., [19]).

Step 2: A priori estimate of the approximate solution.

Firstly, we estimate Equation (12), multiplied by $a_{ki}(t)$ to Equation (12) and sum it to obtain the ODE:

$$\frac{1}{2}\frac{\mathrm{d}}{\mathrm{d}t}\|u_k(t)\|^2+\nu\|u_k(t)\|_V^2=\langle f(t),u_k(t)\rangle+\big(G(t,u_k(t+\theta)),u_k(t)\big), \tag{14}$$

which implies

$$\frac{1}{2}\frac{\mathrm{d}}{\mathrm{d}t}\|u_k(t)\|^2+\nu\|u_k(t)\|_V^2\leq\|f\|_{V'}\,\|u_k(t)\|_V+\|G(t,u_k(t+\theta))\|\,\|u_k(t)\|_V. \tag{15}$$

Using Young and Poincare inequations, we choose suitable constants $\varepsilon_1=\varepsilon_2=\frac{\nu}{4}$, then we obtain

$$\begin{aligned}&\|f\|_{V'}\,\|u_k(t)\|_V+\|G(t,u_k(t+\theta))\|\,\|u_k(t)\|\\&\leq\frac{1}{2\varepsilon_1}\|f(t)\|_{V'}^2+\frac{\nu}{4}\|u_k(t)\|_V^2+\frac{L_G}{2\varepsilon_2}\|u_k(t+\theta)\|_{\mathcal{C}_\gamma(H)}^2,\end{aligned} \tag{16}$$

where $\|u_k(t+\theta)\|_{\mathcal{C}_\gamma(H)}=\sup_{s\in(-\infty,0]}e^{\gamma s}\|u_k(t+s)\|\geq\|u_k(t)\|, t\in[\tau,T]$. Substituting (16) into Equation (15), for $\tau\leq r\leq t\leq T$, we obtain

$$\frac{\mathrm{d}}{\mathrm{d}r}\|u_k(r)\|^2+\nu\lambda_1\|u_k(r)\|^2+\frac{\nu}{2}\|u_k(r)\|_V^2\leq\frac{4}{\nu}\|f(r)\|_{V'}^2+\frac{4L_G}{\nu}\|u_k(r+\theta)\|_{\mathcal{C}_\gamma(H)}^2. \tag{17}$$

Multiplying by $e^{-\nu\lambda_1(t-r)}$ and then integrating it for r over $[\tau,t]$, we obtain

$$\begin{aligned}&\|u_k(t)\|^2+\frac{\nu}{2}\int_\tau^t e^{-\nu\lambda_1(t-r)}\|u_k(r)\|_V^2\mathrm{d}r\\&\leq e^{-\nu\lambda_1(t-\tau)}\|u_k(\tau)\|^2+\int_\tau^t e^{-\nu\lambda_1(t-r)}\left(\frac{4}{\nu}\|f(r)\|_{V'}^2+\frac{4L_G}{\nu}\|u_k(r+\theta)\|_{\mathcal{C}_\gamma(H)}^2\right)\mathrm{d}r.\end{aligned} \tag{18}$$

According to the definition of $\mathcal{C}_\gamma(H)$, we obtain

$$\begin{aligned}\|u_k(t+\theta)\|_{\mathcal{C}_\gamma(H)}^2&=\left(\sup_{s\in(-\infty,0]}e^{\gamma s}\|u_k(t+s)\|\right)^2,\\&\leq\max\left\{\sup_{s\in(-\infty,\tau-t]}e^{2\gamma s}\|u_k(t+s)\|^2,\ \sup_{s\in(\tau-t,0]}e^{2\gamma s}\|u_k(t+s)\|^2\right\}\\&=\max\{J_1(t),J_2(t)+J_3(t)\},\end{aligned} \tag{19}$$

where

$$\begin{aligned}J_1(t)&=\sup_{s\in(-\infty,\tau-t]}e^{2\gamma s}\|u_k(t+s)\|^2,\\J_2(t)&=\sup_{s\in(\tau-t,0]}\left[e^{2\gamma s-\nu\lambda_1(t+s-\tau)}\|u_k(\tau)\|^2\right],\\J_3(t)&=\sup_{s\in(\tau-t,0]}\left[e^{(2\gamma-\nu\lambda_1)s}\int_\tau^{t+s}e^{-\nu\lambda_1(t-r)}\left(\frac{4}{\nu}\|f(r)\|_{V'}^2+\frac{4L_G}{\nu}\|u_k(r+\theta)\|_{\mathcal{C}_\gamma(H)}^2\right)\mathrm{d}r\right].\end{aligned}$$

Now, let us estimate $J_1(t)$, $J_2(t)$, and $J_3(t)$. On one hand, since $\nu\lambda_1<2\gamma$,

$$
\begin{aligned}
J_1(t) = & \sup_{s\in(-\infty,\tau-t]} e^{2\gamma s}\|P_k\phi(t+s-\tau)\|^2 \leq \sup_{s\in(-\infty,\tau-t]} e^{2\gamma s}\|\phi(t+s-\tau)\|^2 \\
= & \sup_{s\in(-\infty,0]} e^{2\gamma[s-(t-\tau)]}\|\phi(s)\|^2 = e^{2\gamma(\tau-t)}\|\phi(s)\|^2_{C_\gamma(H)} \\
\leq & e^{-\nu\lambda_1(t-\tau)}\|\phi(s)\|^2_{C_\gamma(H)}. \qquad (20)
\end{aligned}
$$

On the other hand, by direct computation, we have

$$
J_2(t) \leq e^{-\nu\lambda_1(t-\tau)}\|u_k(\tau)\|^2 \leq e^{-\nu\lambda_1(t-\tau)}\|\phi(s)\|^2_{C_\gamma(H)}, \qquad (21)
$$

$$
J_3(t) \leq \int_\tau^t e^{-\nu\lambda_1(t-r)}\left(\frac{4}{\nu}\|f(r)\|^2_{V'} + \frac{4L_G}{\nu}\|u_k(r+\theta)\|^2_{C_\gamma(H)}\right)\mathrm{d}r. \qquad (22)
$$

Then, Equations (19)–(22) give

$$
\begin{aligned}
& \|u_k(t+\theta)\|^2_{C_\gamma(H)} \\
\leq & e^{-\nu\lambda_1(t-\tau)}\|\phi(s)\|^2_{C_\gamma(H)} + \int_\tau^t e^{-\nu\lambda_1(t-r)}\left(\frac{4}{\nu}\|f(r)\|^2_{V'} + \frac{4L_G}{\nu}\|u_k(r+\theta)\|^2_{C_\gamma(H)}\right)\mathrm{d}r. \qquad (23)
\end{aligned}
$$

By Lemma 2, this implies

$$
\|u_k(t+\theta)\|^2_{C_\gamma(H)} \leq e^{-\left(\nu\lambda_1-\frac{4L_G}{\nu}\right)(t-\tau)}\|\phi(s)\|^2_{C_\gamma(H)} + \frac{4}{\nu}\int_\tau^t e^{-\left(\nu\lambda_1-\frac{4L_G}{\nu}\right)(t-r)}\|f(r)\|^2_{V'}\mathrm{d}r, \qquad (24)
$$

combining Equations (18) and (24); it can be concluded that the $\{u_k(t)\}$ is bounded in $L^\infty(\tau, T; H)$. According to Equation (18), this means

$$
\begin{aligned}
& \frac{\nu}{2}e^{-\nu\lambda_1(t-\tau)}\int_\tau^t \|u_k(r)\|^2_V\mathrm{d}r \\
\leq & \|u_k(\tau)\|^2 + \int_\tau^t e^{-\nu\lambda_1(t-r)}\left(\frac{4}{\nu}\|f(r)\|^2_{V'} + \frac{4L_G}{\nu}\|u_k(r+\theta)\|^2_{C_\gamma(H)}\right)\mathrm{d}r. \qquad (25)
\end{aligned}
$$

By Equation (24), this implies that the $\{u_k(t)\}$ is bounded in $L^2(\tau, T; V)$. In addition, for any $\psi \in V$, we obtain

$$
\langle u_k'(t), \psi\rangle + \langle Au_k(t), \psi\rangle + b(u_k, u_k, \psi) = \langle f(t), \psi\rangle + \langle G(t, u_k(t+\theta)), \psi\rangle.
$$

Using the Holder inequation, we obtain the following result:

$$
\begin{aligned}
\left|\langle u_k'(t), \psi\rangle\right| \leq & |\langle Au_k(t), \psi\rangle| + |b(u, u, \psi)| + |\langle f(t), \psi\rangle| + |\langle G(t, u_k(t+\theta)), \psi\rangle| \\
\leq & \|\psi\|_V(\nu\|u_k(t)\|_V + C_\Omega\|u_k(t)\|\,\|\nabla u_k(t)\| + \|f\|_{V'} + \|G(t, u_k(t+\theta))\|), \\
\leq & \|\psi\|_V(\nu\|u_k(t)\|_V + C_\Omega\|u_k(t)\|\,\|u_k(t)\|_V + \|f\|_{V'} + \|G(t, u_k(t+\theta))\|). \qquad (26)
\end{aligned}
$$

Hence, it follows from Equations (7), (18), (24) and (25) that the sequence $\{u_k'(t)\}$ is bounded in $L^2(\tau, T; V')$.

Step 3: Approximation of approximate solutions.

Now, based on the conclusions of the previous step, since the compactness theorem (see, e.g., [1,11,18]), for all $T > \tau$, there exist subsequences, which we still denote by $\{u_k\}$, such that as $k \to \infty$, the following conditions satisfy:

$$u_k \overset{*}{\rightharpoonup} u \quad \text{in}\, L^\infty(\tau - h, T; H), \tag{27}$$
$$u_k \rightharpoonup u \quad \text{in}\, L^2(\tau, T; V), \tag{28}$$
$$u_k' \rightharpoonup u' \quad \text{in}\, L^2(\tau, T; V'), \tag{29}$$
$$u_k \to u \quad \text{in}\, L^2(\tau, T; H), \tag{30}$$
$$G(t, u_k(t+\theta)) \overset{*}{\rightharpoonup} \eta(t) \quad \text{in}\, L^\infty(\tau, T; (L^2(\Omega))^2). \tag{31}$$

where $\eta(t) \in L^\infty(\tau, T; (L^2(\Omega))^2)$ is the limiting function of $G(t, u_k(t+\theta))$. However, currently, we cannot yet obtain it:

$$G(t, u_k(t+\theta)) \to G(t, u(t+\theta)) \in L^2(\tau, T; (L^2(\Omega))^2). \tag{32}$$

Next, we will prove Equation (32) through conclusions (27)–(31).

From conclusions (27)–(31), we obtain

$$u_k(t) \to u(t), \quad a.e.\, t \in (\tau, T), \quad \text{in}\, H, \tag{33}$$

then for all $s, t \in [\tau, T]$, it implies

$$u_k(t) - u_k(s) = \int_s^t u_k{}'(r)\mathrm{d}r, \quad \text{in}\, V'; \tag{34}$$

therefore, the $\{u_k\}$ is equicontinuous for all $[\tau, T]$ and k in H. By the embedding relation $V \hookrightarrow\hookrightarrow H \hookrightarrow\hookrightarrow V'$, and the Ascoli–Arzela theorem, it yields that $\{u_k\}$ is relatively compact in V', and for all $t \in [\tau, T]$, which implies

$$u_k(t) \to u(t), \quad \text{in}\, \mathcal{C}([\tau, T]; V'). \tag{35}$$

According to conclusions (27)–(31), for any sequence $\{t_k\} \subset [\tau, T]$ that satisfies $t_k \to t$,

$$u_k(t_k) \rightharpoonup u(t), \quad \text{in}\, H. \tag{36}$$

Before proving Equation (32), we need to first prove

$$u_k(t) \to u(t), \quad \text{in}\, \mathcal{C}([\tau, T]; H). \tag{37}$$

Since for all $r \in [s, t] \subset [\tau, T]$, the approximate solution u_k satisfies

$$\begin{aligned} &\|u_k(t)\|^2 + 2\nu \int_s^t \|u_k(r)\|_V^2 \mathrm{d}r \\ =&\|u_k(s)\|^2 + 2\int_s^t \langle f(r), u_k(r)\rangle\rangle \mathrm{d}r + 2\int_s^t (G(r, u_k(r+\theta), u_k(r)))\mathrm{d}r, \end{aligned} \tag{38}$$

we obtain the following result by conclusions (27)–(31),

$$\int_s^t \|G(r, u_k(r+\theta))\|^2 \mathrm{d}r \le C_1(t-s), \quad \forall r \in [s, t] \subset [\tau, T], \tag{39}$$

where C_1 is a positive constant. According to the conclusions of (27)–(31), we verify that the function

$$u \in \mathcal{C}_\gamma(H) \cap L^\infty(\tau, T; H) \cap L^2(\tau, T; V),$$

is a weak solution of Equation (1), and it satisfies

$$\frac{\mathrm{d}}{\mathrm{d}t}(u(t),w)+\nu\langle Au(t),w\rangle+b(u(t),u(t),w)=\langle f(t),w\rangle+(\eta(t),w)\quad\forall w\in V,\tag{40}$$

in addition, for any $r\in[s,t]\subset[\tau,T]$, the energy estimates also satisfy

$$\begin{aligned}&\|u(t)\|^2+2\nu\int_s^t\|u(r)\|_V^2\mathrm{d}r\\=&\|u(\tau)\|^2+2\int_s^t\Big(\langle f(r),u(r)\rangle+(G(t,u(r+\theta)),u(r)\Big)\mathrm{d}r.\end{aligned}\tag{41}$$

Due to the conclusions of (27)–(31) and Equation (39), we obtain

$$\int_s^t\|\eta(r)\|^2\mathrm{d}r\le\liminf_{k\to\infty}\int_s^t\|G(t,u(r+\theta))\|^2\mathrm{d}r\le C_1(t-s);\tag{42}$$

therefore, consider the continuous functions $L_k,L:[\tau,t]\to\mathbb{R}$, which are defined by

$$\begin{aligned}L_k(t)&=\frac{\nu}{2}\|u_k(t)\|_V^2-\int_s^t\langle f(r),u_k(r)\rangle\mathrm{d}r-C_1t,\\L(t)&=\frac{\nu}{2}\|u(t)\|_V^2-\int_s^t\langle f(r),u(r)\rangle\mathrm{d}r-C_1t.\end{aligned}$$

As shown in Equations (38) and (41), it is evident that the functions $L_k(t),L(t)$ are non-increasing and continuous in $[\tau,T]$. According to the conclusions of (27)–(30), we obtain

$$L_k(t)\to L(t)\quad a.e.\quad t\in[\tau,T],\tag{43}$$

from the conclusions of (27)–(30), it is obvious that $\|u(t_0)\|\le\liminf_{k\to\infty}\|u_k(t_k)\|$. To prove

$$\limsup_{k\to\infty}\|u_k(t_k)\|\le\|u(t_0)\|,\tag{44}$$

we assume $t_0>\tau$ and take the sequence $\{\bar{t}_n\}\subset\{t_k\}$ that satisfies (43), which is increasing, and approach the value t_0 from the left when $n\to\infty$. Since $L(\cdot)$ is continuous, there exists N_ε, and when $n>N_\varepsilon$,

$$|L(\bar{t}_n)-L(t_0)|<\varepsilon.$$

Take $k>K(N_\varepsilon)$ such that $t_k>\bar{t}_{N_\varepsilon}$, by the sequence $L(\cdot),L_k(\cdot)$, is non-increasing and satisfies (43); we obtain

$$|L_k(t_k)-L(t_0)|\le|L_k(\bar{t}_{N_\varepsilon})-L(\bar{t}_{N_\varepsilon})|+|L(\bar{t}_{N_\varepsilon})-L(t_0)|<2\varepsilon.$$

At this time, the conclusions of (27)–(30) imply

$$\int_\tau^{t_k}\langle f(r),u_k(r)\rangle\mathrm{d}r\to\int_\tau^t\langle f(r),u(r)\rangle\mathrm{d}r,\quad(k\to\infty).\tag{45}$$

Due to these and functions L_k,L, we have proven Equation (44).

According to the definition of $C_\gamma(H)$, we obtain

$$
\begin{aligned}
&\|u_k(t+\theta)-u(t+\theta)\|_{\mathcal{C}_\gamma(H)}\\
=&\sup_{s\in(-\infty,0]} e^{\gamma s}\|u_k(t+s)-u(t+s)| = \max\{\Phi_1(s),\Phi_2(s)\}\\
\leq&\max\left\{e^{\gamma(\tau-t)}\|P_k\phi-\phi\|_{\mathcal{C}_\gamma(H)}, \sup_{s\in(\tau-t,0]} e^{\gamma s}\|u_k(t+s)-u(t+s)\|\right\},
\end{aligned}
\tag{46}
$$

where

$$
\begin{aligned}
\Phi_1(s) &= \sup_{s\in(-\infty,\tau-t]} e^{\gamma s}\|P_k\phi(t+s-\tau)-\phi(t+s-\tau)\|,\\
\Phi_2(s) &= \sup_{s\in(\tau-t,0]} e^{\gamma s}\|u_k(t+s)-u(t+s)\|,
\end{aligned}
$$

which implies that

$$
\lim_{k\to\infty}\|u_k(t+\theta)-u(t+\theta)\|_{\mathcal{C}_\gamma(H)} = 0. \tag{47}
$$

In addition, the convergence results are obtained by Equations (7), (37) and (47), and conclusions of (27)–(31); therefore, we prove Equation (32). Thus, we have proven Theorem 1. □

3.2. The Uniqueness of Solutions

Theorem 2. *If all the conditions in the Theorem 1 are satisfied, then the function $u \in \mathcal{C}_\gamma(H)\cap L^\infty(\tau,T;H)\cap L^2(\tau,T;V)$ is the unique weak solution of Equation (1).*

Proof. Set $\overline{u}_1$ and $\overline{u}_2$ be the weak solutions of Equation (1). Denote the function $U(t) = \overline{u}_1(t)-\overline{u}_2(t)$; for any $t>\tau$, we have

$$
\frac{1}{2}\frac{\mathrm{d}}{\mathrm{d}t}\|U(t)\|^2+\nu\|\nabla U(t)\|^2+b(U,\overline{u}_1,U) = \big(G(t,\overline{u}_1(t+\theta))-G(t,\overline{u}_2(t+\theta)),U(t)\big). \tag{48}
$$

Furthermore, according to Lemma 1, and Equations (14) and (39), using Young, Holder, and Poincare inequations, we obtain

$$
\begin{aligned}
&\frac{1}{2}\frac{\mathrm{d}}{\mathrm{d}t}\|U(t)\|^2+\nu\|U(t)\|_V^2\\
\leq&C_\Omega\left(\frac{\|U(t)\|^2\|\overline{u}_1(t)\|_V^2}{2\varepsilon_3}+\frac{\varepsilon_3}{2}\|U(t)\|_V^2\right)+L_G\|U(t+\theta)\|_{\mathcal{C}_\gamma(H)}\|U(t)\|.
\end{aligned}
\tag{49}
$$

Integrating Equation (49), we obtain

$$
\begin{aligned}
&\frac{1}{2}\|U(t)\|^2-\frac{1}{2}\|U(\tau)\|^2+\nu\int_\tau^t\|U(r)\|_V^2\mathrm{d}r\\
\leq&C_\Omega\int_\tau^t\left(\frac{\|U(r)\|^2\|\overline{u}_1(r)\|_V^2}{2\varepsilon_3}+\frac{\varepsilon_3}{2}\|U(r)\|_V^2\right)\mathrm{d}r+\int_\tau^t L_G\|U(r+\theta)\|_{\mathcal{C}_\gamma(H)}\|U(r)\|\mathrm{d}r.
\end{aligned}
\tag{50}
$$

Take $\varepsilon_3 = \dfrac{2\nu}{C_\Omega}$; then, according to the definition of $\mathcal{C}_\gamma(H)$, we obtain

$$
\|U(r+\theta)\| = \sup_{s\in(-\infty,0]} e^{\gamma s}\|U(r+s)\| \leq \sup_{z\in(\tau,r)}\|U(z)\|, \quad r\in[\tau,t].
$$

Therefore, we have

$$\sup_{z\in(\tau,t)} \|U(z)\|^2 \le \int_\tau^t \left(\frac{C_\Omega \|\overline{u}_1(r)\|_V^2}{2\nu} + 2L_G\right) \sup_{z\in(\tau,r)} \|U(z)\|^2 \mathrm{d}r, \tag{51}$$

where $\|U(\tau)\|^2 = 0$. By Lemma 2, we conclude that $\|U(t)\|^2 = 0$; therefore, we have proven Theorem 2. □

4. Estimate the Number of Determining Nodes

In this section, we prove that Equation (1) has a finite number of determining nodes.

4.1. Introduction to Relevant Lemmas

Let $\overline{u}_1$ and $\overline{u}_2$ be the two strong solutions of Equation (1) corresponding to the external force and torque f_1 and f_2, respectively, and $f_1, f_2 \in L^2(\tau, T; H)$. The asymptotic strength of the external force and moment is described by its L^2 norm, i.e.,

$$F := \limsup_{t\to+\infty} \left(\int_\Omega |f_i(x,t)|^2\right)^{\frac{1}{2}} \mathrm{d}x, \quad i = 1,2. \tag{52}$$

which can be found in references [12,28]. Therefore, we have the following definition.

Definition 2 ([12,28,29]). *Consider N measuring points x_i in the space $\Omega \subseteq \mathbb{R}^2$, where $i = 1,2,\cdots,N$. Denoted $\Lambda = \{x^1, x^2, \cdots, x^N\}$. Suppose that $\overline{u}_1$ and $\overline{u}_2$ are two strong solutions of Equation (1). If by*

$$\lim_{t\to+\infty} \max_{i=1,2,\cdots,N} |\overline{u}_1(x^i,t) - \overline{u}_2(x^i,t)| = 0, \tag{53}$$

we can obtain

$$\lim_{t\to+\infty} \int_\Omega |\overline{u}_1(x,t) - \overline{u}_2(x,t)|^2 \mathrm{d}x = 0, \tag{54}$$

then the point set Λ is called the definite node set of Equation (1), and the point in Λ is the definite node of Equation (1).

In addition, in order to prove the main conclusions of this section, the following important lemmas (see [11,26,29–31]) should also be used.

Lemma 3. *Let Ω be covered by N identical squares. Remember the point set*

$$\Lambda = \left\{x^1, x^2, \cdots, x^N\right\} \subset \Omega,$$

where the point x^i belongs to and only belongs to one of the squares, then for $\forall u \in D(A)$, there exists the normal number C_Ω, which is only dependent on Ω, such that

$$\|\nabla u\|^2 \le C_\Omega N \eta^2(u) + \frac{C_\Omega}{\lambda_1 N} \|Au\|^2, \tag{55}$$

where $\eta(u) = \max_{i=1,2,\cdots,N} |u(x^i)|$.

Lemma 4. *If $P(t)$ and $Q(t)$ are real-valued functions on $[\tau, +\infty)$ and there exist $T > 0$ and constant C_2, such that*

$$\liminf_{t\to+\infty} \frac{1}{T}\int_t^{t+T} P(r)\mathrm{d}r = C_2 > 0, \quad \limsup_{t\to+\infty} \frac{1}{T}\int_t^{t+T} P^-(r)\mathrm{d}r < \infty, \tag{56}$$

and

$$\lim_{t\to+\infty} \frac{1}{T}\int_t^{t+T} Q^+(r)\mathrm{d}r = 0, \tag{57}$$

where $P^-(t) = \max\{-P(t), 0\}, Q^+(t) = \max\{Q(t), 0\}$. Suppose $\xi(t)$ is the non-negative absolutely continuous function on $[\tau, +\infty)$. If $\xi(t)$ satisfies

$$\frac{\mathrm{d}\xi(t)}{\mathrm{d}t} + P(t)\xi(t) \le Q(t),$$

then $\lim\limits_{t\to+\infty} \xi(t) = 0$.

Next, we prove that if any two strong solutions of Equation (1) have the same asymptotic behavior at a finite number of points in space, then these two solutions will have the same asymptotic behavior almost everywhere in the entire space.

4.2. Main Results

Theorem 3. *Let Ω be covered by N identical squares. The set Λ is defined in Lemma 3, $N > \frac{16C_\Omega^3 C_5}{5\nu^2\lambda_1}$, where $C_5 := C_4\|\phi(s)\|^2 + C_3F^2$ and each point x^i belongs to and only belongs to one of the squares. Let $\overline{u}_1$ and $\overline{u}_2$ be two strong solutions of Equation (1) corresponding to external forces f_1 and f_2, respectively, and f_1 and f_2 have the same asymptotic strength, i.e.,*

$$\lim_{t\to+\infty} \int_\Omega |f_i(x,t)|^2 \mathrm{d}x = 0. \tag{58}$$

Then, the point set Λ is the definite node set of Equation (1).

Proof. Denote $U = \overline{u}_1 - \overline{u}_2, f = f_1 - f_2$ and

$$G(t, U(t+\theta)) = G_1(t, \overline{u}_1(t+\theta)) - G_2(t, \overline{u}_2(t+\theta)).$$

Since $\overline{u}_1$ and $\overline{u}_2$ are the two solutions of Equation (1), in the sense of distribution, we obtain

$$\frac{\partial U}{\partial t} - \nu\Delta U + (U\cdot\nabla)\overline{u}_1 + (\overline{u}_2\cdot\nabla)u = f(t,x) + G(t, U(t+\theta)). \tag{59}$$

Next, we prove that under the condition of Theorem 1, if Equation (53) holds, then there is

$$\lim_{t\to+\infty} \|U(t)\|^2 = 0. \tag{60}$$

Firstly, the inner product of AU with Equation (59), respectively, is obtained with

$$\begin{aligned}&\frac{1}{2}\frac{\mathrm{d}}{\mathrm{d}t}\|\nabla U(t)\|^2 + \nu\|AU\|^2 \\ =& -b(U, \overline{u}_1, AU) - b(\overline{u}_2, U, AU) + (f, AU) + (G(t, U(t+\theta)), AU),\end{aligned} \tag{61}$$

by the Lemma 1 and Young inequality. Take $\varepsilon_3 = \frac{\nu}{4}$, then we can obtain

$$|b(U, u_1, AU)| \leq C_\Omega \|\nabla U\| \, \|\nabla \overline{u}_1\| \, \|AU\| \leq \frac{2C_\Omega^2}{\nu} \|\nabla U\|^2 \|\nabla \overline{u}_1\|^2 + \frac{\nu}{8} \|AU\|^2, \tag{62}$$

$$|b(\overline{u}_2, U, AU)| \leq C_\Omega \|\nabla \overline{u}_2\| \, \|\nabla U\| \, \|AU\| \leq \frac{2C_\Omega^2}{\nu} \|\nabla \overline{u}_2\|^2 \|\nabla U\|^2 + \frac{\nu}{8} \|AU\|^2. \tag{63}$$

Similarly, it is obvious that

$$|(f, Au)| \leq \frac{\nu}{16} \|AU\|^2 + \frac{4}{\nu} \|f\|^2, \tag{64}$$

and

$$\left|(G(t, U(t+\theta)), AU)\right| \leq \frac{\nu}{16} \|AU\|^2 + \frac{4L_G^2}{\nu} \|U(t+\theta)\|_{C_\gamma(H)}^2. \tag{65}$$

By Equation (24), substituting (62)–(65) into Equation (61), we obtain

$$\begin{aligned} &\frac{\mathrm{d}}{\mathrm{d}t} \|\nabla U(t)\|^2 + \frac{5\nu}{4} \|Au\|^2 - \frac{4C_\Omega^2}{\nu} \|\nabla U(t)\|^2 \left(\|\nabla \overline{u}_1\|^2 + \|\nabla \overline{u}_2\|^2\right) \\ \leq &\frac{8L_G^2}{\nu} e^{-\left(\nu\lambda_1 - \frac{4L_G}{\nu}\right)(t-\tau)} \|\phi(s)\|_{C_\gamma(H)}^2 + \frac{8}{\nu} \|f\|^2 + 2\left(\frac{4L_G}{\nu}\right)^2 \int_\tau^t e^{-\left(\nu\lambda_1 - \frac{4L_G}{\nu}\right)(t-r)} \|f(r)\|_{V'}^2 \mathrm{d}r. \end{aligned} \tag{66}$$

By Equation (55) in Lemma 3, we obtain

$$\begin{aligned} &\frac{\mathrm{d}}{\mathrm{d}t} \|\nabla U(t)\|^2 + \left[\frac{5\nu\lambda_1 N}{4C_\Omega} - \frac{4C_\Omega^2}{\nu} \left(\|\nabla \overline{u}_1\|^2 + \|\nabla \overline{u}_2\|^2\right)\right] \|\nabla U(t)\|^2 \\ \leq &\frac{8L_G^2}{\nu} e^{-\left(\nu\lambda_1 - \frac{4L_G}{\nu}\right)(t-\tau)} \|\phi(s)\|_{C_\gamma(H)}^2 + \frac{8}{\nu} \|f\|^2 + 2\left(\frac{4L_G}{\nu}\right)^2 \int_\tau^t e^{-\left(\nu\lambda_1 - \frac{4L_G}{\nu}\right)(t-r)} \|f(r)\|_{V'}^2 \mathrm{d}r \\ &+ \frac{5\nu\lambda_1 N^2}{4} \eta^2(U). \end{aligned} \tag{67}$$

Secondly, we define

$$\begin{cases} \xi(t) := \|\nabla U(t)\|^2, \\ P(t) := \dfrac{5\nu\lambda_1 N}{4C_\Omega} - \dfrac{4C_\Omega^2}{\nu} \left(\|\nabla \overline{u}_1\|^2 + \|\nabla \overline{u}_2\|^2\right). \\ Q(t) := \dfrac{8L_G^2}{\nu} e^{-\left(\nu\lambda_1 - \frac{4L_G}{\nu}\right)(t-\tau)} \|\phi(s)\|_{C_\gamma(H)}^2 + \dfrac{8}{\nu} \|f\|^2 + \dfrac{5\nu\lambda_1 N^2}{4} \eta^2(U) \\ \qquad + 2\left(\dfrac{4L_G}{\nu}\right)^2 \displaystyle\int_\tau^t e^{-\left(\nu\lambda_1 - \frac{4L_G}{\nu}\right)(t-r)} \|f(r)\|_{V'}^2 \mathrm{d}r. \end{cases}$$

Then, the inequality (67) can be expressed as

$$\frac{\mathrm{d}\xi(t)}{\mathrm{d}t} + P(t)\xi(t) \leq Q(t). \tag{68}$$

Next, we verify that $P(t)$ and $Q(t)$ satisfy the conditions of Lemma 4. There exist constants C_3 and C_4 such that

$$\limsup_{t \to +\infty} \frac{1}{T} \int_t^{t+T} \|\nabla \overline{u}_i(r)\|^2 \mathrm{d}r \leq C_5, \quad i = 1, 2, \tag{69}$$

where $C_5 := C_4\|\phi(s)\|^2 + C_3F^2$. Therefore, when $N > \dfrac{16C_\Omega^3 C_5}{5\nu^2\lambda_1}$, $P(r)$ and $P^-(r)$ satisfy

$$\begin{aligned}\liminf_{t\to+\infty}\frac{1}{T}\int_t^{t+T}P(r)\mathrm{d}r \geq&\frac{5\nu\lambda_1 N}{4C_\Omega}-\frac{4C_\Omega^2}{\nu}\limsup_{t\to+\infty}\frac{1}{T}\int_t^{t+T}\|\nabla\overline{u}_i(r)\|^2\mathrm{d}r\\ \geq&\frac{5\nu\lambda_1 N}{4C_\Omega}-\frac{4C_\Omega^2 C_5}{\nu}>0,\end{aligned}$$

and

$$\begin{aligned}\limsup_{t\to+\infty}\frac{1}{T}\int_t^{t+T}P^-(r)\mathrm{d}r \leq&\frac{5\nu\lambda_1 N}{4C_\Omega}+\frac{4C_\Omega^2}{\nu}\limsup_{t\to+\infty}\frac{1}{T}\int_t^{t+T}\|\nabla\overline{u}_i(r)\|^2\mathrm{d}r\\ \leq&\frac{5\nu\lambda_1 N}{4C_\Omega}+\frac{4C_\Omega^2 C_5}{\nu}<+\infty,\end{aligned}$$

they satisfy Equation (56).

By Lemma 4, this implies

$$\lim_{t\to+\infty}\eta(U(t))=0.$$

Combining them, then we have

$$\lim_{t\to+\infty}\frac{1}{T}\int_t^{t+T}\left(\frac{5\nu\lambda_1 N^2}{4}\eta^2(U(r))+\frac{8}{\nu}\|f(r)\|^2\right)\mathrm{d}r=0. \tag{70}$$

Since $\nu^2\lambda_1 > 4L_G$, we obtain

$$\begin{aligned}&\lim_{t\to+\infty}\frac{1}{T}\int_t^{t+T}e^{-(\nu\lambda_1-\frac{4L_G}{\nu})(r-\tau)}\|\phi(s)\|^2_{C_\gamma(H)}\mathrm{d}r\\ =&\lim_{t\to+\infty}\frac{1}{T(\nu\lambda_1-\frac{4L_G}{\nu})}\left(e^{-(\nu\lambda_1-\frac{4L_G}{\nu})(t+T-\tau)}-e^{-(\nu\lambda_1-\frac{4L_G}{\nu})(t-\tau)}\right)\|\phi(s)\|^2_{C_\gamma(H)}\\ =&0.\end{aligned}$$

According to Equation (58), for all $\varepsilon > 0$ there exists $T_1 > \tau$ such that when $t > T_1$, it satisfies

$$\frac{1}{T(\nu\lambda_1-\frac{4L_G}{\nu})}\sup_{z\in[T_1,+\infty)}\|f(z)\|^2\int_\tau^{t+T}[e^{-(\nu\lambda_1-\frac{4L_G}{\nu})(t-r)}-e^{-(\nu\lambda_1-\frac{4L_G}{\nu})(t+T-r)}]\mathrm{d}r<\frac{\varepsilon}{2}; \tag{71}$$

therefore, for $\forall\, T_1 > \tau$, we have

$$\lim_{t\to+\infty}\left(e^{-(\nu\lambda_1-\frac{4L_G}{\nu})(t-r)}-e^{-(\nu\lambda_1-\frac{4L_G}{\nu})(t+T-r)}\right)=0. \tag{72}$$

Hence, for the ε of Equation (71), there exists T_2 such that when $t > T_2$, we have

$$\frac{1}{T(\nu\lambda_1-\frac{4L_G}{\nu})}\int_\tau^{T_0}\|f(r)\|^2\mathrm{d}r\left[e^{-(\nu\lambda_1-\frac{4L_G}{\nu})(t-T_0)}-e^{-(\nu\lambda_1-\frac{4L_G}{\nu})(t+T-T_0)}\right]<\frac{\varepsilon}{2}. \tag{73}$$

Denote $T_0 = \max\{T_1, T_2\}$, then for $\varepsilon > 0$, when $t > T_0$, we have

$$\begin{aligned}
&\frac{1}{T}\int_t^{t+T}\int_\tau^r e^{-(\nu\lambda_1-\frac{4L_G}{\nu})(\rho-r)}\|f(r)\|^2 \mathrm{d}\rho \mathrm{d}r \\
\leq&\frac{1}{T}\int_\tau^{t+T}\int_t^{t+T} e^{-(\nu\lambda_1-\frac{4L_G}{\nu})(\rho-r)}\|f(r)\|^2 \mathrm{d}\rho \mathrm{d}r \\
=&\frac{1}{T(\frac{4L_G}{\nu}-\nu\lambda_1)}\int_\tau^{t+T}\|f(r)\|^2\cdot\left[e^{-(\nu\lambda_1-\frac{4L_G}{\nu})(t+T-r)}-e^{-(\nu\lambda_1-\frac{4L_G}{\nu})(t-r)}\right]\mathrm{d}r \\
\leq&\frac{1}{T(\nu\lambda_1-\frac{4L_G}{\nu})}\int_\tau^{T_0}\|f(r)\|^2\mathrm{d}r\cdot\left[e^{-(\nu\lambda_1-\frac{4L_G}{\nu})(t-T_0)}-e^{-(\nu\lambda_1-\frac{4L_G}{\nu})(t+T-T_0)}\right] \\
&+\frac{1}{T(\nu\lambda_1-\frac{4L_G}{\nu})}\sup_{z\in[T_0,+\infty)}\|f(z)\|^2\int_{T_0}^{t+T}\left[e^{-(\nu\lambda_1-\frac{4L_G}{\nu})(t-r)}-e^{-(\nu\lambda_1-\frac{4L_G}{\nu})(t+T-r)}\right]\mathrm{d}r \\
<&\varepsilon,
\end{aligned} \tag{74}$$

which implies

$$\lim_{t\to+\infty}\frac{1}{T}\int_t^{t+T}\int_\tau^\rho e^{-(\nu\lambda_1-\frac{4L_G}{\nu})(\rho-r)}\|f(r)\|^2 \mathrm{d}\rho \mathrm{d}r=0. \tag{75}$$

By equations (70) and (75), we can see that $Q^+(t)$ satisfies Equation (57).

Finally, by Lemma 4, we obtain

$$\lim_{t\to+\infty}\xi(t)=\lim_{t\to+\infty}\|\nabla U(t)\|^2=0.$$

According to the Poincare inequation, we have proven Equation (60). According to Definition 2, Theorem 3 is proven. □

5. Conclusions

The problem addressed in this paper is the global well-posedness and asymptotic behavior of solutions to non autonomous Navier–Stokes equations with infinite time delay and node determination. This study establishes a mathematical framework based on the function space $C_\gamma(H)$ and demonstrates the well-posedness of Equation (1) under the assumption that the function $G(\cdot,\cdot)$ satisfies Lipschitz continuity with respect to time t. Furthermore, the long-term behavior of strong solutions is shown to be characterized by their values at a finite number of spatial nodes. The result of this paper is to apply the infinite delay term $u(t+\theta)$ to the non-autonomous Navier–Stokes equations and to study the well-posedness and asymptotic behavior of the Navier–Stokes equations with delay effects using relevant existing theoretical results. This result provides theoretical support and specific examples for studying nonlinear PDEs with time delay effects to a certain extent. It not only validates the relevant conclusions obtained from time delay differential equations but also reveals the research methods for nonlinear PDEs of other time delay effects, further verifying some examples given by time delay differential equations (see [23–25]).

However, this method also has some limitations, as the construction of $C_\gamma(H)$ is only a function space established for handling the infinite delay term $u(t+\theta)$, as the asymptotic behavior of function u becomes particularly important at $t\to\infty$ and creates a convergence relationship between the infinite delay terms $u(t+\theta)$ and $u(t)$. In addition, the function $G(\cdot,\cdot)$ itself must satisfy Lipschitz properties, otherwise it will greatly affect the well-posedness of the solution of Equation (1). For the physical meaning of the Navier–Stokes equation itself, we only consider the case where the Reynolds number is particularly small to study the global well-posedness and determining nodes of Equation (1). For other cases, due to the need to consider the pressure p term, the method used in this paper may not be applicable.

The research method presented in this paper has high universality and can be applied to various types of nonlinear PDEs. By adding an infinite delay term $u(t+\theta)$ to the existing conditions of a nonlinear PDE, it becomes a nonlinear PDE with infinite delay, which has a more profound impact on the well-posedness of solutions and other related issues. This provides theoretical support and technical means for solving other complex systems, especially for the study of differential equations with infinite delay. In the current research results, only the system of non-autonomous micro polar fluid flow has been studied for global well-posedness and asymptotic behavior of solutions by adding an infinite delay term $u(t+\theta)$ on the original basis (see [32]).

Due to the existence of time delay factors, the introduction and application of numerical methods need to consider the influence of historical states, which leads to a more complex implementation of the algorithm. In order to solve Navier–Stokes equations with time delay, it is generally necessary to discretize them. Furthermore, determining nodes are the discrete points determined during this process. In the process of analyzing problems, it is usually necessary to calculate analytical and numerical solutions at determined nodes and to strictly control the time step based on the introduced time delay factors in order to avoid the instability of numerical solutions and evaluate the accuracy of numerical methods, ensuring the stability and convergence of the algorithm. By comparing these solutions, we can assess the effectiveness of the selected nodes and discretization methods, thereby improving the efficiency and accuracy of solving Navier–Stokes equations with time delays, ensuring that researchers can better simulate and control fluid systems, and enhance the reliability and performance of engineering design.

Advancements in computational technology open new avenues for research on Navier–Stokes equations with time delay, particularly in exploring time-delay effects in high-dimensional spaces and complex geometries. This includes the behavior of fluids under complex boundary conditions or multiphase flow, particularly in applications such as biomedical engineering and environmental science. In recent years, machine learning has gained prominence in fluid dynamics, offering novel approaches to modeling and real-time control of fluid systems. Integrating time-delay factors with machine learning methods presents a promising direction for developing more accurate fluid models and real-time control strategies, advancing both theoretical understanding and practical applications. These methods can be used to learn fluid behavior from experimental data and predict the system's response under different conditions.

In addition, for delay differential equations, there are various types of delay effects such as discrete delay and state-dependent delay. Future research will focus on investigating the global well-posedness and asymptotic behavior of solutions to differential equations with state-dependent delay $u(t-\sigma(t,u(t+\theta)))$ and generalize the relevant conclusions of abstract functional differential equations with state-dependent delay in reference [20] through several specific partial differential equations. The manuscript on the study of partial differential equations with state-dependent delay is currently in progress.

Author Contributions: Conceptualization, H.G.; methodology, H.G.; validation, H.G. and F.D.; writing—original draft, H.G.; writing—review and editing, H.G. and F.D. All authors have read and agreed to the published version of the manuscript.

Funding: This work is supported by the Research Project of Jingchu University of Technology (Grant Nos. HX20240049), and the NSF of Hubei Province (Grant No. 2022CFB527).

Data Availability Statement: Data sharing is not applicable to this article, as no datasets were generated or analyzed during the current study.

Conflicts of Interest: The authors declare no conflicts of interest.

References

1. Ferreira, L.C.F.; Precioso, J.C. Existence of solutions for the 3D-micropolar fluid system with initial data in Besov–Morrey spaces. *Commun. Math. Sci.* **2013**, *64*, 1699–1710. [CrossRef]
2. Galdi, P.; Rionero, S. A note on the existence and uniqueness of solusions of the micropolar fluid equations. *Int. J. Eng. Sci.* **1997**, *15*, 105–108. [CrossRef]
3. Lukaszewicz, G. *Micropolar Fluids: Theory and Applications, Modeling and Simulation in Science*; Birkhauser: Boston, MA, USA, 1999; pp. 177–215.
4. Lukaszewicz, G.; Tarasinska, A. On H^1-pullback attractors for nonautonomous micropolar fluid equations in a bounded domain. *Nonlinear Anal.-TMA* **2009**, *71*, 782–788. [CrossRef]
5. Foias, C.; Manley, O.; Rosa, R.; Temam, R. *Navier-Stokes Equations and Turbulence*; Encyclopedia of Mathematics and Its Application: Cambridge, UK, 2004; pp. 255–343.
6. Caraballo, T.; Lukaszewicz, G.; Real, J. Pullback attractors for non-autonomous 2D-Navier-Stokes equations in several unbounded domains. *Dynam. Syst.* **2006**, *342*, 263–268.
7. García-Luengo, J.; Marín-Rubio, P.; Real, J. H^2-boundedness of the pullback attractors for non-autonomous 2D Navier-Stokes equations in bounded domains. *Nonlinear Anal.* **2011**, *74*, 4882–4887. [CrossRef]
8. García-Luengo, J.; Marín-Rubio P.; Real, J. Pullback attractors in V for non-autonomous 2D-Navier-Stokes equations and their tempered behaviour. *J. Differ. Equ.* **2012**, *252*, 4333–4356. [CrossRef]
9. García-Luengo, J.; Marín-Rubio, P.; Real, J. Pullback attractors for 2D Navier-Stokes equations with delays and their regularity. *Adv. Nonlinear Stud.* **2013**, *13*, 331–357. [CrossRef]
10. Hoff, D.; Ziane, M. The global attractor and finite determining nodes for the Navier-Stokes equations of compressible flow with singular initial data. *Indiana U. Math. J.* **2003**, *49*, 843–890.
11. Jolly, M.S.; Sadigoy, T.; Titi, E.S. A determining form for the damped driven nonlinear Schröinger equation—Fourier modes case. *J. Differ. Equ.* **2015**, *258*, 2711–2744. [CrossRef]
12. Kakizawa, R. Determining nodes for semilinear parabolic equations *J. Math. Anal. Appl.* **2011**, *378*, 375–386. [CrossRef]
13. Marín-Rubio, P.; Real, J. Attractors for 2D-Navier-Stokes equations with delays on several unbounded domains. *Nonlinear Anal.-TMA* **2007**, *67*, 2784–2799. [CrossRef]
14. Marín-Rubio, P.; Real, J. Pullback attractors for 2D-Navier-Stokes equations with delays in continuous and sub-linear operators. *Discrete Cont. Dyn.-A* **2010**, *26*, 989–1006. [CrossRef]
15. Szopa, P. Determining modes for 2D micropolar fluid flows. *Math. Comput. Model.* **2004**, *42*, 1079–1088. [CrossRef]
16. Marín-Rubio, P.; Real, J.; Valero, J. Pullback attractors for a two-dimensional Navier-Stokes model in an infinite delay case. *Nonlinear Anal.-Theor.* **2011**, *74*, 2012–2030. [CrossRef]
17. Ning, Z.; Shen, C.; Zhao, X.; Li, H.; Lin, C.; Zhang, Y. Nonlinear boundary stabilization of the wave equations with variable coefficients and time dependent delay. *Appl. Math. Comput.* **2014**, 232, 511–520. [CrossRef]
18. Caraballo, T.; Real, J. Attractors for 2D-Navier-Stokes models with delays. *J. Differ. Equ.* **2004**, *205*, 271–297. [CrossRef]
19. Hale, J.K.; Verduyn Lunel, S.M. *Introduction to Functional Differential Equations*; Springer: New York, NY, USA, 1993; pp. 144–195.
20. Hernandez, E.; Fernandes, D; Wu, J. Existence and uniqueness of solutions, well-posedness and global attractor for abstract differential equations with state-dependent delay. *J. Differ. Equ.* **2021**, *302*, 753–806. [CrossRef]
21. Chueshov, I. Finite-Dimensional global attractors for parabolic nonlinear equations with state-dependent dealy. *Commun. Pur. Appl. Anal.* **2015**, *14*, 1685–1704. [CrossRef]
22. Hernandez, E.; Pierri, M.; Wu, J. Existence and uniqueness of $C^{1+\alpha}$-strict solutions for integro-differential equations with state-dependent delay. *J. Differ. Equ.* **2016**, *261*, 6856–6882. [CrossRef]
23. Fu, X.; Liu, X. Existence of periodic solutions for abstract neutral non-autonomous equations with infinite delay. *J. Math. Anal. Appl.* **2007**, *325*, 249–267. [CrossRef]
24. Chang, J. Solutions to non-autonomous integrodifferential equations with infinite delay. *J. Math. Anal. Appl.* **2007**, *331*, 137–151. [CrossRef]
25. Huang, A.; Huo, W.; Ma, J. Finite-Dimensionality and Determining Modes of the Global Attractor for 2D Boussinesq Equations with Fractional Laplacian. *Adv. Nonlinear Stud.* **2018**, *18*, 501–515. [CrossRef]
26. Lukaszewicz, G. Long time behavior of 2D micropolar fluid flows. *Math. Comp. Model. Dyn.* **2001**, *34*, 487–509. [CrossRef]
27. Lukaszewicz, G.; Sadowski, W. Uniform attractor for 2D magneto-micropolar fluid flow in several unbounded domains. *Z. Angew. Math. Phys.* **2004**, *55*, 247–257.
28. Jones, D. On the Number of Determining Nodes for the 2D Navier-Stokes Equations. *J. Math. Anal. Appl.* **1992**, *168*, 72–88. [CrossRef]

29. Foias, C.; Temam, R. Determination of the solutions of the Navier-Stokes equations by a set of nodal values. *Math. Comput.* **1984**, *43*, 117–133. [CrossRef]
30. Lu, Y. Uniform attractors for the closed process and applications to the reaction-diffusion equation with dynamical boundary condition. *Nonlinear Anal.-Real.* **2009**, *71*, 4012–4025. [CrossRef]
31. Sun, W.; Lai, C.; Liang, Y. Determining modes and determining nodes for the 3D non-autonomous regularized magnetohydrodynamics equations. *Discrete Contin. Dyn. Syst. Ser. B* **2023**, *28*, 3373–3392. [CrossRef]
32. Zhao, C.; Sun, W. Global well-posedness and pullback attractors for a two-dimensional non-autonomous micropolar fluid flows with infnite delays. *Commun. Math. Sci.* **2017**, *15*, 97–121. [CrossRef]

mathematics

MDPI

Article

Nonlinear Neutral Delay Differential Equations: Novel Criteria for Oscillation and Asymptotic Behavior

Belal Batiha [1,*], Nawa Alshammari [2], Faten Aldosari [3], Fahd Masood [4] and Omar Bazighifan [5,6,*]

[1] Mathematics Department, Faculty of Science and Information Technology, Jadara University, Irbid 21110, Jordan
[2] Department of Basic Sciences, College of Science and Theoretical Studies, Saudi Electronic University, Riyadh 11673, Saudi Arabia; n.alshammari@seu.edu.sa
[3] Department of Mathematics, College of Science, Shaqra University, P.O. Box 15572, Shaqra 11961, Saudi Arabia; faldosari@su.edu.sa
[4] Department of Mathematics, Faculty of Education and Science, University of Saba Region, Marib 14400, Yemen; fahdmasoud22@gmail.com
[5] Department of Mathematics, Faculty of Education, Seiyun University, Seiyun 50512, Yemen
[6] Jadara Research Center, Jadara University, Irbid 21110, Jordan
* Correspondence: b.bateha@jadara.edu.jo (B.B.); o.bazighifan@gmail.com (O.B.)

Abstract: This research deals with the study of the oscillatory behavior of solutions of second-order differential equations containing neutral conditions, both in sublinear and superlinear terms, with a focus on the noncanonical case. The research provides a careful analysis of the monotonic properties of solutions and their derivatives, paving the way for a deeper understanding of this complex behavior. The research is particularly significant as it extends the scope of previous studies by addressing more complex forms of neutral differential equations. Using the linearization technique, strict conditions are developed that exclude the existence of positive solutions, which allows the formulation of innovative criteria for determining the oscillatory behavior of the studied equations. This research highlights the theoretical and applied aspects of this mathematical phenomenon, which contributes to enhancing the scientific understanding of differential equations with neutral conditions. To demonstrate the effectiveness of the results, the research includes two illustrative examples that prove the validity and importance of the proposed methodology. This work represents a qualitative addition to the mathematical literature, as it lays new foundations and opens horizons for future studies in this vital field.

Keywords: oscillation; non-oscillation; sublinear type; superlinear type; neutral differential equation; second order

MSC: 34C10; 34K11

1. Introduction

In this paper, we study the second-order noncanonical neutral differential equation of the following form:

$$\left(\kappa(\mathrm{s})\left[(y(\mathrm{s})+g_1(\mathrm{s})y^{\gamma_1}(\mathfrak{r}_1(\mathrm{s}))+g_2(\mathrm{s})y^{\gamma_2}(\mathfrak{r}_2(\mathrm{s})))'\right]^{\alpha}\right)'+q(\mathrm{s})y^{\beta}(\sigma(\mathrm{s}))=0,\ \mathrm{s}\geq \mathrm{s}_0. \quad (1)$$

To ensure a comprehensive study of this equation, we assume the following hypotheses:

H1. $\alpha>1$, $\beta>0$, $\gamma_1>1$ *and* $\gamma_2<1$ *are ratios of odd positive integers;*

H2. $g_1, g_2, q\in C([\mathrm{s}_0,\infty),\mathbb{R}^+)$, *and* $q\neq 0$;

H3. $\tau_1, \tau_2, \sigma \in C^1([s_0,\infty),\mathbb{R})$ *satisfy* $\sigma(s) \leq s$, $\tau_1(s) \leq s$, $\tau_2(s) \leq s$, $\sigma'(s) > 0$ *and* $\lim_{s\to\infty} \tau_1(s) = \lim_{s\to\infty} \tau_2(s) = \lim_{s\to\infty} \sigma(s) = \infty$;

H4. $\kappa \in C^1([s_0,\infty),\mathbb{R}^+)$. *We define*

$$\pi(s) = \int_s^\infty \frac{1}{\kappa^{1/\alpha}(v)} dv,$$

and

$$\pi(s,s_0) := \int_{s_0}^s \frac{1}{\kappa^{1/\alpha}(v)} dv < \infty \text{ as } s \to \infty. \tag{2}$$

Below, we provide some basic definitions:

(1) A function $y(s) \in C([s_y,\infty),\mathbb{R})$, $s_y \geqslant s_0$, is said to be a solution of (1) if it has the property $\kappa(s)\left[(y(s) + g_1(s)y^{\gamma_1}(\tau_1(s)) + g_2(s)y^{\gamma_2}(\tau_2(s)))'\right]^\alpha \in C^1[s_y,\infty)$, and it satisfies the Equation (1) for all $s \in [s_y,\infty)$. We consider only those solutions $y(s)$ of (1) that exist on some half-line $[s_y,\infty)$ and satisfy the condition

$$\sup\{|y(s)| : s \geqslant S\} > 0, \text{ for all } S \geq s_y.$$

(2) The solution of (1) is said to be oscillatory if it is neither eventually positive nor eventually negative.
(3) If the solution of (1) is eventually positive or negative, it is non-oscillatory.
(4) The equation is considered oscillatory if all its solutions are oscillatory.

Since the time of Newton, differential equations (DEs) have been one of the basic tools for understanding dynamic systems and modeling natural phenomena, as they are used to describe changes in physical, chemical, and biological systems. With the continuous development of science and the expansion of its applications, the need for more accurate and comprehensive models has emerged. Among these models are delay differential equations (DDEs), which are characterized by taking into account the effect of the temporal memory of systems, making them more efficient in representing many natural phenomena, see [1,2].

However, finding accurate solutions to these equations represents a major challenge that hinders a deep understanding of these phenomena. Therefore, qualitative theories are an essential tool that allows studying the properties of equations without the need to find their detailed solutions. Among these theories, Oscillation Theory stands out, which focuses on studying the oscillatory and non-oscillatory behavior of solutions, in addition to the infinite analysis of the distribution of roots. Recent advancements have further enriched this foundational theory, see Chuanxi and Ladas [3], Kiguradze and Chanturia [4], Bazighifan [5,6], and Masood et al. [7], which provide innovative criteria and methodologies to analyze these complex equations.

The study of oscillation criteria for second-order DEs has been a cornerstone of mathematical analysis due to its wide applicability in physical and engineering systems. Agarwal et al. [8] laid the foundation for oscillation control criteria, and subsequent research [9] extended to include linear and nonlinear equations. Džurina et al. [10] developed further criteria specific to delay differential equations, while Erbe et al. [11] provided criteria for nonlinear equations. Later, Hassan [12] and Grace et al. [13] improved these neutral equations. In recent years, Zhang et al. [14] and Baculíková [15] contributed significantly to the understanding of second-order equations with noncanonical operators and deviating arguments, respectively. Jadlovská [16] extended these findings to include Kneser-type criteria and sublinear neutral terms. Li et al. [17] and Grace et al. [18] introduced advanced differential equations with diverse terms. Finally, Muhib [19] presented important developments in the study of noncanonical neutral equations. For more details, see Moaaz et al. [20], Masood et al. [21], Alsharidi and Muhib [22], and Alemam et al. [23].

Various oscillation criteria for second order NDEs impose specific constraints on their coefficients:

Agarwal et al. [24] and Han et al. [25] studied the oscillation of second-order linear NDEs

$$\left(\kappa(\mathrm{s})(y(\mathrm{s})+g(\mathrm{s})y(\tau(\mathrm{s})))'\right)'+q(\mathrm{s})y(\sigma(\mathrm{s}))=0,$$

introducing new criteria under the condition $0 \leq g(\mathrm{s}) \leq g_0 < \infty$.

Agarwal et al. [26] considered NDEs with a nonlinear term

$$\left(\kappa(\mathrm{s})(y(\mathrm{s})+g_1(\mathrm{s})y^{\gamma_1}(\tau_1(\mathrm{s})))'\right)'+q(\mathrm{s})y(\sigma(\mathrm{s}))=0,$$

where $0 < \gamma_1 \leq 1$. They introduced conditions to ensure oscillation in the cases

$$\int_{\mathrm{s}}^{\infty} \frac{1}{\kappa(v)} \mathrm{d}v = \infty,$$

and

$$\int_{\mathrm{s}}^{\infty} \frac{1}{\kappa(v)} \mathrm{d}v < \infty.$$

Wang et al. [27] investigated the asymptotic properties of second-order nonlinear delay equations

$$\left(\kappa(\mathrm{s})\left[(y(\mathrm{s})-g_1(\mathrm{s})y(\tau_1(\mathrm{s})))'\right]^{\alpha}\right)'+q(\mathrm{s})f(y(\sigma(\mathrm{s})))=0,$$

with a non-positive neutral coefficient, and $f(u) \geq ky^{\alpha}(u)$.

Tamilvanan et al. [28] addressed the oscillatory nature of a similar DEs with a nonlinear neutral term.

$$\left(\kappa(\mathrm{s})(y(\mathrm{s})+g_1(\mathrm{s})y^{\gamma_1}(\tau_1(\mathrm{s})))'\right)'+q(\mathrm{s})y^{\beta}(\sigma(\mathrm{s}))=0.$$

Džurina and Jadlovská [29] introduced criteria to ensure the oscillation of nonlinear equations

$$\left(\kappa(\mathrm{s})\left[y'(\mathrm{s})\right]^{\alpha}\right)'+q(\mathrm{s})y^{\beta}(\sigma(\mathrm{s}))=0.$$

in a noncanonical form.

Džurina et al. [30] and Wu et al. [31] used the Riccati method to study the oscillation in the nonlinear NDEs

$$\left(\kappa(\mathrm{s})\left[(y(\mathrm{s})+g(\mathrm{s})y^{\gamma_1}(\tau(\mathrm{s})))'\right]^{\alpha}\right)'+q(\mathrm{s})y^{\beta}(\sigma(\mathrm{s}))=0.$$

Despite the importance of these models, understanding the oscillatory behavior of their solutions, especially in nonlinear and noncanonical cases, remains a major challenge. Most previous research has focused on linear or quasi-linear forms of these equations, creating a knowledge gap regarding more complex cases.

This research aims to fill this gap by establishing novel and generalized criteria for analyzing the oscillatory behavior of neutral second-order differential equations. Previous studies primarily considered neutral terms of the form

$$u(\mathrm{s}) := y(\mathrm{s})+g_1(\mathrm{s})y(\tau_1(\mathrm{s})),$$

as presented in [25], with some extending to sublinear cases such as

$$\mathrm{u}(\mathrm{s}) := y(\mathrm{s}) + g_1(\mathrm{s}) y^{\gamma_1}(\mathfrak{r}_1(\mathrm{s})),\ \gamma_1 < 1,$$

as presented in [26,28,31]. In contrast, this study introduces a more comprehensive framework that incorporates both sublinear $\gamma_1 < 1$ and superlinear $\gamma_2 > 1$ terms within the generalized relationship:

$$\mathrm{u}(\mathrm{s}) := y(\mathrm{s}) + g_1(\mathrm{s}) y^{\gamma_1}(\mathfrak{r}_1(\mathrm{s})) + g_2(\mathrm{s}) y^{\gamma_2}(\mathfrak{r}_2(\mathrm{s})).$$

This dual consideration of multiple nonlinear terms significantly broadens the scope of oscillation theory for neutral differential equations. Through advanced techniques, including linearization and rigorous analytical methods, new criteria are derived and validated with illustrative examples, demonstrating their effectiveness and applicability. This research contributes to the existing literature by expanding the understanding of oscillatory and asymptotic properties of neutral differential equations, providing a solid foundation for future investigations into more complex systems.

2. Preliminary Results

Let us define

$$\mathrm{u}(\mathrm{s}) := y(\mathrm{s}) + g_1(\mathrm{s}) y^{\gamma_1}(\mathfrak{r}_1(\mathrm{s})) + g_2(\mathrm{s}) y^{\gamma_2}(\mathfrak{r}_2(\mathrm{s})),$$

$$\mu(\mathrm{s},\mathrm{s}_0) := \begin{cases} 1, & \text{if } \alpha = \beta, \\ M_1^{\beta-\alpha}, & \text{if } \alpha < \beta, \\ M_2^{\beta-\alpha} \pi^{\beta-\alpha}(\mathrm{s},\mathrm{s}_1), & \text{if } \alpha > \beta, \end{cases}$$

$$\mu_1(\mathrm{s},\mathrm{s}_0) := \begin{cases} 1, & \text{if } \alpha = \beta, \\ M_3^{\beta-\alpha}, & \text{if } \alpha > \beta, \\ M_4^{\beta-\alpha} \pi^{\beta-\alpha}(\mathrm{s}), & \text{if } \alpha < \beta, \end{cases}$$

$$\mathrm{H}(\mathrm{s}) := \frac{1}{\alpha} C^{\beta} \pi^{\alpha-1}(\sigma(\mathrm{s}),\mathrm{s}_0) q(\mathrm{s}),$$

and

$$\widetilde{\mathrm{H}}(\mathrm{s}) := \rho(\mathrm{s}) \int_{\mathrm{s}}^{\infty} \mu(\sigma(v),\mathrm{s}_0) \mathrm{H}(v) dv.$$

Lemma 1 ([32]). *Let α be a ratio of two odd positive integers, $A > 0$ and B are constants. Then,*

$$Bu - Au^{(\alpha+1)/\alpha} \leq \frac{\alpha^{\alpha}}{(\alpha+1)^{\alpha+1}} \frac{B^{\alpha+1}}{A^{\alpha}},\ A > 0. \tag{3}$$

Lemma 2. *Assume that $y(\mathrm{s})$ is an eventually positive solution of (1). Then, the corresponding function $\mathrm{u}(\mathrm{s})$ satisfies one of two cases eventually:*

$$(\mathrm{N}_1) \ : \ \mathrm{u}(\mathrm{s}) > 0, \kappa(\mathrm{s})(\mathrm{u}'(\mathrm{s}))^{\alpha} > 0, \left(\kappa(\mathrm{s})(\mathrm{u}'(\mathrm{s}))^{\alpha}\right)' < 0,$$
$$(\mathrm{N}_2) \ : \ \mathrm{u}(\mathrm{s}) > 0, \kappa(\mathrm{s})(\mathrm{u}'(\mathrm{s}))^{\alpha} < 0, \left(\kappa(\mathrm{s})(\mathrm{u}'(\mathrm{s}))^{\alpha}\right)' < 0,$$

for $\mathrm{s} \geqslant \mathrm{s}_1 \geqslant \mathrm{s}_0$.

Proof. Assume that $y(s)$ is a positive solution of (1). In view of (H_1)–(H_4), there exists $s_1 \geqslant s_0$ such that $y(\sigma(s)) > 0$, $y(\mathfrak{r}_1(s)) > 0$ and $y(\mathfrak{r}_2(s)) > 0$, for all $s \geqslant s_1$, then,

$$u(s) = y(s) + g_1(s)y^{\gamma_1}(\mathfrak{r}_1(s)) + g_2(s)y^{\gamma_2}(\mathfrak{r}_2(s)) > 0,$$

for all $s \geqslant s_1$. Then, from (1), we obtain

$$\left(\kappa(s)(u'(s))^{\alpha}\right)' = -q(s)(y(\sigma(s)))^{\beta} < 0.$$

From the above inequality, we can obtain that $\kappa(s)(u'(s))^{\alpha}$ is decreasing. Then, $\kappa(s)(u'(s))^{\alpha} > 0$ or $\kappa(s)(u'(s))^{\alpha} < 0$. Hence, the proof is complete. □

Notation 1. *The notation* N_i *denotes the set comprising all solutions that eventually become positive and satisfy condition* (N_i) *for* $i = 1, 2$.

3. Main Results

In this section, we provide key results regarding the monotonic behavior of solutions to Equation (1) and its derivatives. Additionally, we establish conditions that rule out the existence of positive solutions, addressing the cases (N_1) and (N_2) separately.

3.1. Category N_1

In this subsection, we introduce a collection of lemmas focused on the asymptotic properties of solutions belonging to the (N_1) class.

Lemma 3. *Let* $y(s) \in N_1$. *Assume that*

$$\lim_{s\to\infty} g_1(s)\pi^{\gamma_1-1}(s, s_1) = 0, \text{ and } \lim_{s\to\infty} g_2(s) = 0. \tag{4}$$

Then, eventually

(A_{11}) $u(s) \geqslant \kappa^{1/\alpha}(s)u'(s)\pi(s, s_0)$;
(A_{12}) $u(s)/\pi(s, s_0)$ *is decreasing;*
(A_{13}) $u^{\beta-\alpha}(s) \geq \mu(s, s_0)$;
(A_{14}) $y(s) \geq Cu(s)$, *where* $C \in (0, 1)$.

Proof. Let $y(s) \in N_1$. Then, there exists an $s_1 \geq s_0$, such that $y(s) > 0$, $y(\mathfrak{r}_1(s)) > 0$, $y(\mathfrak{r}_2(s)) > 0$ and $y(\sigma(s)) > 0$ for $s \geq s_1$.

(A_{11}) With the monotonicity property of $\kappa^{1/\alpha}(s)u'(s)$, we obtain

$$\begin{aligned} u(s) &= u(s_1) + \int_{s_1}^{s} \frac{\kappa^{1/\alpha}(v)u'(v)}{\kappa^{1/\alpha}(v)} dv \\ &\geq u(s_1) + \kappa^{1/\alpha}(s)u'(s) \int_{s_1}^{s} \frac{1}{\kappa^{1/\alpha}(v)} dv \\ &\geq \kappa^{1/\alpha}(s)u'(s)\pi(s, s_1), \ s \geq s_1. \end{aligned}$$

(A_{12}) Using the above inequality, we deduce that

$$\left(\frac{u(s)}{\pi(s, s_1)}\right)' = \frac{\kappa^{1/\alpha}(s)u'(s)\pi(s, s_1) - u(s)}{\kappa^{1/\alpha}(s)\pi^2(s, s_1)} \leq 0.$$

(A_{13}) We have the following cases:

Case $\alpha \leq \beta$: Since $u'(s) > 0$, there exists a constant $M_1 > 0$, such that

$$u(s) \geq M_1,$$

and therefore,

$$u^{\beta-\alpha}(s) \geq M_1^{\beta-\alpha}.$$

Case $\alpha > \beta$: Since $u(s)/\pi(s, s_1)$ is a decreasing function for $s \geq s_1$ we can find $s_2 \geq s_1$ and a constant $M_2 > 0$ such that

$$u(s) \leq M_2 \pi(s, s_1).$$

Thus

$$u^{\beta-\alpha}(s) \geq M_2^{\beta-\alpha} \pi^{\beta-\alpha}(s, s_1).$$

(A_{14}) From the definition of $u(s)$, we have $u(s) \geq y(s)$. Then, we express $y(s)$ as

$$\begin{aligned} y(s) &= u(s) - g_1(s) y^{\gamma_1}(\tau_1(s)) - g_2(s) y^{\gamma_2}(\tau_2(s)) \\ &\geq u(s) - g_1(s) u^{\gamma_1}(\tau_1(s)) - g_2(s) u^{\gamma_2}(\tau_2(s)). \end{aligned}$$

Now, because $\gamma_1 > 1$, and $\gamma_2 < 1$, and noting that $u' > 0$, we find

$$\begin{aligned} y(s) &\geq u(s) - g_1(s) u^{\gamma_1}(s) - g_2(s) u^{\gamma_2}(s) \\ &= \left[1 - g_1(s) \pi^{\gamma_1 - 1}(s, s_1) \left(\frac{u(s)}{\pi(s, s_1)}\right)^{\gamma_1 - 1} - g_2(s) u^{\gamma_2 - 1}(s)\right] u(s). \end{aligned} \tag{5}$$

Since $u(s)/\pi(s, s_1)$ is decreasing and positive, and $u(s)$ is increasing, there exist two constants, c_1 and c_2 such that

$$\left(\frac{u(s)}{\pi(s, s_1)}\right)^{\gamma_1 - 1} \leq c_1,$$

and

$$u^{\gamma_2 - 1}(s) \leq c_2.$$

So (5) it becomes

$$y(s) \geq \left[1 - c_1 g_1(s) \pi^{\gamma_1 - 1}(s, s_1) - c_2 g_2(s)\right] u(s).$$

By (4), we can choose $C \in (0, 1)$ such that

$$y(s) \geq C u(s).$$

Accordingly, the proof is finished. □

Lemma 4. *Assume that (4) holds. If*

$$\int_{s_0}^{\infty} \frac{1}{\kappa^{1/\alpha}(t)} \int_{s_0}^{t} \mu(\sigma(v), s_0) \pi^{\alpha - 1}(\sigma(v), s_1) q(v) dv dt = \infty, \tag{6}$$

then $N_1 = \varnothing$.

Proof. Let $y \in N_1$. Then, there exists an $s_1 \geq s_0$, such that

$$y(\tau_1(s)) > 0,\ y(\tau_2(s)) \text{ and } y(\sigma(s)) > 0 \text{ for } s \geq s_1 \geq s_0.$$

We begin with the relation

$$\left(\kappa(s)\left(u'(s)\right)^{\alpha}\right)' = \alpha\left(\kappa^{1/\alpha}(s)u'(s)\right)'\left(\kappa^{1/\alpha}(s)u'(s)\right)^{\alpha-1},$$

we can derive

$$\left(\kappa^{1/\alpha}(s)u'(s)\right)' = \frac{1}{\alpha}\left(\kappa(s)\left(u'(s)\right)^{\alpha}\right)'\left(\kappa^{1/\alpha}(s)u'(s)\right)^{1-\alpha}.$$

Using (1) and (A_{14}) gives

$$\begin{aligned}\left(\kappa^{1/\alpha}(s)u'(s)\right)' &= -\frac{1}{\alpha}\left(\kappa^{1/\alpha}(s)u'(s)\right)^{1-\alpha}q(s)y^{\beta}(\sigma(s)) \\ &\leq -\frac{1}{\alpha}C^{\beta}\left(\kappa^{1/\alpha}(s)u'(s)\right)^{1-\alpha}q(s)u^{\beta}(\sigma(s)).\end{aligned}$$

Applying Lemma 3, we deduce

$$\begin{aligned}\left(\kappa^{1/\alpha}(s)u'(s)\right)' &\leq -\frac{1}{\alpha}C^{\beta}\left(\kappa^{1/\alpha}(s)u'(s)\right)^{1-\alpha}q(s)u^{\beta-\alpha}(\sigma(s))u^{\alpha}(\sigma(s)) \\ &\leq -\frac{1}{\alpha}C^{\beta}\left(\kappa^{1/\alpha}(s)u'(s)\right)^{1-\alpha}q(s)\mu(\sigma(s),s_0)u^{\alpha}(\sigma(s)) \\ &\leq -\frac{1}{\alpha}C^{\beta}\left(\frac{u(s)}{\pi(s,s_1)}\right)^{1-\alpha}q(s)\mu(\sigma(s),s_0)u^{\alpha}(\sigma(s)) \\ &\leq -\frac{1}{\alpha}C^{\beta}\left(\frac{u(\sigma(s))}{\pi(\sigma(s),s_1)}\right)^{1-\alpha}q(s)\mu(\sigma(s),s_0)u^{\alpha}(\sigma(s)) \\ &= -\frac{1}{\alpha}C^{\beta}\mu(\sigma(s),s_0)\pi^{\alpha-1}(\sigma(s),s_1)q(s)u(\sigma(s)).\end{aligned}$$

Thus,

$$\left(\kappa^{1/\alpha}(s)u'(s)\right)' \leq -\frac{1}{\alpha}C^{\beta}\mu(\sigma(s),s_0)\pi^{\alpha-1}(\sigma(s),s_1)q(s)u(\sigma(s)). \tag{7}$$

Since $u(s)$ is an increasing function, there exists a constant $M_2 > 0$ such that $u(s) \geq M_2$. Using this in inequality (7), we obtain

$$\left(\kappa^{1/\alpha}(s)u'(s)\right)' \leq -\frac{1}{\alpha}M_2C^{\beta}\mu(\sigma(s),s_0)\pi^{\alpha-1}(\sigma(s),s_1)q(s). \tag{8}$$

Integrating this inequality from s_1 to s, we have

$$\kappa^{1/\alpha}(s)u'(s) \leq \kappa^{1/\alpha}(s)u'(s) - \kappa^{1/\alpha}(s_1)u'(s_1) \leq -\frac{1}{\alpha}C^{\beta}M_2\int_{s_1}^{s}\mu(\sigma(v),s_0)\pi^{\alpha-1}(\sigma(v),s_1)q(v)dv,$$

which implies that

$$u'(s) \leq -\frac{1}{\alpha}\frac{C^{\beta}M_2}{\kappa^{1/\alpha}(s)}\int_{s_1}^{s}\mu(\sigma(v),s_0)\pi^{\alpha-1}(\sigma(v),s_1)q(v)dv.$$

Integrating this inequality from s_1 to s, we have

$$u(s) \leq -\frac{1}{\alpha}C^{\beta}M_2\int_{s_1}^{s}\frac{1}{\kappa^{1/\alpha}(t)}\int_{s_1}^{t}\mu(\sigma(v),s_0)\pi^{\alpha-1}(\sigma(v),s_1)q(v)dvdt.$$

As $s \to \infty$, this leads to a contradiction with the assumption that $u(s)$ is positive. This concludes the proof. □

Lemma 5. *Let (4) hold. Assume that there exists a non-decreasing function* $\rho(s) \in C^1([s_0, \infty,), (0, \infty))$, *and* $\sigma'(s) > 0$. *If*

$$\limsup_{s \to \infty} \left[\widetilde{H}(s) + \int_{s_0}^{s} \left(\rho(v)\mu(\sigma(v), s_0)H(v) - \frac{\kappa^{1/\alpha}(v)[\rho'(v)]^2}{4\sigma'(v)\rho(v)} \right) dv \right] = \infty, \tag{9}$$

then $N_1 = \varnothing$.

Proof. Let $y \in N_1$. Then, there exists an $s_1 \geq s_0$, such that

$$y(s) > 0,\ y(\mathfrak{r}_1(s)) > 0,\ y(\mathfrak{r}_2(s)) \text{ and } y(\sigma(s)) > 0 \text{ for } s \geq s_1 \geq s_0.$$

Using (7), we obtain

$$\left(\kappa^{1/\alpha}(s)u'(s) \right)' \leq -\frac{1}{\alpha} C^{\beta} \mu(\sigma(s), s_0) \pi^{\alpha-1}(\sigma(s), s_1) q(s) u(\sigma(s)).$$

Integrating the above inequality from s to ∞, we have

$$\begin{aligned} \kappa^{1/\alpha}(s)u'(s) &\geq \frac{1}{\alpha} C^{\beta} \int_{s}^{\infty} \mu(\sigma(v), s_0) \pi^{\alpha-1}(\sigma(v), s_1) q(v) u(\sigma(v)) dv \\ &\geq u(\sigma(s)) \int_{s}^{\infty} \mu(\sigma(v), s_0) H(v) dv. \end{aligned} \tag{10}$$

Define

$$\varphi(s) = \rho(s) \frac{\kappa^{1/\alpha}(s)u'(s)}{u(\sigma(s))} \geq \rho(s) \int_{s}^{\infty} \mu(\sigma(v), s_0) H(v) dv > 0. \tag{11}$$

Then

$$\begin{aligned} \varphi'(s) &= \rho'(s) \frac{\kappa^{1/\alpha}(s)u'(s)}{u(\sigma(s))} - \rho(s)\mu(\sigma(s), s_0)H(s) - \rho(s)\sigma'(s) \frac{\kappa^{1/\alpha}(s)u'(s)u'(\sigma(s))}{u^2(\sigma(s))} \\ &\leq \frac{\rho'(s)}{\rho(s)} \varphi(s) - \rho(s)\mu(\sigma(s), s_0)H(s) - \rho(s)\sigma'(s) \frac{\kappa^{1/\alpha}(s)[u'(s)]^2}{u^2(\sigma(s))} \\ &= \frac{\rho'(s)}{\rho(s)} \varphi(s) - \rho(s)\mu(\sigma(s), s_0)H(s) - \frac{\sigma'(s)}{\kappa^{1/\alpha}(s)\rho(s)} \varphi^2(s). \end{aligned} \tag{12}$$

Using Lemma 1, we see that

$$\frac{\rho'(s)}{\rho(s)} w(s) - \frac{\sigma'(s)}{\kappa^{1/\alpha}(s)\rho(s)} w^2(s) \leq \frac{1}{4} \frac{\kappa^{1/\alpha}(s)[\rho'(s)]^2}{\sigma'(s)\rho(s)}.$$

By substituting the above inequality in (13), we obtain

$$\varphi'(s) \leq -\rho(s)\mu(\sigma(s), s_0)H(s) + \frac{1}{4} \frac{\kappa^{1/\alpha}(s)[\rho'(s)]^2}{\sigma'(s)\rho(s)}.$$

Integrating the last inequality from s_2 to s and then using (11), we deduce that

$$\rho(s)\int_s^{\infty}\mu(\sigma(v),s_0)H(v)dv+\int_{s_2}^{s}\left[\rho(v)\mu(\sigma(v),s_0)H(v)-\frac{1}{4}\frac{\kappa^{1/\alpha}(v)[\rho'(v)]^2}{\sigma'(v)\rho(v)}\right]dv\le\varphi(s_2).$$

By applying the lim sup to both sides of this inequality as $s\to\infty$, we reach a contradiction. This concludes the proof. □

By setting $\rho(s)=1$, and considering Lemma 5, we immediately derive the following result.

Corollary 1. *Let (4) hold. If*

$$\limsup_{s\to\infty}\int_{s_0}^{s}\mu(\sigma(v),s_0)H(v)dv=\infty, \tag{13}$$

then $N_1=\varnothing$.

Lemma 6. *Let (4) hold. If*

$$\int_{s_0}^{\infty}\pi^{\beta}(\sigma(v))q(v)dv=\infty, \tag{14}$$

then $N_1=\varnothing$.

Proof. Let $y\in N_1$. Then, there exists an $s_1\ge s_0$, such that

$$y(s)>0,\ y(\tau_1(s))>0,\ y(\tau_2(s))\text{ and }y(\sigma(s))>0\text{ for }s\ge s_1\ge s_0.$$

Using Lemma 3 (A_{14}), the expression in (1) can be transformed into the following inequality

$$\left(\kappa(s)\left(u'(s)\right)^{\alpha}\right)'+C^{\beta}q(s)u^{\beta}(\sigma(s))\le 0. \tag{15}$$

Integrating the last inequality from s_2 to s, we have

$$\begin{aligned}\kappa(s)\left(u'(s)\right)^{\alpha}&\le\kappa(s_2)\left(u'(s_2)\right)^{\alpha}-C^{\beta}\int_{s_2}^{s}q(v)u^{\beta}(\sigma(v))dv\\&\le\kappa(s_2)\left(u'(s_2)\right)^{\alpha}-C^{\beta}u^{\beta}(\sigma(s_2))\int_{s_2}^{s}q(v)dv.\end{aligned} \tag{16}$$

Since $\pi'<0$, we deduce that

$$\int_{s_2}^{s}\pi^{\beta}(\sigma(v))q(v)dv\le\pi^{\beta}(\sigma(s_2))\int_{s_2}^{s}q(v)dv.$$

From (14), it follows that

$$\int_{s_2}^{s}q(v)dv\to\infty\text{ as }s\to\infty.$$

Consequently, from Equation (16), we deduce that $u'(s)\to-\infty$ as $s\to\infty$, which leads to a contradiction. □

3.2. Category N_2

In this subsection, we introduce a collection of lemmas focused on the asymptotic properties of solutions belonging to the (N_2) class.

Lemma 7. *Let $y(s) \in N_2$. Assume that*

$$\lim_{s\to\infty} g_1(s)\left(\frac{\pi(\tau_1(s))}{\pi(s)}\right)^{\gamma_1} = 0, \text{ and } \lim_{s\to\infty} g_2(s)\frac{\pi^{\gamma_2}(\tau_2(s))}{\pi(s)} = 0. \tag{17}$$

Then, eventually

(A_{21}) $u(s) \geqslant -\kappa^{1/\alpha}(s)u'(s)\pi(s)$;
(A_{22}) $u(s)/\pi(s)$ *is increasing;*
(A_{23}) $u^{\beta-\alpha}(s) \geq \mu_1(s,s_0)$;
(A_{24}) $y(s) \geq \widetilde{C}u(s)$, *where* $\widetilde{C} \in (0,1)$.

Proof. Let $y(s) \in N_2$. Then, there exists an $s_1 \geq s_0$, such that $y(s) > 0$, $y(\tau_1(s)) > 0$, $y(\tau_2(s)) > 0$ and $y(\sigma(s)) > 0$ for $s \geq s_1$.

(A_{21}) Since $(\kappa(v)(u'(s))^{\alpha})' < 0$, we get

$$\kappa(v)(u'(v))^{\alpha} \leq \kappa(s)(u'(s))^{\alpha} \text{ for } v \geq s \geq s_1,$$

or equivalently

$$u'(v) \leq \frac{1}{\kappa^{1/\alpha}(v)}\kappa^{1/\alpha}(s)u'(s).$$

Integrating this inequality from s to ∞, we deduce that

$$-u(s) \leq \kappa^{1/\alpha}(s)u'(s)\int_s^{\infty}\frac{1}{\kappa^{1/\alpha}(v)}dv = \kappa^{1/\alpha}(s)u'(s)\pi(s).$$

That is,

$$u(s) \geq -\kappa^{1/\alpha}(s)u'(s)\pi(s).$$

(A_{22}) Using the above inequality, we deduce that

$$\left(\frac{u(s)}{\pi(s)}\right)' = \frac{\kappa^{1/\alpha}(s)u'(s)\pi(s) + u(s)}{\kappa^{1/\alpha}(s)\pi^2(s)} \geq 0.$$

(A_{23}) we have the following cases:

Case $\alpha \geq \beta$: Since $u'(s) < 0$, there exists a constant $M_3 > 0$, such that

$$u(s) \leq M_3,$$

and therefore,

$$u^{\beta-\alpha}(s) \geq M_3^{\beta-\alpha}.$$

Case $\alpha < \beta$: Since $u(s)/\pi(s)$ is an increasing function for $s \geq s_1$, we can find $s_2 \geq s_1$ and a constant $M_4 > 0$ such that

$$u(s) \geq M_4\pi(s).$$

Thus

$$u^{\beta-\alpha}(s) \geq M_4^{\beta-\alpha}\pi^{\beta-\alpha}(s).$$

(A_{24}) From the definition of $u(s)$, we have $u(s) \geq y(s)$. Then, we express $y(s)$ as

$$\begin{aligned} y(s) &= u(s) - g_1(s)y^{\gamma_1}(\tau_1(s)) - g_2(s)y^{\gamma_2}(\tau_2(s)) \\ &\geq u(s) - g_1(s)u^{\gamma_1}(\tau_1(s)) - g_2(s)u^{\gamma_2}(\tau_2(s)). \end{aligned}$$

Now, because $\gamma_1 > 1$, and $\gamma_2 < 1$, and noting that $u' < 0$, we find

$$\begin{aligned} y(s) &\geq u(s) - g_1(s)u^{\gamma_1}(s) - g_2(s)u^{\gamma_2}(s) \\ &= u(s) - g_1(s)\pi^{\gamma_1}(\tau_1(s))\frac{u^{\gamma_1}(\tau_1(s))}{\pi^{\gamma_1}(\tau_1(s))} - g_2(s)\pi^{\gamma_2}(\tau_2(s))\frac{u^{\gamma_2}(\tau_2(s))}{\pi^{\gamma_2}(\tau_2(s))} \\ &\geq u(s) - g_1(s)\pi^{\gamma_1}(\tau_1(s))\frac{u^{\gamma_1}(s)}{\pi^{\gamma_1}(s)} - g_2(s)\pi^{\gamma_2}(\tau_2(s))\frac{u^{\gamma_2}(s)}{\pi^{\gamma_2}(s)} \\ &= \left[1 - g_1(s)\left(\frac{\pi(\tau_1(s))}{\pi(s)}\right)^{\gamma_1} u^{\gamma_1-1}(s) - g_2(s)\frac{\pi^{\gamma_2}(\tau_2(s))}{\pi(s)}\left(\frac{u(s)}{\pi(s)}\right)^{\gamma_2-1}\right]u(s). \end{aligned}$$

Since $u(s)/\pi(s)$ is positive and increasing, and $u(s)$ is decreasing, there exist two constants, c_3 and c_4 such that

$$y(s) \geq \left[1 - c_3 g_1(s)\left(\frac{\pi(\tau_1(s))}{\pi(s)}\right)^{\gamma_1} - c_4 g_2(s)\frac{\pi^{\gamma_2}(\tau_2(s))}{\pi(s)}\right]u(s).$$

By (17), we can choose $\widetilde{C} \in (0,1)$ such that

$$y(s) \geq \widetilde{C}u(s).$$

Accordingly, the proof is finished. □

Lemma 8. *Assume that (17) holds. If*

$$\int_{s_1}^{\infty} \frac{1}{\kappa^{1/\alpha}(t)} \int_{s_0}^{t} \mu_1(\sigma(v), s_0)\pi^{\alpha}(v)q(v)dvdt = \infty, \tag{18}$$

then $N_2 = \varnothing$.

Proof. Let $y \in N_2$. Then, there exists an $s_1 \geq s_0$, such that

$$y(s) > 0,\ y(\tau_1(s)) > 0,\ y(\tau_2(s)) \text{ and } y(\sigma(s)) > 0 \text{ for } s \geq s_1 \geq s_0.$$

We know that

$$\left(\kappa^{1/\alpha}(s)u'(s)\right)' = \frac{1}{\alpha}\left(\kappa(s)(u'(s))^{\alpha}\right)'\left(\kappa^{1/\alpha}(s)u'(s)\right)^{1-\alpha}.$$

Using (1) and (A_{24}) gives

$$\begin{aligned} \left(\kappa^{1/\alpha}(s)u'(s)\right)' &= -\frac{1}{\alpha}\left(\kappa^{1/\alpha}(s)u'(s)\right)^{1-\alpha} q(s)y^{\beta}(\sigma(s)) \\ &\leq -\frac{1}{\alpha}\widetilde{C}^{\beta}\left(\kappa^{1/\alpha}(s)u'(s)\right)^{1-\alpha} q(s)u^{\beta}(\sigma(s)). \end{aligned}$$

Applying Lemma 7, we deduce

$$\begin{aligned}\left(\kappa^{1/\alpha}(s)u'(s)\right)' &\leq -\frac{1}{\alpha}\widetilde{C}^{\beta}\left(\kappa^{1/\alpha}(s)u'(s)\right)^{1-\alpha} q(s)u^{\beta-\alpha}(\sigma(s))u^{\alpha}(\sigma(s)) \\ &\leq -\frac{1}{\alpha}\widetilde{C}^{\beta}\left(\kappa^{1/\alpha}(s)u'(s)\right)^{1-\alpha} q(s)\mu_1(\sigma(s),s_0)u^{\alpha}(\sigma(s)) \\ &\leq -\frac{1}{\alpha}\widetilde{C}^{\beta}\left(\frac{u(s)}{\pi(s)}\right)^{1-\alpha} q(s)\mu_1(\sigma(s),s_0)u^{\alpha}(\sigma(s)) \\ &\leq -\frac{1}{\alpha}\widetilde{C}^{\beta}\left(\frac{u(\sigma(s))}{\pi(\sigma(s))}\right)^{1-\alpha} q(s)\mu_1(\sigma(s),s_0)u^{\alpha}(\sigma(s)) \\ &= -\frac{1}{\alpha}\widetilde{C}^{\beta}\mu(\sigma(s),s_0)\pi^{\alpha-1}(\sigma(s),s_1)q(s)u(\sigma(s)).\end{aligned}$$

Since $u' < 0$, then, $u(\sigma(s)) \geq u(s)$, so that

$$\begin{aligned}\left(\kappa^{1/\alpha}(s)u'(s)\right)' &\leq -\frac{1}{\alpha}\widetilde{C}^{\beta}\left(\frac{u(s)}{\pi(s)}\right)^{1-\alpha} q(s)\mu_1(\sigma(s),s_0)u^{\alpha}(s) \\ &= -\frac{1}{\alpha}\widetilde{C}^{\beta}\pi^{\alpha-1}(s)q(s)\mu_1(\sigma(s),s_0)u(s)).\end{aligned}$$

Thus,

$$\left(\kappa^{1/\alpha}(s)u'(s)\right)' \leq -\frac{1}{\alpha}\widetilde{C}^{\beta}\pi^{\alpha-1}(s)q(s)\mu_1(\sigma(s),s_0)u(s). \tag{19}$$

Since $u(s)/\pi(s)$ is an increasing function, there exists a constant $M_5 > 0$ such that $u(s) \geq M_5\pi(s)$. Using this in inequality (19), we obtain

$$\left(\kappa^{1/\alpha}(s)u'(s)\right)' \leq -\frac{1}{\alpha}M_5\widetilde{C}^{\beta}\mu_1(\sigma(s),s_0)\pi^{\alpha}(s)q(s).$$

Integrating this inequality from s_1 to s, we have

$$\kappa^{1/\alpha}(s)u'(s) \leq -\frac{1}{\alpha}M_5\widetilde{C}^{\beta}\int_{s_1}^{s}\mu_1(\sigma(v),s_0)\pi^{\alpha}(v)q(v)dv,$$

which implies that

$$u'(s) \leq -\frac{1}{\alpha}\frac{M_5\widetilde{C}^{\beta}}{\kappa^{1/\alpha}(s)}\int_{s_1}^{s}\mu_1(\sigma(v),s_0)\pi^{\alpha}(v)q(v)dv.$$

Integrating this inequality from s_1 to s, we have

$$u(s) \leq -\frac{1}{\alpha}M_5\widetilde{C}^{\beta}\int_{s_1}^{s}\frac{1}{\kappa^{1/\alpha}(t)}\int_{s_1}^{t}\mu_1(\sigma(v),s_0)\pi^{\alpha}(v)q(v)dvdt.$$

As $s \to \infty$, this leads to a contradiction with the assumption that $u(s)$ is positive. This concludes the proof. □

Lemma 9. *Assume that (17) hold. If*

$$\limsup_{s\to\infty}\pi(s)\int_{s_0}^{s}\mu_1(\sigma(v),s_0)\pi^{\alpha-1}(v)q(v)dv = \infty, \tag{20}$$

then $N_2 = \varnothing$.

Proof. From (19), we know that

$$\left(\kappa^{1/\alpha}(s)u'(s)\right)' \leq -\frac{1}{\alpha}\widetilde{C}^{\beta}\pi^{\alpha-1}(s)q(s)\mu_1(\sigma(s),s_0)u(s).$$

Integrating the above inequality from s_1 to s, we have

$$\begin{aligned}\kappa^{1/\alpha}(s)u'(s) &\leq -\frac{1}{\alpha}\widetilde{C}^{\beta}\int_{s_1}^{s}\mu_1(\sigma(v),s_0)\pi^{\alpha-1}(v)q(v)u(v)dv\\ &\leq -\frac{1}{\alpha}\widetilde{C}^{\beta}u(s)\int_{s_1}^{s}\mu_1(\sigma(v),s_0)\pi^{\alpha-1}(v)q(v)dv.\end{aligned}$$

Using Lemma 7 (A_{21}), we infer that

$$\kappa^{1/\alpha}(s)u'(s) \leq \frac{1}{\alpha}\widetilde{C}^{\beta}\kappa^{1/\alpha}(s)u'(s)\pi(s)\int_{s_1}^{s}\mu_1(\sigma(v),s_0)\pi^{\alpha-1}(v)q(v)dv,$$

which leads to

$$1 \geq \frac{1}{\alpha}\widetilde{C}^{\beta}\pi(s)\int_{s_1}^{s}\mu_1(\sigma(v),s_0)\pi^{\alpha-1}(v)q(v)dv.$$

This leads to a contradiction with the condition (20).

This concludes the proof. □

Lemma 10. *Let (4) hold. If (14) holds, then,* $N_2 = \varnothing$.

Proof. Let $y \in N_2$. Then, there exists an $s_1 \geq s_0$, such that

$$y(s) > 0,\ y(\tau_1(s)) > 0,\ y(\tau_2(s)) \text{ and } y(\sigma(s)) > 0 \text{ for } s \geq s_1 \geq s_0.$$

Using Lemma 7 (A_{24}), the expression in (1) can be transformed into the following inequality

$$\left(\kappa(s)\left(u'(s)\right)^{\alpha}\right)' + \widetilde{C}^{\beta}q(s)u^{\beta}(\sigma(s)) \leq 0. \tag{21}$$

By applying a similar line of reasoning as in Lemma 6, we arrive at a contradiction. This concludes the proof. □

4. Oscillatory Theorems and Examples

In this section, we present a comprehensive set of theorems that establish oscillation criteria, which are formulated directly by summarizing the results obtained in the main results.

Theorem 1. *Assume that (4) and (17) hold. If both (6) and (18) are satisfied, then, (1) is oscillatory.*

Theorem 2. *Assume that (4) and (17) hold. If both (6) and (20) are satisfied, then, (1) is oscillatory.*

Theorem 3. *Assume that (4) and (17) hold. If both (9) and (20) are satisfied, then, (1) is oscillatory.*

Theorem 4. *Assume that (4) and (17) hold. If both (13) and (20) are satisfied, then, (1) is oscillatory.*

Theorem 5. *Assume that (4) and (17) hold. If (14) is satisfied, then, (1) is oscillatory.*

Example 1. *Consider the equation:*

$$\left(s^6\left[\left(y(s) + \frac{1}{s-1}y^3\left(\frac{1}{4}s\right) + \frac{1}{s-2}y^{1/3}\left(\frac{1}{3}s\right)\right)'\right]^3\right)' + s^5y^3\left(\frac{1}{5}s\right) = 0,\ s \geq 1. \tag{22}$$

Comparing Equation (22) with (1), we deduce the following:

$$\begin{aligned} \alpha &= \beta = \gamma_1 = 3,\ \gamma_2 = \frac{1}{3},\ \kappa(s) = s^6,\ \sigma(s) = \frac{1}{5}s,\ \mathfrak{r}_1(s) = \frac{1}{4}s, \\ \mathfrak{r}_2(s) &= \frac{1}{3}s,\ g_1(s) = \frac{1}{s-1},\ g_1(s) = \frac{1}{s-2},\ \text{and } q(s) = s^5. \end{aligned}$$

Additionally, we have:

$$\mu(s, s_0) = \mu_1(s) = 1,\ \pi(s) = \frac{1}{s} \text{ and } \pi(s, s_0) = \frac{s-1}{s}.$$

Using (4), we compute:

$$\lim_{s\to\infty} g_1(s)\pi^{\gamma_1 - 1}(s, s_1) = \lim_{s\to\infty} \frac{(s-1)^2}{(s-1)s^2} = 0, \text{ and } \lim_{s\to\infty} g_2(s) = \lim_{s\to\infty} \frac{1}{s-2} = 0.$$

From (17), we find:

$$\lim_{s\to\infty} g_1(s)\left(\frac{\pi(\mathfrak{r}_1(s))}{\pi(s)}\right)^{\gamma_1} = \lim_{s\to\infty} \frac{64}{s-1} = 0, \text{ and } \lim_{s\to\infty} \frac{g_2(s)\pi^{\gamma_2}(\mathfrak{r}_2(s))}{\pi(s)} = \lim_{s\to\infty} \frac{3^{1/3}s^{2/3}}{s-2} = 0.$$

Several conditions are verified as follows:
Condition (6):

$$\int_{s_0}^{\infty} \frac{1}{\kappa^{1/\alpha}(t)} \int_{s_0}^{t} \mu(\sigma(v), s_0)\pi^{\alpha-1}(\sigma(v), s_1)q(v)dvdt = \int_{1}^{\infty} \frac{1}{t^{1/3}} \int_{1}^{t} \frac{(v-5)^2}{v^2} v^3 dvdt = \infty.$$

Condition (13):

$$\limsup_{s\to\infty} \int_{s_0}^{s} \pi^{\alpha-1}(\sigma(v), s_1)q(v)dv = \limsup_{s\to\infty} \int_{1}^{s} \frac{(v-5)^2}{v^2} v^3 dv = \infty.$$

Condition (14):

$$\int_{s_0}^{\infty} \pi^{\beta}(\sigma(v))q(v)dv = \int_{1}^{\infty} \frac{125}{v^3} v^3 dv = \infty.$$

Condition (18) leads to

$$\int_{s_0}^{\infty} \frac{1}{\kappa^{1/\alpha}(t)} \int_{s_0}^{t} \mu_1(\sigma(v), s_0)\pi^{\alpha}(v)q(v)dvdt = \int_{1}^{\infty} \frac{1}{u^{1/3}} \int_{1}^{t} \frac{1}{v^3} v^3 dvdu = \infty.$$

Condition (20):

$$\limsup_{s\to\infty} \pi(s) \int_{s_0}^{s} \mu_1(\sigma(v), s_0)\pi^{\alpha-1}(v)q(v)u(v)dv = \limsup_{s\to\infty} \frac{1}{s} \int_{1}^{s} \frac{1}{v^2} v^3 dv = \limsup_{s\to\infty} \frac{s}{2} = \infty.$$

Since the conditions of Theorems 1–5 are satisfied, it follows that every solution of (22) oscillates.

Example 2. *Consider the equation:*

$$\left(s^{10}\left[\left(y(s) + \frac{1}{s}y^5\left(\frac{1}{3}s\right) + \frac{1}{s^2}y^{1/5}\left(\frac{1}{2}s\right)\right)'\right]^5\right)' + s^5 y^5\left(\frac{1}{4}s\right) = 0,\ s \geq 1. \quad (23)$$

Clearly

$$\begin{aligned} \alpha &= \beta = \gamma_1 = 5,\ \gamma_2 = \frac{1}{5},\ \kappa(s) = s^{10},\ \sigma(s) = \frac{1}{4}s,\ \mathfrak{r}_1(s) = \frac{1}{3}s, \\ \mathfrak{r}_2(s) &= \frac{1}{2}s,\ g_1(s) = \frac{1}{s},\ g_1(s) = \frac{1}{s^2},\ \textit{and}\ q(s) = s^5. \end{aligned}$$

Additionally, we have:

$$\mu(s, s_0) = \mu_1(s) = 1,\ \pi(s) = \frac{1}{s}\ \textit{and}\ \pi(s, s_0) = \frac{s-1}{s}.$$

Using (4), we compute:

$$\lim_{s\to\infty} g_1(s)\pi^{\gamma_1 - 1}(s, s_1) = \lim_{s\to\infty} \frac{(s-1)^4}{s^5} = 0,\ \textit{and}\ \lim_{s\to\infty} g_2(s) = \lim_{s\to\infty} \frac{1}{s^2} = 0.$$

From (17), we find:

$$\lim_{s\to\infty} g_1(s)\left(\frac{\pi(\mathfrak{r}_1(s))}{\pi(s)}\right)^{\gamma_1} = \lim_{s\to\infty} \frac{3^5}{s} = 0,\ \textit{and}\ \lim_{s\to\infty} \frac{g_2(s)\pi^{\gamma_2}(\mathfrak{r}_2(s))}{\pi(s)} = \lim_{s\to\infty} \frac{1}{s^2}\frac{2^{1/5}s}{s^{1/5}} = 0.$$

Verification of conditions (6), (13), (14), (18) and (20) proceeds as follows:
Condition (6):

$$\int_1^\infty \frac{1}{t^{1/5}} \int_1^t \frac{(v-4)^4}{v^4} v^5 dv dt = \infty.$$

Condition (13):

$$\limsup_{s\to\infty} \int_1^s \frac{(v-4)^4}{v^4} v^5, dv = \infty.$$

Condition (14):

$$\int_1^\infty \frac{4^5}{v^5} v^5 dv = \infty.$$

Condition (18) leads to

$$\int_1^\infty \frac{1}{t^{1/5}} \int_1^t \frac{1}{v^5} v^5 dv dt = \infty.$$

Condition (20):

$$\limsup_{s\to\infty} \frac{1}{s} \int_1^s \frac{1}{v^4} v^5 dv = \limsup_{s\to\infty} \frac{s^2}{2s} = \infty.$$

Since the conditions of Theorems 1–5 are satisfied, it follows that every solution of (23) oscillates.

5. Conclusions

The study of the oscillatory behavior of solutions of second-order DEs containing neutrality conditions, whether sublinear or superlinear, is a rich and exciting field in applied and theoretical mathematics. This research has made new contributions in this context by developing analytical criteria that highlight the dynamics of these equations and explain the associated oscillation patterns. The results obtained here contribute to a deeper understanding of the mathematical properties of this class of equations, which enhances the ability of researchers to address similar problems in multiple contexts. What distinguishes this work is that it highlights the dual effect of neutrality conditions in shaping the behavior of solutions, which opens up prospects for extending current models to include more complex real-world applications. This research also adds to the existing literature with precise criteria that contribute to assessing the nature of oscillatory solutions, which lays a strong foundation for future studies. It is worth noting that the application of the approach developed in this study to higher-order DEs represents a promising and interesting direction. Exploring oscillatory effects in the context of higher-order equations may reveal new patterns and add further understanding to the mathematical structure of these systems. One of the exciting directions for future studies is to extend these investigations without the constraints $\gamma_1 > 1$ and $\gamma_2 < 1$, as well as without relying on conditions (4) and (17), which would allow for broader applications and deeper insights into more general systems. This research advances the understanding of oscillatory phenomena in NDEs and lays a foundation for expanding these insights into more complex studies.

Author Contributions: Methodology, B.B., N.A. and F.A.; Investigation, O.B. and N.A.; Writing-original draft, F.A. and F.M.; Writing—review & editing, F.M. and O.B. All authors have read and agreed to the published version of the manuscript.

Funding: This research received no external funding.

Data Availability Statement: Data are contained within the article.

Conflicts of Interest: The authors declare no conflicts of interest.

References

1. Cooke, K.L. Differential-Difference Equations. In *International Symposium on Nonlinear Differential Equations and Nonlinear Mechanics*; Academic Press: New York, NY, USA, 1963; pp. 155–171.
2. Hale, J.K. *Theory of Functional Differential Equations*; Springer: New York, NY, USA, 1977.
3. Chuanxi, Q.; Ladas, G. Oscillations of Neutral Differential Equations with Variable Coefficients. *Appl. Anal.* **1989**, *32*, 215–228. [CrossRef]
4. Kiguradze, I.; Chanturia, T.A. *Asymptotic Properties of Solutions of Nonautonomous Ordinary Differential Equations*; Springer: Dordrecht, The Netherlands, 2012.
5. Bazighifan, O. An Approach for Studying Asymptotic Properties of Solutions of Neutral Differential Equations. *Symmetry* **2020**, *12*, 555. [CrossRef]
6. Bazighifan, O. On the Oscillation of Certain Fourth-Order Differential Equations with p-Laplacian Like Operator. *Appl. Math. Comput.* **2020**, *386*, 125475. [CrossRef]
7. Masood, F.; Moaaz, O.; Santra, S.S.; Fernandez-Gamiz, U.; El-Metwally, H. On the monotonic properties and oscillatory behavior of solutions of neutral differential equations. *Demonstr. Math.* **2023**, *56*, 20230123. [CrossRef]
8. Agarwal, R.P.; Shieh, S.-L.; Yeh, C.-C. Oscillation criteria for second-order retarded differential equations. *Math. Comput. Model.* **1997**, *26*, 1–11. [CrossRef]
9. Agarwal, R.P.; Grace, S.R.; O'Regan, D. *Oscillation Theory for Second Order Linear, Half-Linear, Superlinear and Sublinear Dynamic Equations*; Kluwer Academic: Dordrecht, The Netherlands, 2002.
10. Džurina, J.; Stavroulakis, I.P. Oscillation criteria for second-order delay differential equations. *Appl. Math. Comput.* **2003**, *140*, 445–453. [CrossRef]
11. Erbe, L.; Peterson, A.; Saker, S.H. Oscillation criteria for second-order nonlinear delay dynamic equations. *J. Math. Anal. Appl.* **2007**, *333*, 505–522. [CrossRef]
12. Hassan, T.S. Oscillation criteria for second-order nonlinear dynamic equations. *Adv. Differ. Equ.* **2012**, *2012*, 171. [CrossRef]
13. Grace, S.R.; Graef, J.R. Oscillation of second-order nonlinear neutral differential equations with noncanonical operators. *Bull. Malays. Math. Sci. Soc.* **2015**, *38*, 761–778.
14. Zhang, C.; Agarwal, R.P.; Bohner, M.; Li, T. Oscillation of second-order nonlinear neutral dynamic equations with noncanonical operators. *Bull. Malays. Math. Sci. Soc.* **2017**, *38*, 761–778. [CrossRef]
15. Baculíková, B. Oscillation of second-order nonlinear noncanonical differential equations with deviating argument. *Appl. Math. Lett.* **2019**, *91*, 68–75. [CrossRef]
16. Jadlovská, I. Oscillation criteria of Kneser-type for second-order half-linear advanced differential equations. *Appl. Math. Lett.* **2020**, *106*, 106354. [CrossRef]
17. Li, H.; Zhao, Y.; Han, Z. New oscillation criterion for Emden-Fowler type nonlinear neutral delay differential equations. *J. Appl. Math. Comput.* **2019**, *60*, 191–200. [CrossRef]
18. Grace, S.R.; Džurina, J.; Jadlovská, I.; Li, T. An improved approach for studying oscillation of second-order neutral delay differential equations. *J. Inequal. Appl.* **2018**, *2018*, 193. [CrossRef]
19. Muhib, A. On oscillation of second-order noncanonical neutral differential equations. *J. Inequal. Appl.* **2021**, *2021*, 79. [CrossRef]
20. Moaaz, O.; Masood, F.; Cesarano, C.; Alsallami, S.A.; Khalil, E.M.; Bouazizi, M.L. Neutral Differential Equations of Second-Order: Iterative Monotonic Properties. *Mathematics* **2022**, *10*, 1356. [CrossRef]

21. Masood, F.; Cesarano, C.; Moaaz, O.; Askar, S.S.; Alshamrani, A.M.; El-Metwally, H. Kneser-Type Oscillation Criteria for Half-Linear Delay Differential Equations of Third Order. *Symmetry* **2023**, *15*, 1994. [CrossRef]
22. Alsharidi, A.K.; Muhib, A. Oscillation criteria for mixed neutral differential equations. *AIMS Math.* **2024**, *9*, 14473–14486. [CrossRef]
23. Alemam, A.; Al-Jaser, A.; Moaaz, O.; Masood, F.; El-Metwally, H. Second-Order Neutral Differential Equations with a Sublinear Neutral Term: Examining the Oscillatory Behavior. *Axioms* **2024**, *13*, 681. [CrossRef]
24. Agarwal, R.P.; Zhang, C.; Li, T. Some remarks on oscillation of second order neutral differential equations. *Appl. Math. Comput.* **2016**, *274*, 178–181. [CrossRef]
25. Han, Z.; Li, T.; Sun, S.; Sun, Y. Remarks on the paper. *Appl. Math. Comput.* **2010**, *215*, 3998–4007.
26. Agarwal, R.P.; Bohner, M.; Li, T. Oscillation of second-order differential equations with a sublinear neutral term. *Carpathian J. Math.* **2014**, *30*, 1–6. [CrossRef]
27. Li, Q.; Wang, R.; Chen, F.; Li, T. Oscillation of second-order nonlinear delay differential equations with nonpositive neutral coefficients. *Adv. Differ. Equ.* **2015**, *2015*, 35. [CrossRef]
28. Tamilvanan, S.; Thandapani, E.; Džurina, J. Oscillation of second order nonlinear differential equations with sub-linear neutral term. *Differ. Equ. Appl.* **2017**, *9*, 29–35. [CrossRef]
29. Džurina, J.; Jadlovská, I. A sharp oscillation result for second-order half-linear noncanonical delay differential equations. *Electron. J. Qual. Theory Differ. Equ.* **2020**, *2020*, 1–14. [CrossRef]
30. Džurina, J.; Grace, S. R.; Jadlovská, I.; Li, T. Oscillation criteria for second-order Emden–Fowler delay differential equations with a sublinear neutral term. *Math. Nachrichten* **2020**, *293*, 910–922. [CrossRef]
31. Wu, Y.; Yu, Y.; Xiao, J.; Jiao, Z. Oscillatory behaviour of a class of second order Emden-Fowler differential equations with a sublinear neutral term. *Appl. Math. Sci. Eng.* **2023**, *31*, 224609. [CrossRef]
32. Zhang, C.; Agarwal, R.; Bohner, M.; Li, T. New results for oscillatory behavior of even-order half-linear delay differential equations. *Appl. Math. Lett.* **2013**, *26*, 179–183. [CrossRef]

mathematics MDPI

Article

Delay-Embedding Spatio-Temporal Dynamic Mode Decomposition

Gyurhan Nedzhibov

Faculty of Mathematics and Informatics, Konstantin Preslavsky University of Shumen, 9700 Shumen, Bulgaria; g.nedzhibov@shu.bg

Abstract: Spatio-temporal dynamic mode decomposition (STDMD) is an extension of dynamic mode decomposition (DMD) designed to handle spatio-temporal datasets. It extends the framework so that it can analyze data that have both spatial and temporal variations. This facilitates the extraction of spatial structures along with their temporal evolution. The STDMD method extracts temporal and spatial development information simultaneously, including wavenumber, frequencies, and growth rates, which are essential in complex dynamic systems. We provide a comprehensive mathematical framework for *sequential* and *parallel* STDMD approaches. To increase the range of applications of the presented techniques, we also introduce a generalization of delay coordinates. The extension, labeled *delay-embedding* STDMD allows the use of delayed data, which can be both time-delayed and space-delayed. An explicit expression of the presented algorithms in matrix form is also provided, making theoretical analysis easier and providing a solid foundation for further research and development. The novel approach is demonstrated using some illustrative model dynamics.

Keywords: DMD method; spatio-temporal dynamic mode decomposition; Koopman operator; delay embedding

MSC: 65P99; 37M10; 37N99

1. Introduction

Dynamical systems are prevalent in science and engineering, yet analyzing and predicting them remains challenging. While linear systems are well characterized, nonlinear systems are difficult to characterize. They can exhibit an extremely wide range of behaviors, including chaos, and generally do not yield analytical solutions. Koopman operator theory plays an important role in the analysis of such systems [1,2]. The idea is based on transforming the finite-dimensional dynamics of the nonlinear state space into an infinite-dimensional linear dynamical system of functions on the state, represented by the Koopman operator. Through the eigendecomposition of the Koopman operator, we can understand the behavior, stability and long-term dynamics of complex systems. One of the leading algorithms for Koopman spectral analysis is *dynamic mode decomposition* (DMD), introduced by Schmid in [3]. The method comprises a mathematical technique for identifying spatio-temporal coherent structures from high-dimensional data. After its introduction, the method is now used in a variety of fields, including various jets [4,5], epidemiology [6], video processing [7], neuroscience [8], financial trading [9–11], robotics [12] and cavity flows [13,14]. For a review of the DMD literature, we refer the reader to [15–19]. For some recent results on DMD extensions, we recommend [20–42] to the reader.

While standard DMD is a powerful technique for analyzing dynamic systems, it has limitations related to its assumptions, sensitivity to noise, ability to capture long-term dynamics, computational complexity, parameter sensitivity and others. Researchers continue to develop and refine variations in the DMD method to address these shortcomings and improve its applicability to a wide range of data analysis tasks. Over the last few years, several variants of DMD have been proposed. Chen [20] proposed an optimized DMD method that can reduce numerical sensitivity and calculate the modal growth rate and frequency accurately. Williams et al. [21] suggested extended DMD (EDMD), which can produce improved approximations of the leading Koopman eigenfunctions and eigenvalues. Moreover, Le Clainche et al. [22] developed *higher-order* DMD (HODMD), which extends DMD to resolve delayed snapshots. In [23], Le Clainche and Vega introduce *spatio-temporal Koopman decomposition* (STKD), which incorporates higher order DMD and a spatio-temporal approach for the Koopman operator.

One of the modifications of the DMD method, which will play a key role in the exposition of the present work, is the *delay-embedding* DMD (or Hankel DMD) [43,44]. Delay-embedding methods have also been employed for system identification, most notably by the eigensystem realization algorithm (ERA)[45] and in climate science with singular spectrum analysis (SSA) [46]. Brunton et al. [47] developed a variant of this technique called the Hankel alternative view of Koopman (HAVOK) analysis.

In the present work, we consider the *spatio-temporal* DMD (STDMD), a generalization of the DMD method designed to handle spatio-temporal datasets. It extends the framework so that it can analyze data that have both spatial and temporal variations, by extracting spatial structures and their temporal evolution. The STDMD method extracts temporal and spatial development information simultaneously, including wavenumber and spatial growth rate. This can be crucial in complex dynamic systems. The "spatio-temporal" aspect refers to the fact that DMD is applied to data that vary both in space and time, such as sequences of images or sensor measurements collected over time and across multiple spatial locations. In such data, patterns and structures can evolve both spatially and temporally, and the approach aims to capture these spatio-temporal dynamics. Applications of spatio-temporal DMD span various fields, including fluid dynamics, neuroscience, climate science, and engineering, where understanding and predicting complex spatio-temporal behaviors is essential. Some recent publications related to the topic suggest applications in the fields of unsteady shear layer flow [48], wake of a circular cylinder [49], urban flow [50], aerodynamic modeling [51], turbulent flow [52] and binary fluid convection [53].

We provide a comprehensive mathematical framework for sequential and parallel STDMD approaches. A clear expression of the presented algorithms in matrix form is also provided. This facilitates theoretical analysis and provides a solid foundation for further research and development. Furthermore, we introduce a delay coordinate generalization of STDMD, enabling the use of both time-delayed and space-delayed snapshots. This extension, labeled delay-embedding STDMD, can be considered as an alternative approach to the STKD method proposed in [23]. The proposed STDMD approach is compared with the results obtained from STKD.

The following is an outline of the paper: in the rest of Section 1, we describe the DMD and some basic concepts related to it; spatio-tempral DMD approaches are in Section 2; in Section 3, we introduce and discuss the framework for delay-embedding STDM; in Section 4, we present the numerical results; in Section 5, we provide the conclusion.

1.1. Dynamic Mode Decomposition

In this paragraph, a brief introduction to the classical dynamic mode decomposition (DMD) framework is provided. For details, we refer the reader to [16,17,19] and the references therein. Consider the system of time-invariant ordinary differential equations of the form

$$\dot{\mathbf{x}}(t) = f(\mathbf{x}(t)), \tag{1}$$

where $\mathbf{x} \in \mathcal{R}^n$ is the state vector and $f : \mathcal{R}^n \to \mathcal{R}^n$ is a nonlinear map ($n \gg 1$). Let the discrete-time representation of (1) be

$$\mathbf{x}_{k+1} = \mathbf{F}(\mathbf{x}_k), \tag{2}$$

where $\mathbf{x}_k \in \mathcal{R}^n$ is a high-dimensional state vector sampled at $t_k = k\triangle t$ for $k = 0, \ldots, m$, and $\mathbf{F}$ is an unknown map that describes the evolution of the state vector between two subsequent sampling times. The initial condition is defined by $\mathbf{x}(0) = \mathbf{x}_0$.

Suppose that the evolution of the high-dimensional state $\mathbf{x}$ is governed by some underlying low-dimensional dynamics. Then, the DMD computes a data-driven linear approximation to the system (2) as follows: the sequential set of data

$$\mathcal{D} = [\mathbf{x}_0, \ldots, \mathbf{x}_m] \tag{3}$$

is arranged into the following two large data matrices

$$X = [\mathbf{x}_0, \ldots, \mathbf{x}_{m-1}] \quad \text{and} \quad Y = [\mathbf{x}_1, \ldots, \mathbf{x}_m]. \tag{4}$$

The goal of the DMD approach is to find a relationship between the future state $\mathbf{x}_{k+1}$ and the current state $\mathbf{x}_k$, given by

$$\mathbf{x}_{k+1} = A\mathbf{x}_k\,, \tag{5}$$

where $A \in \mathcal{R}^{n \times n}$ is called the DMD operator. The solution of (5) may be expressed simply in terms of the eigenvalues λ_j and eigenvectors ϕ_j of A:

$$\mathbf{x}_k = \sum_{j=1}^{r} \phi_j b_j \lambda_j^k = \Phi \Lambda^k \mathbf{b}\,, \tag{6}$$

where Φ is the eigenvector matrix of A, Λ is the diagonal matrix of eigenvalues $\Lambda = \text{diag}\{\lambda_i\}$, $\mathbf{b} = \Phi^\dagger \mathbf{x}_0$, and $\Phi^\dagger$ is the Moore–Penrose pseudoinverse of Φ. The parameter r is determined by the low-rank eigendecomposition of matrix A.

Therefore, the corresponding continuous-time approximation of the system (1) can be written as

$$\dot{\mathbf{x}} = \mathcal{A}\mathbf{x}\,, \quad \text{with } A = \exp(\mathcal{A}) \tag{7}$$

and the initial condition $\mathbf{x}(0)$. Then, the state-variable evolution in time can be approximated by the following modal expansion

$$\mathbf{x}(t) = \sum_{j=1}^{r} \phi_j b_j \exp(\omega_j t) = \Phi \exp(\Omega t)\mathbf{b}\,, \tag{8}$$

where ϕ_j are also the eigenvectors of the approximated matrix $\mathcal{A}$ and matrix $\Omega = \text{diag}(\omega_j)$ is a diagonal matrix whose entries are

$$\omega_j = \ln(\lambda_j)/\triangle t \tag{9}$$

the eigenvalues of $\mathcal{A}$, with λ_j the eigenvalues of A. The real part of ω_j regulates the growth or decay of the DMD modes, while the imaginary part of ω_j drives oscillations in the DMD modes. In this sense, while the discrete-time eigenvalues λ_i imply stability when they are inside the unit disc in $\mathbf{C}$, the continuous-time eigenvalues ω_i imply stability when they are in the left half-plane of $\mathbf{C}$. Each component b_j of vector $\mathbf{b}$, in (6) and (8), is a complex scalar that represents the i-th modal contribution of initial vector $\mathbf{x}_0$ and can be interpreted as the amplitude of the corresponding DMD mode ϕ_j.

1.2. Reduced-Order DMD Operator

The relation (5) can be rewritten in terms of snapshot matrices

$$Y = AX. \tag{10}$$

Then, the dynamic mode decomposition of data matrix $\mathcal{D}$ is given by the eigendecomposition of A. The DMD finds the best-fit solution A, one that minimizes the least-squares distance in the Frobenius norm

$$\arg\min_{A} \|Y - AX\|_F, \tag{11}$$

where $\|.\|_F$ is the Frobenius norm. The solution A to this optimization problem is given by

$$A \approx YX^{\dagger}, \tag{12}$$

where $X^{\dagger}$ denotes the Moore–Penrose pseudo-inverse of X. This is the same as saying that A minimizes $\|\mathbf{x}_{k+1} - A\mathbf{x}_k\|_2$ across all time steps. The *DMD modes* and *eigenvalues* are intended to approximate the eigenvectors and eigenvalues of A.

In practice, the A matrix can be too large and it is computationally inefficient to explicitly compute $A \approx YX^{\dagger}$. It should be noted that calculating the eigendecomposition of the $n \times n$ matrix A can be prohibitively expensive if n is large, i.e., $n \gg 1$. In such cases, DMD aims at finding a reduced representation of A by $\tilde{A} \in \mathcal{R}^{r\times r}$ with $r \ll n$. Matrix $\tilde{A}$ can be used to construct DMD modes associated with specific temporal frequencies. Thus, we can use the dynamics of low-rank approximation to represent the full state dynamics. This basis transformation takes the form

$$\mathbf{x} = Q\tilde{\mathbf{x}}, \tag{13}$$

where Q is usually a unitary matrix or such that $Q^*Q = I$. The reduced-order model, corresponding to (5), can be derived as follows:

$$\tilde{\mathbf{x}}_{k+1} = A\tilde{\mathbf{x}}_k, \tag{14}$$

where the corresponding reduced-order matrix is

$$\tilde{A} = Q^*AQ, \tag{15}$$

such that $\tilde{A} \in \mathcal{R}^{r\times r}$. The eigenvalues of $\tilde{A}$ and A are equivalent, because of similarity transformation and the eigenvectors are related via a linear transformation.

Let the eigendecomposition of $\tilde{A}$ be

$$\tilde{A}W = W\Lambda \tag{16}$$

where W is the eigenvector matrix and Λ is the diagonal matrix of the associated eigenvalues $\Lambda = \text{diag}\{\lambda_i\}$. Then, the matrix of DMD modes is

$$\Phi = QW \tag{17}$$

which approximates the eigenvector matrix of A.

Some possible choices for the projection matrix Q in (13) are:

(i). The left singular vector matrix of X. A common approach to choosing the transformation matrix Q is

$$Q = U, \tag{18}$$

from the truncated SVD of X:

$$X = U\Sigma V^*, \tag{19}$$

where $U \in \mathcal{R}^{n\times r}, \Sigma \in \mathcal{R}^{r\times r}$ and $V \in \mathcal{R}^{m\times r}$. In this case the reduced order matrix $\tilde{A}$ in (15), can be expresses as

$$\tilde{A} = U^*YV\Sigma^{\dagger}. \tag{20}$$

The DMD modes have the following presentation

$$\Phi = YV\Sigma^{\dagger}W. \tag{21}$$

This approach to implementing the DMD method is called *exact DMD*, since Tu et al. [16] proves that DMD modes computed by (21) are the exact eigenvectors of A. DMD modes computed by (17) are known as projected eigenvectors of A. See [38,39] for some other results.

In this case, the projected matrix of $\mathcal{D}$, in (3), has the following presentation:

$$\tilde{\mathcal{D}} = U^{*}\mathcal{D} = [\tilde{\mathbf{x}}_0, \ldots, \tilde{\mathbf{x}}_m] \tag{22}$$

or in equivalent block-matrix form

$$\tilde{\mathcal{D}} = [UX \mid U\mathbf{x}_m]. \tag{23}$$

If $\mathcal{D}$ is a full-rank matrix, then (23) has the form

$$\tilde{\mathcal{D}} = [\Sigma V^{*} \mid U\mathbf{x}_m]. \tag{24}$$

(ii). The left singular vector matrix of $\mathcal{D}$. We can choose the transformation matrix Q, in (13), to be

$$Q = U_{\mathcal{D}}, \tag{25}$$

where $U_{\mathcal{D}}$ is from the truncated SVD of the full data matrix $\mathcal{D}$:

$$\mathcal{D} = U_{\mathcal{D}}\Sigma_{\mathcal{D}}V_{\mathcal{D}}^{*}, \tag{26}$$

where $U_{\mathcal{D}} \in \mathcal{R}^{n\times r}$, $\Sigma_{\mathcal{D}} \in \mathcal{R}^{r\times r}$ and $V_{\mathcal{D}} \in \mathcal{R}^{m\times r}$, see [22].

Then, the projected matrix of $\mathcal{D}$, in (3), has the following presentation:

$$\tilde{\mathcal{D}} = U_{\mathcal{D}}^{*}\mathcal{D} = [\tilde{\mathbf{x}}_0, \ldots, \tilde{\mathbf{x}}_m] \tag{27}$$

and if $\mathcal{D}$ is a full-rank matrix, then

$$\tilde{\mathcal{D}} = \Sigma_{\mathcal{D}}V_{\mathcal{D}}^{*}. \tag{28}$$

The matrix of DMD modes In this case, is

$$\Phi = U_{\mathcal{D}}W, \tag{29}$$

where W is the eigenvector matrix of $\tilde{A} = U_{\mathcal{D}}^{*}\, A\, U_{\mathcal{D}}$.

1.3. Optimal Amplitudes of DMD Modes

Finding the DMD mode amplitudes that best fit the DMD modes of a collection of data is referred to as the reconstruction problem. In the context of DMD, reduced-order modeling seeks to identify a subset of DMD modes that perform well in data reconstruction for a data set or a variety of data sets.

Let us consider again Equation (6), which represents the DMD reconstruction of data snapshots $\mathcal{D}$. In the standard DMD approach the vector of amplitudes is computed by

$$\mathbf{b} = \Phi^{\dagger}\mathbf{x}_0 \tag{30}$$

as shown in (6). It is possible to improve this estimate with optimization over all snapshots.

It is straightforward to show that (6) has the following equivalent expression:

$$\mathcal{D} = \Phi\,\mathrm{diag}\{b_i\}V_{and}(\lambda), \tag{31}$$

where $V_{and}(\lambda)$ is a Vandermonde matrix

$$V_{and}(\lambda) = \begin{pmatrix} 1 & \lambda_1 & \dots & \lambda_1^m \\ 1 & \lambda_2 & \dots & \lambda_2^m \\ \vdots & \vdots & \ddots & \vdots \\ 1 & \lambda_r & \dots & \lambda_r^m \end{pmatrix}. \tag{32}$$

This demonstrates that the temporal evolution of the dynamic modes is governed by the Vandermonde matrix, which is determined by the r complex eigenvalues λ_i of $\tilde{A}$ which contain information about the underlying temporal frequencies and growth/decay rates.

Therefore, determination of the unknown vector of amplitudes $\mathbf{b}$ can be considered as the following optimization problem:

$$\min_{\mathbf{b}} \|\mathcal{D} - \Phi \operatorname{diag}\{b_i\} V_{and}(\lambda)\|_F^2. \tag{33}$$

Using the truncated SVD of $\mathcal{D} = U_{\mathcal{D}} \Sigma_{\mathcal{D}} V_{\mathcal{D}}^*$, and the definition of the matrix $\Phi = U_{\mathcal{D}} W$ in (17), we bring this problem into the following form:

$$\min_{\mathbf{b}} \|\Sigma_{\mathcal{D}} V_{\mathcal{D}}^* - W \operatorname{diag}\{b_i\} V_{and}(\lambda)\|_F^2 \tag{34}$$

or in equivalent form, by using (27) and (28)

$$\min_{\mathbf{b}} \|\tilde{\mathcal{D}} - W \operatorname{diag}\{b_i\} V_{and}(\lambda)\|_F^2 \tag{35}$$

where W is the eigenvector matrix and λ is the eigenvalues vector of the reduced-order operator (15). This is a convex optimization problem that can be solved using standard methods. For instance, we can represent (35) in matrix form as

$$M\mathbf{b} = \mathbf{h}, \tag{36}$$

where $M \in \mathbf{C}^{r.(m+1)\times r}$ is the coefficient matrix, $\mathbf{h}$ is the forcing term and the unknown amplitude vector $\mathbf{b}$ as given by

$$M = \begin{bmatrix} W \\ W\Lambda \\ \dots \\ W\Lambda^m \end{bmatrix}, \ \mathbf{h} = \begin{bmatrix} \tilde{\mathbf{x}}_0 \\ \tilde{\mathbf{x}}_1 \\ \dots \\ \tilde{\mathbf{x}}_m \end{bmatrix}, \ \text{and } \mathbf{b} = \begin{bmatrix} b_1 \\ b_2 \\ \dots \\ b_r \end{bmatrix}, \tag{37}$$

where $\Lambda = \operatorname{diag}\{\lambda_i\} \in \mathbf{C}^{r\times r}$ is a diagonal matrix formed by the eigenvalues of $\tilde{A}$ in (16). Therefore, we can solve the Equation (36) by least-squares approach

$$\mathbf{b} = M^{\dagger}\mathbf{h}, \tag{38}$$

where the pseudoinverse $M^{\dagger}$ may be computed through SVD of M.

1.4. Delay-Embedding Dynamic Mode Decomposition

Delay-embedding is also an important technique when the temporal or spectral complexity of a dynamical system exceeds the spatial complexity, for example, in systems characterized by a broadband spectrum or spatially undersampled. In this case, we arrive at a "short-and-wide", rather than a "tall-and-skinny", data matrix $\mathcal{D}$, and the standard algorithm fails at extracting all relevant spectral features.

Delay-Embedding DMD (or *Hankel* DMD) overcomes several shortcomings of the standard DMD method by extending its capabilities to handle nonlinear dynamics, non-uniformly sampled data, long-term temporal behavior, high-dimensional datasets, and noisy data. This makes it a more versatile and robust technique for dynamic mode decomposition in various applications. The Takens embedding theorem [54] provides a rigorous framework for analyzing the information content of measurements of a nonlinear dynamical system.

To implement delay-embedding DMD, given the data sequence $\mathcal{D}$ in (3), we stack $s \leq m$ time-shifted copies of the data to form the augmented input matrix. The following Hankel matrix H is formed:

$$\mathcal{D}_{aug} = \begin{pmatrix} \mathbf{x}_1 & \mathbf{x}_2 & \cdots & \mathbf{x}_{m-s+1} \\ \mathbf{x}_2 & \mathbf{x}_3 & \cdots & \mathbf{x}_{m-s+2} \\ \vdots & \vdots & \ddots & \vdots \\ \mathbf{x}_s & \mathbf{x}_{s+1} & \cdots & \mathbf{x}_m \end{pmatrix}, \tag{39}$$

where the applied embedding dimension is s. The augmented data matrix $\mathcal{D}_{aug}$ is then used in place of $\mathcal{D}$ and processed by the standard DMD algorithm. The DMD algorithm prescribed in Equations (3)–(8) is applied to the augmented matrices $X_{aug}, Y_{aug} \in \mathbf{R}^{(n.s)\times(m-s)}$ in place of X and Y, giving eigenvalues Φ_{aug} and modes Λ_{aug}. The first n rows of Φ_{aug} correspond to the current (not shifted) time and are used to forecast $\mathbf{x}(t)$.

Arbabi and Mezić [43] have shown the convergence of this time-shifted approach to the eigenfunctions of the Koopman operator. They also illustrated remarkable improvements in the prediction of simple and complex fluid systems. Further examples and theoretical results on delay-embedding and the Hankel viewpoint of Koopman analysis are given by Brunton et al. [47] and Kamb et al. [44]. They demonstrated that linear time-delayed models are an effective and efficient tool to capture nonlinear and chaotic dynamics.

2. Spatio-Temporal DMD

The idea behind the spatio-temporal extension of the DMD method is to extend the application range of DMD by implementing the simultaneous capture of both spatial and temporal dynamics. This approach is particularly useful for analyzing complex systems where dynamics evolve both in space and time, such as fluid flows, biological systems, and climate phenomena. To our knowledge, the first paper in the literature in which this idea has been attempted is Sharma et al. [55], and later, it was realized by Clainche et al. [23]; see also [56]. In [23], Le Clainche and Vega introduce *spatio-temporal Koopman decomposition* (STKD), which incorporates higher order DMD (HODMD) and a spatio-temporal approach for the Koopman operator. For some applications, see [48,49].

In principle, this expansion can be obtained in two ways:

(i). *Sequential method.* A temporal DMD algorithm is first applied to the snapshot matrix and a spatial DMD algorithm is applied to the spatial modes. Obviously, the order in which temporal and spatial DMDs are applied can be reversed, and the result of the direct and reverse methods is not identical.

(ii). *Parallel method.* Reduced SVD is first applied to the snapshot matrix $\mathcal{D}$, and then, spatial and temporal DMD algorithms are applied to the rescaled left and right singular vector matrices.

In the following, we provide a detailed mathematical description of the *parallel* STDMD and *sequential* STDMD approaches.

2.1. Parallel STDMD

The parallel spatio-temporal DMD method simultaneously decomposes spatio-temporal data across both spatial and temporal dimensions, providing insights into the interplay between spatial and temporal dynamics.

Let us recall that the DMD algorithm presented in Section 1.1 uses a low-rank approximation of the linear mapping that best approximates the dynamics of the data $\mathcal{D}$, in (3), collected for the system. Moreover, if we choose the projection matrix to be the matrix $U_{\mathcal{D}}$ from the truncated SVD of the full data matrix $\mathcal{D}$, as shown in (26)

$$\mathcal{D} = U_{\mathcal{D}}\Sigma_{\mathcal{D}}V_{\mathcal{D}}^*,$$

we obtain the reduced-order model given by the following data matrix

$$\tilde{\mathcal{D}} = [\tilde{\mathbf{x}}_0, \dots, \tilde{\mathbf{x}}_m],$$

which coincides with the scaled right singular vector matrix of $\mathcal{D}$, i.e.

$$\tilde{\mathcal{D}} = \Sigma_{\mathcal{D}} V_{\mathcal{D}}^*,$$

according to (27) and (28). Applying the standard DMD approach to reduced model data $\tilde{\mathcal{D}}$, we obtain the following expansion according to (6):

$$\tilde{\mathbf{x}}_k = W\Lambda^k \mathbf{b}, \tag{40}$$

where W is the eigenvector matrix, $\Lambda = \mathrm{diag}\{\lambda_i\}$ is the diagonal matrix of associated eigenvalues of the corresponding DMD operator, and $\mathbf{b} = W^{-1}\tilde{\mathbf{x}}_0$. For our purposes, we will call W the matrix of *temporal DMD modes* and Λ the matrix of *temporal DMD eigenvalues*.

Using equality (13), by multiplying the left side of Equation (40) by matrix $U_{\mathcal{D}}$, we obtain the *temporal DMD expansion*, in (8):

$$\mathbf{x}_k = \Phi\Lambda^k \mathbf{b}.$$

Following the same idea, we can use the row vectors of the scaled left singular vector matrix $U\Sigma_{\mathcal{D}}$ of $\mathcal{D}$ to obtain a spatial expansion similar to (40). Let us denote

$$\bar{\mathcal{D}} = \Sigma_{\mathcal{D}} U^T = [\bar{\mathbf{y}}_0, \dots, \bar{\mathbf{y}}_n], \tag{41}$$

where $\bar{\mathbf{y}}_i$ is the i-th column vector of $\bar{\mathcal{D}}$. Applying the standard DMD approach to data $\bar{\mathcal{D}}$, we obtain the following expansion, according to (6):

$$\bar{\mathbf{y}}_k = \bar{W}\bar{\Lambda}^k \bar{\mathbf{b}}, \tag{42}$$

where $\bar{W}$ is the eigenvector matrix, $\bar{\Lambda} = \mathrm{diag}\{\bar{\lambda}_i\}$ is the diagonal matrix of associated eigenvalues of the corresponding DMD operator, and $\bar{\mathbf{b}} = \bar{W}^{-1}\bar{\mathbf{y}}_0$. We will call $\bar{W}$ the matrix of *spatial DMD modes* and $\bar{\Lambda}$ the matrix of *spatial DMD eigenvalues*.

From expressions (40) and (42), using (31), obtain

$$\tilde{\mathcal{D}} = W\,\mathrm{diag}\{b_i\} V_{and}(\lambda) \text{ and } \bar{\mathcal{D}} = \bar{W}\,\mathrm{diag}\{\bar{b}_i\} V_{and}(\bar{\lambda}). \tag{43}$$

Then, for the full-data matrix $\mathcal{D}$, using equality

$$\mathcal{D} = (U_{\mathcal{D}}\Sigma_{\mathcal{D}})\Sigma_{\mathcal{D}}^{-1}(\Sigma_{\mathcal{D}} V_{\mathcal{D}}^*),$$

we obtain the matrix form presentation

$$\mathcal{D} = V_{and}^T(\bar{\lambda})\mathrm{diag}\{\bar{b}_i\}\Psi\,\mathrm{diag}\{b_i\} V_{and}(\lambda), \tag{44}$$

where $r \times r$ the matrix

$$\Psi = \bar{W}^T \Sigma_{\mathcal{D}}^{-1} W \tag{45}$$

is the matrix of *spatio-temporal DMD modes*.

The following algorithm (Algorithm 1) summarizes the steps for parallel STDMD:

Algorithm 1: Parallel STDMD algorithm

1. Compute the (reduced) SVD of $\mathcal{D}$, writing $\mathcal{D} = U_{\mathcal{D}}\Sigma_{\mathcal{D}}V_{\mathcal{D}}^*$.
2. Define spatial and temporal data matrices:
$\tilde{\mathcal{D}} = \Sigma_{\mathcal{D}}V_{\mathcal{D}}^*$ and $\bar{\mathcal{D}} = \Sigma_{\mathcal{D}}U^T$.
3. Perform the standard DMD approach to data set $\tilde{\mathcal{D}}$
and compute temporal DMD modes, eigenvalues and amplitudes:
W, Λ and $\mathbf{b}$.
4. Perform the standard DMD approach to data set $\bar{\mathcal{D}}$
and compute spatial DMD modes, eigenvalues and amplitudes:
$\bar{W}, \bar{\Lambda}$ and $\bar{\mathbf{b}}$.
5. Compute the matrix of spatio-temporal DMD modes
$\Psi = \bar{W}^T\Sigma_{\mathcal{D}}^{-1}W$.

The eigenvalues and DMD modes can then be used to reconstruct the full data $\mathbf{x}_k$ in $\mathcal{D}$. Let us denote the elements of snapshot $\mathbf{x}_k$ and matrix Ψ as follows:

$$\mathbf{x}_k = [x_1^{(k)}, x_2^{(k)}, \ldots, x_n^{(k)}]^T \text{ and } \Psi = [\psi_{ij}]_{r\times r}.$$

Then, from (44), for the s-th coordinate of $\mathbf{x}_k$ it follows:

$$x_s^{(k)} = \sum_{i,j=1}^{r} \psi_{ij}\bar{\lambda}_i^s\bar{b}_i\lambda_j^k b_j, \tag{46}$$

where $\bar{\lambda}_i$ and λ_j are the spatial and temporal DMD eigenvalues, respectively.

2.2. Sequential STDMD

In contrast to parallel STDMD, sequential involves decomposing spatio-temporal data sequentially along the temporal axis, capturing both spatial and temporal dynamics separately. This approach enables the identification of spatial structures evolving over time and their corresponding temporal dynamics.

For conventional DMD, the temporal information (temporal growth rate and angular frequency) is explicitly included in the eigenvalue matrix Λ, whereas the spatial information (spatial growth rate and wavenumber) is implicitly hidden in the dynamic mode matrix Φ. Therefore, this study aims to decompose dynamic modes in a certain way to obtain spatial information.

Let us apply the standard DMD method described in Section 1.1 to the input data $\mathcal{D}$ specified in (3), which results in *temporal DMD expansion* (8):

$$\mathbf{x}_k = \Phi\Lambda^k\mathbf{b},$$

where $\Phi = YV\Sigma^{\dagger}W$ is the matrix of (exact) DMD modes, Λ is the matrix of DMD eigenvalues and $\mathbf{b}$ is the vector of amplitudes; see (15)–(21). As we mentioned, this expression is equivalent to (31):

$$\mathcal{D} = \Phi\,\mathrm{diag}\{b_i\}V_{and}(\lambda).$$

Note that the spatial information, such as spatial growth rate and wavenumber, of the dynamic in consideration is implicitly hidden in the dynamic mode matrix Φ. We can use the row vectors of the DMD mode matrix Φ to obtain spatial expansion similar to (40). Let us denote

$$\bar{\mathcal{D}} = \Phi^T = [\bar{\mathbf{y}}_0, \ldots, \bar{\mathbf{y}}_n], \tag{47}$$

where $\bar{\mathbf{y}}_i$ is the i-th column vector of $\bar{\mathcal{D}}$. Applying the standard DMD approach to data $\bar{\mathcal{D}}$, we obtain the following expansion according to (6):

$$\bar{\mathbf{y}}_k = \bar{\Phi}\bar{\Lambda}^k\bar{\mathbf{b}}, \tag{48}$$

where $\bar{\Phi}$ is the eigenvector matrix, $\bar{\Lambda} = \mathrm{diag}\{\bar{\lambda}_i\}$ is the diagonal matrix of associated eigenvalues of the corresponding DMD operator, and $\bar{\mathbf{b}} = \bar{\Phi}^{-1}\bar{\mathbf{y}}_0$.

Then, for the full-data matrix $\mathcal{D}$, we obtain the following matrix form presentation:

$$\mathcal{D} = V_{and}^T(\bar{\lambda})\mathrm{diag}\{\bar{b}_i\}\Psi\,\mathrm{diag}\{b_i\}V_{and}(\lambda), \tag{49}$$

where $r \times r$ matrix

$$\Psi = \bar{W}^T \tag{50}$$

is the matrix of *spatio-temporal DMD modes*. The following algorithm (Algorithm 2) summarizes the steps for sequential STDMD:

Algorithm 2: Sequential STDMD algorithm

1. Perform the standard DMD approach to data set $\mathcal{D}$:
   1.1. Define the data matrices: X and Y;
   1.2. Compute the reduced SVD of X : $X = U\Sigma V^*$;
   1.3. Construct the reduced-order operator: $\tilde{A} = U^*YV\Sigma^\dagger$;
   and compute the eigendecomposition of $\tilde{A}$: $\tilde{A}W = W\Lambda$;
   1.4. Compute the DMD modes, eigenvalues and amplitudes:
   $\Phi = YV\Sigma^\dagger W$, Λ and $\mathbf{b}$.
2. Define the spatial data matrix as transposed DMD modes:
   $\bar{\mathcal{D}} = \Phi^T$.
3. Perform the standard DMD approach to data set $\bar{\mathcal{D}}$ and compute DMD modes, eigenvalues and amplitudes:
   $\bar{\Phi}$, $\bar{\Lambda}$ and $\bar{\mathbf{b}}$.
4. Compute the matrix of spatio-temporal DMD modes
   $\Psi = \bar{\Phi}^T$.

For the reconstruction of snapshots in $\mathcal{D}$, we obtain similar to (46) expression

$$x_s^{(k)} = \sum_{i,j=1}^{r} \psi_{ij}\bar{\lambda}_i^s\bar{b}_i\lambda_j^k b_j, \tag{51}$$

where $x_s^{(k)}$ is the s-th coordinate of state $\mathbf{x}_k$. Note that although the notations of parameters in (51) and (46) are the same, their values are different.

For both cases, in (46) and (51), it is straightforward to obtain the expression for the continuous case, in the form

$$x(s,t) = \sum_{i,j=1}^{r} \psi_{ij}\, e^{\bar{\omega}_i s}\, \bar{b}_i\, e^{\omega_j t}\, b_j = \sum_{i,j=1}^{r} \psi_{ij}\, \bar{b}_i\, b_j\, e^{\bar{\omega}_i s + \omega_j t}, \tag{52}$$

where s denotes the spatial variable. The spatial DMD eigenvalues $\bar{\omega}_i$ give the information about spatial wavenumbers and growth rates, while the temporal DMD eigenvalues ω_j give information about the underlying temporal frequencies and growth rates.

3. Delay-Embedding STDMD

As already mentioned, traditional DMD approaches are limited in their ability to capture the full complexity of nonlinear and non-stationary systems, particularly when dealing with high-dimensional and noisy datasets. Due to the fact that in Algorithms 1 and 2 the standard DMD method is applied sequentially or in parallel, they inherit the disadvantages of the DMD method. To address these limitations, we will propose an extension of STDMD algorithms using the delay-embedding approach described in Section 1.

3.1. *Parallel Delay-Embedding STDMD*

This approach redesigns the input data of the system, creating new state variables. However, the introduction of the new variables is made at the expense of reducing the number of samples in the training data set. Hence, the number of these new variables (number of rows in the Hankel matrix), in (39), has to be a balance between the ability to detect dominant modes and the accuracy of the estimated model. The following algorithm (Algorithm 3) provides a step-by-step implementation of *parallel delay-embedding DMD*:

Algorithm 3: Parallel delay-embedding STDMD

1. Compute the (reduced) SVD of $\mathcal{D}$, writing $\mathcal{D} = U_{\mathcal{D}}\Sigma_{\mathcal{D}}V_{\mathcal{D}}^*$.
2. Define spatial and temporal data matrices:
   $\tilde{\mathcal{D}} = \Sigma_{\mathcal{D}}V_{\mathcal{D}}^*$ and $\bar{\mathcal{D}} = \Sigma_{\mathcal{D}}U^T$.
3. Perform delay-embedding DMD approach to data set $\tilde{\mathcal{D}}$
   and compute temporal DMD modes, eigenvalues and amplitudes:
   W, Λ and $\mathbf{b}$.
4. Perform delay-embedding DMD approach to data set $\bar{\mathcal{D}}$
   and compute spatial DMD modes, eigenvalues and amplitudes:
   $\bar{W}, \bar{\Lambda}$ and $\bar{\mathbf{b}}$.
5. Compute the matrix of spatio-temporal DMD modes
   $\Psi = \bar{W}^T\Sigma_{\mathcal{D}}^{-1}W$.

The implementation of the corresponding algorithm for the sequential STDMD approach is similar, so we will omit it here. We note that although delay-embedding is only applied to the reduced input matrices $\tilde{\mathcal{D}}$ and $\bar{\mathcal{D}}$, the embedding can be applied to the full input data matrix $\mathcal{D}$ as well.

3.2. *Delay-Embedding STDMD vs. STKD*

Le Clainche et al. [23] introduced *spatio-temporal Koopman decomposition* (STKD), which incorporates higher order DMD [56] and a spatio-temporal approach for the Koopman operator. Our goal in this section is to present an alternative approach to STKD. Below, we outline some similarities and differences between the two approaches.

- The STKD scheme is similar to delay-embedding STDMD, with the difference that STKD uses higher order DMD instead of augmented DMD. This implies greater computational complexity in STKD than in STDMD, but on the other hand, it allows easily extending the STKD to higher spatial dimensions when the snapshot matrix becomes a tensor.
- In [23], the spatio-temporal expansion, by STKD, corresponding to (52) has the form

$$x(s,t) = \sum_{i,j-1}^{m,n} a_{ij}q_{ij}\, e^{\hat{\omega}_i s + \tilde{\omega}_j t},$$

where q_{ij} are the normalized spatial modes and a_{ij} are the mode amplitudes. In addition, for STKD, the amplitudes a_{ij} are determined by the optimal amplitudes computation scheme described in (34)–(38). We should note that although the calculation of the amplitudes in STDMD is through the standard Formula (30), which is more cost-efficient, a better approximation of the data is achieved when using the schemes (34)–(38).

Among the main advantages of the schemes proposed in this article are the following:

- The matrix form presentations (44) and (49) of the snapshot matrix $\mathcal{D}$, which offer a structured framework that facilitates easier understanding and implementation.
- Additionally, the structured nature of the matrix representation allows for straightforward generalization to parallel computation architectures, enabling seamless scalability and improved computational efficiency in analyzing large-scale spatio-temporal datasets.
- The STDMD approach, augmented with delay-embedding, offers enhanced computational efficiency compared to STKD.
- By augmenting the dataset with delayed observations, the analysis captures underlying dynamics more effectively, reducing the impact of noise on mode identification and reconstruction.

Overall, the delay-embedding STDMD enhances the accessibility and usability of the proposed approaches, making them more practical and widely applicable to researchers and practitioners in various fields.

4. Numerical Examples

In this section, we will illustrate the introduced approach to delay-embedding spatio-temporal DMD. The considered examples are well known in the literature, and through them, we illustrate the ability of the proposed scheme to accurately calculate spatio-temporal DMD modes and eigenvalues, including spatial wavenumbers and growth rates and temporal frequencies and growth rates. We mainly present the results of the application of parallel delay-embedding STDMD (Algorithm 3). Since both methods use extended data matrices and are computationally comparable, we collate the results obtained by Algorithm 3 with those of the STKDM method presented by Le Clainche in [23]. All numerical experiments and simulations were performed on Windows 7 with MATLAB release R2013a on an Acer Aspire 571G laptop with an Intel(R) Core(TM) i3-2328M CPU at 2.2 GHz and 4 GB of RAM.

Example 1. *Combination of travelling wavetrains.*

We begin by demonstrating the feature extraction technique for delay embedding STDMD for a spatio-temporal signal:

$$x(s,t) = [0.5 + \sin(s)][2\cos(k_1 s - \omega_1 t) + 0.5\cos(k_2 s - \omega_2 t)], \tag{53}$$

defined in a 1D periodic domain, $s \in [0, 2\pi)$. This example was taken from [23] and the same example was also discussed in [57]. It represents a simplified model of the signal proposed in [58] with three basic features in the convective variability of the tropical atmosphere as a function of longitude (s):

(i) *A time-independent profile, $0.5 + \sin(s)$, representing enhanced convective activity over warm oceans over cold oceans such and continental land;*
(ii) *A long-wavelength eastward-propagating wave, $\cos(k_1 s - \omega_1 t)$, representing a large-scale mode of organized convection called Madden-Julian oscillation (MJO);*
(iii) *A short-wavelength westward-propagating wave representing the building blocks of the MJO (so-called convectively coupled equatorial waves).*

The natural time units in (53) are days, so the long wave has a period of 45 days and the period of the short wave is approximately 14 days. These periods are comparable to the timescales observed in nature.

In (53), k_1 and k_2 are integer-valued wavenumbers set to $k_1 = 2$ and $k_2 = 10$, and ω_1 and ω_2 are time-dependent phases for the rationally independent frequencies $\omega_1 = 2\pi/45$ and $\omega_2 = \sqrt{10}\omega_1$. The color map of this pattern is depicted in Figure 1 (left). This pattern is obtained with a spectral spatial and temporal complexity of 12 and 4, respectively. This is because it involves 12 wavenumbers: $\pm k_1, \pm k_2, \pm(k_1 \pm 1)$ and $\pm(k_2 \pm 1)$, and four frequencies: $\pm\omega_1$ and $\pm\omega_2$. This pattern is spatially periodic, with a period equal to 2π, but temporally quasi-periodic.

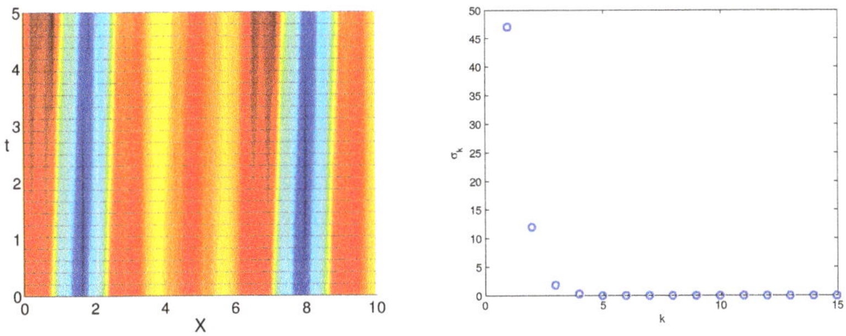

Figure 1. Spatio-temporal color map for the dynamics defined by (54), (**left panel**), and first 15 singular values of the generated data (**right panel**).

In order to apply the delay-embedding STDMD method, we discretize s and t in the sampled intervals $0 \le s \le 10$ and $0 \le t \le 5$, using 50 and 25 points, respectively. Generated data are 50×25, but its rank is 4 (see Figure 1 (right)), which yields unsatisfactory results with the pure temporal DMD method.

Performing delay-embedding STDMD (Algorithm 1), with time-delaying index 2 and spatial-delaying index 3, we identify the correct 12 wavenumbers and 4 frequencies. See the dynamic reconstruction with delayed STDMD (Algorithm 1) in Figure 2. Figure 3 depicts the *amplitude–frequency* and *growth rate–frequency* diagrams. Figure 3 shows the combinations of spatial modes and temporal modes used in the reconstruction of the data in (52). They are grouped along straight lines in the plane, which may be either horizontal or oblique, and correspond to either standing or travelling patterns, respectively. The results are identical to those in [23], where the STKD method is applied to the same example and input data.

Example 2. *Dynamics of two counter-propagating waves*

In this example, we consider the dynamics of two counter-propagating waves

$$x(s,t) = v(s,t) + v(-s,t)\,, \tag{54}$$

where v is defined as

$$v(s,t) = \frac{1}{2}\sum_{-6}^{6} 3^{-|m|} e^{i\,m(10\pi s+30t)}\,. \tag{55}$$

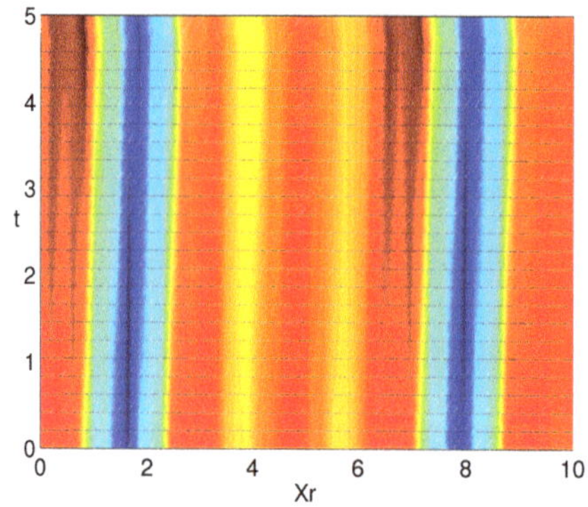

Figure 2. Spatio-temporal color map of reconstructed data computed by delay-embedding STDMD (Algorithm 1).

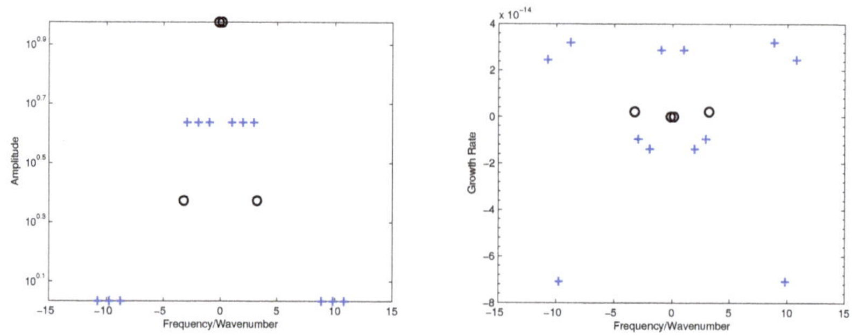

Figure 3. (**Left panel**) Spatial amplitude–wavenumber ('+') and temporal amplitude–frequency ('o'); (**Right panel**) Spatial growth rate–wavenumber ('+') and temporal growth rate–frequency ('o').

The color map of this pattern is depicted in Figure 4. The two counter-propagating waves are visible on the chart, but it is seen that the pattern can also be considered as a modulated *standing waves*, in which the positions of the nodes and crests do not remain constant, but oscillate left and right. The generated data have a low-rank structure, which can be seen from the singular values depicted in Figure 4.

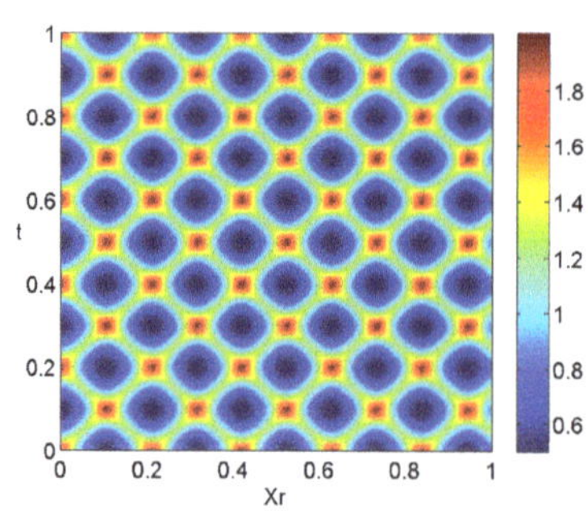

Figure 4. Spatio-temporal color map of reconstructed data computed by delay-embedding STDMD (Algorithm 1).

If we apply the standard DMD approach, we obtain only seven modes and it gives poor reconstruction of the input data. Instead, if we use delay-embedding STDMD (Algorithm 1), with time delay of 2 and spatial delay also of 2, then we obtain 13 modes and reconstruct the input data with greater accuracy. See the dynamic reconstruction with delayed STDMD (Algorithm 1) in Figure 5.

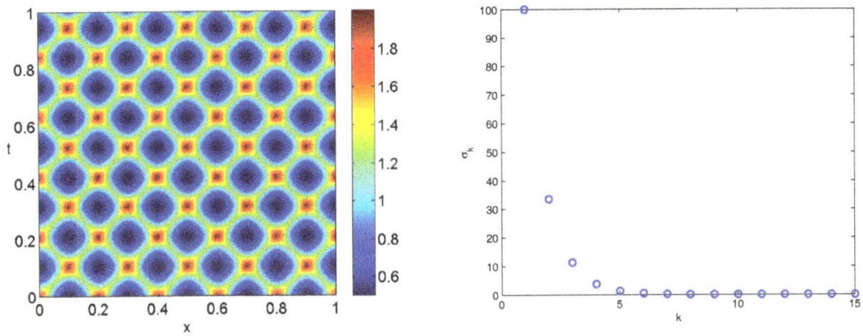

Figure 5. Spatio-temporal color map for the dynamics defined by (54), (**left panel**), and first 15 singular values of the generated data (**right panel**).

Note that, if we use optimal amplitude computation, in Algorithm 1, as shown in (34)–(38), we obtain a better approximation of the dynamics data and reconstruct the snapshots with a relative RMS error $\sim 1.4 \times 10^{-12}$. Figure 6 depicts the *amplitude–frequency* and *growth rate–frequency* diagrams. It shows that the relevant points are aligned in two straight lines, which, according to (54), is consistent with the fact that the pattern is the superposition of two counter-propagating travelling waves.

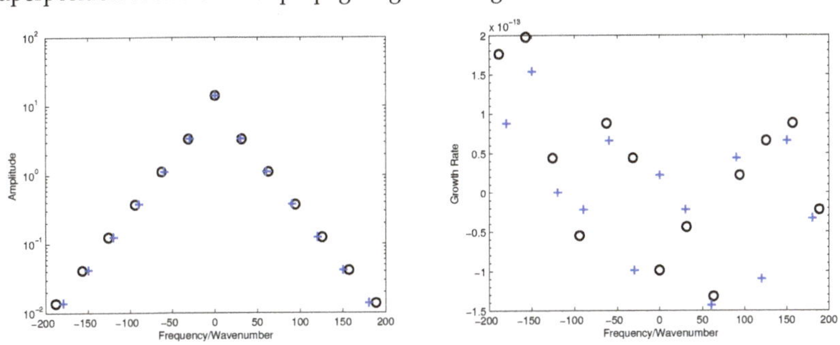

Figure 6. (**Left panel**) Spatial amplitude–wavenumber ('+') and temporal amplitude–frequency ('o'); (**Right panel**) Spatial growth rate–wavenumber ('+') and temporal growth rate–frequency ('o').

Note that the counterpart to Equation (55) is given by

$$v(s,t) = \frac{1}{2} \sum_{-6}^{6} 3^{-|m|} e^{30i\,mt} \cos(10m\pi s)\,, \tag{56}$$

which implies (from the equality $\cos(10m\pi s) = \cos(-10m\pi s)$) that the spatial complexity is 7, while the spectral complexity is 13. It also follows from (56) that the pattern can be seen as modulated standing waves.

5. Conclusions

In this paper, we have provided a detailed exposition of two variants of spatio-temporal dynamic mode decomposition (STDMD), namely the parallel methods STDMD and sequential STDMD. We have introduced the matrix representations underlying these techniques, highlighting their respective computational frameworks for analyzing spatio-temporal data. To address some shortcomings of the presented algorithms, which are inherited from the classic DMD algorithm, we have introduced extensions to these approaches incorporating delay-embedding techniques. Furthermore, we have conducted numerical experiments to validate the efficacy of the proposed extensions in overcoming the identified limitations of traditional DMD methods. Through these experiments, we have illustrated the enhanced performance of delay-embedded STDMD, showcasing its utility in analyzing complex spatio-temporal datasets.

For future work, there are several promising directions that can build upon the methodologies and findings presented in this paper. Firstly, further exploration and refinement of the delay-embedding techniques introduced in our study could lead to more effective approaches for capturing nonlinear dynamics and improving robustness against noise in spatio-temporal DMD analyses. Additionally, investigating the application of our sequential and parallel approaches with delay-embedding across a wide range of spatio-temporal datasets and real-world applications would provide valuable insights into their generalizability and practical utility. Furthermore, exploring hybrid methodologies that combine elements of different spatio-temporal decomposition techniques, such as incorporating machine learning algorithms or Bayesian approaches, could offer new avenues for enhancing the accuracy and interpretability of spatio-temporal analysis. Additionally, future research could focus on the parallel implementation of the approaches introduced in this paper to enhance computational efficiency. Investigating strategies for parallelizing the computation of spatio-temporal DMD algorithms across multiple processing units or distributed computing architectures could significantly reduce computational time and enable the analysis of large-scale datasets. By investigating the parallel implementation of these techniques, future research can enhance their computational efficiency and facilitate their widespread adoption in scientific and engineering domains where timely analysis of spatio-temporal data is critical. Overall, these future directions hold great potential for advancing the state-of-the-art in spatio-temporal DMD methodologies and their applications in diverse fields.

In conclusion, our research contributes to the advancement of spatio-temporal DMD methodologies by introducing extensions that enhance the robustness and accuracy of the analysis. The proposed approaches offer valuable tools for researchers and practitioners in diverse fields, enabling deeper insights into the dynamics of complex spatio-temporal systems. We anticipate that our findings will stimulate further research and development in this area, leading to continued advancements in the analysis and understanding of spatio-temporal phenomena.

Funding: This research received no external funding.

Data Availability Statement: No publicly available data.

Conflicts of Interest: The author declares no conflicts of interest.

References

1. Koopman, B. Hamiltonian systems and transformations in Hilbert space. *Proc. Natl. Acad. Sci. USA* **1931**, *17*, 315–318. [CrossRef]
2. Mezić, I. Spectral properties of dynamical systems, model reduction and decompositions. *Nonlin. Dynam.* **2005**, *41*, 309–325. [CrossRef]
3. Schmid, P.J.; Sesterhenn, J. Dynamic mode decomposition of numerical and experimental data. In Proceedings of the 61st Annual Meeting of the APS Division of Fluid Dynamics, San Antonio, TX, USA, 23–25 November 2008.
4. Rowley, C.W.; Mezić, I.; Bagheri, S.; Schlatter, P.; Henningson, D.S. Spectral analysis of nonlinear flows. *J. Fluid Mech.* **2009**, *641*, 115–127. [CrossRef]
5. Schmid, P.J. Application of the dynamic mode decomposition to experimental data. *Exp. Fluids* **2011**, *50*, 1123–1130. [CrossRef]
6. Proctor, L.J.; Eckhoff, A.P. Discovering dynamic patterns from infectious disease data using dynamic mode decomposition, International health. *Int. Health* **2015**, *7*, 139–145. [CrossRef]
7. Grosek, J.; Kutz, J.N. Dynamic Mode Decomposition for Real-Time Background/Foreground Separation in Video. *arXiv* **2014**, arXiv:1404.7592.
8. Brunton, B.W.; Johnson, L.A.; Ojemann, J.G.; Kutz, J.N. Extracting spatial-temporal coherent patterns in large-scale neural recordings using dynamic mode decomposition. *J. Neurosci. Methods* **2016**, *258*, 1–15. [CrossRef] [PubMed]
9. Mann, J.; Kutz, J.N. Dynamic mode decomposition for financial trading strategies. *Quant. Financ.* **2016**, *16*, 1643–1655. [CrossRef]
10. Cui, L.; Long, W. Trading strategy based on dynamic mode decomposition: Tested in Chinese stock market. *Phys. A Stat. Mech. Its Appl.* **2016**, *461*, 498–508. [CrossRef]

11. Kuttichira, D.P.; Gopalakrishnan, E.A.; Menon, V.K.; Soman, K.P. Stock price prediction using dynamic mode decomposition. In Proceedings of the 2017 International Conference on Advances in Computing, Communications and Informatics (ICACCI), Udupi, India, 13–16 September 2017; pp. 55–60. [CrossRef]
12. Berger, E.; Sastuba, M.; Vogt, D.; Jung, B.; Amor, H.B. Estimation of perturbations in robotic behavior using dynamic mode decomposition. *J. Adv. Robot.* **2015**, *29*, 331–343. [CrossRef]
13. Schmid, P.J. Dynamic mode decomposition of numerical and experimental data. *J. Fluid Mech.* **2010**, *656*, 5–28. [CrossRef]
14. Seena, A.; Sung, H.J. Dynamic mode decomposition of turbulent cavity ows for selfsustained oscillations. *Int. J. Heat Fluid Fluid* **2011**, *32*, 1098–1110. [CrossRef]
15. Mezić, I. Analysis of fluid flows via spectral properties of the Koopman operator. *Annu. Rev. Fluid Mech.* **2013**, *45*, 357–378. [CrossRef]
16. Tu, J.H.; Rowley, C.W.; Luchtenburg, D.M.; Brunton, S.L.; Kutz, J.N. On dynamic mode decomposition: Theory and applications. *J. Comput. Dyn.* **2014**, *1*, 391–421. [CrossRef]
17. Kutz, J.N.; Brunton, S.L.; Brunton, W.; Proctor, J. *Dynamic Mode Decomposition: Data-Driven Modeling of Complex Systems*; SIAM: Philadelphia, PA, USA, 2016; pp. 1–234. ISBN 978-1-611-97449-2.
18. Bai, Z.; Kaiser, E.; Proctor, J.L.; Kutz, J.N.; Brunton, S.L. Dynamic Mode Decomposition for Compressive System Identification, *AIAA J.* **2020**, *58*, 561–574. [CrossRef]
19. Brunton, S.L.; Budišić, M.; Kaiser, E.; Kutz, J.N. Modern Koopman Theory for Dynamical Systems. *SIAM Rev.* **2022**, *64*, 229–340. [CrossRef]
20. Chen, K.K.; Tu, J.H.; Rowley, C.W. Variants of dynamic mode decomposition: Boundary condition, Koopman, and Fourier analyses. *J. Nonlinear Sci.* **2012**, *22*, 887–915. [CrossRef]
21. Williams, M.O.; Hemati, M.S.; Dawson, S.T.M.; Kevrekidis, I.G.; Rowley, C.W. Extending Data-Driven Koopman Analysis to Actuated Systems. *IFAC-PapersOnLine* **2016**, *49*, 704–709. [CrossRef]
22. Le Clainche, S.; Vega, J.M.; Soria, J. Higher order dynamic mode decomposition of noisy experimental data: The flow structure of a zero-net-mass-flux jet. *Exp. Therm. Fluid Sci.* **2017**, *88*, 336–353. [CrossRef]
23. Clainche, S.L.; Vega, J.M. Spatio-Temporal Koopman Decomposition. *J. Nonlinear Sci.* **2018**, *28*, 1793–1842. [CrossRef]
24. Anantharamu, S.; Mahesh, K. A parallel and streaming Dynamic Mode Decomposition algorithm with finite precision error analysis for large data. *J. Comput. Phys.* **2019**, *380*, 355–377. [CrossRef]
25. Sayadi, T.; Schmid, P.J. Parallel data-driven decomposition algorithm for large-scale datasets: With application to transitional boundary layers. *Theor. Comput. Fluid Dyn.* **2016**, *30*, 415–426. [CrossRef]
26. Maryada, K.R.; Norris, S.E. Reduced-communication parallel dynamic mode decomposition. *J. Comput. Sci.* **2022**, *61*, 101599. [CrossRef]
27. Li, B.; Garicano-Menaab, J.; Valero, E. A dynamic mode decomposition technique for the analysis of nonuniformly sampled flow data. *J. Comput. Phys.* **2022**, *468*, 111495. [CrossRef]
28. Smith, E.; Variansyah, I.; McClarren, R. Variable Dynamic Mode Decomposition for Estimating Time Eigenvalues in Nuclear Systems. *arXiv* **2022**, arXiv:2208.10942v1.
29. Jovanovic, M.R.; Schmid, P.J.; Nichols, J.W. Sparsity-promoting dynamic mode decomposition. *Phys. Fluids* **2014**, *26*, 024103. [CrossRef]
30. Guéniat, F.; Mathelin, L.; Pastur, L.R. A dynamic mode decomposition approach for large and arbitrarily sampled systems. *Phys. Fluids* **2014**, *27*, 025113. [CrossRef]
31. Cassamo, N.; van Wingerden, J.W. On the Potential of Reduced Order Models for Wind Farm Control: A Koopman Dynamic Mode Decomposition Approach. *Energies* **2020**, *13*, 6513. [CrossRef]
32. Ngo, T.T.; Nguyen, V.; Pham, X.Q.; Hossain, M.A.; Huh, E.N. Motion Saliency Detection for Surveillance Systems Using Streaming Dynamic Mode Decomposition. *Symmetry* **2020**, *12*, 1397. [CrossRef]
33. Babalola, O.P.; Balyan, V. WiFi Fingerprinting Indoor Localization Based on Dynamic Mode Decomposition Feature Selection with Hidden Markov Model. *Sensors* **2021**, *21*, 6778. [CrossRef]
34. Lopez-Martin, M.; Sanchez-Esguevillas, A.; Hernandez-Callejo, L.; Arribas, J.I.; Carro, B. Novel Data-Driven Models Applied to Short-Term Electric Load Forecasting. *Appl. Sci.* **2021**, *11*, 5708. [CrossRef]
35. Surasinghe, S.S.; Bollt, E.M. Randomized Projection Learning Method for Dynamic Mode Decomposition. *Mathematics* **2021**, *9*, 2803. [CrossRef]
36. Li, C.Y.; Chen, Z.; Tse, T.K.T. A parametric and feasibility study for data sampling of the dynamic mode decomposition: Range, resolution, and universal convergence states. *Nonlinear Dyn.* **2022**, *107*, 3683–3707. [CrossRef]
37. Mezić, I. On Numerical Approximations of the Koopman Operator. *Mathematics* **2022**, *10*, 1180. [CrossRef]
38. Nedzhibov, G. Dynamic Mode Decomposition: A new approach for computing the DMD modes and eigenvalues. *Ann. Acad. Rom. Sci. Ser. Math. Appl.* **2022**, *14*, 5–16. [CrossRef]
39. Nedzhibov, G. On Alternative Algorithms for Computing Dynamic Mode Decomposition. *Computation* **2022**, *10*, 210. [CrossRef]
40. Nedzhibov, G. An Improved Approach for Implementing Dynamic Mode Decomposition with Control. *Computation* **2023**, *11*, 201. [CrossRef]
41. Nedzhibov, G. Online Dynamic Mode Decomposition: An alternative approach for low rank datasets. *Ann. Acad. Rom. Sci. Ser. Math. Appl.* **2023**, *15*, 229–249. [CrossRef]

42. Nedzhibov, G. Extended Online DMD and Weighted Modifications for Streaming Data Analysis. *Computation* **2023**, *11*, 114. [CrossRef]
43. Arbabi, H.; Mezić, I. Ergodic Theory, Dynamic Mode Decomposition, and Computation of Spectral Properties of the Koopman Operator. *SIAM J. Appl. Dyn. Syst.* **2017**, *16*, 2096–2126. [CrossRef]
44. Kamb, M.; Kaiser, E.; Brunton, S.L.; Kutz, J.N. Time-delay observables for Koopman: Theory and applications. *SIAM J. Appl. Dyn. Syst.* **2020**, *19*, 886–917. [CrossRef]
45. Juang, J.N.; Pappa, R.S. An eigensystem realization algorithm for modal parameter identification and model reduction. *J. Guidance Control Dyn.* **1985**, *8*, 620–627. [CrossRef]
46. Vautard, R.; Ghil, M. Singular spectrum analysis in nonlinear dynamics, with applications to paleoclimatic time series. *Phys. D* **1989**, *35*, 395–424. [CrossRef]
47. Brunton, S.L.; Brunton, B.W.; Proctor, J.L.; Kaiser, E.; Kutz, J.N. Chaos as an intermittently forced linear system. *Nat. Commun.* **2017**, *8*, 19. [CrossRef] [PubMed]
48. Lu, W.; Huang, G.; Wang, J.; Hong, S. Spatio-temporal dynamic mode decomposition in a shear layer flow. *Aerosp. Sci. Technol.* **2019**, *91*, 263–271. [CrossRef]
49. Le Clainche, S.; Pérez, J.M.; Vega, J.M. Spatio-temporal flow structures in the three-dimensional wake of a circular cylinder. *Fluid Dyn. Res.* **2018**, *50*, 051406. [CrossRef]
50. Torres, P.; Le Clainche, S.; Vinuesa, R. On the Experimental, Numerical and Data-Driven Methods to Study Urban Flows. *Energies* **2021**, *14*, 1310. [CrossRef]
51. Kou, J.; Zhang, W. Data-driven modeling for unsteady aerodynamics and aeroelasticity. *Prog. Aerosp Sci.* **2021**, *125*, 100725. [CrossRef]
52. Eivazi, H.; Le Clainche, S.; Hoyas, S.; Vinuesa, R. Towards extraction of orthogonal and parsimonious non-linear modes from turbulent flows. *Expert Syst. Appl.* **2022**, *202*, 117038. [CrossRef]
53. Alonso, A.; Mercader, I.; Batiste, O.; Vega, J.M. Analyzing Slightly Inclined Cylindrical Binary Fluid Convection via Higher Order Dynamic Mode Decomposition. *SIAM J. Appl. Dyn. Syst.* **2022**, *21*, 2148–2186. [CrossRef]
54. Takens, F. Detecting strange attractors in turbulence. In *Dynamical Systems and Turbulence*; Lecture Notes in Mathematics; Springer: Berlin/Heidelberg, Germany, 1981; Volume 898; pp. 366–381. [CrossRef]
55. Sharma, A.S.; Mezić, I.; McKeon, B.J. Correspondence between Koopman mode decomposition, resolvent mode decomposition, and invariant solutions of the Navier–Stokes equations. *Phys. Rev. Fluids* **2016**, *1*, 032402. [CrossRef]
56. Vega, J.M.; Le Clainche, S. *Higher Order Dynamic Mode Decomposition and Its Applications*; Elsevier: Amsterdam, The Netherlands, 2020.
57. Giannakis, D.; Slawinska, J.; Zhao, Z. Spatiotemporal Feature Extraction with Data-Driven Koopman Operators. *JMLR Workshop Conf. Proc.* **2015**, *44*, 103–115.
58. Kikuchi, K.; Wang, B. Spatiotemporal wavelet transform and the multiscale behavior of the Madden-Julian oscillation. *J. Clim.* **2010**, *23*, 3814–3834. [CrossRef]

mathematics

MDPI

Article

Asymptotic Behavior of Solutions in Nonlinear Neutral System with Two Volterra Terms

Mouataz Billah Mesmouli [1,*], Abdelouaheb Ardjouni [2] and Hicham Saber [1]

[1] Mathematics Department, College of Science, University of Ha'il, Ha'il 2440, Saudi Arabia; hicham.saber7@gmail.com
[2] Department of Mathematics and Informatics, University of Souk-Ahras, P.O. Box 1553, Souk Ahras 41000, Algeria; abd_ardjouni@yahoo.fr
* Correspondence: m.mesmouli@uoh.edu.sa or mesmoulimouataz@hotmail.com

Abstract: In this manuscript, we generalise previous results in the literature by providing sufficient conditions for the matrix measure to guarantee the stability, asymptotic stability and exponential stability of a neutral system of differential equations. This is achieved by constructing a suitable operator from our system and applying the Banach fixed point theorem.

Keywords: neutral system; fixed points; fundamental matrix; asymptotic stability; exponential stability; matrix measure; volterra term

MSC: 34A34; 34D20; 34K20; 34K40; 45D05; 47H10

1. Introduction

The basic applications of Volterra equation, which was introduced in 1928 by Volterra himself, can be found in [1–3]. After that, the Volterra integro-differential equation appeared, which has several applications in many fields, such as nanohydrodynamics, glass-forming process, diffusion process in general, heat transfer, neutron diffusion, and wind ripple in the desert. More details about these equations and their applications can be found in [4–8].

Many researchers studied the existence of solutions and asymptotic behavior of these equations; for example, in [9–12], the authors considered the exponential stability of continuous, discrete, and stochastic differential equations. In [13–19], the authors dealt with the existence and stability of one or n-dimensional equations.

A wide variety of differential equations were successfully stabilized using Lyapunov's direct method. Over the last century, Lyapunov theory has been a very fruitful field, studying a qualitative theory of differentials and systems. However, the expressions of Lyapunov functionals are very complicated and hard to construct in many problems, as is the case when the differential equation has unbounded terms or when it contains unbounded functional delays. To overcome the shortcomings of Lyapunov's direct method, in recent years, several researchers have investigated different aspects of the qualitative theory of differential equations using the fixed-point method, which was found to be significantly advantageous compared to Lyapunov's direct method; see instance [20–22].

In [23], Dung studied the following problem of mixed linear Levin–Nohel integro-differential equations.

$$\begin{cases} u'(p) + \int_{p-\beta(p)}^{p} c(p,\eta)u(\eta)d\eta + b(p)u(p-\gamma(p)) = 0, \ p \geq p_0, \\ u(p) = \psi(p) \text{ for } p \in [m(p_0), p_0], \end{cases} \tag{1}$$

while the following n-dimensional version of the above problem

$$\begin{cases} u'(p) + \int_{p-\beta(p)}^{p} C(p,\eta)u(\eta)d\eta + B(p)u(p-\gamma(p)) = 0, \ p \geq p_0, \\ u(p) = \psi(p) \text{ for } p \in [m(p_0), p_0], \end{cases} \tag{2}$$

with

$$m(p_0) = \min\left(\inf_{\eta \geq p_0} \{\eta - \beta(\eta)\}, \inf_{\eta \geq p_0} \{\eta - \gamma(\eta)\} \right),$$

has been considered in [19], as well as its asymptotic stability.

In this work, we propose generalizing these problems by considering the following nonlinear neutral differential system with two Volterra terms, in addition to the study of the exponential stability

$$\begin{cases} \left(u(p) - \int_{p-\alpha(p)}^{p} C_1(p,\eta)u(\eta)d\eta\right)' = \int_{p-\beta(p)}^{p} C_2(p,\eta)u(\eta)d\eta \\ \qquad +Q(p,u(p),u(p-\gamma(p))), \ p \geq p_0, \\ u(p) = \psi(p) \text{ for } p \in [\tau(p_0), p_0], \end{cases} \tag{3}$$

with

$$\tau(p_0) = \min\left(\inf_{\eta \geq p_0} \{\eta - \alpha(\eta)\}, \inf_{\eta \geq p_0} \{\eta - \beta(\eta)\}, \inf_{\eta \geq p_0} \{\eta - \gamma(\eta)\} \right),$$

where

- $u : [\tau(p_0), \infty) \longrightarrow \mathbb{R}^n$ and $Q : [p_0, \infty) \times \mathbb{R}^n \times \mathbb{R}^n \longrightarrow \mathbb{R}^n$ are continuous vector functions, such that $Q(p,0,0) \equiv 0$.
- $\alpha, \beta, \gamma : \mathbb{R} \longrightarrow \mathbb{R}^+$ is a continuous real function such that $p - \alpha(p), p - \beta(p), p - \gamma(p) \longrightarrow \infty$ when $n \longrightarrow \infty$.
- $C_1, C_2 : [p_0, \infty) \times [\tau(p_0), \infty) \to \mathbb{R}^{n^2}$ are bounded with a continuous real function such that $C_2(p,p)$ is nonsingular for all $p \in [p_0, \infty)$.

In this context, the main contribution of this paper is to apply the Banach fixed-point theorem to the show stability, asymptotic stability and exponential stability of solutions for the system (3), which is the generalization of the papers [19,23]. The paper is organized as follows. In Section 2, we present some previous results, and construct the integral form of the problem. After this, we prove the stability, asymptotic stability, and exponential stability of solutions for the system (3) in Sections 3–5, respectively. An example is given in Section 6 to illustrate our results, and a conclusion is provided at the end of this article.

2. Preliminaries

We start this section by transforming the system (3) to a more tractable system. Therefore, in the analysis, we use the fundamental matrix solution of

$$y'(p) = C_2(p,p)y(p), \tag{4}$$

from which we obtain a fixed-point mapping.

Throughout this paper, $\mathcal{Q}(p,p_0)$ will denote a fundamental matrix solution of the homogeneous (unperturbed) linear problem (4).

Lemma 1. *We say that u is a solution of the problem (3) if and only if*

$$\begin{aligned} u(p) &= \mathcal{Q}(p,p_0)\left(u(p_0) - \int_{p_0-\alpha(p_0)}^{p_0} C_1(p_0,\eta)u(\eta)d\eta\right) \\ &+ \int_{p_0}^{p} \mathcal{Q}(p,\eta)\left[C_2(\eta,\eta)\left(\int_{\eta-\alpha(\eta)}^{\eta} C_1(\eta,r)u(r)dr - u(\eta)\right)d\eta\right. \\ &+ \left.\int_{\eta-\beta(\eta)}^{\eta} C_2(\eta,r)u(r)dr + Q(\eta,u(\eta),u(\eta-\gamma(\eta)))\right]d\eta \end{aligned} \tag{5}$$

for $p \geq p_0$ *and* $u(p) = \psi(p)$ *for* $p \in [\tau(p_0), p_0]$.

Proof. Let
$$y(p) = u(p) - \int_{p-\alpha(p)}^{p} C_1(p,\eta)u(\eta)d\eta.$$

Then, we can write the system (3) as

$$\begin{aligned} y(p) &= C_2(p,p)y(p) + \int_{p-\beta(p)}^{p} C_2(p,\eta)u(\eta)d\eta \\ &- C_2(p,p)y(p) + Q(p,u(p),u(p-\gamma(p))). \end{aligned}$$

Hence

$$\begin{aligned} y(p) &= \mathcal{Q}(p,p_0)y(p_0) - \int_{p_0}^{p} \mathcal{Q}(p,\eta) \\ &\times \left[\int_{p-\beta(p)}^{p} C_2(p,\eta)u(\eta)d\eta - C_2(\eta,\eta)y(\eta) + Q(\eta,u(\eta),u(\eta-\gamma(\eta)))\right]d\eta, \end{aligned}$$

witch equivalent to (5). □

Lemma 2 ([24]). *The state transition matrix* $\Phi(p,\eta)$ *of Equation (4) satisfies*

$$\|\Phi(p,\eta)\| \leq e^{\int_{\eta}^{p}\mu(C_2(p,r))dr}, p \geq \eta,$$

where $\mu(C_2(p,r))$ *is the Matrix measure of* $C_2(p,r)$.

Let $(\mathcal{S}, \|\cdot\|)$ be the Banach space of vector continuous functions $u : [\tau(p_0),\infty) \longrightarrow \mathbb{R}^n$ with the supremum norm.

$$\|u\| = \sup_{p\in[\tau(p_0),\infty)} |u(p)|,$$

where $|\cdot|$ is the infinity norm for $u \in \mathbb{R}^n$. If A is an $n \times n$ matrix valued function A given by $A(p) := [a_{ij}(p)]$, then we define the norm of A by

$$\|A\| := \sup_{p\in[\tau(p_0),\infty)} |A(p)|,$$

where

$$|A(p)| = \max_{1\leq i\leq n} \sum_{j=1}^{n} |a_{ij}(p)|.$$

Using Lemma 1, we define the operator $F : \Gamma_\epsilon \to \mathcal{S}$ by

$$\begin{aligned} (Fu)(p) &= \mathcal{Q}(p,p_0)\left(\psi(p_0) - \int_{p_0-\alpha(p_0)}^{p_0} C_1(p_0,\eta)\psi(\eta)d\eta\right) \\ &+ \int_{p_0}^{p} \mathcal{Q}(p,\eta)\left[\int_{\eta-\beta(\eta)}^{\eta} C_2(\eta,r)u(r)dr\right. \\ &+ C_2(\eta,\eta)\left(\int_{\eta-\alpha(\eta)}^{\eta} C_1(\eta,r)u(r)dr - u(\eta)\right) \\ &+ Q(\eta,u(\eta),u(\eta-\gamma(\eta)))]d\eta \end{aligned} \tag{6}$$

for $p \in [p_0,\infty)$. Therefore, in this paper, we need the following conditions

(C1) The function Q satisfies

$$\begin{aligned} &|Q(\eta,u_1(\eta),u_1(\eta-\gamma(\eta))) - Q(\eta,u_2(\eta),u_2(\eta-\gamma(\eta)))| \\ &\leq q_1|u_1(\eta) - u_2(\eta)| + q_2|u_1(\eta-\gamma(\eta)) - u_2(\eta-\gamma(\eta))|, \end{aligned}$$

for all $u_1, u_2 \in \mathcal{S}$ and $p \in [p_0, \infty)$.

(C2) There is a positive constant $L \in (0,1)$ such that

$$L := \sup_{p \in [\tau(p_0), \infty)} \int_{p_0}^{p} \left(\|C_2(\eta,\eta)\| \left(\int_{\eta-\alpha(\eta)}^{\eta} \|C_1(\eta,r)\| dr + 1 \right) + \int_{\eta-\beta(\eta)}^{\eta} \|C_2(\eta,r)\| dr + q_1 + q_2 \right) d\eta.$$

3. Stability

Definition 1. *The zero solution of (3) is Lyapunov stable if, for any $\epsilon > 0$ and any integer $p \in [p_0, \infty)$, there exists $\delta > 0$ such that $|\psi(p)| \le \delta$ for $p \in [\tau(p_0), p_0]$ implies $|u(p, p_0, \psi)| \le \epsilon$ for $p \in [p_0, \infty)$.*

Theorem 1. *Suppose the conditions (C1), (C2) and*

$$\int_{\eta}^{p} \mu(C_2(r,r)) dr \le M, \quad p \ge \eta,$$

where M is a positive constant. Then, the zero solution of (3) is stable.

Proof. Let $\epsilon > 0$ be given. Choose $\delta > 0$, such that for

$$\left| \psi(p_0) - \int_{p_0-\alpha(p_0)}^{p_0} C_1(p_0,\eta)\psi(\eta) d\eta \right| \le \delta, \quad \forall p \in [\tau(p_0), p_0],$$

and

$$e^{M}(\delta + L\epsilon) \le \epsilon.$$

Define complete metric space

$$\Gamma_\epsilon = \{ u \in \mathcal{S} : \|u\| \le \delta, \forall p \in [\tau(p_0), p_0] \text{ and } \|u\| \le \epsilon, \forall p \in [p_0, \infty) \}.$$

We first prove that $\digamma$ maps Γ_ϵ into Γ_ϵ. Therefore, using the conditions (C1) and (C2), we have

$$\begin{aligned}
|(\digamma u)(p)| \le{}& \|\mathcal{Q}(p,p_0)\| \left| \psi(p_0) - \int_{p_0-\alpha(p_0)}^{p_0} C_1(p_0,\eta)\psi(\eta) d\eta \right| \\
&+ \int_{p_0}^{p} \|\mathcal{Q}(p,\eta)\| \left[\|C_2(\eta,\eta)\| \left(\int_{\eta-\alpha(\eta)}^{\eta} \|C_1(\eta,r)\| |u(r)| dr + |u(\eta)| \right) \right. \\
&+ \left. \int_{\eta-\beta(\eta)}^{\eta} \|C_2(\eta,r)\| |u(r)| dr + |Q(\eta, u(\eta), u(\eta-\gamma(\eta)))| \right] d\eta \\
\le{}& e^{\int_{p_0}^{p} \mu(C_2(r,r)) dr} \left| \psi(p_0) - \int_{p_0-\alpha(p_0)}^{p_0} C_1(p_0,\eta)\psi(\eta) d\eta \right| \\
&+ \int_{p_0}^{p} e^{\int_{\eta}^{p} \mu(C_2(r,r)) dr} \left[\|C_2(\eta,\eta)\| \left(\int_{\eta-\alpha(\eta)}^{\eta} \|C_1(\eta,r)\| |u(r)| dr + |u(\eta)| \right) \right. \\
&+ \left. \int_{\eta-\beta(\eta)}^{\eta} \|C_2(\eta,r)\| |u(r)| dr + |Q(\eta, u(\eta), u(\eta-\gamma(\eta)))| \right] d\eta \\
\le{}& e^{M}(\delta + L\epsilon) \le \epsilon,
\end{aligned}$$

hence

$$\|\digamma u\| \le \epsilon.$$

We next prove that $\digamma$ is a contraction.

Let $u, v \in \Gamma_\epsilon$; then,

$$\begin{aligned}|(Fu)(p) - (Fv)(p)| &\leq \int_{p_0}^{p} e^{\int_\eta^p \mu(C_2(r,r))dr} \Big[\|C_2(\eta,\eta)\| \Big(\int_{\eta-\alpha(\eta)}^{\eta} \|C_1(\eta,r)\| dr + 1 \Big) \\ &+ \int_{\eta-\beta(\eta)}^{\eta} \|C_2(\eta,r)\| dr + q_1 + q_2 \Big] d\eta \|u - v\| \\ &\leq L\|u - v\|.\end{aligned}$$

Hence,

$$\|Fu - Fv\| \leq L\|u - v\|,$$

since $L \in (0,1)$, then F is a contraction.

Thus, using the fixed point of Banach, F has a unique fixed point u in Γ_ϵ, which is a solution of (3). This proves that the zero solution of (3) is stable. □

4. Asymptotic Stability

Definition 2. *The zero solution of (3) is asymptotically stable if it is Lyapunov stable and if, for any integer $p_0 \geq 0$, there exists $\delta > 0$ such that $|\psi(p)| \leq \delta$ for $p \in [\tau(p_0), p_0]$ implies $|u(p)| \to 0$ as $p \to \infty$.*

Theorem 2. *Assume that the hypotheses (C1), (C2) and*

$$\int_\eta^p \mu(C_2(r,r))dr \to -\infty, \;\; p \geq \eta,, as\; p \to \infty, \tag{7}$$

hold. Then, the zero solution of (3) is asymptotically stable.

Proof. In the last Theorem, we proved that the zero solution of (3) is stable. For a given $\epsilon > 0$, define

$$\Gamma_0 = \{u \in \Gamma_\epsilon \text{ such that } u(p) \to 0, \text{ as } p \to \infty\}.$$

Define $F : \Gamma_0 \to \Gamma_\epsilon$ by (6). We must prove that, for $u \in \Gamma_0$, $(Fu)(p) \to 0$ when $p \to \infty$. Using the definition of Γ_0, $u(p) \to 0$, as $p \to \infty$. Thus, we obtain

$$\begin{aligned}(Fu)(p) &\leq \delta e^{\int_{p_0}^p \mu(C_2(r,r))dr} \\ &\int_{p_0}^{p} e^{\int_\eta^p \mu(C_2(r,r))dr} \Big[\|C_2(\eta,\eta)\| \Big(\int_{\eta-\alpha(\eta)}^{\eta} \|C_1(\eta,r)\| |u(r)| dr + |u(\eta)| \Big) \\ &+ \int_{\eta-\beta(\eta)}^{\eta} \|C_2(\eta,r)\| |u(r)| dr + q_1|u(\eta)| + q_2|u(\eta - \gamma(\eta))| \Big] d\eta\end{aligned}$$

By (7)

$$\delta e^{\int_{p_0}^p \mu(C_2(r,r))dr} \to 0 \text{ when } n \to \infty.$$

Moreover, let $u \in \Gamma_0$ so that, for any $\epsilon_1 \in (0,\epsilon)$, there exists $T \geq p_0$ large enough such that $\eta \geq T - \tau(p_0)$ implies $|u(\eta)|, |u(\eta - \gamma(\eta))| < \epsilon_1$. Hence, we obtain

$$
\begin{aligned}
\Lambda = &\int_{p_0}^{p} e^{\int_{\eta}^{p} \mu(C_2(r,r))dr} \Big[\|C_2(\eta,\eta)\| \Big(\int_{\eta-\alpha(\eta)}^{\eta} \|C_1(\eta,r)\| |u(r)| dr + |u(\eta)| \Big) \\
&+ \int_{\eta-\beta(\eta)}^{\eta} \|C_2(\eta,r)\| |u(r)| dr + q_1 |u(\eta)| + q_2 |u(\eta-\gamma(\eta))| \Big] d\eta \\
\le & e^{\int_{p_0}^{p} \mu(C_2(r,r))dr} \int_{p_0}^{T} e^{\int_{\eta}^{p_0} \mu(C_2(r,r))dr} \Big[\|C_2(\eta,\eta)\| \Big(\int_{\eta-\alpha(\eta)}^{\eta} \|C_1(\eta,r)\| |u(r)| dr + |u(\eta)| \Big) \\
&+ \int_{\eta-\beta(\eta)}^{\eta} \|C_2(\eta,r)\| |u(r)| dr + q_1 |u(\eta)| + q_2 |u(\eta-\gamma(\eta))| \Big] d\eta \\
&+ \int_{T}^{p} e^{\int_{\eta}^{p} \mu(C_2(r,r))dr} \Big[\|C_2(\eta,\eta)\| \Big(\int_{\eta-\alpha(\eta)}^{\eta} \|C_1(\eta,r)\| |u(r)| dr + |u(\eta)| \Big) \\
&+ \int_{\eta-\beta(\eta)}^{\eta} \|C_2(\eta,r)\| |u(r)| dr + q_1 |u(\eta)| + q_2 |u(\eta-\gamma(\eta))| \Big] d\eta \\
\le & L e^{\int_{p_0}^{p} \mu(C_2(r,r))dr} \|u\| + L\epsilon_1.
\end{aligned}
$$

Since (7) holds, then $\Lambda \to 0$, as $p \to \infty$.

Hence, $\digamma$ maps Γ_0 into itself. Using the fixed point of Banach, $\digamma$ has a unique fixed point $u \in \Gamma_0$, which solves (3). □

5. Exponential Stability

Definition 3. *We can say that the zero solution of (3) is exponentially stable if there exists $\sigma, \delta, \lambda > 0$, such that*

$$|u(p)| < \sigma e^{-\lambda(p-p_0)}, \; p \ge p_0, \tag{8}$$

whenever $|\psi(p)| < \delta$ for $p \in [\tau(p_0), p_0]$.

Theorem 3. *Assume that conditions (C1) and (C2) hold if there exists $\lambda > 0$, such that*

$$\mu(C_2(p,p)) \le -\lambda, \; \forall p \ge p_0, \tag{9}$$

and

$$
\begin{aligned}
\sup_{p\in[\tau(p_0),\infty)} &\int_{p_0}^{p} \Big[e^{\lambda\eta} \|C_2(\eta,\eta)\| \int_{\eta-\alpha(\eta)}^{\eta} \|C_1(\eta,r)\| e^{-\lambda r} dr + \|C_2(\eta,\eta)\| \\
&+ e^{\lambda\eta} \int_{\eta-\beta(\eta)}^{\eta} \|C_2(\eta,r)\| e^{-\lambda r} dr + q_1 + q_2 e^{\lambda\gamma(\eta)} \Big] d\eta \le \frac{1}{2}
\end{aligned}
\tag{10}
$$

hold. Then, the zero solution of (3) is exponentially stable.

Proof. Since the condition (9) holds. We define Γ_e, the closed subspace of $\mathcal{S}$, as

$$\Gamma_e = \Big\{ u \in \mathcal{S} : \text{such that } |u(p)| \le \sigma e^{-\lambda(p-p_0)}, \; \forall p \ge \tau(p_0) \text{ and } \sigma \ge 2\delta \Big\}.$$

We will show that $\digamma(\Gamma_e) \subset \Gamma_e$. Then, using (9), we have

$$
\begin{aligned}
(Fu)(p) &\leq e^{\int_{p_0}^{p} \mu(B(r,r))dr}\delta + \int_{p_0}^{p} e^{\int_{\eta}^{p} \mu(B(r,r))dr} \\
&\times \left[\|C_2(\eta,\eta)\| \int_{\eta-\alpha(\eta)}^{\eta} \|C_1(\eta,r)\| \sigma e^{-\lambda(r-p_0)}dr + \|C_2(\eta,\eta)\| \sigma e^{-\lambda(\eta-p_0)} \right. \\
&\left. + \int_{\eta-\beta(\eta)}^{\eta} \|C_2(\eta,r)\| \sigma e^{-\lambda(r-p_0)}dr + +q_1\sigma e^{-\lambda(\eta-p_0)} + q_2\sigma e^{-\lambda(\eta-\gamma(\eta)-p_0)} \right] d\eta \\
&\leq e^{-\lambda(p-p_0)}\delta + \int_{p_0}^{p} e^{-\lambda(p-\eta)} \\
&\times \left[\|C_2(\eta,\eta)\| \int_{\eta-\alpha(\eta)}^{\eta} \|C_1(\eta,r)\| \sigma e^{-\lambda(r-p_0)}dr + \|C_2(\eta,\eta)\| \sigma e^{-\lambda(\eta-p_0)} \right. \\
&\left. + \int_{\eta-\beta(\eta)}^{\eta} \|C_2(\eta,r)\| \sigma e^{-\lambda(r-p_0)}dr + q_1\sigma e^{-\lambda(\eta-p_0)} + q_2\sigma e^{-\lambda(\eta-\gamma(\eta)-p_0)} \right] d\eta \\
&= e^{-\lambda(p-p_0)}\delta + \sigma e^{-\lambda(p-p_0)} \\
&\times \int_{p_0}^{p} \left[e^{\lambda\eta} \|C_2(\eta,\eta)\| \int_{\eta-\alpha(\eta)}^{\eta} \|C_1(\eta,r)\| e^{-\lambda r}dr + \|C_2(\eta,\eta)\| \right. \\
&\left. + e^{\lambda\eta} \int_{\eta-\beta(\eta)}^{\eta} \|C_2(\eta,r)\| e^{-\lambda r}dr + q_1 + q_2 e^{\lambda\gamma(\eta)} \right] d\eta
\end{aligned}
$$

since (10) holds. Then, we have

$$
|(Fu)(p)| \leq \frac{1}{2}\sigma e^{-\lambda(p-p_0)} + \frac{1}{2}\sigma e^{-\lambda(p-p_0)} = \sigma e^{-\lambda(p-p_0)}.
$$

Then $F(\Gamma_e) \subset \Gamma_e$.

Hence, F has a unique fixed point $u \in \Gamma_e$, which solves (3). Then, the zero solution of (3) is exponentially stable. □

6. Example

Consider the two-dimensional nonlinear neutral differential system of the form

$$
\begin{cases}
\left(u(p) - \int_{p-\frac{1}{1+p^2}+1}^{p} C_1(p,\eta)u(\eta)d\eta \right)' = \int_{p-\frac{1}{1+p^2}+12}^{p} C_2(p,\eta)u(\eta)d\eta \\
\qquad +Q(p,u(p),u(p-\ln 2^8)),\ p \geq 0, \\
u(p) = \psi(p) \text{ arbitrary for } p \in \left[-\frac{1}{3}, 0\right],
\end{cases}
\tag{11}
$$

where

$$
C_1(p,\eta) = \begin{pmatrix} -2 & \sin(p-\eta) \\ \sin(p-\eta) & -2 \end{pmatrix},
$$

$$
C_2(p,\eta) = \frac{1}{8}\begin{pmatrix} -1 & \frac{1}{2}\cos(p-\eta) \\ \frac{1}{2}\cos(p-\eta) & -1 \end{pmatrix},
$$

and

$$
Q(p,x,y) = \begin{pmatrix} \frac{1}{4}x_2 \sin t \\ \frac{1}{2}y_1 \sin t \end{pmatrix} \Longrightarrow q_1 = \frac{1}{4},\ q_2 = \frac{1}{2}.
$$

Since for $A = (a_{ij})_{n\times n} \in \mathbb{R}^{n\times n}$, we have

$$
\mu(A) = \max_{1\leq j\leq n} \left\{ a_{jj} + \sum_{i\neq j}^{n} |a_{ij}| \right\}.
$$

Then

$$
\mu(C_2(p,\eta)) = \frac{1}{8}(-2+\cos(p-\eta)) \leq -\frac{1}{8},
$$

$$|C_1(p,\eta)| = \max_{1\le i\le n} \sum_{j=1}^{n} |C_{2ij}(p,\eta)| = \frac{1}{16}\left(-1+\frac{1}{2}\sin(p-\eta)\right) \Rightarrow \|C_1(p,\eta)\| \le 1,$$

$$|C_2(p,\eta)| = \max_{1\le i\le n} \sum_{j=1}^{n} |C_{2ij}(p,\eta)| = \frac{1}{8}\left(-1+\frac{1}{2}\cos(p-\eta)\right) \Rightarrow \|C_2(p,\eta)\| \le \frac{1}{16},$$

and

$$\begin{aligned}
L \;:=\; & \sup_{p\in[\tau(p_0),\infty)} \int_{p_0}^{p} \left(\|C_2(\eta,\eta)\| \left(\int_{\eta-\alpha(\eta)}^{\eta} \|C_1(\eta,r)\| dr + 1 \right) \right. \\
& \left. + \int_{\eta-\beta(\eta)}^{\eta} \|C_2(\eta,r)\| dr + q_1 + q_2 \right) d\eta \\
= \; & \sup_{p\in[\frac{-1}{3},\infty)} \int_{0}^{p} \left(\frac{1}{16}\left(\left(\frac{1}{1+\eta^2} - 1 \right) + 1 \right) + \frac{1}{16}\left(\frac{1}{1+\eta^2} - 12 \right) + \frac{3}{4} \right) d\eta \\
= \; & \sup_{p\in[\frac{-1}{3},\infty)} \int_{0}^{p} \left(\frac{1}{16}\frac{1}{1+\eta^2} + \frac{1}{16}\frac{1}{1+\eta^2} \right) d\eta \\
= \; & \sup_{p\in[\frac{-1}{3},\infty)} \frac{1}{8}\tan^{-1}\eta = \frac{\pi}{16} < 1.
\end{aligned}$$

Therefore, using Theorem 2, system (11) is asymptotically stable.

7. Conclusions

This paper investigated the stability, asymptotic stability, and exponential stability using the Banach fixed point theorem. The matrix measure, with some conditions, was the key tool used to tackle these three types of stability for the system (3). The considered system contains two Volterra terms and a nonlinear term; hence, the obtained results generalise the findings of [19,23]. Our work is another example of the advantage of using the fixed-point method instead of the Lyapunov's method.

Author Contributions: Methodology, M.B.M.; formal analysis, M.B.M.; investigation, M.B.M.; writing—original draft preparation, M.B.M.; writing—review and editing, M.B.M.; visualization, M.B.M; project administration, M.B.M.; funding acquisition, A.A.; supervision, A.A.; writing—review and editing, H.S.; funding acquisition, A.A. All authors have read and agreed to the published version of the manuscript.

Funding: This research has been funded by the Deputy for Research & Innovation, Ministry of Education through Initiative of Institutional Funding at University of Ha'il-Saudi Arabia through project number IFP-22 060.

Data Availability Statement: Not applicable.

Acknowledgments: This research has been funded by the Deputy for Research & Innovation, Ministry of Education through Initiative of Institutional Funding at University of Ha'il-Saudi Arabia through project number IFP-22 060.

Conflicts of Interest: The authors declare no conflict of interest.

References

1. Levin, J.J.; Nohel, J.A. On a nonlinear delay equation. *J. Math. Anal. Appl.* **1964**, *8*, 31–44. [CrossRef]
2. Levin, J.J.; Nohel, J.A. On a system of integro-differential equations occurring in reactor dynamics. *J. Math. Mech.* **1960**, *9*, 347–368.
3. Volterra, V. Sur la théorie mathématique des phénomès héréditaires. *J. Math. Pures Appl.* **1928**, *7*, 249–298.
4. Chitour, Y.; Mazanti, G.; Sigalotti, M. Stability of non-autonomous difference equations with applications to transport and wave propagation on networks. *Net. Heterog. Med.* **2016**, *11*, 563–601. [CrossRef]
5. Gu, K.; Kharitonov, V.; Chen, J. *Stability of Time-Delay Systems*; Birkhauser: Boston, FL, USA, 2003.
6. Hante, F.M.; Leugering, G.; Seidman, T.I. Modeling and Analysis of Modal Switching in Networked Transport Systems. *Appl. Math. Optim.* **2009**, *59*, 275–292. [CrossRef]

7. Kuang, Y. *Delay Differential Equations with Applications in Population Dynamics*; Academic Press: San Diego, CA, USA, 1993.
8. Schmidt, E.J.P.G. On the modelling and exact controllability of networks of vibrating strings. *SIAM J. Control Optim.* **1992**, *30*, 229–245. [CrossRef]
9. Altun, Y. A new result on the global exponential stability of nonlinear neutral volterra integro-differential equation with variable lags. *Math. Nat. Sci.* **2019**, *5*, 29–43. [CrossRef]
10. Diblík, J.; Khusainov, D.Y.; Baštinec, J.; Sirenko. A.S. Exponential stability of perturbed linear discrete systems. *Adv. Differ. Equ.* **2016**, *2016*, 2. [CrossRef]
11. Luo,J. Fixed points and exponential stability for stochastic Volterra–Levin equations. *J. Comput. App. Math.* **2010**, *234*, 934–940. [CrossRef]
12. Mesmouli, M.B.; Tunç, C. Matrix measure and asymptotic behaviors of linear advanced systems of differential equations. *Bol. Soc. Mat. Mex.* **2021**, *27*, 56. [CrossRef]
13. Bohner, M.; Tunç, O. Qualitative analysis of integro-differential equations with variable retardation. *Discret. Contin. Dyn. Syst. Ser. B* **2022**, *27*, 639–657. [CrossRef]
14. Jin, C.H.; Luo, J.W. Stability of an integro-differential equation. *Comput. Math. Appl.* **2009**, *57*, 1080–1088. [CrossRef]
15. Khelil, K.A.; Ardjouni, A.; Djoudi, A. Stability in linear delay Levin-Nohel difference equations. *Trans. Natl. Acad. Sci. Azerb. Ser. Phys. Tech. Math. Sci. Math.* **2019**, *39*, 1–12.
16. Mesmouli, M.B.; Ardjouni, A.; Djoudi, A. Stability in nonlinear Levin-Nohel integro-differential equations. *Nonlinear Stud.* **2015**, *22*, 705–718.
17. Mesmouli, M.B.; Ardjouni, A.; Djoudi, A. Stability solutions for a system of nonlinear neutral functional differential equations with functional delay. *Dyn. Syst. Appl.* **2016**, *25*, 253–262.
18. Mesmouli, M.B.; Ardjouni, A.; Djoudi, A. Stability in System of Impulsive Neutral Functional Differential Equations. *Mediterr. J. Math.* **2021**, *18*, 32. [CrossRef]
19. Mesmouli, M.B.; Ardjouni, A.; Djoudi, A. Stability conditions for a mixed linear Levin-Nohel integro-differential system. *J. Integral Equations Appl.* **2022**, *34*, 349–356. [CrossRef]
20. Burton T.A. Stability by fixed point theory or Liapunov theory: A Comparaison. *Fixed Point Theory* **2003**, *4*, 15–32.
21. Burton T.A. Liapunov functionals, fixed points, and stability by Krasnoselskii's theorem. *Nonlinear Stud.* **2001**, *9*, 181–190.
22. Abdulazeeza, S.T.; Mohammed, S.A.; Modanli, M. A comparison between applications of the Lyapunov's second (direct) method and fixed point theory. *Gene Lett. Math.* **2019**, *7*, 61–78. [CrossRef]
23. Dung, N.T. New stability conditions for mixed linear Levin-Nohel integro-differential equations. *J. Math. Phys.* **2013**, *54*, 082705. [CrossRef]
24. Peng, S.; Zhu, S. Periodic solutions of functional differential equations with infinite delay. *Chin. Ann. Math.* **2002**, *23A*, 371–380.

mathematics MDPI

Article

Criteria on Exponential Incremental Stability of Dynamical Systems with Time Delay

Yingying Lang [1,*,†] **and Wenlian Lu** [1,2,3,†]

[1] School of Mathematical Sciences, Fudan University, Shanghai 200433, China; wenlian@fudan.edu.cn
[2] Shanghai Center for Mathematical Sciences, Fudan University, Shanghai 200433, China
[3] Shanghai Key Laboratory for Contemporary Applied Mathematics, Shanghai 200433, China
* Correspondence: yylang18@fudan.edu.cn; Tel.: +86-1391-266-9933
† These authors contributed equally to this work.

Abstract: Incremental stability analysis for time-delay systems has attracted more and more attention for its contemporary applications in transportation processes, population dynamics, economics, satellite positions, etc. This paper researches the criteria for exponential incremental stability for time-delay systems with continuous or discontinuous right-hand sides. Firstly, the sufficient conditions for exponential incremental stability for time-delay systems with continuous right-hand sides are studied, and several corollaries for specific cases are provided. As for time-delay systems with discontinuous right-hand sides, after expounding the relevant conditions for the existence and uniqueness of the Filippov solution, by using approximation methods, sufficient conditions for exponential incremental stability are obtained. The conclusions are applied to linear switched time-delay systems and Hopfield neural network systems with composite right-hand sides.

Keywords: time-delay system; exponential incremental stability; discontinuous right-hand sides; Filippov solutions

MSC: 34K20

1. Introduction

Stability analysis in mathematics mainly refers to the relevant research on the long-term performance of the dynamical system's steady state. With more and more applications of neural networks and complex systems, the stability analysis of differential equations, including time-delay dynamical systems, has attracted more and more attention from academia and industry. Incremental stability [1,2] has been presented to be a perfect instrument for stability analysis, which is able to address problems of synchronization of coupled systems.

Incremental stability means that as time approaches infinity, the solutions of the dynamical system in different initial states will approach each other, that is, the state variables of the system with different initial states will gradually converge to the same trajectory. This property has a very wide range of applications in different fields of academia and industry. In recent years, due to the increasing potential application value in many frontier fields, such as PI-controlled missiles, Ref. [3] as well as the synchronization problem of network dynamics [4–6], there is already a lot of literature available on incremental stability, e.g., Refs. [7,8] provided a systematic exposition and discussion of related issues, and Ref. [3] provided specific examples of incremental stability-related applications.

In dynamical system analysis, the theoretical research on differential equations with discontinuous right-hand sides has also been highly valued because of its wide application. In some fields, such as mechanical engineering, electronic engineering, and automatic control theory, many problems rely on relevant theories of these 'discontinuous' differential equations [9]. Among them, switched systems, as a type of differential equation with discontinuous right-hand functions, are particularly commonly used in the field of automatic control, thus driving the development of related theories [10–13].

In 1964, Filippov [14] studied the motion of Coulomb friction oscillators and proposed a differential equation with a discontinuous right-hand side. In order to study the trajectory of the solution, 'differential inclusion' and set-valued mapping were introduced, and the existence and uniqueness of the solution of the discontinuous differential equation were discussed. A detailed discussion on this type of discontinuous differential equation can be found in reference [15]. Before we study the compressibility of the system, we need to first ensure the existence and uniqueness of the Carathéodory solution of the system. Filippov's theory mainly focuses on the existence and uniqueness of the solution of the non-smooth dynamical system. The relevant conclusions have been listed in [15].

Research on time-delay differential equations first began in the early 20th century by Volterra [16,17]. The ordinary differential equations with time delay are commonly used in contemporary applications, gradually pushing the relevant theories of time-delay systems to integrity and maturity and producing rich results. There are many important achievements emerging one after another. It is worth mentioning Hale and Verduyn Lunel's comprehensive work [18], which discussed in detail the properties of the solutions for some time-delay differential equations, e.g., uniqueness, continuous dependence of parameters, continuity and compactness of solutions, stability and invariance, etc. At the same time, some concrete analyses and methods on the properties of these solutions for time-delay systems were proposed in the literature [19–23], among which, Ref. [20] includes an introductory chapter that provides detailed examples of time-delay differential equations used to control computer systems, transportation processes, population dynamics, economics, satellite positions, urban transportation, and so on.

Set-valued dynamical systems, also named Filippov systems, whose right-hand sides are set-valued mappings, are widely used in these applications mentioned above. These set-valued dynamical systems are perfect instruments to represent the time-delay differential equations with discontinuous right-hand sides [20,24–28] or control systems with time delay [20,29,30]. Therefore, naturally, a large amount of the literature has discussed the problems along these lines. One of the most important achievements in this field is [31], in which Haddad focused on upper semicontinuous dynamics, elaborated on the existence and compactness of the solution set, and also proved the upper semicontinuity of the solution. Haddad's work [31] is given under functional differential inclusion, where the corresponding time-delay term acts on the infinite-dimensional space of continuous functions.

In recent years, there have been many related analytical studies and achievements on the incremental stability of Filippov systems. In the case that the local Lipschisz condition is satisfied, Ref. [32] provided a sufficient condition for the local stability of Filippov solutions. Ref. [33] used the concept of Filippov solutions to analyze a class of time-delay dynamical systems with discontinuous right-hand sides. In the sense of the Filippov solution, Ref. [34] proposed the conditions for global asymptotic stability of the error system of the time-delay neural network with a discontinuous activation function. While [35] put forward an approximation method and gave the specific sufficient conditions for the exponential incremental stability of the switched system.

In this paper, first, several preliminary definitions are given in Section 2. In Section 3, we research the criteria on the exponential incremental stability of the solutions for time-delay systems with continuous right-hand sides, involving several specific cases, and relevant corollaries are provided. Then, in Section 4, under the hypothesis that the system has a unique solution, we extend the sufficient conditions for exponential incremental stability to the time-delay system with a discontinuous right-hand side in the sense of the Filippov solution by using a sequence of 'continuous systems' to approach the corresponding Filippov system. In this section, we also provide the conditions for the existence and uniqueness of the solution for the time-delay dynamical system before stability analysis in Section 4.1. The applications on linear switched systems and Hopfield neural network systems with time delay are given in Section 5, respectively, and corresponding numerical examples are given in Section 6.

2. Preliminaries

Here, we first introduce some primary definitions, including matrix measure and multiple norms, incremental stability property, exponential incremental stability, and so on.

Definition 1 (Definition 1 in [35]). *For any real matrix $A \in \mathbb{R}^{n\times n}$ and a given norm $\|\cdot\|$, we define the corresponding matrix measure $v(A)$ as*

$$v(A, \|\cdot\|) = \lim_{h\to 0^+} \frac{\|I + hA\| - 1}{h}.$$

The matrix measure above can be considered as the one-sided directional derivative of the induced matrix norm function $\|\cdot\|$, evaluated at the point I, in the direction of A.

In the following parts, we will study the incremental stability property of time-delay systems under multiple norms. Here, we also list the definitions of multiple norms with subscript $\chi(t)$ and the corresponding measures. Note that the function $\chi(t)$ is a piecewise right-continuous function.

Definition 2. *For real matrix $A \in \mathbb{R}^{n\times n}$ and the matrix norm $\|\cdot\|_{\chi(t)}$, (the corresponding vector measure $|\cdot|_{\chi(t)}$), we here define the corresponding matrix measure $\mu_{\chi(t)}(A)$ as follows:*

$$\mu_{\chi(t)}(A) = \lim_{h\to 0^+} \frac{\|I + hA\|_{\chi(t)} - 1}{h}.$$

If $\lim_{h\to 0^+} |x|_{\chi(t+h)}(\lim_{h\to 0^-} |x|_{\chi(t+h)})$ exists, then we denote the right (left) limit of the norm $|\cdot|_{\chi(t)}$ at time point t by $|\cdot|_{\chi(t\pm)}$. We say the norm $|\cdot|_{\chi(t)}$ is continuous at t, if and only if $|\cdot|_{\chi(t+)} = |\cdot|_{\chi(t-)} = |\cdot|_{\chi(t)}$, that is, $|\cdot|_{\chi(t)}$ is right-continuous and left-continuous as well. If there exists $D > 0$, such that $|x|_{\chi(t)} < D|x|_{\chi(s)}$ holds for all $t, s \in \mathbb{R}^+$, we say $|\cdot|_{\chi(t)}$ is uniformly equivalent.

Then, we extend the definition for matrix measure in the sense of multiple norms. Consider the time-varying nature of $\chi(t)$, as follows:

Definition 3 (Definition 3 in [36]). *If the following limit exists, the switched matrix measure with respect to vector norm $|\cdot|_{\chi(t)}$ is defined as follows:*

$$v_{\chi(t)}(A) = \overline{\lim_{h\to 0^+}} \frac{1}{h} \sup_{|x|_{\chi(t)}=1} |(I_n + hA)x|_{\chi(t+h)} - 1$$

where $\overline{\lim}$ stands for the upper superior.

Remark 1. *The definition of multiple matrix norms $\|\cdot\|_{\chi(t)}$ can be thought of as matrix norms induced by vector norm $|\cdot|_{\chi(t)}$: for a matrix A,*

$$\|A\|_{\chi(t)} = \sup_{|x|_{\chi(t)}=1} |Ax|_{\chi(t)}$$

This implies that, if $\chi(t)$ is constant over an internal $[a, a+\delta)$, then it holds that $v_{\chi(t)}(A) = \mu_{\chi(t)}(A)$ in $[a, a+\delta)$.

According to the existence of the switched matrix measure, the definition is as follows,

Definition 4 ([36]). *Define the partial differential of the switched norm $|\cdot|_{\chi(t)}$ as follows,*

$$\overline{\partial}_t(|\cdot|_{\chi(t)}) = \overline{\lim_{h\to 0^+}} \sup_{|x|_{\chi(t)}=1} \frac{|x|_{\chi(t+h)} - 1}{h}$$

If $\overline{\partial}_t(|\cdot|_{\chi(t)})$ exists at t, we say the multiple norm $|\cdot|_{\chi(t)}$ is right regular at time t.

According to the 'right regular' property, we have the following proposition [36]:

Proposition 1 ([36]). *If the multiple norm $|\cdot|_{\chi(t)}$ is right regular, then*

1. *The multiple norm $|\cdot|_{\chi(t)}$ is right-continuous at time t;*
2. *$\nu_{\chi(t)}(\cdot)$ exists at time t.*

For a clearer statement in the following part, we define a transaction function between norms $|\cdot|_{\chi}$ and $|\cdot|_{\chi'}$,

Definition 5. *Function $C(\chi, \chi') > 0$ is the transaction function between norms $|\cdot|_{\chi}$ and $|\cdot|_{\chi'}$, satisfying that*

$$|\cdot|_{\chi} \le C(\chi, \chi')|\cdot|_{\chi'}.$$

Definition 6. *If the function $C(\chi(t), \chi(t'))$ is well-defined for all t and t', we say the multiple norm $|\cdot|_{\chi(t)}$ is equivalent for all t.*

Here, we consider the following dynamical time-delay system:

$$\begin{cases} \dot{x} = f(x, x_{\tau_1(t)}, \ldots, x_{\tau_m(t)}, r(t)),\ t \ge t_0 \\ x(s) = \phi(s),\ s \in [t_0 - \overline{\tau}, t_0] \end{cases} \tag{1}$$

where $x \in \mathbb{R}^n$, $x_{\tau_k(t)} = x(t - \tau_k(t))(k = 1, \ldots, m)$ is the time-delay term, each τ_k is a bounded function, $\max_k sup_{t\in[t_0,\infty)} \tau_k(t) = \overline{\tau}$, function $r(t) : [t_0, +\infty) \to \mathbb{R}$ is an upper continuous staircase function, $f = (f_1, \ldots, f_n) : \mathbb{R}^{n\times(m+1)} \times [t_0, +\infty) \to \mathbb{R}^n$. The function $\phi(\cdot)$ represents the initial value function, and $\phi(\cdot) \in C^1([t_0 - \overline{\tau}, t_0], \mathbb{R}^n)$. Let $x(t; \phi, r_t)$ be the solution of system (1).

Then, we will research the sufficient conditions for incremental stability for time-delay dynamical system (1), which is defined as follows.

We have the following definition for several types of incremental stability (IS):

Definition 7. *Let $\phi(t; t_0, x_0)$ be the solution of system (1) with the initial time t_0 and initial value function $x_0(\cdot)$. If there exist a function $\beta(s, t)$ of class $\mathcal{KL}$, and some norm $|\cdot|^{\infty}_{[t_0-\overline{\tau},t_0]}$ induced by vector norm $|\cdot|$, defined as $|\varphi|^{\infty}_{[t_0-\overline{\tau},t_0]} = \sup_{s\in[t_0-\overline{\tau},t_0]} |\varphi(s)|$, such that for any initial function $x_0(\cdot), y_0(\cdot)$,*

$$|\phi(t + t_0; x_0, t_0) - \phi(t + t_0; y_0, t_0)| \le \beta(|x_0 - y_0|^{\infty}_{[t_0-\overline{\tau},t_0]}, t),$$

then, we say that system (1) is Incrementally Asymptotically Stable (δAS) in the region $\Sigma \subset \mathbb{R}^n$. If $\beta(s, t)$ is independent of initial time t, then we say system (1) is Incrementally Uniformly Asymptotically Stable (δUAS). If function $\beta(s, t)$ is of class $\mathcal{EKL}$, then we say system (1) is Incrementally Uniformly Exponentially Asymptotically Stable (δUEAS).

Moreover, if there exists a constant M and $c > 0$ such that $\beta(\cdot, \cdot)$ of class $\mathcal{KL}$ satisfies (2) with some norm $|\cdot|$, then system (1) is said to be exponentially incrementally stable.

$$\beta(|x_0 - y_0|^{\infty}_{[t_0-\overline{\tau},t_0]}, t) = Me^{-ct}|x_0 - y_0|^{\infty}_{[t_0-\overline{\tau},t_0]}, \tag{2}$$

3. Contraction Theory for Time-Delay Systems

Here, we list the following hypothesis, denoted by Assumption 1, including the Carathéodory condition to guarantee the existence and uniqueness of the solution of the time-delay dynamical system (1) with a continuous right-hand side.

Assumption 1. *Dynamical time-delay system* (1) *satisfies the following conditions:*

1. $f(x, x_{\tau_1(t)}, \ldots, x_{\tau_m(t)}, r(t))$ *is continuously differentiable with respect to x, and continuous with respect to* $(x, x_{\tau_1(t)}, \ldots, x_{\tau_m(t)}, r)$ *except for the switching time points* $\{t_1, \ldots, t_j, \ldots\}$.
2. $\tau_k(t)$ *is upper bounded and has a positive lower bound for each k, and* $\max_k \sup_{t\in[t_0,\infty)} \tau_k(t) = \overline{\tau}$, $\min_k \inf_{t\in[t_0,\infty)} \tau_k(t) = \underline{\tau}$.
3. $f_i : \mathbb{R}^{n\times(m+1)} \times [t_0, +\infty) \to \mathbb{R}$ $(i = 1, \ldots, n)$ *is locally Lipschitz.*

Thus, under Assumption 1, system (1) has a unique solution. (Refer to the Reference [37] for details.)

Here, we try to research the contraction property for time-delay system (1). First, enlightened by Ref. [38], we prove the following lemma:

Lemma 1. *Assume that* $|\cdot|_{\chi(t)}$ *is right regular,* $\chi(t)$ *is a right-continuous staircase function with discontinuities in* $\{t_1, \ldots, t_j, \ldots\}$ *and* $|\cdot|_{\chi(t)} \le C_0 |\cdot|_{\chi(t')}$ *holds for any* $t, t' \ge t_0$. $x(t)$ *is continuous,* t_0 *is the initial time, and* $\overline{\tau} = \max_k \sup_{s\ge t_0} \tau_k(s)$. *For the following time-delay system:*

$$\dot{x}(t) = A(t)x(t) + \sum_{k=1}^{n} B_k(t)x(t-\tau_k(t))$$

where $x(t) \in \mathbb{R}^n$, $A(t), B_k(t) \in \mathbb{R}^{n\times n}(k = 1, 2, \ldots, m)$ *is piecewise continuous with respect to t, and the discontinuities belong to* $\{t_1, t_2, \ldots, t_i, \ldots\}$, *which is a countable set. If there exists a piecewise right-continuous function* $m(t) > 0$ *whose discontinuities belong to* $\{t_1, t_2, \ldots, t_i, \ldots\}$, *and matrix-valued functions* $B_k^{(1)}(t)$, $B_k^{(2)}(t)$ *such that*

$$\nu_{\chi(t)}(A(t) + \sum_{k=1}^{m} B_k^{(1)}(t)) + \sum_{k=1}^{m} \|B_k^{(2)}(t)\|_{\chi(t)} \frac{m(t)}{m(t-\tau_k(t))} + \sum_{k=1}^{m} \tau_k(t) \|B_k^{(1)}(t)\|_{\chi(t)} (\tilde{A}^k(t) + \tilde{B}^k(t)) \le -\frac{D^+ m(t)}{m(t)}$$

where D^+ *represents the Dini derivative, and*

$$\tilde{A}^k(t) = \sup_{t-\tau_k(t)\le s\le t} \|A(s)\|_{\chi(s)} \frac{m(t)}{m(s)},$$

$$\tilde{B}^k(t) = \sup_{t-\tau_k(t)\le s\le t} \|B_k(s)\|_{\chi(s)} \frac{m(t)}{m(s-\tau_k(s))}.$$

Then, for each $t \in [t_j, t_{j+1})$, *we have*

$$|x(t)|_{\chi(t_j)} m(t) \le \sup_{t_0-\overline{\tau}\le s\le t} |x(s)|_{\chi(t_j)} m(s) \le C_0 \sup_{t_0-\overline{\tau}\le s\le t_j} |x(s)|_{\chi(t_j-)} m(s)$$

Proof. Let $V(t) = \sup_{t_0-\overline{\tau}\le\theta\le t} |x(\theta)|_{\chi(\theta)} m(\theta)$. Assume that $V(t)$ is strictly increasing at time point t^*, it implies that $V(t^*) = |x(t^*)|_{\chi(t^*)} m(t^*)$. There exists j such that $t^* \in [t_j, t_{j+1})$, and here we calculate the Dini derivative of $|x(t)|_{\chi(t_j)} m(t)$,

$$D^+[|x(t)|_{\chi(t_j)} m(t)] = \dot{m}(t)|x(t)|_{\chi(t_j)} + m(t) \lim_{h\to 0} \frac{|x(t+h)|_{\chi(t_j)} - |x(t)|_{\chi(t_j)}}{h},$$

in which $\dot{x}(t)$ can be rewritten as

$$\begin{aligned}\dot{x}(t) &= A(t)x(t) + \sum_{k=1}^{m} B_k(t)x(t-\tau_k(t)) \\ &= [A(t) + \sum_{k=1}^{m} B_k^{(1)}(t)]x(t) + \sum_{k=1}^{m} B_k^{(1)}(t)\int_t^{t-\tau_k(t)} \dot{x}(s)ds + \sum_{k=1}^{m} B_k^{(2)}(t)x(t-\tau_k(t))\end{aligned}$$

Thus, we have

$$\begin{aligned}&\overline{\lim}_{h\to 0}\frac{|x(t+h)|_{\chi(t_j)} - |x(t)|_{\chi(t_j)}}{h} \\ &= \overline{\lim}_{h\to 0}\frac{1}{h}\Big[\Big|x(t) + h(A(t) + \sum_{k=1}^{m} B_k^{(1)}(t))x(t) + h\sum_{k=1}^{m} B_k^{(1)}(t)\int_t^{t-\tau_k(t)} \dot{x}(s)ds \\ &\quad + h\sum_{k=1}^{m} B_k^{(2)}(t)x(t-\tau_k(t))\Big|_{\chi(t_j)} - |x(t)|_{\chi(t_j)}\Big] \\ &= \overline{\lim}_{h\to 0}\frac{1}{h}|x(t)|_{\chi(t_j)}\Big[\|I + h(A(t) + \sum_{k=1}^{m} B_k^{(1)}(t))\|_{\chi(t_j)} - 1\Big] + \sum_{k=1}^{m}\|B_k^{(1)}(t)\|_{\chi(t_j)}\int_{t-\tau_k(t)}^{t} |\dot{x}(s)|_{\chi(t_j)}ds \\ &\quad + \sum_{k=1}^{m}\|B_k^{(2)}(t)\|_{\chi(t_j)}|x(t-\tau_k(t))|_{\chi(t_j)} \\ &= \nu_{\chi(t_j)}(A(t) + \sum_{k=1}^{m} B_k^{(1)}(t))|x(t)|_{\chi(t_j)} + \sum_{k=1}^{m}\|B_k^{(1)}(t)\|_{\chi(t_j)}\int_{t-\tau_k(t)}^{t} |\dot{x}(s)|_{\chi(t_j)}ds \\ &\quad + \sum_{k=1}^{m}\|B_k^{(2)}(t)\|_{\chi(t_j)}|x(t-\tau(t))|_{\chi(t_j)}\end{aligned}$$

that is,

$$\begin{aligned}&D^+[|x(t)|_{\chi(t_j)}m(t)] \\ &= \frac{\dot{m}(t)}{m(t)}|x(t)|_{\chi(t_j)}m(t) + \nu_{\chi(t_j)}(A(t) + \sum_{k=1}^{m} B_k^{(1)}(t))|x(t)|_{\chi(t_j)}m(t) \\ &\quad + \sum_{k=1}^{m}\|B_k^{(2)}(t)\|_{\chi(t_j)}|x(t-\tau_k(t))|_{\chi(t_j)} \\ &\quad + \sum_{k=1}^{m}\|B_k^{(1)}(t)\|_{\chi(t_j)}m(t)\int_{t-\iota_k(l)}^{t} |A(s)x(s) + \sum_{k=1}^{m} B_k(s)x(s-\tau_k(s))|_{\chi(t_j)}ds \\ &= \frac{\dot{m}(t)}{m(t)}|x(t)|_{\chi(t_j)}m(t) + \nu_{\chi(t_j)}(A(t) + \sum_{k=1}^{m} B_k^{(1)}(t))|x(t)|_{\chi(t_j)}m(t) \\ &\quad + \sum_{k=1}^{m}\|B_k^{(2)}(t)\|_{\chi(t_j)}|x(t-\tau_k(t))|_{\chi(t_j)}m(t-\tau_k(t))\frac{m(t)}{m(t-\tau_k(t))} \\ &\quad + \sum_{k=1}^{m}\|B_k^{(1)}(t)\|_{\chi(t_j)}\int_{t-\tau_k(t)}^{t} \|A(s)\|_{\chi(t_j)}|x(s)|_{\chi(t_j)}m(s)\frac{m(t)}{m(s)} \\ &\quad + \sum_{k=1}^{m}\|B_k(s)\|_{\chi(t_j)}|x(s-\tau_k(s))|_{\chi(t_j)}m(s-\tau_k(s))\frac{m(t)}{m(s-\tau_k(s))}ds\end{aligned}$$

Let

$$\tilde{A}^k(t) = \sup_{t-\tau_k(t)\le s\le t}\|A(s)\|_{\chi(t_j)}\frac{m(t)}{m(s)}$$

$$\tilde{B}^k(t) = \sup_{t-\tau_k(t)\le s\le t}\|B_k(s)\|_{\chi(t_j)}\frac{m(t)}{m(s-\tau_k(s))}$$

then, for $t = t^*$, we have

$$D^+V(t) \leq \Bigg[\frac{\dot{m}(t)}{m(t)} + v_{\chi(t_j)}(A(t) + \sum_{k=1}^{m} B_k^{(1)}(t)) + \sum_{k=1}^{m} \tau_k(t)\|B_k^{(1)}(t)\|_{\chi(t_j)}(\tilde{A}^k(t) + \tilde{B}^k(t)) + \sum_{k=1}^{m} \|B_k^{(2)}(t)\|_{\chi(t_j)} \frac{m(t)}{m(t-\tau_k(t))}\Bigg] V(t) \leq 0$$

which is contradictory to the hypothesis that $V(t)$ is strictly increasing at t^*. Therefore, $V(t)$ is decreasing for $t \in [t_j, t_{j+1})$, that is,

$$V(t) \leq V(t_j)$$

that is,

$$|x(t)|_{\chi(t_j)} m(t) \leq \sup_{t_0-\overline{\tau}\leq s\leq t_j} |x(s)|_{\chi(t_j)} m(s) \leq C_0 \sup_{t_0-\overline{\tau}\leq s\leq t_j} |x(s)|_{\chi(t_j-)} m(s)$$

The lemma is proved. □

With the conclusion in Lemma 1, we can select a proper function $m(t) > 0$, and prove the following theorem for exponential incremental stability property of system (1).

Theorem 1. *Suppose that Assumption 1 holds for time-delay system* (1). $\chi(t)$ *is a right-continuous staircase function with discontinuities in* $\{t_1, \ldots, t_j, \ldots\}$. *Let* $N(t) = \#\{j : t \geq t_j, j = 1, 2, \ldots\}$, *and there exist that*

1. *A constant* $T_0 > 0$,
2. *Positive constants* $\gamma_k (k = 0, 1, \ldots)$, $\gamma_0 \leq \gamma_1 \leq \ldots$,
3. $C(\chi(t), \chi(t')) \leq C_0$ *for any* $t, t' \geq t_0$,

such that the following conditions hold:

Let $A(t) = (\partial f/\partial x)(x, x_{\tau_1}, \ldots, x_{\tau_m}, r(t))$, $B_k(t) = (\partial f/\partial x_{\tau_k})(x, x_{\tau_1}, \ldots, x_{\tau_m}, r(t))$, $k = 1, \ldots, m$ *be piecewise continuous with respect to t, and the discontinuities belong to* $\{t_1, t_2, \ldots, t_i, \ldots\}$. *There exist matrix-valued functions* $B_k^{(1)}(t)$, $B_k^{(2)}(t)$, $B_k^{(1)}(t) + B_k^{(2)}(t) = B_k(t)$ *such that*

$$v_{\chi(t)}(A(t) + \textstyle\sum_{k=1}^{m} B_k^{(1)}(t)) + \sum_{k=1}^{m} \tau_k(t)\|B_k^{(1)}(t)\|_{\chi(t)}(\tilde{A}^k(t) + \tilde{B}^k(t)) + \sum_{k=1}^{m} \|B_k^{(2)}(t)\|_{\chi(t)} \dfrac{\exp\left((\gamma_{N(t)} - \gamma_{N(t-\tau_k(t))})t\right)}{\exp\left(\gamma_{N(t-\tau_k(t))}\tau_k(t)\right)} \leq -\gamma_{N(t)} \quad (3)$$

where

$$\tilde{A}_t^k = \sup_{t-\tau_k(t)\leq s\leq t} \|A(s)\|_{\chi(t)} \exp\left(\gamma_{N(t)}t - \gamma_{N(s)}s\right)$$
$$\tilde{B}_t^k = \sup_{t-\tau_k(t)\leq s\leq t} \|B_k(s)\|_{\chi(t)} \exp\left(\gamma_{N(t)}t - \gamma_{N(s-\tau_k(s))}(s - \tau_k(s))\right).$$

and for any $t > T_0$,

$$\frac{1}{t}\Bigg[\sum_{i=0}^{N(t)-1} [(\gamma_{i+1} - \gamma_i)t_{i+1} + \log \beta_{i+1}] + \gamma_0 t_0 - \gamma_{N(t)}t\Bigg] \leq -c \quad (4)$$

where $\beta_k = C(\chi(t_k), \chi(t_k-))$, *then system* (1) *is exponentially incrementally stable.*

Proof. For any initial state x_0, y_0, denote the corresponding initial function by $x_0(\cdot), y_0(\cdot)$, $x_0(\cdot), y_0(\cdot) \in C([t_0 - \overline{\tau}, t_0], \mathbb{R}^m)$. Here, we define a function $\varphi_\lambda(\cdot)$ as $\varphi_\lambda(s) = (1-\lambda)x_0(s) + \lambda y_0(s), \lambda \in [0,1], s \in [t_0 - \overline{\tau}, t_0]$, which is the initial value function of the initial state φ_λ. Let $\varphi_0 = x_0, \varphi_1 = y_0$. $f(x, x_{\tau_1}, \ldots, x_{\tau_m}, r(t))$ is continuous with respect to $(x, x_{\tau_1}, \ldots, x_{\tau_m}, r)$ except for the switching time points $\{t_j\}$, and is continuously differentiable with respect to x, so we have the solution $\psi(t, \lambda) = x(t; \varphi_\lambda, r_t)$, which is continuously differentiable with respect to φ_λ. Let $\omega = \partial\psi/\partial\lambda$, thus we can conclude that ω is well-defined and continuous. From chain rule, $\omega(t,\lambda)$ is the solution of the following system:

$$\begin{cases} \dot{\omega} = \frac{\partial^2\psi}{\partial\lambda\partial t} = \frac{\partial f}{\partial\lambda} = \frac{\partial f}{\partial x}\omega + \sum_{k=1}^{m} \frac{\partial f}{\partial x_{\tau_k}}\omega_{\tau_k} \\ \omega(s,\lambda) = \frac{\partial\varphi_\lambda}{\partial\lambda}(s), s \in [t_0 - \overline{\tau}, t_0] \end{cases}$$

$\partial\psi/\partial\lambda$ is well-defined and continuous, with condition (3), from the proof of Lemma 1, select a piecewise right-continuous function $m(t) = \exp(\gamma_{N(t)}t) > 0$ whose discontinuities belong to $\{t_1, t_2, \ldots, t_i, \ldots\}$, we have

$$m(t)|\omega(t,\lambda)|_{\chi(t)} \leq V(t) \leq V(t_j) = \sup_{t_0-\overline{\tau}\leq s\leq t_j} m(s)|\omega(s,\lambda)|_{\chi(t_j)}$$

holds for any $t \in [t_j, t_{j+1})$. Thus, under the condition (4), we have

$$\begin{aligned} & m(t)|\omega(t,\lambda)|_{\chi(t)} \leq V(t) \leq V(t_j) = \sup_{t_0-\overline{\tau}\leq s\leq t_j} m(s)|\omega(s,\lambda)|_{\chi(t_j)} \\ \leq & \exp\left((\gamma_j - \gamma_{j-1})t_j\right) \cdot \beta_j \sup_{t_0-\overline{\tau}\leq s\leq t_j} m(s)|\omega(s,\lambda)|_{\chi(t_j-)} \\ \leq & \exp\left((\gamma_j - \gamma_{j-1})t_j\right) \cdot \beta_j \sup_{t_0-\overline{\tau}\leq s\leq t_{j-1}} m(s)|\omega(s,\lambda)|_{\chi(t_{j-1})} \\ \leq & \prod_{j=1}^{N(t)} \exp\left((\gamma_j - \gamma_{j-1})t_j\right) \cdot \beta_j \cdot \sup_{t_0-\overline{\tau}\leq s\leq t_0} m(s)|\omega(s,\lambda)|_{\chi(t_0)} \\ \leq & \prod_{j=1}^{N(t)} \exp\left((\gamma_j - \gamma_{j-1})t_j\right) \cdot \beta_j \cdot \sup_{\theta\in[t_0-\overline{\tau},t_0]} m(\theta) \sup_{t_0-\overline{\tau}\leq s\leq t_0} |\omega(s,\lambda)|_{\chi(t_0)} \end{aligned}$$

then, we have

$$|\omega(t,\lambda)|_{\chi(t)} \leq \exp\left(\sum_{j=1}^{N(t)}(\gamma_j - \gamma_{j-1})t_j + \log\beta_j\right)\exp\left(\gamma_0 t_0 - \gamma_{N(t)}t\right) \sup_{t_0-\overline{\tau}\leq s\leq t_0} |\omega(t_0,\lambda)|_{\chi(t_0)} \leq e^{-ct} \sup_{t_0-\overline{\tau}\leq s\leq t_0} |\omega(t_0,\lambda)|_{\chi(t_0)}.$$

Therefore, together with the condition (4), we conclude that the time-delay system (1) is incrementally uniformly asymptotically stable:

$$\begin{aligned} & |x(t;y_0,r_t) - x(t;x_0,r_t)|_{\chi(t_0)} \leq C_0|x(t;y_0,r_t) - x(t;x_0,r_t)|_{\chi(t)} \\ \leq & C_0\left|\int_0^1 \frac{\partial\psi(t,\lambda)}{\partial\lambda}d\lambda\right|_{\chi(t)} \leq C_0\int_0^1 |\omega(t,\lambda)|_{\chi(t)}d\lambda \\ \leq & C_0 e^{-ct}\int_0^1 \sup_{t_0-\overline{\tau}\leq s\leq t_0} |\omega(t_0,\lambda)|_{\chi(t_0)}d\lambda \\ \leq & C_0 e^{-ct} \sup_{\theta\in[t_0-\overline{\tau},t_0]} |x_0(\theta) - y_0(\theta)|_{\chi(t_0)} \end{aligned}$$

□

Actually, the key thought of Theorem 1 is replacing the time-delay term $B_k(t)x_{\tau_k}(t)$ with $B_k^{(1)}(t)x_{\tau_k}(t) + B_k^{(2)}(t)x(t) + B_k^{(2)}(t)\int_t^{t-\tau_k(t)} \dot{x}(s)ds$. In some special cases, we can set $B_k^{(1)}(t) = 0$ or $B_k^{(2)}(t) = 0$ for $k = 1, 2, \ldots, m$, which infers the following corollaries.

Corollary 1. *Suppose that Assumption 1 holds. $\chi(t)$ is a right-continuous staircase function with discontinuities in $\{t_1, \ldots, t_j, \ldots\}$. Let $N(t) = \#\{j : t > t_j, j = 1, 2, \ldots\}$, and there exist*

1. *A constant $T_0 > 0$,*
2. *Positive constants $\gamma_k (k = 0, 1, \ldots)$, $\gamma_0 \leq \gamma_1 \leq \ldots$,*

3. $C(\chi(t), \chi(t')) \leq C_0$ *for any* $t, t' \geq t_0$,

such that the following conditions hold:

Let $A(t) = (\partial f/\partial x)(x, x_{\tau_1}, \ldots, x_{\tau_m}, r(t))$, $B_k(t) = (\partial f/\partial x_{\tau_k})(x, x_{\tau_1}, \ldots, x_{\tau_m}, r(t))$, $k = 1, \ldots, m$ *be piecewise continuous with respect to* t, *and the discontinuities belong to* $\{t_1, t_2, \ldots, t_i, \ldots\}$,

$$\nu_{\chi(t)}(A(t)) + \sum_{k=1}^{m} \|B_k(t)\|_{\chi(t)} \frac{\exp\left(\gamma_{N(t)} t\right)}{\exp\left(\gamma_{N(t-\tau_k(t))}(t - \tau_k(t))\right)} \leq -\gamma_{N(t)}$$

and for any $t > T_0$,

$$\frac{1}{t}\left[\sum_{i=0}^{N(t)-1} [(\gamma_{i+1} - \gamma_i)t_{i+1} + \log \beta_{i+1}] + \gamma_0 t_0 - \gamma_{N(t)} t\right] \leq -c,$$

where $\beta_k = C(\chi(t_k), \chi(t_k-))$, *then system* (1) *is exponentially incrementally stable.*

Corollary 2. *Suppose that Assumption 1 holds.* $\chi(t)$ *is a right-continuous staircase function with discontinuities in* $\{t_1, \ldots, t_j, \ldots\}$. *Let* $N(t) = \#\{j : t \geq t_j, j = 1, 2, \ldots\}$, *and there exist*

1. *A constant* $T_0 > 0$,
2. *Positive constants* $\alpha_k > 0 (k = 0, 1, \ldots)$,
3. $C(\chi(t), \chi(t')) \leq C_0$ *for any* $t, t' \geq t_0$,

such that the following conditions hold:

Let $A(t) = (\partial f/\partial x)(x, x_{\tau_1}, \ldots, x_{\tau_m}, r(t))$, $B_k(t) = (\partial f/\partial x_{\tau_k})(x, x_{\tau_1}, \ldots, x_{\tau_m}, r(t))$, $k = 1, \ldots, m$, *there exist matrix-valued functions* $B_k^{(1)}(t)$, $B_k^{(2)}(t)$, $B_k^{(1)}(t) + B_k^{(2)}(t) = B_k(t)$ *such that*

$$\nu_{\chi(t)}(A(t) + \sum_{k=1}^{m} B_k(t)) + \sum_{k=1}^{m} \tau_k(t) \|B_k(t)\|_{\chi(t)} (\tilde{A}^k(t) + \tilde{B}^k(t)) \leq -\gamma_{N(t)}$$

where

$$\tilde{A}_t^k = \sup_{t-\tau_k(t) \leq s \leq t} \|A(s)\|_{\chi(t)} \exp\left(\gamma_{N(t)} t - \gamma_{N(s)} s\right)$$

$$\tilde{B}_t^k = \sup_{t-\tau_k(t) \leq s \leq t} \|B_k(s)\|_{\chi(t)} \exp\left(\gamma_{N(t)} t - \gamma_{N(s-\tau_k(s))}(s - \tau_k(s))\right)$$

and for any $t > T_0$,

$$\frac{1}{t}\left[\sum_{i=0}^{N(t)-1} [(\gamma_{i+1} - \gamma_i)t_{i+1} + \log \beta_{i+1}] + \gamma_0 t_0 - \gamma_{N(t)} t\right] \leq -c,$$

where $\beta_k = C(\chi(t_k), \chi(t_k-))$, *then system* (1) *is exponentially incrementally stable.*

4. Incremental Stability for Time-Delay Dynamical Systems with Discontinuous Right-Hand Sides

Here, we consider the time-delay dynamical systems [39] with discontinuous right-hand sides using multiple norms, formulated as follows:

$$\dot{x} = f(x(t), x_{\tau_1}(t), \ldots, x_{\tau_m}(t), r(t)) \tag{5}$$

where $x, x_{\tau_1}, \ldots, x_{\tau_m} \in \mathbb{R}^n$, $x_{\tau_k}(t) = x(t - \tau_k(t)), (k = 1, \ldots, m)$ represents the time-delay term. The right-hand function f may be discontinuous with respect to $(x, x_{\tau_1}, \ldots, x_{\tau_m})$. The solution of the system (5) can be defined as a solution of the following differential inclusion, which is named a (time-delay) Filippov system,

$$\begin{cases} \dot{x} \in F(x(t), x_{\tau_1}(t), \ldots, x_{\tau_m}(t), r(t)), \ t \in [0, T] \\ x(s) = \phi(s), s \in [t_0 - \overline{\tau}, t_0] \end{cases} \tag{6}$$

where $x_{\tau_k}(t) = x(t - \tau_k(t))$, $\tau_k(t)$ is non-negative for $t \in [t_0, T]$, $T \in (t_0, +\infty]$, $\overline{\tau} = \max_k \sup_{s \geq t_0} \tau_k(s)$, the initial function $\phi(\cdot)$ is defined on $[t_0 - \overline{\tau}, t_0]$, and F is a set-valued mapping defined as follows,

$$\begin{aligned} F(x(t), x_{\tau_1}(t), \ldots, x_{\tau_m}(t), r(t)) &= \mathcal{K}[f](x(t), x_{\tau_1}(t), \ldots, x_{\tau_m}(t), r(t)) \\ &= \bigcap_{\epsilon>0} \bigcap_{\mu(P)=0} \overline{co}\{f(B((x, x_{\tau_1}, \ldots, x_{\tau_m}), \epsilon) \setminus P, r(t))\}, \end{aligned}$$

where $\mu(\cdot)$ stands for the Lebesgue measure, $B((x, x_{\tau_1}, \ldots, x_{\tau_m}), \epsilon) = \{(y, y_{\tau_1}, \ldots, y_{\tau_m}) : |(y^\top, y_{\tau_1}^\top, \ldots, y_{\tau_m}^\top)^\top - (x^\top, x_{\tau_1}^\top, \ldots, x_{\tau_m}^\top)^\top| \leq \epsilon\}$ represents the ϵ-neighborhood of $(x, x_{\tau_1}, \ldots, x_{\tau_m})$ with the given vector norm $|\cdot|$, and $\overline{co}$ represents convex closure.

4.1. Existence and Uniqueness of the Solution

Before the main theorem, the existence and uniqueness of the Cauchy problem of the Filippov system (6) should be proved first. Herein, several of the existing results on dynamical systems without time-delay terms are presented as follows. Readers are referred to [15,37,40] for the details. For some dynamical systems without time-delay terms, formulated as follows,

$$\dot{x} = f(x, t)$$

in which $x \in \mathbb{R}^n$, we have the corresponding Filippov system,

$$\dot{x} = F(x, t) = \mathcal{K}[f](x, t) = \bigcap_{\epsilon>0} \bigcap_{\mu(P)=0} \overline{co}\{f(B(x, \epsilon) \setminus P, t)\} \tag{7}$$

Then, from Definition 4 and 5 in [40]. We have concluded that under the following Assumption 2, it can be guaranteed that system (7) has at least one solution.

Assumption 2 ([40]). *The set-valued mapping $F : \mathbb{R}^n \times \mathbb{R}^+ \rightrightarrows \mathbb{R}^n$ satisfies that for all $(x, t) \in \mathbb{R}^n \times \mathbb{R}^+$, $F(x, t)$ is non-empty, bounded, convex, and closed, and F is upper semicontinuous at (x, t).*

In Assumption 2, 'upper semicontinuity' for the set-valued mapping F is defined as follows.

Definition 8 (Section 1, Chapter 2 in [37]). *A set-valued mapping $F : \mathbb{R}^n \times \mathbb{R}^+ \rightrightarrows Y$ is called upper semicontinuous at $(x, t) \in \mathbb{R}^n \times \mathbb{R}^+$ if and only if for any neighborhood $\mathcal{U}$ of $F(x, t)$, $\exists \delta > 0$, such that $\forall (\tilde{x}, \tilde{t}) \in B((x, t), \delta)$, $F(\tilde{x}, \tilde{t}) \subset \mathcal{U}$.*

Assumption 3. *With respect to a given Euclid norm $|\cdot|$ defined on a n-dimensional space, we have the following hypothesis:*

1. *For any $(x, y_1, \ldots, y_m, r) \in \mathbb{R}^{n \times (m+1)} \times \mathbb{R}$, $F(x, y_1, \ldots, y_m, r(t))$ is non-empty, convex, closed in $\mathbb{R}^n$, and set-valued mapping F is upper semicontinuous with respect to $(x, y_1, \ldots, y_m, r)$.*
2. *(Linearly increasing) There exists $\alpha > 0$ such that*

$$\sup\{|v| : v \in F(x, y_1, \ldots, y_m, r)\} \leq \alpha(|x| + |y_1| + \ldots + |y_m| + |r| + 1)$$

holds for any $(x, y_1, \ldots, y_m, r) \in \mathbb{R}^{n \times (m+1)} \times \mathbb{R}$. With Gronwall inequality [41], it can easily be seen as equivalent to: there exists $\Theta > 0$ such that

$$\sup\{|v| : v \in F(x, y_1, \ldots, y_m, r)\} \leq \Theta$$

holds for any $(x, y_1, \ldots, y_m, r) \in \mathbb{R}^{n \times (m+1)} \times \mathbb{R}$.

3. *Function* $\tau_k : [t_0, T] \to [0, \infty)$ $(k = 1, \ldots, m)$ *is continuously differentiable and bounded, with its upper bound* $\overline{\tau} := \max\{\tau_k(t) : t \in [t_0, T],\ k = 1, \ldots, m\}$ *and lower bound* $\underline{\tau} = \min\{\tau_k(t) : t \in [t_0, T],\ k = 1, \ldots, m\} > 0$.
4. *The initial function* $\phi(\cdot) \in L^\infty([t_0 - \overline{\tau}, t_0], \mathbb{R}^n)$ *is measurable.*
5. *For any* $(x, y_1, \ldots, y_m, r) \in \mathbb{R}^{n\times(m+1)} \times \mathbb{R}^n \times \mathbb{R}^+$, *there exists continuous function* $h(\cdot) : \mathbb{R}^+ \to \mathbb{R}^+$, *such that* $|F(x_1, y_1, \ldots, y_m, r(t)) - F(x_2, y_1, \ldots, y_m, r(t))| \le h(|x_1 - x_2|)$ *holds.*

First, we fix a continuous initial function $\phi(\cdot) \in L^\infty([t_0 - \overline{\tau}, t_0], \mathbb{R}^n)$, then select a measurable function $\psi : [t_0 - \overline{\tau}, t_0] \to \mathbb{R}^n$ such that $\psi(s) \in \mathcal{K}[\phi](s)$ holds for $s \in [t_0 - \overline{\tau}, t_0]$ almost everywhere. For $t \in [t_0, t_0 + \underline{\tau}]$, consider the following differential inclusion [42]:

$$\begin{cases} \dot{x}(t) \in F(x(t), \psi(t - \tau_1(t)), \ldots, \psi(t - \tau_m(t)), r(t)) \\ x(0) = \phi(0) \end{cases}, \tag{8}$$

From Assumption 3, together with Assumption 2 and the conclusion for the existence of the solution of system (8), the inclusion (6) has at least one solution defined in $[t_0, t_0 + \underline{\tau}]$.

Therefore, similarly, the solution can be extended to $[t_0, +\infty)$. Assume, as an inductive step, that the solution x is defined on $[t_0 - \overline{\tau}, t_0 + N\underline{\tau}]$, for some $N = 1, 2, \ldots$. Then, one can consider the vector $\alpha = x(t_0 + N\underline{\tau})$ as the initial state of the following differential inclusion,

$$\begin{cases} \dot{x}(t) \in F(x(t), \psi(t - \tau_1(t)), \ldots, \psi(t - \tau_m(t)), r(t)) \\ x(0) = \phi(0) \end{cases} t \in [t_0 + N\underline{\tau}, t_0 + (N+1)\underline{\tau}] \text{ almost everywhere.}$$

Then, one can extend $x(t), t \in [t_0 - \overline{\tau}, t_0 + N\underline{\tau}]$ to a right neighborhood of $t_0 + N\underline{\tau}$, the interval $[t_0 - \overline{\tau}, t_0 + (N+1)\underline{\tau}]$. That is, we have the following lemma,

Lemma 2. *If the time-delay Filippov system* (6) *satisfies Assumption 3, then, the system* (6) *has at least on solution in* $[t_0, T]$, $T \in (0, +\infty]$.

Then, when it comes to the problem of uniqueness, enlightened by Chapter 2, Section 10, Theorem 1 in [15], we similarly research the conditions for uniqueness of the solution of system (6).

Theorem 2. *Suppose that function* $f(x(t), x_{\tau_1}(t), \ldots, x_{\tau_m}(t), r(t))$ *defined on region* $D \subset \mathbb{R}^n \times \mathbb{R}^n \times \mathbb{R}^+$ *is discontinuous on zero measure set* M, *and there exists an integral function* $l(t)$ *such that* $|f(x, x_{\tau_1}, \ldots, x_{\tau_m}, r)| \le l(t)$ *holds for any* $(x, x_{\tau_1}, \ldots, x_{\tau_m}, r) \in D$, *and* $l(t) < \infty$ *almost everywhere. Let* $\epsilon_0 > 0$, *for any* $(x_0, x_{\tau_1}, \ldots, x_{\tau_m}, r), (y_0, y_{\tau_1}, \ldots, y_{\tau_m}, r)$ *satisfying that* $|x_0 - y_0| < \epsilon_0$ *and* $|x_{\tau_k} - y_{\tau_k}| \le |x_0 - y_0|, (k = 1, \ldots, m)$,

$$(x_0 - y_0) \cdot (f(x_0, x_{\tau_1}, \ldots, x_{\tau_m}, t) - f(y_0, y_{\tau_1}, \ldots, y_{\tau_m}, r(t))) \le l(t)|x_0 - y_0|^2 \tag{9}$$

Then, under the simplest convex definition (Page 50 in [15]), equation $\dot{x} = f(x, x_{\tau_1}, \ldots, x_{\tau_m}, r(t))$ *is right-unique on* D.

Proof. If for all $t \in \mathbb{R}^+$, any $\epsilon_0 > 0$, $x(\cdot)$ and $y(\cdot)$ satisfying that $|x(\cdot) - y(\cdot)|^\infty_{[t-\overline{\tau}, t]} \le |x(t) - y(t)| < \epsilon_0$, on the basis of (9), we have

$$(x(t) - y(t)) \cdot (f(x(t), x_{\tau_1}(t), \ldots, x_{\tau_m}(t), r(t)) - f(y(t), y_{\tau_1}(t), \ldots, y_{\tau_m}(t), r(t))) \le l(t)|x(t) - y(t)|^2,$$

holds. Thus, we have

$$\begin{aligned} \frac{1}{2}\frac{d}{dt}|x(t) - y(t)|^2 &= (x(t) - y(t))(\dot{x}(t) - \dot{y}(t)) \\ &= (x(t) - y(t)) \cdot (f(x(t), x_{\tau_1}(t), \ldots, x_{\tau_m}(t), r(t)) - f(y(t), y_{\tau_1}(t), \ldots, y_{\tau_m}(t), r(t))) \\ &\le l(t)|x(t) - y(t)|^2. \end{aligned}$$

Therefore, similar to the proof of Theorem 1, in Section 10, Chapter 2 in [15], it can be seen that

$$\frac{d}{dt}\left(|x(t)-y(t)|^2 e^{-L(t)}\right) \leq 0$$

where $L(t) = \int_{t_0}^{t} l(s)ds$, that is, $|x(t)-y(t)|^2 e^{-L(t)}$ is decreasing with respect to time t. If $|x(\cdot)-y(\cdot)|^{\infty}_{[t_0-\overline{\tau},t_0]} = \sup\{|x(t)-y(t)| : t \in [t_0-\overline{\tau}, t_0]\} = 0$, then $|x(t)-y(t)| = 0$ holds for $t > t_0$, then we obtained the right uniqueness of the solution of system (6). □

If system (5) is a switched system, according to Theorem 2, one can prove the right uniqueness of the solution.

Here, we formulate a switched system with time delay, that is, the right-hand function is switched with respect to $(x, x_{\tau_1}, \ldots, x_{\tau_m})$.

$$f(x,t) = f_i(x, x_{\tau_1}, \ldots, x_{\tau_m}, r(t)),\ (x, x_{\tau_1}, \ldots, x_{\tau_m}, t) \in R_i \tag{10}$$

in which $f_i : \mathbb{R}^{n\times(m+1)} \times \mathbb{R}^+ \to \mathbb{R}^n$, regions $R_i \subset \mathbb{R}^{n\times(m+1)} \times \mathbb{R}^+$, $i = 1, \ldots, K$. All of the regions R_i have non-empty interiors. The discontinuities are composed of several smooth hypersurfaces of dimension $d(d < (m+1)n+1)$. Suppose that $\{S_i\}_{i=1}^N$ is a sequence $((m+1)n)$-dimensional smooth hypersurfaces, $S_i = \{(x, x_{\tau_1}, \ldots, x_{\tau_m}, t) \in \mathbb{R}^{n\times(m+1)} \times \mathbb{R}^+ \mid \phi_i(x, x_{\tau_1}, \ldots, x_{\tau_m}, t) = 0\}$, in which $\phi_i(x, x_{\tau_1}, \ldots, x_{\tau_m}, t) \in C^1(\mathbb{R}^{n\times(m+1)} \times \mathbb{R}^+, \mathbb{R})$, the continuous region of the function f is a sequence of connected regions, whose boundaries are the switching surfaces. Suppose that the switching surfaces never intersect each other. Denote one of the connected continuous region of f by $G_i^+(G_i^-)$, then it satisfies that

1. $\partial G_i^+(\partial G_i^-) \subset \bigcup_k S_k$;
2. $f(x, x_{\tau_1}, \ldots, x_{\tau_m}, r(t))$ is continuous in $G_i^+(G_i^-)$;
3. $\phi_i(x, x_{\tau}, \ldots, x_{\tau_m}, t) > 0 (< 0)$ holds in G_i^+ (G_i^-).

in which G_i^+ and G_i^- are two different regions with their common boundary on S_i.

Take a switched system defined as (10) with $K = 2$, $N = 1$ as an example.In the domain G, consider one of the switching hypersurface S, $f^+(x, x_{\tau_1}, \ldots, x_{\tau_m}, r(t))$ and $f^-(x, x_{\tau_1}, \ldots, x_{\tau_m}, r(t))$ represent the limiting values of the function $f(x, x_{\tau_1}, \ldots, x_{\tau_m}, r(t))$ at point $(x, x_{\tau_1}, \ldots, x_{\tau_m}, t)$ from the regions G^+ and G^-, respectively. $f_N^+(x, x_{\tau_1}, \ldots, x_{\tau_m}, r(t))$ and $f_N^-(x, x_{\tau_1}, \ldots, x_{\tau_m}, r(t))$ represent the projections of the vectors $f^+(x, x_{\tau_1}, \ldots, x_{\tau_m}, r(t))$ and $f^-(x, x_{\tau_1}, \ldots, x_{\tau_m}, r(t))$ onto the normal vector to S directed from G^+ to G^-, respectively, at the point $(x, x_{\tau_1}, \ldots, x_{\tau_m}, t)$.

Together with Theorem 2, according to bimodal time-delay systems, we have the following conclusion:

Theorem 3. *Under the notations defined above, for all* $t \in [t_0, +\infty)$ *and point* $(x, x_{\tau_1}, \ldots, x_{\tau_m}, t) \in S$, *if the inequality* $f_N^-(x, x_{\tau_1}, \ldots, x_{\tau_m}, r(t)) - f_N^+(x, x_{\tau_1}, \ldots, x_{\tau_m}, r(t)) > 0$ *is fulfilled, then right uniqueness of Filippov solution for the bimodal system* (10) *(*$K = 2$, $N = 1$*) occurs. (Possibly different inequalities for different* $(x, x_{\tau_1}, \ldots, x_{\tau_m})$ *and* t*.)*

Proof. We use the conclusion in Theorem 2 to prove Theorem 3 above.

For any point $(z, z_{\tau_1}, \ldots, z_{\tau_m}, t)$ on the switching surface S, and $(x, x_{\tau_1}, \ldots, x_{\tau_m}, t) \in R_1$, $(y, y_{\tau_1}, \ldots, y_{\tau_m}, t) \in R_2$, which satisfy that $|y_{\tau_k} - z_{\tau_k}| \leq |y - z|$, $|x_{\tau_k} - z_{\tau_k}| \leq |x - z|$, $|x_{\tau_k} - y_{\tau_k}| \leq |y - x|$. Since $\partial f_1/\partial x$, $\partial f_2/\partial x$ and $\partial f_1/\partial x_{\tau_i}$, $\partial f_2/\partial x_{\tau_i}$ $(i = 1, \ldots, m)$ are bounded, this implies that there exist $l, k_i > 0$ $(i = 1, \ldots, m)$ such that

$$\begin{aligned} &|f(x, x_{\tau_1}, \ldots, x_{\tau_m}, r(t)) - f_1(z, z_{\tau_1}, \ldots, z_{\tau_m}, r(t))| \leq l|x - z| + \sum_{i=1}^{m} k_i |x_{\tau_i} - z_{\tau_i}|, \\ &|f(y, y_{\tau_1}, \ldots, y_{\tau_m}, r(t)) - f_2(z, z_{\tau_1}, \ldots, z_{\tau_m}, r(t))| \leq l|y - z| + \sum_{i=1}^{m} k_i |y_{\tau_i} - z_{\tau_i}|. \end{aligned} \tag{11}$$

Similar to the proof of Theorem 2 in Chapter 2 in [15], if $f_N^-(x, x_{\tau_1}, \ldots, x_{\tau_m}, r(t)) - f_N^+(x, x_{\tau_1}, \ldots, x_{\tau_m}, r(t)) > 0$ holds, then

$$(x-z)(f_1(z, z_{\tau_1}, \ldots, z_{\tau_m}, r(t)) - f_2(z, z_{\tau_1}, \ldots, z_{\tau_m}, r(t))) \leq 0. \tag{12}$$

The inequality (12) still holds if vector $x - y$ is substituted with vector $x - z$, which is in the same direction. Together with (11) and (12), it infers that

$$\begin{aligned}
&(x-y)(f(x, x_{\tau_1}, \ldots, x_{\tau_m}, r) + f_2(z, z_{\tau_1}, \ldots, z_{\tau_m}, r) - f_1(z, z_{\tau_1}, \ldots, z_{\tau_m}, r) - f(y, y_{\tau_1}, \ldots, y_{\tau_m}, r)) \\
\leq &|y-x| \cdot \Big(|f(x, x_{\tau_1}, \ldots, x_{\tau_m}, r) - f_1(z, z_{\tau_1}, \ldots, z_{\tau_m}, r)| + |f(y, y_{\tau_1}, \ldots, y_{\tau_m}, r) - f_2(z, z_{\tau_1}, \ldots, z_{\tau_m}, r)| \Big) \\
< &|y-x| \cdot (l|x-z| + \sum_{i=1}^{m} k_i |x_{\tau_i} - z_{\tau_i}| + l|y-z| + \sum_{i=1}^{m} k_i |y_{\tau_i} - z_{\tau_i}|).
\end{aligned}$$

That is, if $|y_{\tau_i} - z_{\tau_i}| \leq |y-z|$, $|x_{\tau_i} - z_{\tau_i}| \leq |x-z|$, $|x_{\tau_i} - y_{\tau_i}| \leq |y-x|$ $(i = 1, \ldots, m)$, it holds that

$$(x-y)(f(x, x_{\tau_1}, \ldots, x_{\tau_m}, r(t)) - f(y, y_{\tau_1}, \ldots, y_{\tau_m}, r(t))) < 2(l + \sum_{i=1}^{m} k_i)|y-x|^2.$$

Thus, together with Theorem 2, at any point $(z, z_{\tau_1}, \ldots, z_{\tau_m}, t)$ in the domain, right uniqueness of the Filippov solution for system (10) $(K = 2, N = 1)$ occurs for $t \in [t_0, +\infty)$. □

4.2. Criteria for Incremental Stability for Filippov Systems with Time Delay

Here, with the conclusions above, we then research the conditions of incremental stability for time-delay systems with discontinuous right-hand sides.

$$\dot{x}(t) = f(x, x_{\tau_1}, \ldots, x_{\tau_m}, r(t)) \tag{13}$$

where $x_{\tau_k}(t) = x(t - \tau_k(t))$, $\tau_k(t)$ $(k = 1, 2, \ldots, m)$ is a bounded function with respect to time t, the function $f(x, x_{\tau_1}, \ldots, x_{\tau_m}, r(t)) = (f_1, f_2, \ldots, f_n) : \mathbb{R}^{n \times (m+1)} \times \mathbb{R}^+ \to \mathbb{R}^n$ is discontinuous with respect to $(x, x_{\tau_1}, \ldots, x_{\tau_m}, t)$ on a zero measure set. $r(t)$ is a piecewise right-continuous switched function, with its discontinuities in $\{t_1, t_2, \ldots, t_j, \ldots\}$.

Then, according to the discontinuous right-hand side $f(x, x_{\tau_1}, \ldots, x_{\tau_m}, r(t))$, with corresponding set-valued mapping $F(x, x_{\tau_1}, \ldots, x_{\tau_m}, r(t)) = \mathcal{K}[f](x, x_{\tau_1}, \ldots, x_{\tau_m}, r(t))$, we construct a sequence of functions $\{f^p(x, x_{\tau_1}, \ldots, x_{\tau_m}, r(t))\}_{p=1}^{\infty}$ satisfying the following conditions, denoted by Condition $C_{time-delay}(\Sigma)$, where $\Sigma \in \mathbb{R}^{n \times (m+1)}$:

1. $f^p(x, x_{\tau_1}, \ldots x_{\tau_m}, r(t)) = (f_1^p, f_2^p, \ldots, f_m^p) : \mathbb{R}^{n \times (m+1)} \times \mathbb{R}^+ \to \mathbb{R}^n$ is continuous and continuously differentiable with respect to $(x, x_{\tau_1}, \ldots x_{\tau_m})$, and continuous with respect to $(x, x_{\tau_1}, \ldots x_{\tau_m}, r)$. Moreover, $f_i^p, i = 1, \ldots, m$ satisfies local Lipschitz conditions for $(x, x_{\tau_1}, \ldots x_{\tau_m}) \in \Sigma$.
2. For each $t \geq t_0$ and compact set $\Sigma \subset \mathbb{R}^{n \times (m+1)}$,

   $$\lim_{m \to \infty} d_H\{Graph(f^p(\Sigma, r(t))), Graph(F(\Sigma, r(t)))\} = 0$$

   holds, where $F(x, x_{\tau_1}, \ldots x_{\tau_m}, r(t)) = \mathcal{K}[f](x, x_{\tau_1}, \ldots x_{\tau_m}, r(t))$ and d_H represents the Hausdorff metric. $Graph(F)$ and $Graph(f^p)$ are considered on $\mathbb{R}^{m \times (n+1)} \times [t_0, +\infty)$, where $Graph(F(x, x_{\tau_1}, \ldots x_{\tau_m}, r(t))) = \{(x, t, y) : y \in F(x, x_{\tau_1}, \ldots x_{\tau_m}, r(t)), (x, x_{\tau_1}, \ldots x_{\tau_m}) \in \Sigma, t \geq t_0\}$, and so it is with $Graph(f^p(x, x_{\tau_1}, \ldots x_{\tau_m}, r(t)))$.
3. For any compact set $\Sigma \subset \mathbb{R}^{m \times (n+1)}$, there exists measure $w(\cdot)$, defined as $w(\Sigma) = q(\lambda(\Sigma))$, in which λ represents the Lebesgue measure, q is a measurable function mapping $\mathbb{R}^+$ to $\mathbb{R}^+$, such that $|f^p(x, x_{\tau_1}, \ldots x_{\tau_m}, t)| \leq w(\Sigma)$ holds for each $(x, x_{\tau_1}, \ldots x_{\tau_m}) \in \Sigma$ and $t \geq t_0$.

Thus, we have the following conclusion on incremental stability of time-delay systems with discontinuous right-hand sides:

Theorem 4. *Suppose that system* (13) *has a unique solution, and there exists a sequence of functions* $\{f^p\}_{p=1}^{\infty}$ *satisfying Condition* $C_{time-delay}(\Sigma)$. $\chi(t)$ *is a right-continuous staircase function with discontinuities in* $\{t_1, \ldots, t_j, \ldots\}$. *Let* $N(t) = \#\{j : t \geq t_j, j = 1, 2, \ldots\}$, *and suppose that there exist*

1. *A constant* $T_0 > 0$,
2. *Positive constants* $\gamma_k (k = 0, 1, \ldots)$, $\gamma_0 \leq \gamma_1 \leq \ldots$,
3. $C(\chi(t), \chi(t')) \leq C_0$ *for any* $t, t' \geq t_0$,

such that the following conditions hold:

Let $A^p(t) = (\partial f^p / \partial x)(x, x_{\tau_1}, \ldots, x_{\tau_m}, r(t))$, $B_k^p(t) = (\partial f^p / \partial x_{\tau_k})(x, x_{\tau_1}, \ldots, x_{\tau_m}, r(t))$, $k = 1, \ldots, m$, *there exist matrix-valued functions* $B_{1k}^p(t)$, $B_{2k}^p(t)$, $B_{1k}^p(t) + B_{2k}^p(t) = B_k^p(t)$ *such that*

$$\nu_{\chi(t)}(A^p(t) + \sum_{k=1}^{m} B_{1k}^p(t)) + \sum_{k=1}^{m} \tau_k(t) \|B_{1k}^p(t)\|_{\chi(t)} (\tilde{A}_k^p(t) + \tilde{B}_k^p(t)) + \sum_{k=1}^{m} \|B_{2k}^p(t)\|_{\chi(t)} \frac{\exp\left(\gamma_{N(t)} t\right)}{\exp\left(\gamma_{N(t-\tau_k(t))}(t - \tau_k(t))\right)} \leq -\gamma_{N(t)}$$

where

$$\tilde{A}_k^p(t) = \sup_{t-\tau_k(t) \leq s \leq t} \|A^p(s)\|_{\chi(t)} \exp\left(\gamma_{N(t)} t - \gamma_{N(s)} s\right)$$
$$\tilde{B}_k^p(t) = \sup_{t-\tau_k(t) \leq s \leq t} \|B_k^p(s)\|_{\chi(t)} \exp\left(\gamma_{N(t)} t - \gamma_{N(s-\tau_k(s))}(s - \tau_k(s))\right).$$

and for any $t > T_0$,

$$\frac{1}{t}\left[\sum_{i=0}^{N(t)-1} [(\gamma_{i+1} - \gamma_i) t_{i+1} + \log \beta_{i+1}] + \gamma_0 t_0 - \gamma_{N(t)} t\right] \leq -c,$$

where $\beta_k = C(\chi(t_k), \chi(t_k-))$, *then system* (6) *is exponentially incrementally stable in* Σ *for* $t \in [t_0, +\infty)$.

Proof. First, we construct a sequence of functions satisfying Condition $C_{time-delay}(\Sigma)$, and the corresponding sequence of time-delay system:

$$\dot{x}(t) = f^p(x, x_{\tau_1}, \ldots x_{\tau_m}, r(t)) \tag{14}$$

in which, according to Condition $C_{time-delay}(\Sigma)$, $f_i, i = 1, \ldots, m$ satisfy local Lipschitz conditions, so it can be seen that (14) has a unique solution for $t \in \mathbb{R}^+$.

Therefore, from Theorem 1, for each p, system (14) is exponentially incrementally stable.

Denote any two of the solutions of (6) with different initial function $x_0(\cdot)$ and $y_0(\cdot)$ by $x(t)$ and $y(t)$. Then, here, try to approximate $x(t)$ and $y(t)$ by two sequences of solutions of (14), denoted by x^p and y^p, respectively. The initial functions $x_0(s)$ and $y_0(s)$ here are defined for $s \in [t_0 - \overline{\tau}, t_0]$, where $\overline{\tau} = \max_k \sup_{s \in [t_0, +\infty)} \tau_k(s)$.

With f^p satisfying condition $C_{time-delay}(\Sigma)$, for each given T, $t_0 \leq t \leq T$, we have $x^p(t)$ and $\dot{x}^p(t)$ are bounded regarding $(x_0(\cdot), T)$. It is the same with $y^p(t)$. Thus, $x^p(t)$ $(y^p(t))$ is uniformly bounded on $[t_0, T]$, and $\dot{x}^p(t)$ $(\dot{y}^p(t))$ is uniformly bounded on $[t_0, T]$ as well.

Because of Condition 1 in $C_{time-delay}(\Sigma)$, $x^p(t)$ $(y^p(t))$ is continuous with respect to t. Together with Condition 3 in $C_{time-delay}(\Sigma)$, we conclude that $x^p(t)$ $(y^p(t))$, $p \in \mathbb{N}^+$ are equicontinuous for $t \in [t_0, T]$.

Here, we present the Arzela–Ascoli lemma (similar to Theorem 2.2 in [43]):

Lemma 3. *(Arzela–Ascoli Lemma) X is a compact set on* $\mathbb{R}^n$*. If a sequence* $\{f_n\}_1^\infty$ *in* $C(X)$ *is bounded and equicontinuous, then it has a uniformly convergent subsequence.*

From Lemma 3, one can find a sub-sequence of $\{x^p(t)\}_{p\in\mathbb{N}^+}$ and $\{y^p(t)\}_{p\in\mathbb{N}^+}$ (still denoted by $x^m(t)$ and $y^m(t)$) satisfying that $x^p(t)$ (y^p(t)) uniformly converges to a continuous function $x^*(t)$ ($y^*(t)$) on $[t_0, T]$, $T \in (t_0, +\infty]$. For all $k \in \mathbb{N}^+$, one can find a subsequence $\{x^{kj}(t)\}_{j\in\mathbb{N}^+}$ of $\{x^p(t)\}_{p\in\mathbb{N}^+}$ such that $|x^{kj}(t) - x^*(t)| < \frac{1}{j}$ holds on the interval $[t_0, t_0 + k + 1]$. Then, by diagonal selection principle, select a new subsequence $\{x^{kk}(t)\}_{k\in\mathbb{N}^+}$ such that $\{x^{kk}(t)\}_{k\in\mathbb{N}^+}$ uniformly converges to a continuous function $x^*(t)$ on $[t_0, T]$, $T \in (t_0, +\infty]$. It is the same with $x^*_{\tau_k}(t)$, for $k = 1, \ldots, m$.

The system $\dot{x}^p(t) = f^p(x, x_{\tau_1}, \ldots, x_{\tau_m}, r(t))$ has a unique solution. $x^p(t)$ satisfies Lipschitz condition:

$$|x^p(t) - x^p(t')|_{\mathcal{X}(t_0)} \leq L|t - t'|_{\mathcal{X}(t_0)}$$

where $t, t' \in [t_0, T]$, $L > 0$. Because of norm equivalence, the Lipschitz condition above also holds with other norms defined in $\mathbb{R}^n$. Therefore, $x^*(t)$ ($y^*(t)$) also satisfies the Lipschitz condition, that is, $\dot{x}^*(t)$ ($\dot{y}^*(t)$) exists and is bounded and measurable for $[t_0, T)$, $T \in (t_0, +\infty]$.

We then have the conclusion that $\dot{x}^p(t)$ ($\dot{y}^p(t)$) weakly converges to $\dot{x}^*(t)$ ($\dot{y}^*(t)$) on the space $L_1([t_0, T], \mathbb{R}^n)$, the demonstrations are as follows.

$C_0^\infty([t_0, T], \mathbb{R}^n)$ is dense in the Banach space $L^\infty([t_0, T], \mathbb{R}^n)$, which is the conjugate space $L_1([t_0, T], \mathbb{R}^n)$. Therefore, the following equation

$$\int_{t_0}^{T} \langle \dot{x}^p(t) - \dot{x}^*, q(t)\rangle dt = -\int_{t_0}^{T} \langle \dot{q}(t), x^p(t) - x^*\rangle dt.$$

holds for each $q(t) \in C_0^\infty([t_0, T], \mathbb{R}^n)$. Since $\{\dot{x}^p(t)\}$ is bounded for each p, from the Lebesgue-dominant convergence theorem we have

$$\lim_{p\to\infty} \int_{t_0}^{T} \langle \dot{x}^p(t) - \dot{x}^*, q(t)\rangle dt = -\int_{t_0}^{T} \langle \dot{q}(t), \lim_{p\to\infty} x^p(t) - x^*(t)\rangle dt = 0.$$

That is, $\{\dot{x}^p(t)\}$ weakly converges to $\dot{x}^*(t)$ on the space $L_1([t_0, T], \mathbb{R}^n)$.

With Mazur's convexity theorem [43], one can find a_l^n (b_l^n) with $\sum_{l=1}^m a_l^m = 1$ ($\sum_{l=1}^m b_l^m = 1$) such that $\dot{\tilde{x}}^p$ converges to $\dot{x}^*(t)$ almost everywhere on $[t_0, T]$, where $\tilde{x}^p(t) = \sum_{l=1}^p a_l^p x^p$. Notice that $\tilde{x}^p$ is in the convex closure of $\{x^p\}$, $\dot{\tilde{x}}^p$ converges to $\dot{x}^*$ uniformly. So it is with $\dot{\tilde{y}}^p(t)$ with $\tilde{y}^p(t) = \sum_{l=1}^p b_l^p y^p$, and it is the same with $\{\dot{x}^p_{\tau_k}(t)\}$ and $\{\dot{x}^*_{\tau_k}(t)\}$.

Recall Condition 3 in $C_{time-delay}(\Sigma)$. For $\Sigma \in \mathbb{R}^n$, it holds that

$$\lim_{p\to\infty} d_H\{Graph(f^p(\Sigma, t)), Graph(F(\Sigma, t))\} = 0, \forall t \geq t_0,$$

With $\dot{\tilde{x}}^p(t)$ in the convex closure of $\{f^p(x^p, x^p_{\tau_1}, \ldots, x^p_{\tau_m}, r(t))\}$, for any $\epsilon > 0$, there exists $N > 0$ such that $\dot{x}^p(t) \in B(F(x^*, x^*_{\tau_1}, \ldots, x^*_{\tau_m}, r(t)), \epsilon)$ for all $p > N$ and $(x^*, x^*_{\tau_1}, \ldots, x^*_{\tau_m})$, $(x^p, x^p_{\tau_1}, \ldots, x^p_{\tau_m}) \in \Sigma$, $t \in [t_0, T]$.

Since ϵ can be arbitrarily small, it can be seen that $\dot{x}^*(t) \in F(x^*, x^*_{\tau_1}, \ldots, x^*_{\tau_m}, r(t))$ with $x^* \in \Sigma$, which infers that the solution of (6) equals to $x^*(t)$ in Σ almost everywhere on $[t_0, T]$. For $x(t)$ and x^*, both are continuous because $\tilde{x}^p$ converges to x^* uniformly on $[t_0, T]$, it can be seen that x^* is the solution of (6). So it is with $y^*(t)$.

Because system (6) has a unique solution, $x(t) = x^*(t)$ and $y(t) = y^*(t)$ almost everywhere for $t \geq t_0$. That is, x^p converges to $x(t)$ uniformly in $[t_0, T]$, $T \in (t_0, +\infty]$. A similar proof can be applied to $y^p(t)$ and $y(t)$.

For $\{f^p(x, x_{\tau_1}, \ldots, x_{\tau_m}, r(t))\}$ is exponentially incrementally stable from Theorem 1, there exists some $M > 0$ and $\alpha > 0$,

$$|x^p(t)-y^p(t)|_{\chi(t_0)} \le Me^{-\alpha(t-t_0)} \sup_{s\in[t_0-\overline{\tau},t_0]} |x_0(s)-y_0(s)|_{\chi(t_0)}$$

for all $p \in \mathbb{N}^+$ and $t \ge t_0$. For each given $t \ge t_0$, let $\epsilon(t) = 3Me^{-\alpha(t-t_0)} \sup_{s\in[t_0-\overline{\tau},t_0]} |x_0(s) - y_0(s)|_{\chi(t_0)}$, there exists some $p_0(\epsilon,t)$ with which $|x^p(t)-x(t)|_{\chi(t_0)} \le \epsilon/3$ and $|y^p(t) - y(t)|_{\chi(t_0)} \le \epsilon/3$ hold for $p \ge p_0(\epsilon,t)$, which implies that

$$\begin{aligned} |x(t)-y(t)|_{\chi(t_0)} &\le |x(t)-x^p(t)|_{\chi(t_0)} + |y(t)-y^p(t)|_{\chi(t_0)} + |x^p(t)-y^p(t)|_{\chi(t_0)} \\ &\le \epsilon = 3Me^{-\alpha(t-t_0)} \sup_{s\in[t_0-\overline{\tau},t_0]} |x_0(s)-y_0(s)|_{\chi(t_0)}. \end{aligned}$$

This completes the proof. □

Remark 2. *Similar to Theorem 4, Corollary 1 and Corollary 2 can also be extended to discontinuous cases.*

5. Applications

In this section, with the conclusion in Theorem 4, the applications to switched time-delay systems and Hopfield time-delay systems are given.

5.1. Linear Switched Time-Delay System

Consider the following linear switched time-delay system:

$$\dot{x}(t) = f(x, x_{\tau_1}, \dots, x_{\tau_m}, t) = \begin{cases} A_1(t)x(t) + \sum_{k=1}^m B_{1k}(t)x(t-\tau_k(t)) + J_1(t), & \phi(x, x_{\tau_1}, \dots, x_{\tau_m}) > 0 \\ A_2(t)x(t) + \sum_{k=1}^m B_{2k}(t)x(t-\tau_k(t)) + J_2(t), & \phi(x, x_{\tau_1}, \dots, x_{\tau_m}) < 0 \end{cases}. \tag{15}$$

in which $x(t) \in \mathbb{R}^n$, $A_1(t), A_2(t) \in \mathbb{R}^{n\times n}$, $B_{1k}(t), B_{2k}(t) (k = 1,\dots,m) \in \mathbb{R}^{n\times n}$ is piecewise continuous, bounded matrix-valued functions, whose discontinuities are in $\{t_1, t_2 \dots .t_i, \dots\}$. Take a simple bimodal system as an example, with the switching surface $S = \{(x, x_{\tau_1}, \dots, x_{\tau_m}) : \phi(x, x_{\tau_1}, \dots, x_{\tau_m}) = 0\}$.

In order to guarantee the uniqueness of the Filippov solution for system (15), the linear time-delay system satisfies the following hypothesis:

Assumption 4. *The linear time-delay system* (15) *satisfies:*

1. *The right-hand function of system* (15) *satisfies Assumption 3.*
2. *For each point $(x, x_{\tau_1}, \dots, x_{\tau_m}) \in S$, the time-delay system* (15) *satisfies*

$$\frac{\partial \phi}{\partial x}(x, x_{\tau_1}, \dots, x_{\tau_m}) \cdot \left((A_1(t) - A_2(t))x + \sum_{k=1}^m (B_{1k}(t) - B_{2k}(t))x_{\tau_k} + J_1(t) - J_2(t) \right) < 0$$

Under the definitions and Assumption 4 above, from Lemma 2 and Theorem 3, it can be obtained that system (15) *has a unique solution.*

Assumption 5. *Suppose that in the continuous regions, the right-hand side $f(x, x_{\tau_1}, \dots, x_{\tau_m}, t)$ satisfies the conditions for exponential incremental stability in Theorem 1, which are formulated as follows.*

Let $N(t) = \#\{j : t \ge t_j, j = 1,2,\dots\}$, $\chi(t)$ be a right-continuous staircase function with its discontinuous points belonging to $\{t_1,\dots,t_j,\dots\}$, and there exist

1. *A constant $T_0 > 0$,*
2. *Positive constants $\gamma_k (k = 0,1,\dots)$, $\gamma_0 \le \gamma_1 \le \dots$,*
3. *$C(\chi(t),\chi(t')) \le C_0$ for any $t,t' \ge t_0$,*
4. *Matrix $B_{1k}^{(1)}, B_{1k}^{(2)}, B_{2k}^{(1)}, B_{2k}^{(2)} \in \mathbb{R}^{n\times n}$ satisfying that $B_{1k}^{(1)}(t) + B_{1k}^{(2)}(t) - B_{1k}(t)$ and $B_{2k}^{(1)}(t) + B_{2k}^{(2)}(t) = B_{2k}(t)$,*

such that the following conditions are satisfied:

$$\begin{aligned}L_1(t) =&\nu_{\chi(t)}(A_1(t) + \sum_{k=1}^{m} B_{1k}^{(1)}(t)) + \sum_{k=1}^{m} \tau_k(t)(\tilde{A}_{1k}(t) + \tilde{B}_{1k}(t))\|B_{1k}^{(1)}(t)\|_{\chi(t)} \\ &+ \sum_{k=1}^{m} \|B_{1k}^{(2)}(t)\|_{\chi(t)} \frac{\exp(\gamma_{N(t)}t)}{\exp(\gamma_{N(t-\tau_k(t))}(t-\tau_k(t)))} \leq -\gamma_{N(t)} \\ L_2(t) =&\nu_{\chi(t)}(A_2(t) + \sum_{k=1}^{m} B_{2k}^{(1)}(t)) + \sum_{k=1}^{m} \tau_k(t)(\tilde{A}_{2k}(t) + \tilde{B}_{2k}(t))\|B_{2k}^{(1)}(t)\|_{\chi(t)} \\ &+ \sum_{k=1}^{m} \|B_{2k}^{(2)}(t)\|_{\chi(t)} \frac{\exp(\gamma_{N(t)}t)}{\exp(\gamma_{N(t-\tau_k(t))}(t-\tau_k(t)))} \leq -\gamma_{N(t)}\end{aligned}$$

in which, for $i = 1, 2$,

$$\begin{aligned}\tilde{A}_{ik}(t) &= \sup_{t-\tau_k(t)\leq s\leq t} \|A_i(s)\|_{\chi(t)} \exp(\gamma_{N(t)}t - \gamma_{N(s)}s) \\ \tilde{B}_{ik}(t) &= \sup_{t-\tau_k(t)\leq s\leq t} \|B_{ik}(s)\|_{\chi(t)} \exp(\gamma_{N(t)}t - \gamma_{N(s-\tau_k(s))}(s-\tau_k(s)))\end{aligned}$$

and for all $t > T_0$,

$$\frac{1}{t}\left[\sum_{i=0}^{N(t)-1} [(\gamma_{i+1} - \gamma_i)t_{i+1} + \log\beta_{i+1}] + \gamma_0 t_0 - \gamma_{N(t)}t\right] \leq -c, \tag{16}$$

where $\beta_k = C(\chi(t_k), \chi(t_k-))$.

Thus, together with Theorem 4, we have the following corollary on incremental stability for bimodal linear time-delay systems.

Corollary 3. *Suppose that time-delay system (15) satisfies Assumptions 4 and 5. Meanwhile, in the neighborhood of switching surface S, that is, when $-\delta/2 < \phi(x, x_{\tau_1}, \ldots, x_{\tau_m}) < \delta/2$, let $w = (A_1(t) - A_2(t))x(t) + \sum_{k=1}^{m}(B_{1k}(t) - B_{2k}(t))x(t-\tau_k(t)) + J_1(t) - J_2(t)$, if it is satisfied that*

$$\begin{aligned}&pL_1(t) + (1-p)L_2(t) + \frac{1}{\delta}\nu_{\chi(t)}\left(w \cdot \frac{\partial\phi}{\partial x}\right) + \frac{1}{\delta}\sum_{k=1}^{m}\left\|w \cdot \frac{\partial\phi}{\partial x_{\tau_k}}\right\|_{\chi(t)} \frac{\exp(\gamma_{N(t)}t)}{\exp(\gamma_{N(t-\tau_k(t))}(t-\tau_k(t)))} \\ &+ p(1-p)\sum_{k=1}^{m}\tau_k(t)\Big[(\|B_{1k}^{(1)}\|_{\chi(t)} - \|B_{2k}^{(1)}\|_{\chi(t)})(\tilde{A}_2^k(t) - \tilde{A}_1^k(t) + \tilde{B}_{2k}(t) - \tilde{B}_{1k}(t)) \\ &+ \frac{1}{\delta}\|pB_{1k}^{(1)} + (1-p)B_{2k}^{(1)}\|_{\chi(t)}\Big(\sup_{t-\tau_k(t)\leq s\leq t}\left\|w \cdot \frac{\partial\phi}{\partial x}\right\|_{\chi(t)} \frac{\exp(\gamma_{N(t)}t)}{\exp(\gamma_{N(s)}s)} + \left\|w \cdot \frac{\partial\phi}{\partial x_{\tau_k}}\right\|_{\chi(t)} \frac{\exp(\gamma_{N(t)}t)}{\exp(\gamma_{N(s-\tau_k(s))}(s-\tau_k(s)))}\Big)\Big] \\ &\leq -\gamma_{N(t)}\end{aligned} \tag{17}$$

holds for $-\frac{\delta}{2} < \phi(x, x_{\tau_1}, \ldots, x_{\tau_m}) < \frac{\delta}{2}$ and $p = \sigma(\phi(x, x_{\tau_1}, \ldots, x_{\tau_m})/\delta) \in [0, 1]$, then the linear switched time-delay system (15) is exponentially incrementally stable.

Proof. With the conclusion in Theorem 4, by constructing a sequence of time-delay systems with continuous right-hand sides satisfying Condition $\mathcal{C}_{time-delay}(\Sigma)$ as follows, we can prove the exponential incremental stability property of system (15):

$$\begin{aligned}\dot{x} = f^\delta =&\sigma\left(\frac{\phi(x, x_{\tau_1}, \ldots, x_{\tau_m})}{\delta}\right)[A_1(t)x(t) + \sum_{k=1}^{m} B_{1k}(t)x(t-\tau_k(t)) + J_1(t)] \\ &+ \left(1 - \sigma\left(\frac{\phi(x, x_{\tau_1}, \ldots, x_{\tau_m})}{\delta}\right)\right)[A_2(t)x(t) + \sum_{k=1}^{m} B_{2k}(t)x(t-\tau_k(t)) + J_2(t)]\end{aligned} \tag{18}$$

in which $\sigma(\cdot)$ is defined as

$$\sigma(\rho) = \begin{cases} 1, & \rho > 1/2, \\ \rho + 1/2, & \rho \in [-1/2, 1/2], \\ 0, & \rho < -1/2. \end{cases}$$

let $w = (A_1(t) - A_2(t))x(t) + \sum_{k=1}^{m}(B_{1k}(t) - B_{2k}(t))x(t - \tau_k(t)) + J_1(t) - J_2(t)$ and $p = \sigma(\phi(x, x_{\tau_1}, \ldots, x_{\tau_m})/\delta)$, the partial derivative of the right-hand function f^δ with respect to x and x_{τ_k} are as follows,

$$\frac{\partial f^\delta(x, x_{\tau_1}, \ldots, x_{\tau_m}, r(t))}{\partial x} = \sigma(\frac{\phi(x, x_{\tau_1}, \ldots, x_{\tau_m})}{\delta})A_1(t) + [1 - \sigma(\frac{\phi(x, x_{\tau_1}, \ldots, x_{\tau_m})}{\delta})]A_2(t) + \frac{1}{\delta}w \cdot \frac{\partial \phi}{\partial x}$$
$$\frac{\partial f^\delta(x, x_{\tau_1}, \ldots, x_{\tau_m}, r(t))}{\partial x_{\tau_k}} = \sigma(\frac{\phi(x, x_{\tau_1}, \ldots, x_{\tau_m})}{\delta})B_{1k}(t) + [1 - \sigma(\frac{\phi(x, x_{\tau_1}, \ldots, x_{\tau_m})}{\delta})]B_{2k}(t) + \frac{1}{\delta}w \cdot \frac{\partial \phi}{\partial x_{\tau_k}}$$

Thus, it needs to satisfy

$$\begin{aligned} L(f^\delta, t) = & \nu_{\chi(t)}\left(pA_1 + (1-p)A_2 + \frac{1}{\delta}w \cdot \frac{\partial \phi}{\partial x} + \sum_{k=1}^{m}[pB_{1k}^{(1)} + (1-p)B_{2k}^{(1)}]\right) \\ & + \sum_{k=1}^{m} \tau_k(t)(\tilde{U}_k(t) + \tilde{V}_k(t))\left\|pB_{1k}^{(1)} + (1-p)B_{2k}^{(1)}\right\|_{\chi(t)} \\ & + \sum_{k=1}^{m}\left\|pB_{1k}^{(2)} + (1-p)B_{2k}^{(2)} + \frac{1}{\delta}w \cdot \frac{\partial \phi}{\partial x_{\tau_k}}\right\|_{\chi(t)} \frac{\exp(\gamma_{N(t)}t)}{\exp(\gamma_{N(t-\tau_k(t))}(t - \tau_k(t)))} \le -\gamma_{N(t)} \end{aligned}$$

in which

$$\tilde{U}_k(t) = \sup_{t-\tau_k(t) \le s \le t} \|\frac{\partial f^\delta}{\partial x}(x(s), x_{\tau_1}(s), \ldots, x_{\tau_m}(s), s)\|_{\chi(t_j)} \exp(\gamma_{N(t)}t - \gamma_{N(s)}s)$$
$$\tilde{V}_k(t) = \sup_{t-\tau_k(t) \le s \le t} \|\frac{\partial f^\delta}{\partial x_\tau}(x(s), x_{\tau_1}(s), \ldots, x_{\tau_m}(s), s)\|_{\chi(t_j)} \exp(\gamma_{N(t)}t - \gamma_{N(s-\tau_k(s))}(s - \tau_k(s)))$$

where $t \in [t_j, t_{j+1})$. That is,

$$\begin{aligned} & \le pL_1(t) + [1-p]L_2(t) + \frac{1}{\delta}\nu_{\chi(t)}\left(w \cdot \frac{\partial \phi}{\partial x}\right) + \frac{1}{\delta}\sum_{k=1}^{m}\left\|w \cdot \frac{\partial \phi}{\partial x_{\tau_k}}\right\|_{\chi(t)} \frac{\exp(\gamma_{N(t)}t)}{\exp(\gamma_{N(t-\tau_k(t))}(t - \tau_k(t)))} \\ & + p(1-p)\sum_{k=1}^{m}\tau_k(t)\Big[(\|B_{1k}^{(1)}\|_{\chi(t)} - \|B_{2k}^{(1)}\|_{\chi(t)})(\tilde{A}_2^k(t) - \tilde{A}_1^k(t) + \tilde{B}_{2k}(t) - \tilde{B}_{1k}(t)) \\ & + \frac{1}{\delta}\|pB_{1k}^{(1)} + (1-p)B_{2k}^{(1)}\|_{\chi(t)}\left(\sup_{t-\tau_k(t) \le s \le t}\left\|w \cdot \frac{\partial \phi}{\partial x}\right\|_{\chi(t)} \frac{\exp(\gamma_{N(t)}t)}{\exp(\gamma_{N(s)}s)} + \left\|w \cdot \frac{\partial \phi}{\partial x_{\tau_k}}\right\|_{\chi(t)} \frac{\exp(\gamma_{N(t)}t)}{\exp(\gamma_{N(s-\tau_k(s))}(s - \tau_k(s)))}\right)\Big] \end{aligned}$$

Together with (17), it infers that $L(f^\delta, t) \le -\gamma_{N(t)}$, that is, system (18) is exponentially incrementally stable for each $\delta = \frac{1}{m}, m \in \mathbb{N}^+$. From Theorem 4, it can be proved that the time-delay system is exponentially incrementally stable. □

Here, let $B_{1k}^{(1)} = B_{2k}^{(1)} = 0, (k = 1, \ldots, m)$, we have the following corollary, which is a variant of Corollary 3.

Corollary 4. *Let $N(t) = \#\{j : t \ge t_j, j = 1, 2, \ldots\}$, and suppose that system (15) satisfies Assumption 4, and there exist*

1. *A constant $T_0 > 0$,*
2. *Positive constants $\gamma_k (k = 0, 1, \ldots)$, $\gamma_0 \le \gamma_1 \le \ldots$,*
3. *$C(\chi(t), \chi(t')) \le C_0$ for any $t, t' \ge t_0$,*

such that the following conditions are satisfied:

$$L_1(t) = \nu_{\chi(t)}(A_1(t)) + \sum_{k=1}^{m} \|B_{1k}(t)\|_{\chi(t)} \frac{\exp(\gamma_{N(t)}t)}{\exp(\gamma_{N(t-\tau_k(t))}(t-\tau_k(t)))} \leq -\gamma_{N(t)}$$
$$L_2(t) = \nu_{\chi(t)}(A_2(t)) + \sum_{k=1}^{m} \|B_{2k}(t)\|_{\chi(t)} \frac{\exp(\gamma_{N(t)}t)}{\exp(\gamma_{N(t-\tau_k(t))}(t-\tau_k(t)))} \leq -\gamma_{N(t)}$$

and for all $t > T_0$,

$$\frac{1}{t}\left[\sum_{i=0}^{N(t)-1}[(\gamma_{i+1}-\gamma_i)t_{i+1} + \log\beta_{i+1}] + \gamma_0 t_0 - \gamma_{N(t)}t\right] \leq -c,$$

where $\beta_k = C(\chi(t_k), \chi(t_k-))$. Moreover, in the neighborhood of switching surface S, that is, when $-\delta/2 < \phi(x, x_{\tau_1}, \ldots, x_{\tau_m}) < \delta/2$, let $w = (A_1(t) - A_2(t))x(t) + \sum_{k=1}^{m}(B_{1k}(t) - B_{2k}(t))x(t-\tau_k(t)) + J_1(t) - J_2(t)$, if it is satisfied that

$$pL_1(t) + (1-p)L_2(t) + \frac{1}{\delta}\nu_{\chi(t)}\left(w \cdot \frac{\partial\phi}{\partial x}\right) + \frac{1}{\delta}\sum_{k=1}^{m}\left\|w \cdot \frac{\partial\phi}{\partial x_{\tau_k}}\right\|_{\chi(t)} \frac{\exp(\gamma_{N(t)}t)}{\exp(\gamma_{N(t-\tau_k(t))}(t-\tau_k(t)))} \leq -\gamma_{N(t)}$$

holds for $-\delta/2 < \phi(x, x_{\tau_1}, \ldots, x_{\tau_m}) < \delta/2$ and $p = \phi(x, x_{\tau_1}, \ldots, x_{\tau_m})/\delta \in [0,1]$, then the linear switched time-delay system (15) is exponentially incrementally stable.

5.2. Hopfield Neural Network Systems with Time Delay

Consider the following Hopfield neural network system with time delay:

$$\dot{x}(t) = -D(t)x(t) + T(t)g(x(t)) + S(t)u(x_\tau(t))) + J(t) \tag{19}$$

where $x = (x_1, x_2, \ldots, x_n)^\top$ is the state variable, the time-delay term $x_\tau(t) = x(t-\tau(t))$. For any $t \in \mathbb{R}^+$, $D(t) = diag\{d_1(t), \ldots, d_n(t)\}$, $T(t) = (T_{ij}(t)) \in \mathbb{R}^{n,n}$, $S(t) = (S_{ij}(t)) \in \mathbb{R}^{n,n}$, $J = (J_1, J_2, \ldots, J_n) \in \mathbb{R}^n$ is the input vector, $g(x) = (g_1(x_1), g_2(x_2), \ldots, g_n(x_n))^\top$, $u(x) = (u_1(x_1), u_2(x_2), \ldots, u_n(x_n))^\top$.

Here, we list the following hypothesis, denoted by Condition $\mathcal{C}_2$:

1. There exists $\tilde{D} = diag\{D_1, D_2, \ldots, D_n\}$, $D_i > 0$, such that $d_i(\cdot)$ is continuous and $\frac{d_i(\zeta_1)-d_i(\zeta_2)}{\zeta_1-\zeta_2} \geq D_i$ holds for $i = 1, 2, \ldots, n$ and $\zeta_1 \neq \zeta_2$.
2. $g_i(\cdot)$ is non-decreasing and non-trivial in any compact set in $\mathbb{R}$, and each $g_i(\cdot)$ has only finite discontinuous points. Therefore, in any compact set in $\mathbb{R}$, except a finite points ρ_k, where there exist finite right and left limits $g_i(\rho_k^+)$ and $g_i(\rho_k^-)$ with $g_i(\rho_k^+) > g_i(\rho_k^-)$, $g_i(\cdot)$ is continuous.
3. $u_i(\cdot)$ is non-decreasing and non-trivial in any compact set in $\mathbb{R}$, and each $u_i(\cdot)$ has only finite discontinuous points. Therefore, in any compact set in $\mathbb{R}$, except a finite points η_k, where there exist finite right and left limits $u_i(\eta_k^+)$ and $u_i(\eta_k^-)$ with $u_i(\eta_k^+) > u_i(\eta_k^-)$, $u_i(\cdot)$ is continuous.
4. Here, define a matrix measure $\nu_{\xi,1}(A) = \max_j[a_{jj} + \sum_{i\neq j}|\xi_i\xi_j^{-1}a_{ij}|]$ for matrix $A = (a_{ij})$, with respect to vector norm $|\cdot|_{\xi,1}$ and matrix norm $\|A\|_{\xi,1} = \|\xi A\xi^{-1}\|_1$, where $\xi = diag\{\xi_1, \ldots, \xi_n\}$. There exists a positive diagonal matrix $\xi(r(t)) = diag\{\xi_1(r(t)), \ldots, \xi_n(r(t))\}$ such that

$$\nu_{\xi(r(t)),1}(T) = \max_j\{T_{jj}(t) + \sum_{i\neq j}|\xi_i(r(t))\xi_j(r(t))^{-1}T_{ij}(t)|\} \leq 0$$

holds for $t \in \mathbb{R}^+$.

Therefore, we have the following corollary:

Corollary 5. *Suppose the system (19) has a unique solution for $t \in \mathbb{R}^+$, and satisfies Condition $\mathcal{C}_2$ above. Let $N(t) = \#\{j : t \geq t_j, j = 1, 2, \ldots\}$, and there exists*

1. *Positive piecewise right-continuous function* $m(t) > 0$*,*
2. *A constant* $T_0 > 0$*,*
3. *Positive constants* $\alpha_k > 0 (k = 0, 1, \ldots)$*,*
4. $C(r(t), r(t')) \leq C_0$ *for any* $t, t' \geq t_0$*,*

such that in the continuous regions of g and u,

$$\nu_{\xi(r(t)),1}\Big(-D(t) + T(t)\frac{\partial g}{\partial x}(x, x_\tau)\Big) + \frac{\exp(\gamma_{N(t)} t)}{\exp(\gamma_{N(t-\tau(t))}(t - \tau(t)))}\|S(t)\frac{\partial u}{\partial x_\tau}(x, x_\tau)\|_{\xi(r(t)),1} \leq -\gamma_{N(t)} \tag{20}$$

Let $K_i = \min_k[g_i(\rho_k+) - g_i(\rho_k-)]$*,* $M_i = \max_k[u_i(\gamma_k+) - u_i(\gamma_k-)]$*, and* $K = \min_i K_i$*,* $M = \max_i M_i$*,*

$$K \cdot \nu_{\xi(r(t)),1}(T(t)) + M \cdot \frac{\exp(\gamma_{N(t)} t)}{\exp(\gamma_{N(t-\tau(t))}(t - \tau(t)))}\|S(t)\|_{\xi(r(t)),1} < 0 \tag{21}$$

For any $t > T_0$*,*

$$\frac{1}{t}\left[\sum_{i=0}^{N(t)-1}[(\gamma_{i+1} - \gamma_i)t_{i+1} + \log \beta_{i+1}] + \gamma_0 t_0 - \gamma_{N(t)} t\right] \leq -c,$$

where $\beta_k = C(r(t_k), r(t_k-))$*, then system* (19) *is exponentially incrementally stable.*

Proof. Suppose that system (19) has a unique solution for $t \in \mathbb{R}^+$, then we construct a sequence of 'continuous systems' as follows,

$$\dot{x}(t) = f^\delta(x, x_\tau, t) = -D(t)x(t) + T(t)\tilde{g}(x(t)) + S(t)\tilde{u}(x_\tau(t)))$$

where $\tilde{g}(x) = (\tilde{g}_1(x_1), \tilde{g}_2(x_2), \ldots, \tilde{g}_n(x_n))^\top$, $\tilde{u}(x) = (\tilde{u}_1(x_1), \tilde{u}_2(x_2), \ldots, \tilde{u}_n(x_n))^\top$. For each i, denote one of the discontinuous points of $g_i(x)$ by ρ_i, and one of the discontinuous point of $u_i(x)$ by η_i.

Function $\tilde{g}^\delta(x)$ is formulated as follows, if $x_i \notin [\rho_i - \frac{\delta}{2}, \rho_i + \frac{\delta}{2}]$, $\tilde{g}_i^\delta(x_i) = g_i(x_i)$, and if $x_i \in [\rho_i - \frac{\delta}{2}, \rho_i + \frac{\delta}{2}]$,

$$\tilde{g}_i^\delta(x_i) = \frac{g_i(\rho_i + \frac{\delta}{2}) - g_i(\rho_i - \frac{\delta}{2})}{\delta}[x_i - \rho_i + \frac{\delta}{2}] + g_i(\rho_i - \frac{\delta}{2}).$$

Function $\tilde{u}(x)$ is similarly constructed. It can be seen that when $\delta \to 0$, the function sequence $f^\delta(x, x_\tau, t)$ converges to the Filippov differential inclusion of the right-hand side of (19), that is, $\{f^\delta(x, x_\tau, t)\}$ satisfies Condition $C_{time-delay}(\mathbb{R}^{n\times 2})$. Let $\bar{g}_i(\rho_i, \delta) = \frac{g_i(\rho_i + \frac{\delta}{2}) - g_i(\rho_i - \frac{\delta}{2})}{\delta}$, $\bar{u}_i(\eta_i, \delta) = \frac{u_i(\eta_i + \frac{\delta}{2}) - u_i(\eta_i - \frac{\delta}{2})}{\delta}$. Here, denote the Jacobi matrix of functions $\tilde{g}^\delta(\cdot)$ and $\tilde{u}^\delta(\cdot)$ by matrix G^δ and U^δ. In the neighborhood of the discontinuous point,

$$G^\delta = \frac{\partial \tilde{g}(x)}{\partial x}|_{x=(\rho_1, \rho_2, \ldots, \rho_n)} = diag\{\bar{g}_1(\rho_1, \delta), \bar{g}_2(\rho_2, \delta), \ldots, \bar{g}_n(\rho_n, \delta)\}$$
$$U^\delta = \frac{\partial \tilde{u}(x_\tau)}{\partial x_\tau}|_{x_\tau=(\eta_1, \eta_2, \ldots, \eta_n)} = diag\{\bar{u}_1(\eta_1, \delta), \bar{u}_2(\eta_2, \delta), \ldots, \bar{u}_n(\eta_n, \delta)\}$$

that is, we have

$$\frac{\partial f^\delta(x, x_\tau, t)}{\partial x} = -D(t) + T(t)G^\delta,$$
$$\frac{\partial f^\delta(x, x_\tau, t)}{\partial x_\tau} = S(t)U^\delta,$$

In the continuous regions, the function sequence $\{f^\delta(x, x_\tau, t)\}$ satisfies (20), and $v_{\xi(r(t)),1}(T(t)) < 0$. Meanwhile, in the neighborhood of the discontinuities, together with the condition (21), it holds that,

$$\begin{aligned}
&v_{\xi(r(t)),1}(-D(t) + T(t)G^\delta) + \frac{\exp\left(\gamma_{N(t)}t\right)}{\exp\left(\gamma_{N(t-\tau(t))}(t-\tau(t))\right)}\|S(t)U^\delta\|_{\xi(r(t)),1} \\
\leq & v_{\xi(r(t)),1}(-D(t)) + v_{\xi(r(t)),1}(T(t)G^\delta) + \frac{\exp\left(\gamma_{N(t)}t\right)}{\exp\left(\gamma_{N(t-\tau(t))}(t-\tau(t))\right)}\|S(t)U^\delta\|_{\xi(r(t)),1} \\
\leq & v_{\xi(r(t)),1}(-D(t)) + \min_i \bar{g}_i(\rho_i, \delta) v_{\xi(r(t)),1}(T(t)) \\
& + \max_i \bar{u}_i(\eta_i, \delta) \frac{\exp\left(\gamma_{N(t)}t\right)}{\exp\left(\gamma_{N(t-\tau(t))}(t-\tau(t))\right)}\|S(t)\|_{\xi(r(t)),1} \\
\leq & -\gamma_{N(t)}
\end{aligned}$$

for $\delta \to 0$. Therefore, if there exists a large enough number $m_0 > 0$, such that for each $m > m_0$, $m \in \mathbb{N}^+$,

$$v_{\xi(r(t)),1}(-D(t) + T(t)G^\delta) + \frac{\exp\left(\gamma_{N(t)}t\right)}{\exp\left(\gamma_{N(t-\tau(t))}(t-\tau(t))\right)}\|S(t)U^\delta\|_{\xi(r(t)),1} \leq -\gamma_{N(t)}$$

holds for $\delta = 1/m$. According to Theorems 1 and 4, the time-delay system (19) is exponentially incrementally stable. □

6. Numerical Experiments

6.1. Linear Time-Delay System

Consider a linear switched time-delay system formulated as follows:

$$\dot{x}(t) = \begin{cases} A_1x(t) + B_1x(t-\tau(t)) + J_1, & z^\top x > 0 \\ A_2x(t) + B_2x(t-\tau(t)) + J_2, & z^\top x < 0 \end{cases} \tag{22}$$

where $x, x_\tau \in \mathbb{R}^2$. The switching surface of system (22) is $\{x : \phi(x) = z^\top x = 0\}$ where $z = [1,3]^\top$.

Let $\tau(t) = 1$ and

$$A_1 = \begin{bmatrix} -6 & 1 \\ 0 & -7 \end{bmatrix}, A_2 = \begin{bmatrix} -7 & -2 \\ -1 & -10 \end{bmatrix}, B_1 = B_2 = \begin{bmatrix} -1 & 0 \\ 0 & 1 \end{bmatrix}, J_1 = \begin{bmatrix} -1 \\ -2 \end{bmatrix}, J_2 = \begin{bmatrix} 0 \\ 1 \end{bmatrix}.$$

Here, we first prove that system (22) has a unique solution for $t \in [1, +\infty)$. On the switching surface $\{x : \phi(x) = z^\top x = 0\}$, we have

$$\frac{d\phi}{dx}(x) \cdot \left((A_1 - A_2)x + J_1 - J_2\right) = [1,3]^\top \left(\begin{bmatrix} 1 & 3 \\ 1 & 3 \end{bmatrix} x(t) + \begin{bmatrix} -1 \\ -3 \end{bmatrix}\right) = -4,$$

According to Assumption 4, the uniqueness of the Filippov solution for (22) occurs for $t \in [0, +\infty)$. Let $\gamma_{N(t)} = 1 - 1/2^{[t]}$ and the number $[t]$ represents the floor of time t. So, for $t > 1$,

$$\begin{aligned}
L_1(t) = & \ v_2(A_1) + \|B_1\|_2 \frac{e^{\gamma_{N(t)}t}}{e^{\gamma_{N(t)-1}(t-1)}} = -5.75 + \frac{e^{(1-1/2^{[t]})t}}{e^{(1-1/2^{[t-1]})(t-1)}} < -3.5 < -1 + \frac{1}{2^{[t]}} \\
L_2(t) = & \ v_2(A_2) + \|B_2\|_2 \frac{e^{\gamma_{N(t)}t}}{e^{\gamma_{N(t)-1}(t-1)}} = -6.35 + \frac{e^{(1-1/2^{[t]})t}}{e^{(1-1/2^{[t-1]})(t-1)}} < -4 < -1 + \frac{1}{2^{[t]}}
\end{aligned}$$

where $\|\cdot\|_2$ stands for 2-norm. Then, for $-\delta/2 < \phi(x) < \delta/2$ and $p = \phi(x)/\delta + 1/2 \in [0,1]$,

$$pL_1(t) + (1-p)L_2(t) + \frac{1}{\delta}\nu_2\left(\left(\begin{bmatrix} 1 & 3 \\ 1 & 3 \end{bmatrix}x(t) + \begin{bmatrix} -1 \\ -3 \end{bmatrix}\right)\cdot[1,3]\right) < -1.5 < -\gamma_{N(t)},$$

and for all $t > T_0$,

$$\frac{1}{t}\left[\sum_{i=0}^{N(t)-1}[(\gamma_{i+1}-\gamma_i)t_{i+1} + \log\beta_{i+1}] + \gamma_0 t_0 - \gamma_{N(t)}t\right] \le \frac{1}{t}\left[\sum_{i=0}^{N(t)-1}[\frac{1}{2^{i+1}}(i+1)] - (1-\frac{1}{2^{[t]}})t\right] \le -0.5$$

Thus, from Corollary 4, the switched time-delay system (22) is exponentially incrementally asymptotically stable.With the initial state $x_0(s) = [5\times(0.5+s)^2, 6\times(1-s)-1.5]$ and $y_0(s) = [-3\times(1+s)^3-2, -3\times(1-s)]$ for $s\in[0,1]$, the corresponding solution of system (22) are $x(t) = (x_1(t), x_2(t))$ and $y(t) = (y_1(t), y_2(t))$, respectively.

Figure 1 shows the dynamical trajectories of two of the solutions with the initial function defined as $x_0(\cdot)$ and $y_0(\cdot)$ for system (22). Moreover, Figure 2 shows the errors between the two dynamical trajectories of their segments.

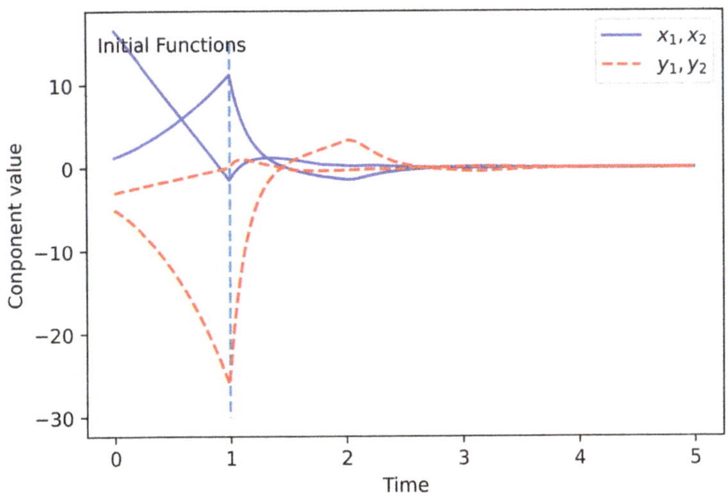

Figure 1. Dynamical trajectories of the solutions for time-delay system (22).

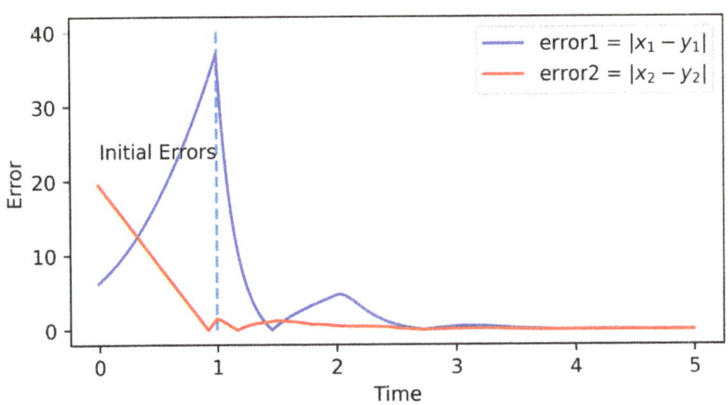

Figure 2. A diagram for exponential incremental uniform stability (the error of each segment) of time-delay system (22).

6.2. Hopfield Neural Network with Time Delay

Here, we take an example of the Hopfield system with time delay for illustration. The system is formulated as follows,

$$\dot{x}(t) = D(t)x(t) + T(t)g(x(t)) + \sigma(t)S(t)u(x_\tau(t))) + J(t) \tag{23}$$

where $x = [x_1, x_2]^\top$ is the state vector, $\sigma(t)$ is the switched function with respect to time t, takes value between 0 and 1. The parameter matrix are

$$\sigma(t) = \begin{cases} 0 & t \in [kT_0, kT_0 + \frac{1}{2}T_0) \\ 1 & t \in [kT_0 + \frac{1}{2}T_0, (k+1)T_0) \end{cases}, \quad \tau(t) = \begin{cases} t & t \leq 0.2 \\ 0.1 \times |\sin(\pi t/0.4)| + 0.1 & t > 0.2 \end{cases}$$

$$D(t) = \begin{bmatrix} -0.3 + 0.1 \times \sin(t) & 0 \\ 0 & -0.3 + 0.1 \times \cos(t) \end{bmatrix}, \quad J(t) = \begin{bmatrix} 10\sin(2t) \\ -10\sin(2t) \end{bmatrix},$$

$$T(t) = \begin{bmatrix} -5 - \sin(t) & 2.5 + \cos(t) \\ 2.5 - \cos(t) & -5 - \sin(t) \end{bmatrix}, S(t) = \begin{bmatrix} 0.1 \times \sin(t) & 0.1 + 0.1 \times \cos(t) \\ 0.1 - 0.1 \times \cos(t) & 0.1 \times \sin(t) \end{bmatrix}$$

$$g_i(x) = \begin{cases} x + 2.5 & x > 0 \\ x - 2.5 & x < 0 \end{cases}, \quad u_i(x) = \begin{cases} x + 1 & x > 0 \\ x - 1 & x < 0 \end{cases}, \quad i = 1, \ldots, n$$

where $k \in \mathbb{N}_{\geq 0}$, $T_0 = 1$. According to the uniqueness conditions for the Filippov solution of the time-delay system, Lemma 2 and Theorem 3, it can be seen that (23) has a unique solution in compact set $\Sigma \in \mathbb{R}^2$.

Here, define the norm with subscript $\sigma(t)$ as $|x|_0 = 0.8|x_1| + |x_2|$, $|x|_1 = |x_1| + |x_2|$, $\beta_{01} = 1.25$, $\beta_{10} = 1$, then $\nu_0(T) < -0.5$, $\nu_1(T) = -2.5 + \sqrt{2} < -1$, $\|S\|_1 < 0.3$, $\|S\|_0 < 0.25$, therefore, let $N(t) = j, t \in [t_{j-1}, t_j)$, $\gamma_j = \max\{1/4, (1/2) - (1/2)^j\}$, $t_j = (T_0/2) \cdot j$, $j = 1, 2, \ldots$, such that in the continuous region of the right-hand side of system (23), it holds that

$$\alpha_{N(t)} + \nu_0(-D(t) + T(t)) < 0$$

$$\alpha_{N(t)} + \nu_1(-D(t) + T(t)) + \frac{\exp\left(\gamma_{N(t)} t\right)}{\exp\left(\gamma_{N(t-\tau(t))}(t - \tau(t))\right)} \|S(t)\|_1 < 0.5 - 1 + 0.25 < 0$$

As for condition (21), after calculation, we have $K = 5$, $M = 2$; thus, condition (21) holds for $\sigma(t) = 0, 1$. Moreover, for $t > 10$, we have

$$\sum_{i=0}^{N(t)-1} [(\gamma_{i+1} - \gamma_i)t_{i+1} + \log \beta_{i+1}] + \gamma_0 t_0 - \gamma_{N(t)} t \leq 1.75 + \log(1.25)t - 0.49t < -0.25t$$

Together with Corollary 5, the switched time-delay system (23) is exponentially incrementally asymptotically stable. With the initial state $x_0(s) = [5 \times (0.5 + s)^2, 6 \times (1 - s) - 1.5]$ and $y_0(s) = [-2 * (1 + s)^2 - 2, -3 \times (1 - s)]$ for $s \in [0, 0.5]$, the corresponding solution of system (23) are $x(t) = (x_1(t), x_2(t))$ and $y(t) = (y_1(t), y_2(t))$, respectively. When $t > 0.5$, $\sigma(t) = 1$ and time lag occurs.

Figure 3 shows the dynamical trajectories of two of the solutions with the initial function defined as $x_0(\cdot)$ and $y_0(\cdot)$ for system (23). Moreover, Figure 4 shows the errors between the two dynamical trajectories of their segments.

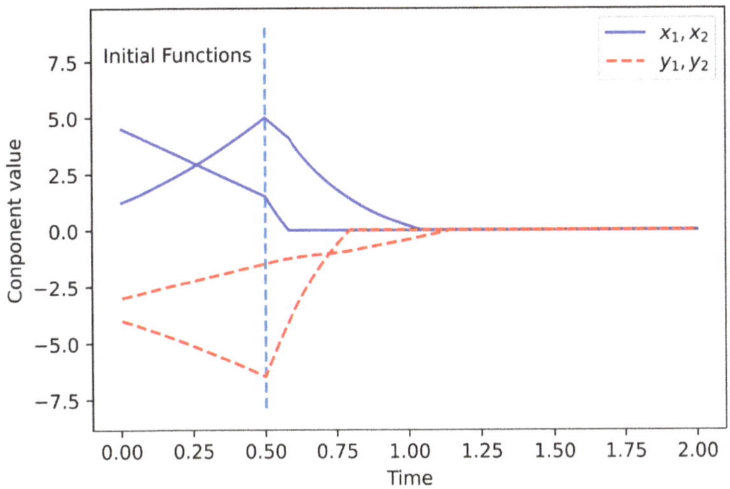

Figure 3. Dynamical trajectories of the solutions for time-delay system (23).

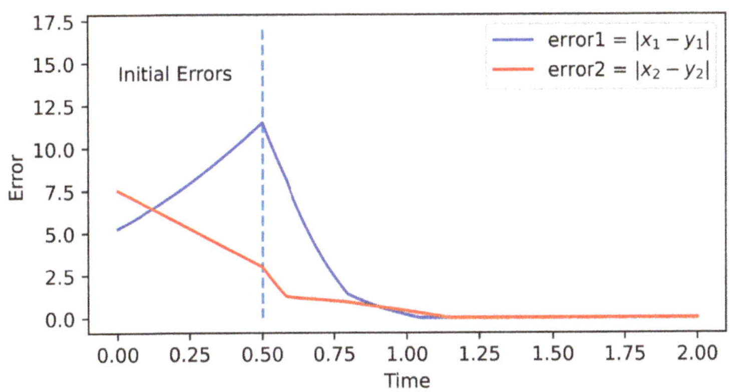

Figure 4. A diagram for exponential incremental uniform stability (the error of each segment) for system (23).

7. Conclusions

This paper researches the criteria for incremental stability for time-delay dynamical systems, including systems with continuous right-hand sides and systems with discontinuous right-hand sides, respectively. In this paper, the corresponding sufficient conditions for the exponential incremental stability of solutions for time-delay dynamical systems with continuous right-hand sides are proposed and proved. Before studying sufficient conditions for incremental stability of the systems with discontinuous right-hand sides, we first provide the conditions for the existence and uniqueness of the Filippov solution. Then, by constructing a sequence of systems with continuous right-hand sides and using the approximation method, sufficient conditions for exponential incremental stability of the systems with discontinuous right-hand sides are obtained.

There still needs to be much further work. Our theorem can be helpful for applications in other more complex scenarios and we may propose more corollaries for some more complex systems in the future. Furthermore, we may seek some other approaches to construct "continuous systems" to approximate discontinuous systems.

Author Contributions: Conceptualization, W.L.; methodology, Y.L. and W.L.; software, Y.L.; validation, Y.L. and W.L.; formal analysis, Y.L.; investigation, Y.L.; resources, W.L.; data curation, W.L.; writing—original draft preparation, Y.L.; writing—review and editing, W.L.; visualization, Y.L.; supervision, W.L.; project administration, W.L.; funding acquisition, W.L. All authors have read and agreed to the published version of the manuscript.

Funding: This work is jointly supported by the National Natural Sciences Foundation of China under Grant (No. 62072111), Shanghai Municipal Science and Technology Major Project under Grant 2018SHZDZX01. This work is conducted in joint accordance with the ZJLab and the Science and Technology Commission of Shanghai Municipality (No. 19JC1420101).

Institutional Review Board Statement: This work is conducted in joint accordance with the ZJLab and the Science and Technology Commission of Shanghai Municipality (No. 19JC1420101).

Informed Consent Statement: Not applicable.

Data Availability Statement: No new data were created.

Acknowledgments: We here thank Hao Qiang for his assistance with some preliminary research.

Conflicts of Interest: The authors declare no conflict of interest.

Notations

$\lvert \cdot \rvert_{\chi(t)}$	Vector norm with subscript $\chi(t)$
$\lVert \cdot \rVert_{\chi(t)}$	Matrix norm induced by $\lvert \cdot \rvert_{\chi(t)}$
$\nu_{\chi(t)}$	Matrix measure induced by $\lvert \cdot \rvert_{\chi(t)}$
$\chi(t)$	A right-continuous staircase function with respect to t, with switching points belonging to $\{t_j\}$
$r(t)$	A piecewise right-continuous function with respect to t, with switching points $\{t_j\}$
t_0	The initial time
$\overline{\tau}$	The upper bound of τ_k: $\max_k sup_{t\in[t_0,\infty)}\tau_k(t) = \overline{\tau}$
$\underline{\tau}$	The lower bound of τ_k: $\min_k inf_{t\in[t_0,\infty)}\tau_k(t) = \underline{\tau}$
$N(t)$	$N(t) = \#\{j : t \geq t_j, j = 1,2,\ldots\}$

References

1. Pavlov, A.; Pogromsky, A.; Wouw, N.V.D.; Nijmeijer, H. Convergent dynamics, a tribute to Boris Pavlovich Demidovich. *Syst. Control Lett.* **2004**, *52*, 257–261. [CrossRef]
2. Rüffer, B.S. Convergent systems vs. incremental stability. *Syst. Control Lett.* **2013**, *62*, 277–285. [CrossRef]
3. Fromion, V.; Scorletti, G.; Ferreres, G. Nonlinear performance of a PI controlled missile: An explanation. *Int. J. Robust Nonlinear Control. IFAC-Affil. J.* **1999**, *9*, 485–518. [CrossRef]
4. Hamadeh, A.; Stan, G.B.; Sepulchre, R.; Goncalves, J. Global State Synchronization in Networks of Cyclic Feedback Systems. *IEEE Trans. Autom. Control* **2012**, *57*, 478–483. [CrossRef]
5. Russo, G.; Di Bernardo, M. Correction to Section V-B of "Contraction Theory and the Master Stability Function: Linking Two Approaches to Study Synchronization in Complex Networks" [Feb 09 177-181]. *Circuits Syst. Express Briefs IEEE Trans.* **2014**, *61*, 915. [CrossRef]
6. Kim, H.; Persis, C.D. Output synchronization of Lur'e-type nonlinear systems in the presence of input disturbances. *IEEE Conf. Decis. Control* **2015**, 4145–4150.
7. Promion, V. Some results on the behavior of Lipschitz continuous systems. In Proceedings of the 1997 European Control Conference (ECC), Brussels, Belgium, 1–7 July 1997; pp. 2011–2016.
8. Lohmiller, W.; Slotine, J.J.E. On contraction analysis for non-linear systems. *Automatica* **1998**, *34*, 683–696. [CrossRef]
9. Andronov, A.A.; Vitt, A.A.; Khaikin, S.E. *Vibration Theory*; Fizmatgiz: Moscow, Russia, 1959. (In Russian)
10. Barbashin, E.A. *Introduction to Stability Theory*; Nauka: Moscow, Russia, 1967. (In Russian)
11. Neimark, Y.I. *Points Mapping Method in the Theory of Nonlinear Vibrations*; Nauka: Moscow, Russia, 1972. (In Russian)
12. Bautin, N.N.; Leontovich, E.A. *Methods and Techniques of Qualitative Study of Dynamic Systems in a Plane*; Nauka: Moscow, Russia, 1976. (In Russian)
13. Gelig, A.K.; Leonov, G.A.; Yakubovich, V.A. *Stability of Nonlinear Systems with Nonunique Equilibrium State*; Nauka: Moscow, Russia, 1978. (In Russian)
14. Filippov, A. Differential equations with discontinuous right-hand side. *Am. Math. Soc. Transl.* **1964**, *42*, 199–231.
15. Filippov, A.F. *Differential Equations with Discontinuous Right-Hand Sides*; Kluwer Academic: Boston, MA, USA, 1988.
16. Volterra, V. Sur la théorie mathématique des phénom enes héréditaires. *J. Math. Pures Appl.* **1928**, *7*, 249–298.

17. Volterra, V. *Theorie Mathematique de la Lutte Pour la vie*; Gauthier-Villars: Paris, France, 1931.
18. Hale, J.K.; Lunel, S.V. *Introduction to Functional Differential Equations(Applied Mathematical Sciences, 99)*; Springer: Berlin, Germany, 1993.
19. Cooke, K.L. Differential—Difference equations. In *International Symposium on Nonlinear Differential Equations and Nonlinear Mechanics*; Academic Press: Cambridge, MA, USA, 1963; pp. 155–171.
20. Nihtilä, M.T. Analysis and synthesis of time delay systems: H. Gorechi, S. Fuksa, P. Grabowski and A. Korytowski. *Automatica* **1991**, *27*, 1065–1067. [CrossRef]
21. Kaminogo, T. Kneser's property and boundary value problems for some retarded functional differential equations. *Tohoku Math. J.* **1978**, *30*, 471–486. [CrossRef]
22. Kaminogo, T. Topological properties of solution mappings in functional differential equations. *Nonlinear Anal. Theory Methods Appl.* **1997**, *30*, 871–876. [CrossRef]
23. Tunç, C. Qualitative properties in nonlinear Volterra integro-differential equations with delay. *J. Taibah Univ. Sci.* **2017**, *11*, 309–314. [CrossRef]
24. Deimling, K. *Multivalued Differential Equations*; De Gruyter: Berlin, Germany; New York, NY, USA, 1992.
25. Haddad, T.; Haddad, T. Delay perturbed state-dependent sweeping process. *Appl. Anal.* **2016**, *95*, 270–282. [CrossRef]
26. Marques, M.D.P.M.; Dzonou, R. Dynamics of a particle with friction and delay. *Comptes Rendus Mec.* **2017**, *346*, 237–246. [CrossRef]
27. Pust, L.; Pešek, L. Influence of delayed excitation on vibrations of turbine blades couple. *Appl. Comput. Mech.* **2013**, *7*, 39–52.
28. Smirnov, G.V. *Introduction to the Theory of Differential Inclusions*; University of Porto: Porto, Portugal, 2002.
29. Ali, M.; Hou, Z.; Noori, M. Stability and performance of feedback control systems with time delays. *Comput. Struct.* **1998**, *66*, 241–248. [CrossRef]
30. Callender, A.B.; Hartree, D.R.; Porter, A.R. Time-Lag in a Control System. *Philos. Trans. R. Soc. A* **1936**, *235*, 415–444.
31. Haddad, G. Topological properties of the sets of solutions for functional differential inclusions. *Nonlinear Anal. Theory Methods Appl.* **1981**, *5*, 1349–1366. [CrossRef]
32. Bacciotti, A.; Ceragioli, F. Optimal Regulation and Discontinuous Stabilization. *IFAC Proc. Vol.* **2001**, *34*, 39–44. [CrossRef]
33. Lu, W.; Chen, T. Almost periodic dynamics of a class of delayed neural networks with discontinuous activations. *Neural Comput.* **2008**, *20*, 1065–1090. [CrossRef] [PubMed]
34. Liu, X.; Cao, J. Synchronization control of discontinuous neural networks via approximation. In Proceedings of the 2010 Chinese Control and Decision Conference, Xuzhou, China, 26–28 May 2010; pp. 782–787.
35. Fiore, D.; Hogan, S.J.; di Bernardo, M. Contraction analysis of switched systems via regularization. *Automatica* **2016**, *73*, 279–288. [CrossRef]
36. Lu, W.; Bernardo, M. Contraction and incremental stability of switched Carathéodory systems using multiple norms. *Automatica* **2016**, *70*, 1–8. [CrossRef]
37. Aubin, J.P.; Bayen, A.M.; Saint-Pierre, P. *Viability Theory*; Springer: Berlin/Heidelberg, Germany, 2009.
38. Qiang, H.; Lu, W. *The Coupling Mechanism and Dynamic Behavior of Complex Network Systems*; Fudan University: Shanghai, China, 2021.
39. Ortiz-Robinson, N.; Rios, V. Qualitative Properties of the Solution Set for Time-Delayed Discontinuous Dynamics. *Set-Valued Var. Anal.* **2020**, *28*, 327–344. [CrossRef]
40. Liu, B.; Lu, W.; Chen, T. New conditions on synchronization of networks of linearly coupled dynamical systems with non-Lipschitz right-hand sides. *Neural Netw.* **2012**, *25*, 5–13. [CrossRef]
41. Ortiz-Robinson, N.; Rios, V. Forward Euler Solutions and Weakly Invariant Time-Delayed Systems. *Abstr. Appl. Anal.* **2012**, *3*, 327–344. [CrossRef]
42. Forti, M.; Nistri, P.; Papini, D. Global exponential stability and global convergence in finite time of delayed neural networks with infinite gain. *IEEE Trans. Neural Netw.* **2005**, *16*, 1449–1463. [CrossRef]
43. Haddad, G. Monotone viable trajectories for functional differential inclusions. *J. Differ. Equ.* **1981**, *42*, 1–24. [CrossRef]

mathematics

MDPI

Article

Exponential Stability of Nonlinear Time-Varying Delay Differential Equations via Lyapunov–Razumikhin Technique

Natalya O. Sedova [1,*] and Olga V. Druzhinina [2,3]

1 Department of Mathematics, Information and Aviation Technology, Ulyanovsk State University, 432017 Ulyanovsk, Russia
2 Federal Research Center "Computer Science and Control" of Russian Academy of Sciences, 119333 Moscow, Russia
3 V.A. Trapeznikov Institute of Control Sciences of Russian Academy of Sciences, 117997 Moscow, Russia
* Correspondence: sedovano@ulsu.ru

Abstract: In this article, some new sufficient conditions for the exponential stability of nonlinear time-varying delay differential equations are given. An extension of the classical asymptotical stability theorem in terms of a Lyapunov–Razumikhin function is obtained. The condition of non-positivity of the time derivative of a Razumikhin function is weakened. Additionally, the resulting sufficient asymptotic stability conditions allow us to guarantee uniform exponential stability and evaluate the exponential convergence rate of the system solutions. The effectiveness of the results is demonstrated by some examples.

Keywords: time-varying system; delay differential system; Razumikhin condition; exponential stability

MSC: 34K20

1. Introduction

There have been a number of developments in searching for the stability criteria for nonlinear delay differential systems, but most of these have been restricted to finding asymptotic stability conditions.

As noted in [1], this may be caused by the fact that 'a "geometric" view of nonlinear dynamics leads one to adopt the view that notions of stability should be invariant under (nonlinear) changes of variables'. For this reason, 'exponential stability is not a natural mathematical notion when nonlinear coordinate changes are allowed. This is why the notion of asymptotic stability is important' [1].

However, in some cases it is necessary not only to establish the fact of asymptotic stability, but also to know the rate of convergence in the asymptotic stability property—for example, in order to guarantee some asymptotic properties of solutions to a cascaded system based on an analysis of the properties of its isolated subsystems [1]. In practical applications, it is also important to guarantee a certain rate of convergence of some characteristics of the system.

At the same time, the exponential stability of nonlinear systems is not easily verified. Moreover, for systems with delay, even in the linear case, there are difficulties in estimating the rate of convergence of solutions (see, for example, references in [2]).

Therefore, researchers are attracted by the problem of obtaining requirements for the Lyapunov function, which can guarantee estimates for the convergence of solutions.

The specificity of using finite-dimensional functions to analyze the stability properties of systems with delay is that the derivative of the Lyapunov function is estimated not in the entire neighborhood of the origin, but only within its part.

The idea of such a modification of the requirements for the derivative was simultaneously proposed by N.N. Krasovskii and B.S. Razumikhin [3,4]. Subsequently, the conditions that determine a part of the neighborhood of zero for estimating the derivative were called Razumikhin conditions.

On one hand, these conditions simplify the practical verification of the relevant requirements that guarantee one type of stability or another. On the other hand, the absence of an estimate for the derivative of the Lyapunov–Razumikhin function along the entire solution makes it difficult to estimate the rate of decrease of the function itself, and, consequently, the estimate of the rate of convergence of solutions.

Therefore, for equations with delay, such estimates are mainly obtained using the Lyapunov–Krasovskii functionals [5,6]. Similar results using the functions instead the functionals have occurred from time to time and have become more frequent in the last decade; in this case, mainly autonomous or linear equations are considered (see, e.g., references in [7]).

The purpose of this paper is to establish sufficient conditions for the exponential stability of nonlinear time-varying delay differential systems, under less restrictive assumptions on the Lyapunov–Razumikhin function (the function $V(t,x)$ below) than those made in the literature so far.

Namely, the time-derivative of the constructed Razumikhin function is allowed to be neither sign-definite (as in the classical asymptotic stability theorem) nor semidefinite (as in some more general theorems, see e.g., [8]). Moreover, a new upper estimate on the rate of decreasing of the function is obtained.

It is important to note that, in this paper, consideration is given only to deterministic systems. Nowadays, practical control systems need to meet several important requirements, for example, time delays, stochastic perturbations, time-varying parameters, and impulse effects. The research problem of stability analysis for related systems has received a great deal of attention.

The Lyapunov–Razumikhin method was originally developed to study the stability of deterministic systems with delay. However, the Razumikhin technique has also been a powerful and effective method for investigating the stability of other types of delay systems. In 1996, X. Mao extended the technique to stochastic functional differential equations to investigate p-th moment exponential stability [9]. In the past several decades, a large number of works on this topic have been reported in the literature (e.g., [10–12]).

In particular, several novel criteria of the moment exponential stability are derived for the related systems; see, for example, [13–16] and references therein.

An analysis of these results shows that Razumikhin-type theorems for deterministic systems can be appropriately developed and extended to stochastic delay systems with additional features and effects. Taking into account the behavior of a specific system leads to using special tools and adding certain conditions to ensure stability. Therefore, when studying a system of a certain type, it is easier to rely on results for deterministic systems than to derive stability conditions from the available results for systems of another type. Therefore, the development of the Razumikhin method for deterministic continuous systems plays an important role both in theory and applications.

The paper is organized as follows. In Section 2, we introduce notation, definitions, and other preliminaries. Section 3 gives new sufficient conditions for uniform asymptotic stability and uniform exponential stability in terms of the Lyapunov–Razumikhin functions. Section 4 contains a remark on necessary conditions for uniform asymptotic stability, which are relevant to the results obtained. In Section 5, we consider scalar linear time-varying equations and show the effectiveness of the exponential stability theorem using some particular examples. Some more examples of nonlinear equations are given in Section 6. Section 7 discusses some known related results. Concluding remarks are given in the final section.

2. Preliminaries

The following notation will be used throughout the paper: R^+ is the set of all non-negative real numbers; R^n is the n-dimensional vector space and $|x|$ is a norm of a vector

$x \in R^n$; time delay is denoted by r ($r > 0$), $R^+ = [0, +\infty)$; R^n denotes the n-dimensional space of vectors $x = (x_1, \ldots, x_n)^\top$ with the norm $|x|$; $C = C([-r, 0], R^n)$ is the Banach space with the supremum-norm $\| \cdot \|$. For a continuous function $x(t) \in C([t_0 - r, t_0 + \bar{t}), R^n)$ ($t_0 \in R^+$, $\bar{t} > 0$) an element $x_t \in C$ is defined for any $t \in [t_0, t_0 + \bar{t})$ by $x_t(s) = x(t+s)$, $-r \leq s \leq 0$, and $\dot{x}(t)$ stands for the right-hand derivative.

Consider the nonlinear system described by a time-varying delay differential equation of the form:

$$\dot{x}(t) = f(t, x_t), \tag{1}$$

where $x(t) \in R^n$, $f(t,x) : R^+ \times C \to R^n$ is a given nonlinear function satisfying $f(t, 0) = 0$ for all $t \in R^+$. Then (1) admits the zero solution.

In the following, we assume that the Carathéodory-type conditions from [17] are imposed on Equation (1). We denote the solution of (1) with initial conditions $t_0 \in R^+$ and $\varphi_0 \in C$ by $x(t; t_0\varphi_0)$.

In addition, we use the following standard definition:

Definition 1. *The zero solution of* (1) *is said to be uniformly exponentially stable (UES) if there exist constants* Δ, δ, *and* r *such that*

$$\|\varphi_0\| < r,\ t \geqslant t_0 \ \Rightarrow\ |x(t; t_0\varphi_0)| \leqslant \Delta \|\varphi_0\| e^{-\delta(t-t_0)}.$$

We say that the zero solution is globally uniformly exponentially stable (GUES) if $r = \infty$.

From now on, to shorten expressions, instead of saying the zero solution of the equation is GUES, we say that the equation is GUES.

We also use the well-known concepts of uniform asymptotic stability (UAS) and global uniform asymptotic stability (GUAS).

Let $V(t,x) : R^+ \times R^n \to R$ be a given function. Now, let $x(t)$ be a solution of (1) starting from (t, φ), and denote by $V'(t, \varphi)$ the upper right-hand derivative of $V(t, x(t))$ [18]:

$$\overline{\lim_{h \to 0^+}} \frac{V(t+h, x(t+h; t, \varphi)) - V(t, \varphi(0))}{h}. \tag{2}$$

Suppose that $V(t,x)$ is locally Lipschitzian in x (uniformly in $t \in R^+$). Then, the derivative (2) is bounded and is equal to the upper Dini derivative of $V(.)$ (along the trajectory of (1)):

$$\overline{\lim_{h \to 0^+}} \frac{V(t+h, \varphi(0) + hf(t, \varphi)) - V(t, \varphi(0))}{h},$$

where $f(.)$ is the right-hand side function of (1).

Obviously, a continuously differentiable function satisfies the equality

$$V'(t, \varphi) = \frac{\partial V(t, \varphi(0))}{\partial t} + \sum_{i=1}^{n} \frac{\partial V(t, \varphi(0))}{\partial x_i} X_i(t, \varphi).$$

In the sequel, we assume that $V(t,x)$ is continuous in t and locally Lipschitzian in x (uniformly in t).

We also define the class of functions $\mathcal{K} = \{a \in C(R^+, R^+), \sigma(u)$ is continuous, strictly increasing, and $a(0) = 0\}$. A *class-*$\mathcal{K}_\infty$ *function* is a function $a \in \mathcal{K}$ which is unbounded.

As is known, the idea that made it possible to obtain constructive results on stability in terms of functions for systems with delays was that it is sufficient to check the sign of the derivative V' at each time not on the whole set C, but only on its subset [3,4]. As a rule, one of two sets is used:

$$\Omega_t(V) = \{\varphi \in C : V(t+s, \varphi(s)) \leqslant V(t, \varphi(0)),\ -r \leqslant s \leqslant 0\},$$

$$\Omega_t(V, \eta) = \{\varphi \in C : V(t+s, \varphi(s)) \leqslant \eta(V(t, \varphi(0))),\ -r \leqslant s \leqslant 0\},$$

where $\eta \in \mathcal{K}$ is such that $\eta(u) > u$ for $u > 0$.

The following Razumikhin-type result of N.N. Krasovskii became the basis for further studies of the asymptotic stability of delay systems in terms of functions.

Theorem 1. *Suppose that there is a function $V : R^+ \times R^n \to R^+$ such that:*

1. $a_1(|x|) \leqslant V(t,x) \leqslant a_2(|x|)$;
2. *if $t \in R^+$ and $\varphi \in \Omega_t(V,\eta)$ then $V'(t,\varphi) \leqslant -a_3(|x|)$;*

for some functions $a_i \in \mathcal{K}$.

Then Equation (1) *is UAS.*

It can be proved in the standard way that if $a_i \in \mathcal{K}_\infty$, then the uniform asymptotic stability will be global (GUAS).

3. Main Result

First, we prove the following lemma, which provides an upper bound for the behavior of the function $V(t,x)$ along solutions of Equation (1).

Lemma 1. *Suppose that there exist numbers $\bar{a} > 0$, $\underline{a} \in R$, and the functions $\eta \in \mathcal{K}$, $V \in C^1(R^+ \times R^n, R^+)$, and $p \in C([-r,+\infty), R)$, such that the following conditions are met:*

1. *for all $t \in [-r,+\infty)$ and $s \in [0,r]$ the following inequalities $\underline{a} \leqslant \int_t^{t+s} p(\theta)d\theta \leqslant \bar{a}$ hold;*
2. $\eta(u) \geqslant e^{\bar{a}}u$ *for* $u > 0$:
3. $V'(t,\varphi) \leqslant -p(t)V(t,\varphi(0))$ *whenever $t \in R^+$ and $\varphi \in \Omega_t(V,\eta)$.*

Then, for any solution $x(t) = x(t;t_0,\varphi_0)$ of Equation (1) *and for all $t \geqslant t_0$ the estimation*

$$V(t,x(t)) \leqslant \max_{-r\leqslant s\leqslant 0} V(t_0+s,\varphi_0(s))e^{-(\int_{t_0}^{t} p(\theta)d\theta + a)}$$

is valid with $a = \min\{0,\underline{a}\}$.

Proof. We define the function $v(t) = V(t,x(t))$ along an arbitrary solution $x(t) = x(t;t_0,\varphi_0)$, and the function $u(t) = v(t) - \max_{-r\leqslant s\leqslant 0} v(t_0+s)e^{-\left[\int_{t_0}^{t} p(\theta)d\theta + a\right]}$. It is clear that $u(t_0) \leqslant 0$. We define $t^* = \inf\{t \geqslant t_0 : \ u(t) > 0\} \geqslant t_0$. Then, $u(t^*) = 0$, while $u(t) \leqslant 0$ for $t \in [t_0 - r, t^*)$, and $u(t) > 0$ for $t \in (t^*, t^*+\varepsilon)$. So we have $\dot{u}(t^*) > 0$. Notice that $\dot{u}(t^*) = \dot{v}(t^*) + p(t^*)\max_{-r\leqslant s\leqslant 0} v(t_0+s)e^{-\left[\int_{t_0}^{t^*} p(\theta)d\theta + a\right]} \leqslant \dot{v}(t^*) + p(t^*)v(t^*)$. On the other hand,

$$v(t^*) = \max_{-r\leqslant s\leqslant 0} v(t_0+s)e^{-\left[\int_{t_0}^{t^*} p(\theta)d\theta + a\right]},$$

and for all $s \in [-r,0]$ we have

$$\begin{aligned} v(t^*+s) &\leqslant \max_{-r\leqslant s\leqslant 0} v(t_0+s)e^{-\left[\int_{t_0}^{t^*+s} p(\theta)d\theta + a\right]} \\ &= \max_{-r\leqslant s\leqslant 0} v(t_0+s)e^{-\left[\int_{t_0}^{t^*} p(\theta)d\theta + a\right]}e^{\int_{t^*+s}^{t^*} p(\theta)d\theta + a} \\ &\leqslant v(t^*)e^{\bar{a}} \leqslant \eta(v(t^*)). \end{aligned}$$

Then, item 3 of the theorem implies $\dot{u}(t^*) \leqslant 0$. The obtained contradiction proves that $u(t) \leqslant 0$, which was to be proved. □

Based on the lemma just proved, it is easy to obtain the following result:

Theorem 2. *In addition to the conditions of Lemma 1, suppose that for some $T > 0$, $A > 0$ and for all $t \in R^+$, we have the estimate*

$$\int_t^{t+T} p(\theta)d\theta \geqslant A.$$

Then, for an arbitrary solution $x(t) = x(t; t_0, \varphi_0)$ of Equation (1) and for all $t \geqslant t_0$, there holds

$$V(t, x(t)) \leqslant M \max_{-r \leqslant s \leqslant 0} V(t_0 + s, \varphi_0(s))e^{-\frac{A}{T}(t-t_0)}$$

with $M = e^{A-\underline{a}-a}$.

In addition:

1. *if $a_1(|x|) \leqslant V(t,x)$ ($a_1 \in \mathcal{K}$) then Equation (1) is asymptotically stable;*
2. *if $a_1(|x|) \leqslant V(t,x) \leqslant a_2(|x|)$ (a_1, $a_2 \in \mathcal{K}$) then Equation (1) is UAS;*
3. *if $a_1(|x|) \leqslant V(t,x) \leqslant a_2(|x|)$ (a_1, $a_2 \in \mathcal{K}$), and there exist constants c, $c_1 > 0$, and $c_2 \in (0,1)$ such that $a_1^{-1}(Ma_2(s)) \leqslant cs$ and $a_1^{-1}(c_1 a_2(s)) \leqslant c_2$, then Equation (1) is UES.*

Proof. Indeed, it follows from the additional condition that for $t \geqslant T$ the inequality $\int_{t_0}^{t_0+t} p(\theta)d\theta \geqslant A(t/T - 1) + \underline{a}$ is valid. Thus, we can immediately get the required estimate for $V(t, x(t))$.

Then, item 1 implies $a_1(|x(t)|) \leqslant V(t, x(t)) \leqslant M \max_{-r\leqslant s\leqslant 0} V(t_0 + s, \varphi_0(s))e^{-\frac{A}{T}(t-t_0)}$, and item 2 implies $a_1(|x(t)|) \leqslant V(t, x(t)) \leqslant M \max_{-r\leqslant s\leqslant 0} V(t_0 + s, \varphi_0(s))e^{-\frac{A}{T}(t-t_0)} \leqslant Ma_2(\|\varphi_0\|)e^{-\frac{A}{T}(t-t_0)}$. The assertions of items 1 and 2 follow directly from these estimates.

It remains to prove item 3. We define the function $v(t) = \max_{-r\leqslant s\leqslant 0} V(t+s, x(t+s))$ along an arbitrary solution $x(t) = x(t; t_0, \varphi_0)$. Note that the resulting estimate for V implies $v(t + t_1) \leqslant Me^{-\frac{A}{T}(t_1-r)}v(t) \leqslant c_1 v(t)$ for every $t \geqslant t_0$ and a sufficiently large value t_1. Therefore, $a_1(\|x_{t+t_1}\|) \leqslant c_1 a_2(\|x_t\|)$ and $\|x_{t+t_1}\| \leqslant c_2\|x_t\|$. Further, take an arbitrary $t > t_0$ and, following the idea of the proof from [19], denote by N the lower integer part of $(t - t_0)/t_1$. Then $t - Nt_1 \in [t_0, t_0 + t_1)$, and $\|x_t\| \leqslant c_2\|x_{t-t_1}\| \leqslant c_2^2\|x_{t-2t_1}\| \leqslant \cdots \leqslant c_2^N\|x_{t-Nt_1}\|$. Moreover, the inequality $v(t) \leqslant Mv(t_0)$ implies $\|x_{t-Nt_1}\| \leqslant a_1^{-1}(Ma_2(\|\varphi_0\|) \leqslant c\|\varphi_0\|$. Thus, $\|x_t\| \leqslant c_2^N c\|\varphi_0\| \leqslant c_2^{\frac{t-t_0}{t_1}} c\|\varphi_0\| \leqslant c\|\varphi_0\|e^{-\delta(t-t_0)}$, where $\delta = \delta(c_2) = \frac{1}{t_1}\log\frac{1}{c_2} > 0$. This implies the last assertion of the theorem. □

Remark 1. *If we replace $\mathcal{K}$ by $\mathcal{K}_\infty$ in the conditions of items 1–3, then we obtain the conditions for global uniform asymptotic (exponential) stability.*

Remark 2. *It is easy to see that the condition $\alpha_1|x|^m \leqslant V(t,x) \leqslant \alpha_2|x|^m$ implies*

$$|x(t)| \leqslant \Delta_1\|x_{t_0}\|e^{-\delta_1(t-t_0)}$$

with $\Delta_1 = (\alpha_2 e^{A-\underline{a}-a}/\alpha_1)^{1/m}$, $\delta_1 = \frac{A}{Tm}$. In this case, $a_1^{-1}(c_1 a_2(s)) = (c_1\alpha_2/\alpha_1)^{1/m}$, hence the second inequality in item 3 holds for an arbitrary $c_2 \in (0,1)$ (it suffices to put $c_1 = c_2^m(\alpha_1/\alpha_2)$). Moreover, $\delta(c_2) \to \gamma/m = \delta_1$ for $c_2 \to 0$.

Remark 3. *Recall the definition of GUAS(a_0) [1], which qualifies the speed of convergence in the GUAS property, and serves to relax exponential stability (here we modify it according to the type of equation considered). We say that the zero solution to the Equation (1) is GUAS(a_0) for a given $a_0 \in \mathcal{K}_\infty$ if there exists a class-$\mathcal{K}_\infty$ function a and a positive constant $\delta > 0$ so that $|x(t; t_0, \varphi_0)| \leqslant a_0(e^{-\delta(t-t_0)}a(\|\varphi_0\|))$ holds for all $\varphi_0 \in C$ (recall that GUAS is always equivalent to the existence of some a and a_0 like this.) We see that due to the exponential estimate for $V(t, x(t))$, item 2 of Theorem 2 actually implies GUAS(a_1^{-1}).*

Corollary 1. *Let the conditions of Theorem 2 hold for $t \geqslant \bar{t} > 0$. Then all statements remain true.*

Proof. For the proof, we use the assumptions on the right-hand side of Equation (1) and results from [17].

By Assumption 2 from [17], for each compact $K \subset C$ there exists a locally Lebesgue-integrable function $L_K(t)$ and $N(K) > 0$ such that for all $\varphi \in K$ and $t \in R^+$ the estimate $|f(t,\varphi)| \leqslant L_K(t)\|\varphi\|$ holds, and $\int_t^{t+1} L_K(s)ds \leqslant N(K)$. In addition, for an arbitrary $a > 0$ every solution $x(t)$ of Equation (1) is contained in some compact $K(q) \subset C$ as long as $|x(t)| \leqslant a$ [17].

Now, let $x(t) = x(t; t_0\varphi_0)$ be an arbitrary solution of (1). It is clear that it suffices to check the case $t_0 < \bar{t}$. If

$$\|x_t\| \leqslant a \text{ for all } t \in [t_0, \bar{t}] \qquad (*)$$

then

$$\|x_{\bar{t}}\| \leqslant \|\varphi_0\| + \max_{\bar{t}-r \leqslant s \leqslant \bar{t}} \int_{t_0}^{s} |f(\theta, x_\theta| d\theta \leqslant$$

$$\|\varphi_0\| + \int_{t_0}^{\bar{t}} L_a(\theta)\|x_\theta\| d\theta.$$

The Grönwall–Bellman inequality now implies

$$\|x_{\bar{t}}\| \leqslant \|\varphi_0\| e^{N_a \bar{t}}.$$

It remains to note that inequality $(*)$ will be satisfied whenever $\|\varphi_0\| \leqslant a e^{-N_a \bar{t}}$. □

Remark 4. *Note that if $V(t,x) \leqslant a_2(|x|)$ ($a_2 \in \mathcal{K}$), then the estimate for the derivative in Theorem 2 can be replaced by the following one: $V'(t,\varphi) \leqslant -p(t)a_3(|\varphi(0)|)$ for all $t \in R^+$ and $\varphi \in \Omega_t(V,\eta)$, where $a_3 \in \mathcal{K}$. Indeed, in this case we set $U(t,x) = \Lambda(V(t,x))$, where Λ is some C^1 positive definite proper function such that $\Lambda'(s)a_3(a_2^{-1}(s)) \geqslant \Lambda(s)$. Then, the function U satisfies the conditions of Lemma 1.*

4. A Remark on Necessary Conditions for Uniform Asymptotic Stability

In this section, the discussion will center on the integral conditions for the function $p(t)$ that ensure the exponential convergence of the function $V(t,x(t)$ to zero (Theorem 2). In fact, these conditions are equivalent to a restriction on the antiderivative of $p(t)$, which naturally arises in the analysis of linear ordinary differential equations with time-varying coefficients. Here, we give a statement showing that, in the nonlinear case, a similar estimate for the right-hand side is a necessary condition for uniform asymptotic stability.

Note that the requirements imposed on integrals of $p(t)$ to be bounded from below, which are specified in Theorem 2, are equivalent to the following condition (see [20]):

$$\exists a > 0 \text{ and } b \text{ such that } \int_{t_0}^{t} p(\theta)\, d\theta \geqslant a(t - t_0) + b \text{ for every } t_0,\ t \geqslant t_0, \qquad (3)$$

and (3) is equivalent to GUES for the scalar ordinary differential equation $\dot{y}(t) = -p(t)y(t)$.

Moreover, for GUES of the linear system $\dot{y}(t) = -P(t)y(t)$ with a symmetric positive semidefinite matrix $P(t)$, it is necessary and sufficient that (3) be satisfied for $p(t) = |P(t)x|$ and every unit vector $x \in R^n$ [21].

If the inequality $x^\top P(t)x \geqslant 0$ is violated, then the estimate (3) provides sufficient GUES conditions via a quadratic time-varying Lyapunov function [20]. Note that for a linear system, GUAS and GUES are equivalent.

Z. Artstein ([22] Theorem 6.2) showed that the growth condition (3) is necessary in a very general situation for ordinary differential equations. There holds a similar statement for Equation (1):

Theorem 3. *Suppose that Equation (1) is uniformly stable. Then, the equation is uniformly asymptotically stable only if there exists a compact neighborhood of zero $W \subset R^n$ such that for every $\delta > 0$ there are numbers $a > 0$ and b such that*

$$\int_{t_0}^{t} |f(\theta,\varphi)|d\theta \geqslant a(t-t_0)+b$$

for every $t_0 \in R^+, t \geqslant t_0$ *and every* $\varphi \in C$ *such that* $\varphi(s) \equiv c$, $|c| \geqslant \delta$, *and* $c \in W$.

Proof. Assumptions about the right-hand side of Equation (1) ensure the positive precompactness of (1) in an appropriate function space and the existence of the so-called limiting equations; in addition, for every limiting equation and every pair (t_0, φ_0) the initial-value problem has a unique solution [23].

Using the relationships of uniform asymptotic stability of Equation (1) and stability properties of the corresponding limiting equations ([23] Theorem 6), we can now repeat the proof of Theorem 6.2 from [22] with slight modifications. □

It should be emphasized that the necessary condition for UAS from Theorem 3 without additional assumptions is not sufficient, even for ordinary differential equations ([22] Theorem 6.3) (see also Section 5).

5. Application: Scalar Linear Time-Varying Equations

In this section, we consider the scalar linear differential equation

$$\dot{x}(t) = -a(t)x(t) + b(t)x(t-\tau(t)), \tag{4}$$

where $a(t)$, $b(t)$, and $\tau(t)$ are piecewise continuous, $0 \leqslant \tau(t) \leqslant r$.

Note that by Theorem 3, the uniform asymptotic stability of the Equation (4) implies the condition

$$\int_{t_0}^{t} |-a(\theta)+b(\theta)|d\theta \geqslant a_0(t-t_0)+b_0 \tag{5}$$

for every $t_0 \in R^+, t \geqslant t_0$, and some numbers $a_0 > 0$ and b_0.

There have been a lot of investigations concerning sufficient stability conditions for Equation (4).

Most of the results obtained in this line of study impose restrictions on the sign of coefficients. For example, by Theorem 1, an Equation (4) is uniformly asymptotically stable if $p_l(t) = a(t) - q|b(t)| \geqslant p_0 > 0$ for some $q > 1$ and $p_0 > 0$; it is also clear that for GUES of Equation (4), it is sufficient for the function $p_l(t)$ to satisfy the conditions of Theorem 2. In both cases, an arbitrary (bounded) delay is allowed. Moreover, if no restrictions are imposed on the delay, then for constant coefficients, the condition is the best possible.

For Equation (4) with time-varying a and b as well as with a time-varying delay, sufficient GUES conditions can be refined through information about the nature of the delay variation. However, in this case, the conditions known so far usually also imply that some function depending on a, b, and $\tau(t)$ must retain its sign (at least for large values of t); see [24,25] and references therein.

Note that the effect of delay variation can have a decisive influence on the stability even for Equation (4) with constant coefficients: one can give an example such that for each fixed member of the range of the delay function, the associated autonomous equation is exponentially stable, yet the time-varying equation considered is unstable [26]. However, the exact form of the relation "delay–time" is usually unknown; thus, in practice, it is more convenient to check the conditions that are valid for all delay values from a given range.

Equation (4) with $a(t) \equiv 0$ has a separate and even richer history of study going back to the work of Myshkis (see e.g., [27]), and this study is still ongoing. Following A.D. Myshkis, various forms of the so-called "3/2-criterion" were obtained, which establish an upper bound either for the coefficient $b(t)$ or for the integral of it; see some discussion and references in [28,29]. However, in those results, the lower bound for $b(t)$ (at least for the limit as t tends to infinity) remains zero.

In [30], the assertion is proved that if the equation $\dot{x}(t) = -b(t)x(t)$ is GUES and a certain additional integral condition for $b(t)$ is satisfied, then Equation (7) is GUES.

Note that the equation $\dot{x}(t) = -b(t)x(t)$ is GUES if and only if (3) hold for $b(t)$ (see Section 4), while for the equation $\dot{x}(t) = -b(t)x(t-\tau(t))$ this condition is not sufficient and additional upper bounds are required. For example, even for constant values $b(t) \equiv b > 0$ and $\tau(t) \equiv r$ the equation $\dot{x}(t) = -bx(t-r)$ is GUAS only if $br < \pi/2$; for time-varying non-negative functions $b(t)$ and $\tau(t)$, this condition turns into restrictions imposed on their supremum or some integral (see, e.g., [27]).

But even such conditions stop working as soon as the coefficient $b(t)$ is allowed to change sign. The authors of [25] investigate whether sufficiently small bounds r for the delay and b_0 for the integral $\int_{t-\tau(t)}^{t} |b(s)|ds \leqslant b_0$ and exponential stability of $\dot{x}(t) = -b(t)x(t)$ cause exponential stability of the equation $\dot{x}(t) = -b(t)x(t-\tau(t))$ with an oscillating coefficient $b(t)$. They provide an example showing that, unlike the case of the equation with $b(t) \geq 0$, such r and b_0 cannot be found in the general case.

Thus, the study of the stability of linear delay equations with sign-changing coefficients is a rather challenging problem. Even for the scalar Equation (4) there are only a few results of this kind; see [25] and references therein.

Next, we deduce sufficient GUES conditions for several examples of Equation (4) using Theorem 2, and compare the conditions with those obtained by some other methods.

Example 1. *Consider the scalar equation*

$$\dot{x}(t) = -x(t) + b(t)x(t-\tau(t)) \tag{6}$$

with $0 \leqslant \tau(t) \leqslant r$.

The classical theorem (Theorem 1) implies GUAS of (1) *for* $|b(t)| < 1$; *the same inequality follows from other results (see, e.g., [24] and references therein).*

Let $b(t)$ *be a periodic function of period* 1 *given by*

$$b(t) = \begin{cases} 0, & t \in [0,c), \\ d, & t \in [c,1), \end{cases}$$

where $c \in (0,1)$ *and* $d > 1$.

For the derivative of the function $V(x) = |x|$ *by virtue of the Equation* (1) *for* $\eta(s) = qs$ $(q > 1)$, *we obtain the estimate from Lemma 1 with* $p(t) = 1 - q|b(t)|$. *If* $r \leqslant 1$, *then* $\bar{a} = \min\{r,c\}$, *and if* $n-1 < r \leqslant n$ *with integer* $n > 1$, *then* $\bar{a} = nc$. *For* $T = 1$, *we get* $A = c + (1-c)(1-qd) = 1 - qd(1-c)$. *Then, by Theorem 2 the conditions* $q \geqslant e^{\bar{a}}$, $A > 0$ *are sufficient for GUES of Equation* (1).

In Table 1 we compare the results for Equation (1) *obtained using various assertions.*

Table 1. Comparison of some sufficient conditions for GUAS (GUES) of Equation (1).

Method	Stability Conditions	Convergence Rate
[31]	$(1-c)d < \frac{1-e^{-1}}{2} \approx 0.3161$ GUAS	–
[32]	$(1-c)d < 1, r < -\ln[(1-c)d]$, GUAS	–
[33]	$(1-c)d < e^{-c}$, $e^{-c} > e^{-1} \approx 0.3679$ GUES	$A/(1+r)$, $(A = 1 - e^{c}d(1-c))$
Theorem 2	$(1-c)d < e^{-\bar{a}}$ $\bar{a} = \begin{cases} nc \text{ if } \max\{c, n-1\} < r \leqslant n \\ (n \in \{1,2,\ldots,\}) \\ r \text{ if } r < c \end{cases}$ GUES	A $(A = 1 - e^{\bar{a}}d(1-c))$

Note that the conditions of GUAS from [32] follow from the estimates obtained using Theorem 2. Thus, the number d can be large enough, provided that c and r are small enough. A comparison of the conditions for r, c, and d shows that for large values of r, Theorem 2 gives more restrictive conditions than [33], and vice versa for small ones.

Example 2. *Consider the scalar equation*

$$\dot{x}(t) = -b(t)x(t-\tau(t)) \tag{7}$$

with a bounded $b(t)$ and a time-varying delay $\tau(t) \in [0, r]$.

Using the function $V(x) = |x|$, we find that the estimation in condition 3 of Lemma 1 holds for $p(t) = b(t) - |b(t)| q \int_{t-r}^{t} |b(s)| ds$, where $\eta(u) = qu$ and $q \geqslant e^{\bar{a}}$. We denote $\hat{b} = \sup_{t \in R^+} |b(t)|$, then $p(t) \geqslant b(t) - qr\hat{b}^2$ and $\int_t^{t+\bar{T}} p(\theta) d\theta \geqslant A = \bar{b} - qr\bar{T}\hat{b}^2$. Moreover, in condition 1 of Lemma 1, the number $\bar{a}$ can be chosen to be equal to $r\hat{b}$. Thus, if the zero solution of the equation $\dot{x}(t) = -b(t)x(t)$ is GUES, then the GUES of Equation (7) is guaranteed for sufficiently small values of r (at least for $0 \leqslant r < \bar{b}/(e^{r\hat{b}}\hat{b}^2\bar{T})$.

To compare known GUES conditions with the conditions of Theorem 2, consider a special case of Equation (7) (see ([30] Example 2) and ([25] Example 4)) with the function

$$b(t) = \begin{cases} \alpha, & 2n \leqslant t \leqslant 2n+1, \\ -\beta, & 2n+1 \leqslant t \leqslant 2n+2, \end{cases} \tag{8}$$

where $0 < r \leqslant 1$, $\alpha > \beta > 0$, and $n = 0, 1, 2, \ldots$.

For (7), (8) with a constant delay, the condition of GUES is obtained in the form

$$\frac{(2e^{\beta} - e^{-(\alpha-\beta)} - 1)\alpha r}{1 - e^{-(\alpha-\beta)}} < 1 \tag{9}$$

in [30], and in the form

$$r\alpha \max\left\{\frac{\alpha}{\alpha-\lambda}, \frac{\beta}{\lambda-\beta}\right\} e^{\lambda} < 1 \text{ for some } \lambda \in (\beta, \alpha) \tag{10}$$

in [25].

From Theorem 2, we get the conditions $A\frac{qr^2}{2}(\alpha-\beta)^2 + (\alpha-\beta) - qr(\alpha^2+\beta^2) > 0$ and $q \geqslant e^{r(\alpha-\beta^2 qr)}$. Table 2 lists some numerical values of the parameters α, β, and r and indicates whether the conditions of Theorem 2 or Equations (9) or (10) are satisfied for these sets.

Table 2. Fulfillment of sufficient GUES conditions for (7), (8) with different values of the parameters α, β, and r.

Values of (α, β, r)	Theorem 2	(9) [30]	(10) [25]
(0.6, 0.2, 0.6)	+	+	+
(0.6, 0.3, 0.5)	+	–	–
(0.6, 0.3, 0.4)	+	+	–
(0.6, 0.3, 0.6)	–	–	–

Comparing the results for Equation (7) with $b(t)$ given by (8), we observe that the conditions do not follow from each other and may or may not be satisfied depending on the parameter values. In addition, the conditions obtained using Theorem 2 remain applicable in the case of variable delay, including a state-dependent one.

Note that all the mentioned stability conditions are sufficient. Not every pair of conditions can be compared; one or the other may win, depending on the particular equation. However, it is worth noting that the previously obtained results discussed in this section were obtained using methods that make significant use of linearity of the equation under study. The results of this paper are obtained on the basis of Lyapunov–Razumikhin functions and are applicable to more general time-varying equations (see Section 6 for some examples of nonlinear equations).

Example 3. *Consider the system*

$$\dot{x}(t) = -\sin^2 t \cdot x(t) + bx(t - \tau(t)), \ \tau(t) \in [0, r]. \tag{11}$$

We study the stability conditions for this equation with arbitrary values of $r > 0$ and $b > 0$. For $b \geqslant 1/2$, the necessary condition GUES of the Equation (11) does not hold for $r = 0$. Numerical experiments show that the solutions of Equation (11) for $b \geqslant 1/2$ increase indefinitely for all $r > 0$. Using the function $V(x) = |x|$, we find that the estimation in condition 3 of Lemma 1 holds for $p(t) = \sin^2 t - q|b|$, and the conditions of Theorem 2 are satisfied for Equation (11) whenever $\eta = 1/2 - q|b| > 0$ and $q \geqslant e^{1/2+r\eta}$. In this case, for all solutions of the equation, the estimate $|x(t)| \leqslant M\|x_{t_0}\|e^{-\eta(t-t_0)}$ is valid with $M = e^{1+\pi\eta}$. The given GUES conditions are satisfied, for example, for $b = 0.2$, $r = 6$, $q \geqslant 2.243$, $\eta \leqslant 0.0513$, and $M \geqslant 3.2$. It can also be noted that none of the GUES conditions given in [24,25] are not applicable here.

From Figure 1, we find that Equation (11) is GUES with the decay rate guaranteed by our conditions: for the selected parameter values, the norm $|x(t)|$ is less than $M\|x_{t_0}\|e^{-\eta(t-t_0)}$. The above GUES conditions remain valid for the equation $\dot{x}(t) = -\sin^2 t \cdot x(t) + \sum_{i=1}^{N} b_i(t)x(t - \tau_i(t))$ with $\sum_{i=1}^{N} |b_i(t)| \leqslant b$ and $0 \leqslant \tau_i(t) \leqslant r$ for all $i = 1, \ldots, N$ (see an example with $N = 2$ in Figure 1a). For comparison, the time evolutions of other functions that estimate the decay rate of solutions are also shown. These functions are calculated using formulas from ([33] Theorem 1). It is clearly seen that our estimate of M is very conservative and much worse than the estimate by [33], but the decay rate estimate gives a better result (0.0513 versus 0.0176). We also see that for $b \geqslant 0.5$ the solutions of Equation (11) diverge (Figure 1b).

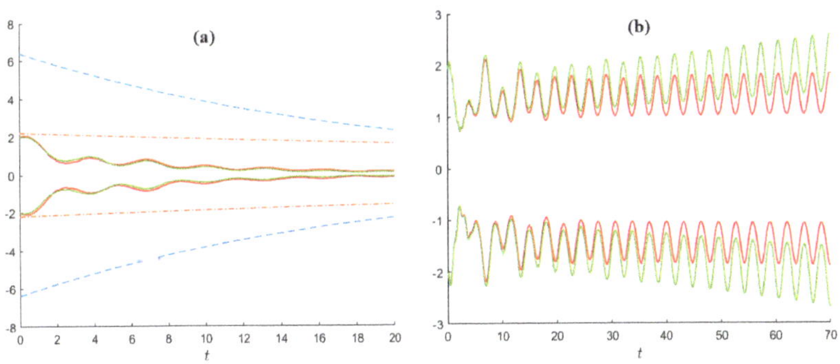

Figure 1. Evolution of the states with $t_0 = 0$, $\varphi_1(s) = -2(1 + \frac{1}{3}s\cos^2(3s))$, and $\varphi_2(s) = 2(1 + \frac{1}{3}s\sin^2(6s))$: (**a**) for Equation (7) with $b = 0.2$ and $\tau(t) = 6(1 - 0.2\cos^2 t)$ (red line); for the equation $\dot{x}(t) = -\sin^2 t \cdot x(t) + b_1(t)x(t - \tau_1(t)) + b_2(t)x(t - \tau_2(t))$ with $b_1(t) = 0.1(1 - 0.2\sin^2 t)$, $b_2(t) = 0.1(1 - 0.1\cos^2 t)$, $\tau_1(t) = 4(1 - 0.5\sin t)$, and $\tau_2(t) = 6/(1 + \sin^2 t)$ (green line); the blue dashed lines indicate the time evolution of the functions $\pm M\|x_{t_0}\|e^{-\eta(t-t_0)}$, the orange dash-dotted lines indicate the time evolution of functions estimating the decay rate of solutions by ([33] Theorem 1). (**b**) for Equation (7) with $\tau(t) \equiv r = 6$ and $b = 0.5$ (red line) or $b = 0.52$ (green line).

6. Nonlinear Examples

Example 4. *Consider the system*

$$x(t) = f(t, x_t) + g(t, x_t), \tag{12}$$

where $x(t) \in R^n$, and suppose that for some $\delta > 0$ the inequality $\|\varphi\| < \delta$ implies $f_i(t,\varphi)\varphi_i(0) \leqslant -a_i(t)\varphi_i^2(0)$ and $|g_i(t,\varphi)| \leqslant b_i(t)|\varphi_i(0)|$ for all $i = 1,\ldots,n$. Using the function $V(x) = \max_{i\in\{1,\ldots,n\}} |x_i|$, we obtain that system (12) *is UES whenever $p(t) = \min_{1\leqslant i\leqslant n}(a_i(t) - qb_i(t))$ satisfies the conditions of Theorem 2 for some $q > 1$.*

It should be pointed out that the idea of generalizing "linear" results to a certain class of nonlinear systems using the direct Lyapunov method is used quite often; see e.g., [29].

Example 5. *Let $\mu_i \geqslant 0$, $f_i : R^+ \times C \to R$ and $g_i : R^+ \times C \to R$ be continuous and locally Lipschitz uniformly in t and take non-negative values for non-negative φ ($i = 1,\ldots,n$). Define $f(t,\varphi) = (f_1(t,\varphi),\ldots,f_n(t,\varphi))^\top$, $g(t,\varphi) = diag(g_1(t,\varphi),\ldots,g_n(t,\varphi))$, and $\mu = diag(\mu_1,\ldots,\mu_n)$, and consider the system*

$$\dot{x}(t) = f(t,x_t) - (\mu + g(t,x_t))x(t), \tag{13}$$

arising in models of population dynamics [34].

It is also assumed that $x(t) \in R^n$ takes non-negative values and there exist matrices L^k ($k = 0,1,\ldots,m+1$) such that $f(t,\varphi) \leqslant \sum_{k=0}^m L^k\varphi(-r_k) + \int_{-r_{m+1}}^0 L^{m+1}(s)\varphi(s)ds$ with $r_0 = 0$, $0 < r_i \leqslant r$ for $k = 1,\ldots,m$ [34]. Let us denote $L = \sum_{k=0}^m L^k + \int_{-r_{m+1}}^0 L^{m+1}(s)ds$. In [34], the exponential convergence of positive solutions of (13) *is proved under the condition that $\mu - L$ is a nonsingular M-matrix. Let us use the function $V(x) = \max_{i\in\{1,\ldots,n\}} |x_i|$. Estimating the derivative of this function by virtue of system* (13) *and applying Theorem 2 with a constant $p(t)$ (see also Theorem 4 below), we obtain a sufficient condition for the exponential convergence of positive solutions of* (13) *in the form:*

$$\min_{i\in\{1,\ldots,n\}} (\mu_i - \sum_{j=1}^n L_{ij}) > 0. \tag{14}$$

Notice that whenever all $L_{ii} = 0$, which corresponds to most specific models, condition (14) *means that the matrix $\mu - L$ is strictly diagonally dominant. This implies that $\mu - L$ is a nonsingular M-matrix [35]. It is easy to see how, for system* (13) *with time-varying parameters, condition* (14) *can be generalized using Theorem 2.*

7. Discussion

On one hand, Razumikhin's conditions simplify the practical checking of the corresponding requirements that guarantee one type of stability or another, since the resulting estimate of the derivative does not depend on the history of the system; this circumstance, in turn, gives more "freedom" for delay in comparison with the method of functionals. On the other hand, the absence of an estimate for the derivative of the Lyapunov function along the entire solution makes it difficult to estimate the rate of convergence of solutions.

To obtain an estimate for the convergence of solutions based on Theorem 1, one can use a special structure of the time-dependent Lyapunov function, so that the convergence to zero of the function itself implies a certain rate of convergence of solutions (see, for example, [36]).

Another approach is to modify the requirements for the function $V(t,x)$. A significant number of modifications of Razumikhin-type theorems are based on ideas representing the so-called comparison principle. Two types of comparison theorems [37] give rise to two types of sufficient stability conditions.

In the first case, the estimate of the derivative is constructed over the entire domain, and therefore, it has the form of a functional. Accordingly, the comparison equation is a delay equation. In the second case, the derivative of the function $V(t,x)$ is estimated over some set in the spirit of Razumikhin's conditions, but to determine this set, it is necessary to know the solutions of the comparison equation [37]. In the first case, to apply the result, it is necessary to obtain information about the properties of solutions of some delay equation; in the second one, it is necessary to find a solution to a (nonlinear) ordinary differential equation.

Therefore, it is natural to try to obtain more specific forms both for estimates of the derivative of the function $V(t,x)$ and for Razumikhin-type conditions. The particular form of the proposed comparison equations makes it possible to obtain more constructive requirements that provide suitable properties for the solutions of these equations and, at the same time, do not lead to the "trivial" stability conditions that follow from the classical theorems. In this case, the requirements for the Lyapunov function are easier to check in specific applications, and sometimes it is also possible to obtain information about the convergence of solutions.

The results which do not make use of any Razumikhin conditions, but use a functional as an estimate of the derivative, mainly go back to the following statement:

Lemma 2 (Halanay's lemma, [38]). *Let $v(t)$ be a piecewise C^1 non-negative valued function that admits constants $r > 0$, $0 < \beta < \alpha$ such that $\dot{v}(t) \leqslant -\alpha v(t) + \beta \max_{t-r \leqslant s \leqslant t} v(s)$ holds for all $t \geqslant t_0$. Then, the inequality $v(t) \leqslant \max_{-r \leqslant s \leqslant 0} v(t_0 + s) e^{-\gamma(t-t_0)}$ holds for all $t \geqslant t_0$ with $\gamma \in (0, \alpha - \beta)$ be the root of the equation $\gamma = \alpha - \beta e^{\gamma r}$.*

There are a number of extensions of Halanay's lemma to the time-varying case; they are formulated in different forms and under different assumptions, depending, among other things, on the purpose of use (e.g., [31,32,39–41]). Moreover, in a number of cases, the proposed conditions imply classical requirements for the Lyapunov–Razumikhin function, which ensure (asymptotic) stability.

The requirements on the derivative in such results are relaxed due to the fact that the proposed conditions do not impose restrictions on the values of the system parameters themselves, such as delay and norms of the system coefficients, but instead involve integration of the time-varying parameters.

The second approach, which is based on the use of Razumikhin's conditions, uses the following result in most cases:

Theorem 4. *Suppose that there exists a function $V : R^+ \times R^n \to R^+$, numbers $\gamma > 0$ and $q > 1$, and functions a_1, $a_2 \in \mathcal{K}$ such that $a_1(|x|) \leqslant V(t,x) \leqslant a_2(|x|)$, and $V'(t,\varphi) \leqslant -\gamma V(t, \varphi(0))$ whenever $t \in R^+$ and $\max_{-r \leqslant s \leqslant 0} V(t+s, \varphi(s)) \leqslant qV(t, \varphi(0))$. Then, along any solution $x(t) = x(t; t_0, \varphi_0)$ of (1), the following inequality*

$$V(t, x(t)) \leqslant \max_{-r \leqslant s \leqslant 0} V(t_0 + s, \varphi_0(s)) e^{-\min(\gamma, \ln q/r)(t-t_0)}$$

holds for all $t \geqslant t_0$. If, in addition, $a_1|x|^m \leqslant V(t,x) \leqslant a_2|x|^m$ for some integer $m > 0$, then Equation (1) is GUES.

This statement is proved in various ways and used in a number of papers (see [7] and references therein). Some estimates for the convergence of the function $V(t,x)$ along solutions use other Razumikhin-type conditions. For discussion of a number of such results, see [8]. Note that, in such statements, the estimate of the derivative of a (non-negative) function $V(t,x)$ is usually non-positive on the entire time interval. The question arises whether it is possible to allow the sign of the estimate of the derivative to change, and at the same time to ensure the (asymptotic) stability of the zero solution of this equation.

One of the main ideas to combine these requirements is to use integral constraints on the parameters of the system studied (including the delay). As a result, it turns out that a delay system can be asymptotically stable even if the system is described by an equation with an unstable zero solution on some (short) time intervals. Therefore, a "classical" function for such a system cannot exist.

The first result allowing usage of an indefinite time-derivative of the function $V(t,x)$ under a Razumikhin-type condition was probably given in [42]: sufficient conditions for uniform stability are justified therein, provided that on the set $\Omega_t(V)$ the estimate

$$V'(t,\varphi) \leqslant \psi(t)V(t,\varphi(0)), \tag{15}$$

is valid, where $\int_0^\infty \max\{\psi(s),0\}ds < \infty$, and for uniform asymptotic stability, the estimate $\int_{t_0}^t \max\{-\psi(s),0\}ds \geqslant \varepsilon(t-t_0)$ is additionally required for some $\varepsilon > 0$ and sufficiently large values of t. It is clear that such a function $\psi(t)$ does not have to be negative all the time. On the other hand, the conditions of [42] cannot be satisfied if, for example, $\psi(t)$ is periodic and $\psi(t) > 0$ for all t from $[a,b] \subset [0,T]$ where T is the period and $b > a$. For such functions $\psi(t)$ in (15), sufficient conditions for uniform asymptotic stability and exponential stability were obtained in [33]: inequality (15) should be verified on the set $\Omega_t(V,\eta)$, wherein the functions ψ and η are linked by a certain relation. Note that Theorem 2 implies Theorem 4 for $p(t) \equiv \gamma$.

The results obtained here are close to the Razumikhin-type asymptotic stability theorem from [33], but another approach is used and other exponential stability conditions are obtained. It should be mentioned at this point that in [33] the estimate of the decay rate of solutions decreases with increasing delay, while in the estimate of Theorem 2 an increase in delay can lead to an increase in the number M. Thus, the results of [33] and Theorem 2 complement each other.

8. Conclusions

This paper has dealt with the problem of uniform exponential stability for nonlinear time-varying delay systems. We apply the Razumikhin method to establish sufficient conditions for exponential stability, and propose an extension of the Razumikhin approach for time-varying systems. Namely, the time-derivative of the constructed Razumikhin function is allowed to be indefinite, and a new upper estimate on the rate of decreasing of the function is also obtained.

The statements deduced can be seen as extensions of those in some earlier work discussed in the previous section, as well as some known sufficient conditions for the exponential stability of linear delay equations. The application of the exponential stability conditions derived here to specific examples shows that the previous related results are either inapplicable or give some other exponential estimates for the solutions.

We note that the use of the Razumikhin method gives rise to stability conditions that are sufficient but not necessary. Therefore, such stability conditions may be overly conservative. Various approaches have been taken to reduce the conservatism of the method, and numerous results have been obtained in this area. However, no universally good stability criterion exists; which criterion is better depends on what a specific system is.

The simple examples given in the paper show that Theorem 2 can be less conservative than other methods.

The method used in this paper for estimating the function V along solutions of a differential equation can be extended to wider classes of differential equations. It can also be used to solve other problems. For example, in [39], similar estimates are used for sufficient conditions for practical stability (exponential stability is a special case; see ([39] Remark 1)). Parenthetically, in [39] the coefficient of V in the estimate of the derivative is negative.

In [16], methods from [33] are extended to stochastic systems, as well as to studying other types of stability, in particular input-to-state stability and integral input-to-state stability. In [14], the ideas of [33] were developed for impulsive stochastic systems with delay. For such systems, it is necessary not only to construct estimates for a function V on continuity intervals, but also to take into account the change in this function at impulse moments. The most important feature of the results from [14] is that time-derivatives of Razumikhin functions are allowed to be unbounded.

We also note the recent work [43], in which the reaction–diffusion epidemic model with a delayed impulse is studied. For this model, a new synchronization criterion is obtained. In this case, the Lyapunov–Krasovskii functional is used, but the estimate for the derivative also has the form $V' \leqslant -\gamma V$ with $\gamma > 0$.

Therefore, the results obtained in this paper can be extended both to other types of equations and the study of other qualitative properties. In the future, the estimates of Razumikhin functions will be refined and used to study other types of stability.

Author Contributions: Conceptualization, N.O.S. and O.V.D.; methodology, N.O.S.; validation, O.V.D.; formal analysis, N.O.S. and O.V.D.; investigation, N.O.S. and O.V.D.; resources, N.O.S. and O.V.D.; data curation, N.O.S. and O.V.D.; writing—original draft preparation, N.O.S.; writing—review and editing, N.O.S. and O.V.D. All authors have read and agreed to the published version of the manuscript.

Funding: This research received no external funding.

Institutional Review Board Statement: Not applicable.

Informed Consent Statement: Not applicable.

Data Availability Statement: Not applicable.

Conflicts of Interest: The authors declare no conflict of interest.

Abbreviations

The following abbreviations are used in this manuscript:

GUAS	Global uniform asymptotic stability
GUES	Global uniform exponential stability

References

1. Sontag, E.D. Input to state stability: Basic concepts and results. In *Nonlinear and Optimal Control Theory*; Springer: Berlin/Heidelberg, Germany, 2008; pp. 163–220.
2. Zevin, A.A.; Poslavskii, S.Y. Two-sided bounds for the largest Lyapunov exponent and exponential stability criteria for nonlinear systems with arbitrary delays. *Autom. Remote Control* **2012**, *73*, 74–82. [CrossRef]
3. Krasovskii, N.N. On the asymptotical stability of systems with aftereffect. *Prikl. Mat. Mekh.* **1956**, *20*, 513–518. (In Russian)
4. Razumikhin, B.S. On the stability of delay systems. *Prikl. Mat. Mekh.* **1956**, *20*, 500–512. (In Russian)
5. Aleksandrov, A.; Aleksandrova, E.; Zhabko, A. Asymptotic stability conditions and estimates of solutions for nonlinear multiconnected time-delay systems. *Circuits Syst. Signal Process.* **2016**, *35*, 3531–3554. [CrossRef]
6. Gomez, M.; Egorov, A.V.; Mondié, S. A Lyapunov matrix based stability criterion for a class of time-delay systems. *Vestnik S.-Petersburg Univ. Ser. 10. Prikl. Mat. Inform. Prots. Upr.* **2017**, *13*, 407–416. [CrossRef]
7. Efimov, D.; Aleksandrov, A. On estimation of rates of convergence in Lyapunov–Razumikhin approach. *Automatica J.* **2020**, *116*, 108928. [CrossRef]
8. Andreev, A.S.; Sedova, N.O. The method of Lyapunov-Razumikhin functions in stability analysis of systems with delay. *Autom. Remote Control* **2019**, *80*, 1185–1229. [CrossRef]
9. Mao, X. Razumikhin-Type theorems on exponential stability of stochastic functional differential equations. *Stoch. Process. Appl.* **1996**, *65*, 233–250. [CrossRef]
10. Gu, H.; Gao, C. Razumikhin-Type Theorems on p-th Moment Stability for Stochastic Switching Nonlinear Systems with Delay. *J. Appl. Math. Phys.* **2016**, *4*, 1237–1244. [CrossRef]
11. Rehák, B.; Lynnyk, V. Synchronization of a Network Composed of Stochastic Hindmarsh–Rose Neurons. *Mathematics* **2021**, *9*, 2625. [CrossRef]
12. Zou, Z.; Song, Y.; Zhao, C. Razumikhin Theorems on Polynomial Stability of Neutral Stochastic Pantograph Differential Equations with Markovian Switching. *Mathematics* **2022**, *10*, 3048. [CrossRef]
13. Hu, W. Stability of Impulsive Stochastic Delay Systems with Markovian Switched Delay Effects. *Mathematics* **2022**, *10*, 1110. [CrossRef]
14. Hu, W.; Zhu, Q.; Karimi, H.R. Some improved Razumikhin stability criteria for impulsive stochastic delay differential systems. *IEEE Trans. Autom. Control* **2019**, *64*, 5207–5213. [CrossRef]

15. Vinodkumar, A.; Senthilkumar, T.; Hariharan, S.; Alzabut, J. Exponential stabilization of fixed and random time impulsive delay differential system with applications. *Math. Biosci. Eng.* **2021**, *18*, 2384–2400. [CrossRef]
16. Zhou, B.; Luo, W. Improved Razumikhin and Krasovskii stability criteria for time-varying stochastic time-delay systems. *Automatica* **2018**, *89*, 382–391. [CrossRef]
17. Sedova, N.O. On the principle of reduction for the nonlinear delay systems. *Autom. Remote Control* **2011**, *72*, 1864–1875. [CrossRef]
18. Hale, J.K. *Theory of Functional Differential Equations*; Springer: New York, NY, USA, 1977.
19. Panteley, E.; Loria, A. A new characterisation of exponential stability. In Proceedings of the 19th International Symposium on Mathematical Theory of Networks and Systems (MTNS), Budapest, Hungary, 5–9 July 2010; Volume 5, pp. 1487–1489.
20. Zhou, B. On asymptotic stability of linear time-varying systems. *Automatica* **2016**, *68*, 266–276. [CrossRef]
21. Morgan, A.P.; Narendra, K.S. On the uniform asymptotic stability of certain linear nonautonomous differential equations. *SIAM J. Control Optim.* **1977**, *15*, 5–24. [CrossRef]
22. Artstein, Z. Uniform asymptotic stability via limiting equations. *J. Differ. Equ.* **1978**, *27*, 172–189. [CrossRef]
23. Druzhinina, O.V.; Sedova, N.O. Method of limiting equations for the stability analysis of equations with infinite delay in the Carathéodory conditions: II. *Differ. Equ.* **2014**, *50*, 715–725. [CrossRef]
24. Adıvar, M.; Raffoul, Y.N. Inequalities and exponential decay in time varying delay differential equations. *Math. Comput. Model.* **2011**, *54*, 794–802. [CrossRef]
25. Berezansky, L.; Braverman, E. On exponential stability of linear delay equations with oscillatory coefficients and kernels. *Differ. Integr. Equ.* **2022**, *35*, 559–580. [CrossRef]
26. Louisell, J. Delay differential systems with time-varying delay: New directions for stability theory. *Kybernetika* **2001**, *37*, 239–251.
27. Myshkis, A.D. *Linear Differential Equations with a Retarded Argument*; Nauka: Moscow, Russia, 1951. (In Russian)
28. Stavroulakis, J.I.; Braverman, E. Oscillation, convergence, and stability of linear delay differential equations. *J. Differ. Equ.* **2021**, *293*, 282–312. [CrossRef]
29. Yoneyama, T. On the 3/2 stability theorem for one-dimensional delay-differential equations. *J. Math. Anal. Appl.* **1987**, *125*, 161–173. [CrossRef]
30. Berezansky, L.; Braverman, E. On exponential stability of a linear delay differential equation with an oscillating coefficient. *Appl. Math. Lett.* **2009**, *22*, 1833–1837. [CrossRef]
31. Mazenc, F.; Malisoff, M.; Niculescu, S.-I. Stability analysis for systems with time-varying delay: Trajectory based approach. In Proceedings of the 54th IEEE Conference on Decision and Control, Osaka, Japan, 15–18 December 2015; pp. 1811–1816.
32. Mazenc, F.; Malisoff, M. Extensions of Razumikhin's theorem and Lyapunov–Krasovskii functional constructions for time-varying systems with delay. *Automatica* **2017**, *78*, 1–13. [CrossRef]
33. Zhou, B.; Egorov, A.V. Razumikhin and Krasovskii stability theorems for time-varying time-delay systems. *Automatica* **2016**, *71*, 281–291. [CrossRef]
34. Pertsev, N.V. On exponentially decreasing estimates of solutions to nonlinear delay functional differential equations used in population dynamics models. *Dinamicheskie Sistemy (Simferopol')* **2020**, *10*, 70–83. (In Russian)
35. Berman, A.; Plemmons, R. *Nonnegative Matrices in the Mathematical Sciences*; Academic Press: New York, NY, USA, 1969.
36. Sun, Y.J.; Hsieh, J.G.; Hsieh, Y.C. Exponential stability criterion for uncertain retarded systems with multiple time-varying delays. *J. Math. Anal. Appl.* **1996**, *201*, 430–446. [CrossRef]
37. Lakshmikantam, V.; Martynyuk, A.A. Development of Lyapunov's direct method for systems with aftereffect. *Prikl. Mekh.* **1993**, *29*, 2–16. (In Russian)
38. Halanay, A. *Differential Equations, Stability, Oscillations Time Lag*; Academic Press: New York, NY, USA, 1966.
39. Hou, C.; Gao, F. Criteria for quantitative stability for a class of Razumikhin-type retarded functional differential equations. *J. Math. Anal. Appl.* **1999**, *238*, 558–566. [CrossRef]
40. Xu, B.G. Decay estimates for retarded dynamic systems. *Int. J. Syst. Sci.* **1999**, *30*, 427–439. [CrossRef]
41. Tian, H. Numerical and analytic dissipativity of the θ-method for delay differential equations with a bounded variable lag. *Int. J. Bifurc. Chaos* **2004**, *14*, 1839–1845. [CrossRef]
42. Ning, C.; He, Y.; Wu, M.; Jinhua She, J. Improved Razumikhin-type theorem for input-to-state stability of nonlinear time-delay systems. *IEEE Trans. Autom. Control* **2014**, *59*, 1983–1988. [CrossRef]
43. Rao, R.; Lin, Z.; Ai, X.; Wu, J. Synchronization of epidemic systems with Neumann boundary value under delayed impulse. *Mathematics* **2022**, *10*, 2064. [CrossRef]

MDPI AG
Grosspeteranlage 5
4052 Basel
Switzerland
Tel.: +41 61 683 77 34

Mathematics Editorial Office
E-mail: mathematics@mdpi.com
www.mdpi.com/journal/mathematics

www.ingramcontent.com/pod-product-compliance
Lightning Source LLC
Chambersburg PA
CBHW061630210926
51850CB00009B/2500
* 9 7 8 3 7 2 5 8 5 5 5 3 7 *